CHILDREN OF THE SEVEN SANDS

Kish

Arabian Gulf

Sir
Abu Nayr

Delma   Sir
         Bani Yas   Abu   Abu Dhabi
                         Al Abyad
         Ruwais

UNITED ARAB
EMIRATES

Published by **Motivate Media Group**

Dubai: Media One Tower, Dubai Media City
PO Box 2331, Dubai, UAE | Tel: (+971 4) 427 3000
books@motivate.ae | booksarabia.com

Abu Dhabi: Makeen Tower, 9th Street, Al Zahiyah
PO Box 43072, Abu Dhabi, UAE | Tel: (+971 2) 657 3490

Riyadh: Al Hamad Tower, King Fahad Road
Al Olaya, Riyadh | Tel: (+966 11) 834 3595

London: Acre House, 11/15 William Road,
London NW1 3ER

Directors: Obaid Humaid Al Tayer, Ian Fairservice
Publisher: Ian Fairservice
Publishing Director: Robin Harvie
Publishing Manager: Vaarunya Bhalla
Senior Editor: Aswathy Sathish
Art Director: Noel De La Pena
Publishing Coordinator: Mariam Aldhuhoori
General Manager – Production: Sunil Kumar

© Alexander McNabb and Motivate Media Group 2025

All photographs belong to the author unless specified.
Book design and illustrations by Maya Smadi.

All rights reserved. No part of this publication may be reproduced in any material form (including photocopying or storing in any medium by electronic means) without the written permission of the copyright holder. Applications for the copyright holder's written permission to reproduce any part of this publication should be addressed to the publishers. In accordance with the International Copyright Act 1956 and the UAE Federal Copyright Law No. (7) of 2002, Concerning Copyrights and Neighbouring Rights, any person acting in contravention of this copyright will be liable to criminal prosecution and civil claims for damages.

Note: All information in this book has been verified by the author and is accurate at the time of publication. This book is the author's work, and he assumes full responsibility for it. The maps in this book represent no authority on borders. They have been specifically designed for the sole purpose of illustrating the geographical extent of the areas discussed in the book. They have neither any purpose nor any relevance beyond this use.

ISBN: 978 1 86063 598 4

Media Regulatory Office Approval Number: MC-02-01-1298254

CHILDREN OF THE SEVEN SANDS

The History of the United Arab Emirates

Alexander McNabb

Consulting Editor: Peter Hellyer

To the Emirati people,
with apologies for the inconvenience.

*"He who does not know his past
cannot make the best of his present and future,
for it is from the past that we learn."*

– Sheikh Zayed Al Nahyan
Founding Father and first President of the UAE

Chronology of key events mentioned in the book

130,000–125,000 BCE — Emergence of anthropologically modern man from Africa

17,000 BCE — The Gulf Oasis sees slowly rising water levels

8500 BCE — Emergence of aceramic Palaeolithic communities on Gulf shores

5500 BCE — Start of the Arabian Bifacial Neolithic Culture (as evidenced from Ubaid ceramics)

3600–2600 BCE — The Hafit Culture (as evidenced from Jemdet Nasr ceramics)

2600–2000 BCE — The Umm Al Nar Culture

2000–1600 BCE — The Wadi Suq Culture

1600–1000 BCE — Iron Age I

1000–600 BCE — Iron Age II

600–300 BCE: — Iron Age III

300 BCE–250 CE — The Early Pre-Islamic Period

250–600 CE — The period of Sasanian rule, which coincides with the Hellenistic Period

600 CE	Commencement of the Islamic Period
1300	The settlement of Hormuz Island
1500	Start of the Portuguese conquests
1600	The beginnings of the Arab rebellion against the Portuguese
1700	The beginnings of British East India Company dominance
1790	Saudi influence spreads
1809	The first British/Qawasim punitive expedition
1819	The second British/Qawasim punitive expedition
1903	Curzon holds a durbar aboard RIMS *Argonaut* at Sharjah
1932	The establishment of Sharjah Airport
1948	Peace is established between Dubai and Abu Dhabi after a period of unrest
1968	Britain announces its intention to withdraw from the Trucial States by 1971
1971	The Emirates of Abu Dhabi, Dubai, Sharjah, Ajman, Fujairah and Umm Al Quwain comes together to form the United Arab Emirates following the departure of Britain. Ras Al Khaimah joins the Union a few months later in February 1972

Preface

This is an amazing story, one like no other. It is the story of a nation born on a handshake, of cities raised from sand and of a people who have traded with the world since the dawn of history. A young nation focused relentlessly on the future, it can now perhaps afford to take pause and reflect a little on its past. And what a past it is!

The human history of the UAE stretches back 130,000 years, which is basically where I started this book. It is a remarkable history by any standard: harsh, desolate, colourful and filled with despair and rapture by turns. There is rarely a quiet moment in the country's past and I can only hope I have done it justice and that you don't find dull moments in my recounting of the kaleidoscopic and often sanguinary avalanche of events that have shaped the place we know today as the Emirates.

From the very dawn of humanity, this arid land has been home to people striving to eke out a living from desperately meagre resources. Battling the climate and frequently each other, they emerged as stone age traders and went on to become the founders of humanity's first intercontinental trading network and conquerors of the Seven Seas.

Falling to the technologically advanced, fast-expanding and frequently brutal European empires (some of the stories of the activities of the Portuguese contained in this book may upset those of a delicate constitution), the descendants of the Arab traders of Julfar went on, Phoenix-like, to become the driving force behind the modern world's largest ports and airports, greatest airlines, glittering global cities and some of its most ambitious and successful international companies.

One of the two routes originally taken by modern humans emerging from Africa to populate the Earth is today a place where humans are planning to emerge from Earth and populate the planets.

The period of British dominance that defined much of the 1800s and 1900s – the period of the Trucial States, which was to give birth to the UAE as a nation – is perhaps the most written-about and yet least understood element of the country's history. It would have made a brilliant Ealing Comedy[1] – something along the lines of *Passport to Pimlico* or *The Titfield Thunderbolt*. For Arab readers, a comparison to a classic Egyptian comedy would perhaps resonate just as well. The resourceful and wily local rulers pitted against the bureaucratic, arrogant British administrators always seem to find a way of getting the better over their overbearing foes and the little guy somehow gets the last laugh.

It is not how the British are used to seeing themselves and I am sure I will be charged with being too soft on the locals and terribly anti-Imperialist, but the truth of the matter is that the British arrived in Southeastern Arabia sailing under a false flag and departed a century and a half later, having little to leave behind other than a note saying how terribly sorry they were for the inconvenience. For what it's worth, I do not consider that to necessarily be the worst of colonial legacies: look at the Belgians in the Congo or the French in North Africa. British involvement in the Emirates was more the stuff of black and white comedy rather than white on black massacre.

I first became fascinated by the history of the UAE when I found out that the little suburb of the city of Sharjah in which I lived was actually home to some of the most influential people and events in the modern history of the nation. Like peeling back an onion, the more I found out, the more fascinating facts and stories emerged, and everyday places became magical, infused with meaning derived from a deep and rich past that we all too often miss as we rush by today.

You'll perhaps have heard or even believed that there's no depth, no culture to the Emirates. That's not true, not by a long chalk. There's an incredible, colourful and glorious history awaiting you in this book – the story of this land of the Emirates is profound and complex, gory and terrible, mean and tragic and proud and triumphant by turns. It is reflected in monuments and sites still to be found today, hiding in plain sight.

What is true is that the people of this young nation, founded in 1971, went through a period where remembering the past meant harking back to a brutal, pestilential existence. Set against a backdrop of newfound wealth and luxury, you could see why any return to revisit that past would have limited appeal. Now, as the Emirates comes of age and finds its place in the world, is perhaps a good time to take a look at the events and people that lie behind the dazzling modern cities and snaking networks of roads that strike out through the shifting sands.

There are roots here in the desert and, believe me, they are deeper than you'd ever have imagined.

Contents

Chronology of key events 10

Preface 13

Introduction: An Amazing History 18

Chapter 1: The Emergence of Man 30

Chapter 2: The End of Eden 36

Chapter 3: The Lords of Magan 46

Chapter 4: Death in the Mountains .55

Chapter 5: The Impossible Desert Forge 65

Chapter 6: The Rise of Mleiha 72

Chapter 7: Here Lie 10,000 Men 80

Chapter 8: Schism, Rift and War 88

Chapter 9: Lords of the Seven Seas .97

Chapter 10: The Portuguese Sword and Cross 111

Chapter 11: The Company and the Prophet 124

Chapter 12: The Arrival of Albion 141

Chapter 13: Exile and the Kingdom 154

Chapter 14: The Trucial Coast 167
Chapter 15: The Father of the Gazelle. 182
Chapter 16: War in the Sands 197
Chapter 17: Of Perpetual Peace 213
Chapter 18: The Rise of the Tribes and Zayed the Great 224
Chapter 19: The Protectorate and the Darbar 244
Chapter 20: Troubled Times in Sharjah 263
Chapter 21: The Passing of the Pearls 280
Chapter 22: Look Up to the Blue Sky. 295
Chapter 23: Oil, Rebellion and War 308
Chapter 24: The Buraimi Incident 334
Chapter 25: Founded on a Handshake. 358
Chapter 26: The Act of Union 371
Chapter 27: Winds of Change. 390

Endnotes 403
Author's notes. 423

Introduction

AN AMAZING HISTORY

"There lie the men who lived in the age of ignorance."

- P. V. Glob

On 25 November 1819, sails appeared on the blue horizon off the dusty port town of Ras Al Khaimah, the capital of the Al Qasimi maritime federation, nestled at the mouth of the Arabian Gulf. The Qawasim (the plural of Al Qasimi) were a seafaring powerhouse drawn from the Huwala people, the Arabs who dominated the waters of the Gulf from Sharjah and Ras Al Khaimah on the southern shore through the islands of Qeshm and Hormuz to Bandar Lingeh and other ports on the northern, Persian, coast. They had done so for hundreds of years, nigh on a thousand years, in fact. The evangelistic and opportunistic Portuguese smashed the Arab global trading network in the early 1500s, now the British in their turn were to demand the Huwala give way to the might of Albion.[1]

A long series of confrontations and skirmishes in the warm waters of the Gulf had taken place between Qawasim boats and those flying the British flag, beginning in the late 1700s and finally leading to the East India Company successfully prosecuting a case with His Majesty's Government for a decisive blow against their aggressive competitors. Since the mid-1700s, when the Portuguese had ceded to English maritime might, the Company had been fending off the argumentative Qawasim – now they were going to put the whole affair to an end.

Shots were fired by lookouts manning Ras Al Khaimah's coastal watchtowers and there would have been a sharp outbreak of panic as the townspeople prepared to defend themselves against whatever malign force this was gathering on their shores. Eagle-eyed observers would have relayed the news: the ships were flying British colours and they were led by men-of-war.[2] Throughout that day and the next, more sail joined until a force of some eleven warships hove to in view of the town.

Some would have taken to the beach to shout defiance at the British flotilla, while more cautious souls would have battened down goods and shuttered shops and storehouses. Many would have remembered the last great British force to gather against Ras Al Khaimah back in 1809, which had swept the coast with terrified anticipation and consumed the town in a great conflagration that had burned a funeral pyre for many of its people.

The men prepared to fight, but nothing happened on that day or the next. The defenders relaxed. It was not until fully a week later, on 2 December, following the arrival of troop transports, that shocked reports would have reached the Al Qasimi Sheikh of Ras Al Khaimah – the British had landed two miles south of the town.

The bombardment of Ras Al Khaimah commenced three days later, on 5 December, with a deadly combination of cannon fire from seawards and the batteries of guns and mortars from the landed troops. Red-hot six-inch iron shot smashed into adobe walls and scudded down sandy streets, cracking timber and bone alike as the flames licked at tinder-dry woodwork supporting brittle, coral-walled buildings. Between the larger houses, most of the people of the town lived in basic huts made from woven palm fronds, *areesh*. The town's desperate defenders were short on ammunition, often resorting to firing foraged rocks from their decrepit cannon.

The result was a foregone conclusion. Despite a spirited resistance, the town was battered into submission by overwhelming force from land and sea. When British bluecoats stormed Ras Al Khaimah on the morning of 9 December 1819, they were unopposed. The fighting men of the town had fled in the night to join their women and children in the date plantations of the mountainous hinterland.

The British sent three ships up to the northern port of Rams and bombarded it before landing there and taking the final surrender of the Qawasim at Dhayah Fort. Over the following days, the punitive force travelled down the shore of the Gulf, bombarding every town they encountered: Jazirat Al Hamra, Umm Al Quwain, Ajman, Al Fisht, Sharjah, Abu Hail and Dubai. Every settlement was visited by devastating violence that seemingly appeared from nowhere, blazing a trail of fire and death along the whole coast.

The stunned rulers of the devastated communities were then invited to sign a treaty with the British – the General Treaty for the Cessation of Plunder and Piracy by Land and Sea, Dated February 5, 1820. Having had a sharp taste of the alternative to the British 'pacification', they duly came as bid and signed the treaty and the Trucial States, as they were to become known, embarked on a period of peace and prosperity under the watchful eye of the British government in Bombay and its sternly enforced 'Pax Britannica'.[3]

Staying away from internal affairs

As usual, the British were to be drawn further into the affairs of those they had conquered than they at first had wished. Bombay (then within British India) had established a naval patrol of the Trucial Coast to enforce the treaty, a Native Residency Agent was eventually installed in Sharjah to manage the relationships between the coastal sheikhs and to protect the interests of British subjects, mainly Indians, trading in the area. This eventually, just after World War II, became a full residency and a British Resident, reporting to the Arabian Gulf Political Residency in Bahrain, took the place of the Native Residency Agent.

With a series of successive agreements enacted over the seventy years following the 1820 treaty, the Trucial States fully ceded their international relations and defence to Britain. But, significantly, the British had no interest whatsoever in becoming embroiled in the interior of these emirates. This wild and reckless place had no benefit to offer other than conflict and bloodshed, dominated by warring Bedouin tribes and their constant and complicated faction fighting.

The British consistently limited their interests and involvements to the relationship with the coastal Sheikhs and their communities, intervening only when the maritime truce was breached, an increasingly rare occurrence. They saw the coastal Sheikhs as paramount and travel to the arid interior beyond a few miles of the coast was generally considered (quite rightly) an unpleasant and dangerous pastime. The occasional brave soul would attempt the journey, in the 1800s adventurers such as Captain Atkins Hamerton, who reached Al Ain in 1840, then later Colonel S. B. Miles. In the 1900s, adventurers such as Bertram Thomas, St John Philby and Sir Wilfred Thesiger stood out. These rare desert wanderers with their leathery skin and far-seeing eyes were celebrated figures of their time and their writings reinforced the British romance of the Bedouin as 'noble savages', never more colourful or popular than

T. E. Lawrence's famous memoir of his time fighting in the Arab Revolt during World War I, *Seven Pillars of Wisdom*.

If the Government in Bombay and, from 1948 onwards following Indian independence, the Foreign Office in London had no desire to concern itself with the interior, the Trucial Sheikhs had no such qualms. They jockeyed for position and forged alliances, marrying to cement their bonds with the tribes and going to war to protect their allies and put down insurrections against their rule, as far as it extended. Rulers would be strengthened or weakened by their status among the tribes: Zayed the Great of Abu Dhabi,[4] for instance, enjoyed remarkable influence over the affairs of the interior and built himself as the central figure of a powerful tribal confederation in the latter half of the 1800s, while up the coast from Abu Dhabi, Sultan bin Saqr Al Qasimi in the 1900s enlisted the formidable Bedouin Bani Qitab tribe, which dominated the northern interior.

As a result of this, the interior of the Trucial States was generally neglected by outside forces and influences, right up to the establishment of the Trucial Oman Levies in 1951. The Levies, to be renamed the Trucial Oman Scouts in 1956, were a British funded and commanded force brought together to suppress trade in arms and slaves and bring some semblance of order to the interior. Some thirteen years after the Scouts' foundation, the interior having been rendered at least accessible, the first archaeologists ventured into Abu Dhabi and then the oasis town of Al Ain and the plains surrounding the great outcrop of Jebel Hafit. What they found was to mark the start of a series of often bewildering discoveries that are still, today, helping us to rewrite the history of this perplexing region.

The great neglect

While Bertram Thomas was writing *Arabia Felix* and St John Philby was advising at the court of King Abdulaziz Al Saud, archaeologists were marvelling at their discoveries of the Sumerian civilisation of Mesopotamia (modern-day Iraq), which had begun in the mid-1800s. One of the most prominent of all archaeologists of his time, Leonard Woolley had hosted a young T. E. Lawrence at his dig at Carchemish, an important Hittite city being excavated before World War I in northern Syria. After the war, Woolley moved on to perhaps his finest achievement, the excavation of Ur of the Chaldees, the great Sumerian city. Like many of his peers, Woolley was fascinated by the traces of Biblical places and names he found in the ancient world and his work essentially focused Westward. The Romans, the Phoenicians, the Greeks all sailed the Mediterranean and traded and warred in that sea. The Arabian Gulf was of little interest, far less its arid interior with its tribes of Bedouin raiders.

Other archaeologists found great monuments in Persia and a fascination with all things Persian briefly gripped Europe, influencing artistic movements such as Art Deco. The Classical World was where it was at and neo-Classicism (and Orientalism) not only brought eastern influences to decoration and art, but found their way into the expression of the Nazi and Fascist New World Orders. Even the Indus Valley, then in northern India, was to be investigated and the Harappan Culture brought to light.

All of this activity has led to a number of assumptions about the ancient world which our recent discoveries in the seemingly barren land of south-east Arabia – the UAE and Oman – are now challenging. We now believe that the very origin of the Sumerian people was in the Gulf. We now know that the water-bearing technology, the *qanat*, previously held to be of Iranian origin, was actually an Iron Age innovation of Southeastern Arabian origin, the *falaj* – a technology evolved through the long cultivation of palm groves and other crops in this desert country. We know that the area was a centre for regional trade throughout the millennia, a source of valuable diorite, copper and bronze for Sumer – that the land of the emirates was the homeland of the fabled Magan people and of the thirty-two Lords of Magan, whose might the son of the Sumerian King Sargon was to eventually destroy. With our new-found knowledge, we now believe the origin of the biblical flood legend also had its genesis here in the prehistoric Arabian Gulf – and we can now also see that the Gulf was once, back in the mists of time, a lush and fertile valley, home to the garden of Eden itself.

This and more has come to light as the interior of the UAE and Oman have been opened up to archaeological study. A 7,500-year-old locus of regional trade, a connecting point between great civilisations and the home to lost ancient cities, the United Arab Emirates has reluctantly yielded its earliest secrets and, in the past twenty years alone, our understanding of the history of the Ancient Near East has been totally reborn. Even today, we are making new finds which are still transforming our understanding of the region's history – finds in Marawah, Dalma and Ghagha in Abu Dhabi since 2019 have pushed back our understanding of the timelines of early trade and commerce in the region by over two millennia. The oldest pearling village in the Gulf on Umm Al Quwain's Sinniyah Island was only revealed to media in 2023, and the finds we are making there are already playing havoc with our assumptions and theories about the early communities of the Gulf – and also about the early Christian communities that made this region home.

One of the first archaeological digs in the Gulf took place not in the UAE, however, but in Bahrain. The team from Denmark working there in the early 1950s were invited to come and dig by the Ruler of Abu Dhabi. He had some interesting humps to show them.

The rest, as they say, is history.

From Dilmun to Magan

The ancient Sumerian civilisation uncovered by Woolley and others was almost unbelievably rich in artefacts and clues to the Sumerian way of life. Sumer was not only the first urban society to emerge in human history, but the wealth of what its people left as a legacy stands out as perhaps only equalled by that of the Egyptians. Their writing, the Sumerian Cuneiform script, meant that they left a great deal more than artefacts behind them – they left histories and ideas, poems, royal boasts and epic stories. Even arguments over payment for goods.

They also left records of other ancient places – the paradisiacal land of Tilmun or Dilmun and the faraway wealth of the lands of Magan and Meluhha. Historians squabbled over where these places mentioned in Sumerian scripts actually were for decades, but it is now generally accepted that Dilmun relates to an area encompassing Bahrain and the eastern coast of Saudi Arabia, and that Magan comprises the land of Southeastern Arabia – the UAE and Oman. Meluhha is today identified as being the Indus Valley Civilisation in what is today Pakistan.

Dilmun was linked by the Sumerians to the idea of an earthly paradise and so has been conjectured by a number of scholars to be the origin of the Garden of Eden – certainly it's hard to move in Bahrain today without encountering Dilmun hotels, Delmon printing presses, Delmun cafes, Dilmon cold stores and myriad other businesses carrying variations of the ancient name.

It is the reason that Danish historian Peter Glob travelled to Bahrain in the early 1950s to excavate there. He went in search of the Garden of Eden, and unwittingly became a pioneer in the exploration of the Sumerians' eastern sphere of influence. His specialisation was actually in artefacts preserved in Danish bogs and yet he was to discover in the arid, shifting sands a world that was far more influential and far-reaching. And although he never did conclusively find Eden, he helped us to locate it years after his passing.

Peter Glob was a colourful figure – he was famous in Denmark for the excavation of bog bodies such as the Grauballe Man and Tollund Man, and his investigations of Bronze Age antiquities in Denmark's bogs. As the Director of the Danish National Museum, he was persuaded to move to Aarhus in Jutland in 1949 to take up the chair of prehistoric archaeology at Aarhus University. The post would also involve Glob becoming the director of Aarhus' obscure Forhistorisk Museum, in return for which Aarhus' mayor agreed to fund his post at the university for two years.

Glob was joined at the museum by the English Assyriologist, Geoffrey Bibby. Bibby had spent his war in the Faroe Islands, working for British intelligence and had met Glob – who had been an active member of the resistance – after the liberation of Copenhagen. Bibby went to Bahrain in 1947 to work for the Iraq Petroleum Company (IPC was a pioneer in the exploration of the Gulf's vast potential oil resources) but when his wife Vibeke, who was from Aarhus, became pregnant, the couple returned to Denmark and Bibby took up a post at the Aarhus museum in 1950.

Geoffrey and Vibeke Bibby regaled Glob with tales of far-flung Bahrain, the tiny island in the Gulf that was home to a hundred thousand graves.[5]

Glob was fascinated and decided to mount an expedition. Letters were sent to Bahrain's administration in 1953 and, in due course, the British Resident, Sir Charles Belgrave KBE, replied with good news. Not only would the Ruler of Bahrain consent to the expedition, he was prepared to help fund it with a grant of 1,000 pounds, a munificent sum at the time. Belgrave was travelling to London with the Ruler to attend the coronation of Queen Elizabeth II, he noted, but could be reached at the Travellers Club in Pall Mall.

In the summer of that year, Glob was excavating in Greenland and managed to capture a large white falcon. Arriving in Bahrain that autumn, he presented Bahrain's Ruler, Sheikh Salman, with the distinctive bird, a gift that quickly became the talk of the town. After that moment, the Danes could do no wrong and Glob and Bibby found doors opening left, right and centre. They based themselves in the old Portuguese fort, Qalat Al Bahrain, setting up an expedition headquarters made from local palm frond houses – the same type of *areesh* houses that the British had set afire in Ras Al Khaimah in 1819, and which were the commonplace dwelling of the semi-settled peoples of the Gulf since time immemorial, often filling the spaces between the more permanent structures of the wealthy or community storehouses.

Glob lost no time in adopting national dress and enjoyed cutting a colourful figure in his robes and sandals – Danish journalists took to the distinctive archaeologist and the expedition to Bahrain quickly garnered national media coverage. The results of the first digs were no less than spectacular: finds of fine statuary and ceramics were yielded up by Bahrain's tumuli as the relics and buildings of the lost Sumerian trading entrepôt of Dilmun emerged. Annual expeditions ran from January to April, and the team from Aarhus grew as Bahrain started to offer up its long-lost history as a major centre of Sumerian trade and commerce.

A friend of Bibby's from his Iraq Petroleum days used to visit the Danes at their dig in Bahrain and became interested in their work. The Abu Dhabi-based Temple (Tim) Hillyard, who worked for British

Petroleum (BP) but was seconded to the oil exploration company, Abu Dhabi Marine Areas Ltd (ADMA), thought there were sites in Abu Dhabi worth visiting. He helped smooth the way for Glob and his team to visit Abu Dhabi. This included getting permission from the Political Resident, the Ruler of Abu Dhabi and finally from BP for the team to dig in the company's concession area. By January 1958, everything was in place for the visit.

Those were the days when oil men regularly sat down with Sheikhs in their *majlis* and so it was that Hillyard engaged the Ruler of Abu Dhabi, Sheikh Shakhbut bin Sultan Al Nahyan, in conversation about the Danes and their digs in Bahrain, showing Shakhbut colourful images from media coverage of the finds. The Sheikh not only gave his agreement to their visit, but pointed to a likely location, an island close to Abu Dhabi which had a number of mounds that had been surveyed by an oil company some twenty years prior. Hillyard knew of the island and what he believed to be a recently constructed water cistern there. He thought it of limited interest, but Shakhbut was insistent and so he visited the island and conducted a preliminary survey. Hillyard wrote to Glob soon after, outlining the ruins he found there and telling him, "The Ruler whose appetite for antiquities has been whetted by seeing your own and Bibby's article in the *Illustrated London News* urges me to press you to see the place and to give him your opinions."

Glob and Bibby mounted the first archaeological expedition to the Trucial States from 15 February to 29 March 1959, on a budget of 2,000 pounds (which they overspent). They lived once again in a house built from *areesh* on the island. Their supply of water was brought in from Dubai in oil drums (tainted, consequently, by oil). Abu Dhabi's bustling souk had little to offer Western palates in 1959 and so they brought most of their provisions from ADMA's stores on Das Island, including placing orders for such luxuries as five tins of salmon, three pounds each of steak, pork cutlets and lamb chops, four pounds of cheese and six packets of cream crackers.

A team of some fourteen local workers was brought in to help with the dig and were paid five rupees a day.

The first season convinced the men that they had unearthed a burial site dating certainly to the first millennium BCE but it wasn't until their second season in the following year that they found large troves of pottery that led them to conclude they had stumbled upon a new Bronze Age culture dating back to the third millennium BCE.

The island they had made their home was called Umm Al Nar (also rendered Umm an-Nar, meaning 'Mother of Fire') and it was to give its name to a culture that defined the Bronze Age in the United Arab Emirates and Oman, flourishing between 2600 and 2000 BCE. Little did they know at the time, but they had stumbled on relics of the faraway land the Sumerians knew as Magan.

Zayed
The work being carried out on Umm Al Nar by the Danish team fascinated Sheikh Shakhbut. He visited the dig along with his two brothers, Zayed and Khalid.

"We have mounds like this in Al Ain," Zayed told Glob. "Hundreds of them."

Glob was polite, but he was also incredulous. The collection at Umm Al Nar comprised a significant find of twenty-nine burial mounds. To claim hundreds of such mounds must surely be in the tradition of Bedouin exaggeration. "Come to Al Ain yourself, you'll see," Zayed told him.

Sure enough, Zayed telegrammed them an invitation to visit Al Ain on 7 March 1959, and the men set off across the desert sands in their jeep a few days later. Zayed took them to Nudud Al Jahal – a huge, barren plain overlooked by the looming mountain of Jebel Hafit to the south of the Al Ain oasis. He swept a hand across the landscape as an astonished Glob peered at a collection of some 200 burial mounds. Glob and Bibby were staggered. "There," Glob told Zayed, "lie the men who lived in the Age of Ignorance."[6]

It was an archaeologist following in Glob and Bibby's footsteps who would give a date to these burials and the craggy mountain that overlooked them would give a name to this fascinating new culture.

Karen Frifelt led expeditions to Abu Dhabi, Hili and Al Ain for the Aarhus Museum in the late 1960s, but it wasn't until she was preparing a Festschrift (a collection of articles from colleagues in honour of a notable academic) for Glob's sixtieth birthday in 1970 that she linked the distinctive pottery finds that Glob's team had taken from the burials in Al Ain to the Sumerian Jemdet Nasr period (3100–2900 BCE). The discovery led to a renewed focus on the beehive graves of Al Ain in the next two years – and the naming of a new cultural period in the UAE's history, the Hafit Period. Dated between 3200 and 2600 BCE and immediately preceding the Umm Al Nar period, the Hafit finds provided a deep insight into an even more ancient period of human settlement – and a strong early link to the Sumerians.

As word of the early successes of the Aarhus expeditions spread (some thirty archaeologists participated in the Museum's extensive work in the region), others travelled to the Trucial States to explore what was clearly a fresh and new field of study. Universities from Iraq, the UK, France, Spain and Germany sent teams from the 1970s onwards.

The mysteries of the United Arab Emirates' past were beginning to reveal themselves for the first time. And it is only now that we can start to appreciate the amazing realities that have so long been neglected as this young nation has emerged onto the world stage. The Emirates' focus on the challenges of the future have meant, frankly, that its people have failed to appreciate the wealth that lies in its past.

Today, for the first time, we can gather the wealth of research we have amassed so far and build a truly holistic picture of the Emirates' human history. And it is never less than amazing.

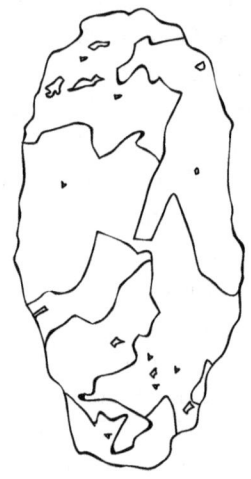

Chapter 1

THE EMERGENCE OF MAN

"No one ought to feel surprise at much remaining as yet unexplained in regard to the origin of species."

- Charles Darwin

On the surface you would think geneticists and archaeologists would have relatively little in common, but when it comes to mapping the origins of mankind, they are happy enough bedfellows – although given to outbreaks of academic squabbling.

They have now come to agree that the likely origins of what we call anatomically modern humans (*Homo sapiens* or, broadly, us) lie in Africa, somewhere between 150,000 and 200,000 years ago. They have also agreed that mankind left Africa to populate the planet through two 'corridors' – a northern corridor through Egypt and Sinai and the Levant, and a southern corridor through East Africa and across to Yemen, then through the Gulf peninsula and from there expanding northwards and eastwards. The two disciplines agree on the dispersal patterns and we have been mapping human genomes to find that our 'trees' of dispersal agree broadly with the archaeological evidence we have found. As a race we, *Homo sapiens*, were 'born' in Africa; we migrated and likely intermingled with Neanderthals (and possibly other hominids such as the Denisovans) on the way – and we evolved to become different colours and have different 'racial' characteristics, pretty much along the lines you'd expect from the process of natural selection that Darwin outlined, to much heated condemnation, in 1859.

One of the most important recent finds in this study, driven by the complex interaction between sciences, lies in the Emirate of Sharjah, under an overhang on the side of a rocky outcrop called Jebel Faya. There, archaeologists from the German University of Tübingen struck lucky as they dug into layers of sediment to uncover strata after strata of human activity, nicely divided by layers of fine sand.

As they dug down, the centuries accumulated until, finally, they came across a 'toolkit' – an assemblage of flint tools that they dated using an accurate dating technique used where carbon dating is not possible and known as single-grain optically-stimulated luminescence (OSL). The results came back and caused consternation: by the layering they had guessed they were 'going early' but the flint tools they had unearthed dated back to at least 125,000 years ago. Here, at Faya, was evidence that anatomically modern humans had, indeed, made the journey across the

Bab Al Mandab Straits separating Djibouti and Yemen and then slowly made their way north until here, in Faya, they had taken shelter from the elements and worked their flint hand axes and scrapers.

The finds from the site, known as Faya-1, are today on display at the Mleiha Archaeological Centre in Sharjah. And they are the oldest known evidence of anatomically modern humanity found in Arabia.

A different world

125,000 years ago, the world was a different place, gripped by Ice Ages: the Pleistocene era – which ran from 2.5 million years ago to about 9700 BCE. A range of human precursor species have been identified, leading up to what we call anatomically modern humans, and stone tools used by these early ancestors have been found dating back to some 3.5 million years ago.

The Pleistocene Ice Age, a world of mammoths and a range of gargantuan species (or 'megafauna'), was a time of wildly varying climactic change. Northern Europe, Asia and much of North America were covered in thick ice sheets and sea levels globally were something like 150 metres lower than they are today. That meant that the route north out of Africa to present day Yemen was a land route – in fact, the Red Sea would have been little more than a series of shallow lakes shimmering across a wide valley floor.[1]

This new race made their way across the Red Sea. Their progress would have been slow: the Pleistocene era brought vast changes to climate in the eastern Gulf Peninsula – confronting the mountains of Yemen, they would have moved along the coast, perhaps braving the interior during periods of monsoon and temperate, wet climate.[2] But just as quickly as the rains of winter swept the land, periods of bitter aridity would follow and beat them back to the coast: a long ebb and flow of early humanity chased scant (and sometimes rich) resources and lived off the land as hunter-gatherers. They would have slowly explored northwards until, reaching the tip of the peninsula, they would enjoy the wetter climate of the coastal littoral to the east of the Hajar Mountains with its frequent rainfall and fertile land. And they doubtless would have explored the passes running through the mountains: to the north these cut from Sohar to Buraimi, Shinas to Hatta and inland to Madam and from Fujairah through Masafi to Dhaid.

It is directly between these last two routes that Mleiha and the rocky outcrop of Jebel Faya lie, a brief shelter in the dusty plain overlooked by the Hajar mountains, a gravel bed that traps the waters running off the great rocky slopes of the Hajar and gives springs of clean, fresh water throughout the year.

The tools found at Faya are distinctive and have links in their form and type to tools of a similar age found in Sudan, giving us confidence in the idea of a virile southern trajectory rather than a leakage east of the people embarking on the Levantine path to Europe. This idea has been strengthened by work from other sites. From Faya they would have crossed to Iran and spread north and east, claiming the world as their own and changing its face – for better or worse – forever.[3]

Gulf, gone

How would they have navigated the sea of the Arabian Gulf in their journey north? They would have walked across it, is the simple answer. No miracles were involved, although the act of crossing ancient lands that then became seas would be remembered – the memories and legends finally recorded as tales of seas that parted to allow human migrations.

125,000 years ago, the familiar sea we know today as the Arabian Gulf (Americans and some others call it the Persian Gulf) simply did not exist. Even today, the Gulf is a shallow sea, never deeper than 100 metres and frequently – especially at its southern and northern shores – less than twenty-five metres deep. Taking Pleistocene era sea levels into account, the Arabian Gulf simply was not a sea. Instead our early explorers would have found a relatively shallow, temperate valley – warm, wet, fertile and fed by the great Tigris and Euphrates rivers flowing lazily down from the very top of the long, gently-sloping plain and washing up against the promontory of Musandam, flowing around it to gush down into the chasm of the Gulf of Oman somewhere between Fujairah and the coast of south-eastern Iran. It would likely have been a wide, slow-flowing river (From present day Basra to fully three quarters down the Gulf, the river would have fallen a depth of only around forty metres) with great lakes forming on its path. And it likely ended in a great waterfall down into the sea beyond. There is every chance that a rich sedimentary deposit would have formed over the millennia as the river turned its last corner around the Straits of Hormuz to meet the depleted ocean. But as that ocean rose, the valley would have flooded.

The rivers and lakes of the valley would have trended towards the north of the Gulf basin because of the strong tectonic forces that are still lifting the Arabian peninsula– even today, shipping in the Gulf sticks to the northern corridor because the southern Gulf is so shallow – the sea off the west coast of the Emirates is only ten metres deep and it is not until you get further out, beyond Sharjah's island of Sir Abu Nu'ayr, that twenty-metre depths start to be found.

The great enigma

The early finds at Jebel Faya point clearly to the opportunistic migration of humankind north out of Africa and from there to the world beyond. But one mystery is why we found traces of their passing 125,000 years ago and then, for many millennia to come, we find nothing. The archaeological record of the Arabian peninsula goes quiet after Faya-1 and it is not until the onset of the era we know as the Holocene (about 10,000 BCE) that we start to see significant traces of settlement in the area again. In that whole time, the region was barren. Barely a single sign of humanity has so far been found.

So what happened? Where did the people go? And why did the Gulf "go dark"?

The answer lies in the world's changing climate. As glaciers gripped the north, arid dunes and desert wastelands formed in Arabia, lashed by tremendous drying winds that flung choking clouds of sand in continuous stinging dust storms that literally rendered the region uninhabitable.[4] Fleeing north down to the temperate and well-watered basin of the Gulf Oasis, and from there striking out to populate Asia, humanity found more welcoming climates. For over 100,000 years, we find virtually no trace of human existence in the south-eastern Gulf with sparse finds across that whole period until, suddenly, humankind reappears in abundance with the emergence of what we now call the 'Arabian bifacial' era.

After their long absence from what they would have seen as the barren highlands, the humans return. Chipping away at their flint tools, these returning visitors to the region had refined the bludgeoning hand axes and scrapers of their ancestors and now made exquisite knapped-stone arrowheads and spear-points. These were lashed to wooden shafts and used to hunt wild game. The tribes learned to herd animals and husband them in the newly temperate lands of what we call the Holocene Optimum – a period of warm, wet weather that transformed the deserts with their stinging sandy winds into a blossoming, temperate zone. Wildlife thrived and with the new wealth of game came its greatest predator: man.

The repopulation of the south-eastern Gulf was driven by a major change in the world's climate as the Pleistocene, the last ice age, gave way to the post-glacial Holocene era, the melting of the glaciers drove the world's water levels up to the point that not only did the rising sea turn the lakes of the Gulf Oasis salty, it flooded the area. Relentlessly, the ebbing and flowing sea levels rose – from about 70,000 BCE to 8000 BCE – by about 150 metres. That massive rise, taking place over almost 60 millennia, would have been a creeping, insidious movement of the seas, likely interspersed with periods of more rapid rises – flooding events – which reclaimed the fertile valley of the Gulf to form the sea we know today.

To the people fleeing the lush valley-basin of the Holocene Arabian Gulf, it meant the end of Eden.

Chapter 2

THE END OF EDEN

"May the waters rise up from it into your great basins. May your city drink water aplenty from them. May Dilmun drink water aplenty from them. May your pools of salt water become pools of fresh water. May your city become an emporium on the quay for the Land."

– The promise of Enki, the Lord of Sweet Waters, to his daughter, Ninsikila, by Ninhursag, the Earth Mother: from the Sumerian creation myth, 'Enki and Ninhursag'.

Even today, the Arabian Gulf is the shallowest sea of any significance on Earth.[1] In the late Pleistocene, as a land-locked valley, its slope down from the inhospitable desert lands of the Arabian Peninsula would have been gentle, leading to a lush and fertile land. On the northern, Persian, coast the land rose precipitously to encounter the forbidding barrier of the Zagros Mountains.

The Gulf Basin would have started to the north west as a gradual slope, a wedge-shaped depression about the size of the UK, dipping down lazily from the coasts of what are today Kuwait, Bahrain, Qatar and the UAE, deepening towards the coast of what is today Iran. There would likely have been a series of deep depressions, which would have formed huge lake systems as the waters of the great Tigris, Euphrates and Karun rivers combined into the Ur-Schatt river system, which made its torpid way towards the straits of Hormuz. Here it is likely that the waters would have been constrained by great silt deposits to the northern side, cutting a channel around the Musandam before fanning out across the shallows to splash into the Gulf of Oman.[2]

Falling northwards from the Arabian peninsula towards the Straits of Hormuz would have been river systems, springs feeding from the coast of what is today Abu Dhabi and Bahrain, flowing down to meet the great rivers and lakes. Here, in these rich and verdant lands, wildlife would have gathered in incredible profusion around the precious waters.

If you have ever visited Dubai's Al Qudra Lakes, perhaps even Sharjah's Wasit Wetland Centre, you would get a taste of what it might have felt like on the shores of the great river system and the lakes of the Gulf valley. Silt from the river would have formed as it meandered the shallow track to the mouth of the basin, birds would carry seeds and ghaf, jujube, date palms and others would have grown densely in the wetlands. Wildlife would have abounded in this wide, fecund plain.

This lush land, sandwiched between the dry desert escarpment of Arabia to the south and the forbidding Zagros Mountains to the north, was remembered by the Sumerians as their land of Eden.

Gradually, however, as sea levels rose (from around 18,000 BCE onwards), the landscape would start to change. At about 11,500 BCE, as the Pleistocene ice age gives way to the temperate Holocene, the sea had an unstoppable foothold on the land and the great Gulf Oasis flooded.

There are a number of elements in the Sumerian creation myth, the story of Enki and Ninhursag, that made their way into our Abrahamic faiths. Set in the wondrous and innocent land of Dilmun, where "… the raven was not yet cawing, the partridge not cackling. The lion did not slay, the wolf was not carrying off lambs, the dog had not been taught to make kids curl up, the pig had not learned that grain was to be eaten," the story the Sumerians recorded tells of the flooding of this wondrous land, a seminal human event that was appropriated in turn as a fact of history by the Hebrews, who retold the Sumerian story of a land of plenty at the heart of man's very beginnings.

Enki fashions his companion Ninhursag out of his own rib, again a root to the story of origin recorded in the Bible, and of the garden of Eden. Enki, styled 'the lord of sweet waters', consumes fruit of the land and loses the love of Ninhursag – the animal involved is a fox, not a snake.

The Sumerian land of Dilmun has been linked to Bahrain and the area of Eastern Saudi Arabia facing the island, but would more easily associate with the whole region beyond Bahrain, that lost valley where mankind settled until the rising sea levels of a changing world forced them to move to the highlands. As that mythical land was lost to the floods, the city known to the later Sumerians would emerge from the lost land of Dilmun. As, indeed, would the land of Magan – the modern Emirates and Oman.

There is little doubt that this land of Eden was where the waters of what we call the Arabian Gulf wash today.[3] The story of the Great Flood of the Bible is now asserted by academics to have its origins in the flooding of the Arabian Gulf Oasis.[4]

By now it is likely that the humans of Eden would have been semi-nomadic or even settled. They would have become pastoralists, herders of animals, as well as being opportunistic hunter-gatherers. The rising sea would have nudged them northwards and also likely south and westwards, some would have relocated further up the great Ur-Schatt river while some would have taken to settling around the springs and rivers tumbling down the slopes from the sandy highlands. Those freshwater springs still persist today, welling up into the salty waters of the Gulf from its floor: pearl divers told tales into the late 1900s of locations in the Gulf sea where they could upend a bucket on the sea floor and come up with a miraculous pail of fresh water. When the Gulf was a valley, those springs would have formed river systems pouring down into the wetlands below.

By around 8000 BCE, the climate in Southeastern Arabia changed: the monsoon rains became heavier and the climate more humid and temperate. This 'climatic optimum' lasted for the next five millennia, with the notable exception of the 'dark millennium', but the wetter weather systems meant that humans could once again return to Faya and the lands around it.[5]

The rising sea filled the basin and eradicated not only Eden itself, but any trace of thousands of years of human existence and development. It is at this time that we see the emergence of our first identifiable Neolithic population centres on the mainland: the beginning of the development of the cities of Ur and Uruk in Mesopotamia and the first signs of the emergence of the Arabian Bifacial tradition in the southern Gulf – the UAE and Oman.[6]

Seemingly out of nowhere, some sixty communities appear in what had previously been a totally barren period on the archaeological map of the Holocene era in Southeastern Arabia.[7] After a sparsity stretching almost 100,000 years, we see rich evidence of human occupation emerging across the area between 8500 and 6000 BCE – virtually all of the archaeological evidence we have of early human settlement around the shores of the Arabian Gulf links to this sudden appearance – again, consistent with human occupation in that lush valley of Eden being forced away to the uplands to escape the encroaching sea.

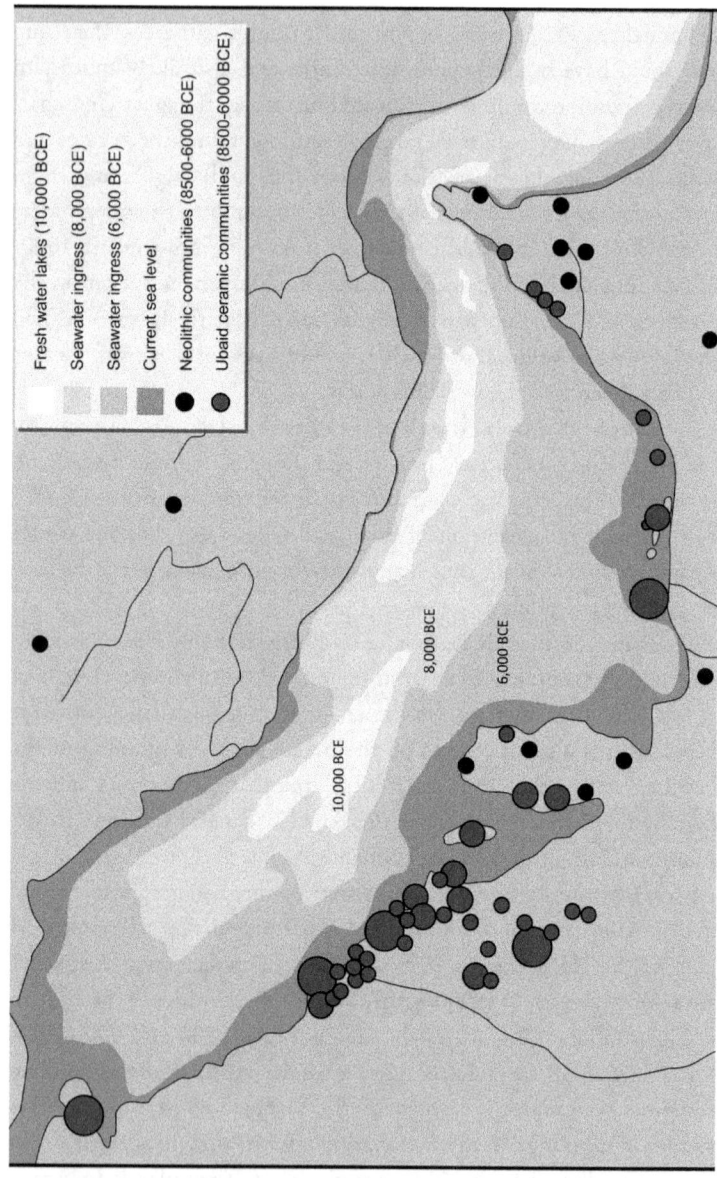

Human Emergence from the Ur Schatt

Rising sea levels forced a migration of humanity from the fertile, lush valley of the Arabian Gulf Oasis to the uplands that surrounded the great water system, from freshwater lakes in 10,000 BCE (shown here in white) to rising sea levels in 8,000 BCE (grey) to the flooding of 6,000 BCE which filled much of the basin, apart from shallow marshes around the shoreline we know today. The emergence of human population centres, particularly linked to the Ubaid Sumerian culture, takes place almost entirely between 8,500 and 6,000 BCE.

Not surprisingly, these new emerging communities were linked. Arabian Bifacial tools have been found alongside distinctively Ubaid era ceramics in the UAE and Oman, which have been traced to a Sumerian origin (using petrographic analysis). As the populations of Sumer gathered to form the first urban communities, fishermen and traders took to using Sumerian reed boats to navigate the Gulf. By the end of the Ubaid period, about the time social and political hierarchies were forming in Sumer, Dilmun (modern-day Bahrain and eastern Saudi Arabia) was emerging as a maritime and mercantile hub, and trading settlements were established along the shores of the Gulf.[8] At the time of the emergence of the Sumerian civilisation, around 6000 BCE, the modern-day island of Bahrain would still have been physically linked to the mainland of what is today the Eastern Province of Saudi Arabia.[9]

By 5000 BCE, the Arabian Gulf was a sea of roughly the scale we know today, although water levels were still slowly rising. Living on its shores and islands, banished from Eden by the Great Floods, the Neolithic people of the Arabian Bifacial era basked in the fresh winds and rains of a more temperate time. We can identify late Stone Age communities in Yemen, southern Oman and along the southern coast of the Gulf living during a period we can define as between the sixth and early fourth millennium BCE. They were makers of fine, sophisticated flint tools, axes, spearheads and arrowheads. They were pastoralists, living nomadic lives herding cattle, sheep and goats in an area watered by the monsoon rains with freshwater lakes forming, even deep into the Rub Al Khali – today one of the world's most forbidding deserts.[10]

And then, as we enter the fourth millennium BCE (4000–3000 BCE), our human record goes, once again, dark.

The dark millennium

The semi-nomadic stone age peoples of the region led their herds to fresh water and grazing, knapping their flint tools and weapons and hunting enthusiastically and opportunistically throughout the interior. They were fishermen, too, not only feasting on freshly caught fish, but molluscs, dugongs and turtles. They fished with both hooks and nets and hunted with flint-headed spears and arrows. Their communities grew and they explored the temperate, welcoming land with its flowing seasonal waterways and lakes fed by the monsoon rains which swept the whole region at the time.

Sometime around 4000 BCE, the climate altered dramatically. The winds changed and the monsoons retreated southwards. The temperate conditions gave way to blazing sun and the greenery withered and browned. Life, so abundant and fecund in the well-watered desertscape, fed by the snaking wadis and home to verdant oases, quickly became marginal and desperate. Dotted across the stony hillside of Jebel Buhais, on the margins of the road between Madam and Mleiha in Sharjah's interior, we find the signs of the impact of that change on the human population of the area. From the fifth millennium BCE to the fourth, Jebel Buhais is rich in evidence of late stone age (or Neolithic) people and clues to the way they lived abound, but then the clues simply stop. No burials, no artefacts. It is as if humankind simply stopped going to Buhais, which up until that point had been a locus of seasonal travel. In fact, there is no other site in the west coast or western interior of the Emirates that shows any evidence of human occupation for much of the period between 4000 and 3200 BCE. Nothing. Dead.

The sudden aridity was the result of a change in the Holocene climate: the temperate, wet phase of the climatic optimum came to an end and there is evidence of springs which stopped flowing at precisely this time: analysis of stalagmites in Omani caves has shown that the water simply dried up. Similarly, a spring located at Jebel Buhais was shown by archaeologists to have dried up at the same time.

The coastal areas on the western shore were also abandoned. It appears as if humankind, those that survived the sudden drought that now gripped the land, moved through the mountain passes to the east coast where wet seasonal weather triggered by the airflow over the Hajar Mountains meeting the Indian Ocean persisted. There is ample evidence of human continuity on the east coast, whereas the west appears barren and abandoned throughout the entire period.[11] Even fishermen to the west would have seen a decline in freshwater resources as the aquifers running down from the mountains dried up.

From all the evidence, the land we know today as the Emirates died for almost a thousand years, desiccated and whipped by sandstorms and harsh desert winds and home to only the hardiest of desert fauna and flora. Any trace of humankind is entirely absent from our current archaeological record of the area.

Humanity returns

Gradually, the weather changed again and ushered in a new temperate era. The monsoons would never return to Arabia, but seasonal rains washed the mountains and the wadis once again blossomed into life in the winter and spring. As water seeped back into the land, so did the people. From their long refuge on the east coast, this population would bring with them new knowledge and habits. They buried their dead in beehive-shaped tombs in the lowlands of mountains and along ridges and other raised formations away from the flowing waters of the wadis. These were the 'people from the Age of Ignorance' Zayed showed to the wide-eyed Glob and Bibby on the plain overlooked by Jebel Hafit in 1959. They populated the mountain areas of Southeastern Arabia and brought the 'Dark Millennium' to an end when they moved west once again. They were farmers, herders, hunters and fishers – and traders. We can date their epoch from 3200 BCE to 2600 BCE, which we now call the Hafit Period after the location of those first archaeological finds from 1959 which pointed to their existence in the foothills of Jebel Hafit.

These returning people brought with them from the eastern mountains an important new discovery: metallurgy. In their time sheltering from the aridity of the west coast, they had found the greenish deposits dotting the Hajar Mountains and had stumbled, somehow, on the strange properties of these rocks when heated. Perhaps knowledge of smelting came from the North – we know that copper was smelted in Serbia as long ago as 5000 BCE and also in Anatolia. Perhaps someone had found the strange shapes of melted ore in the ashes of a campfire and set out to examine this new phenomenon: we will never know quite what happened. But the Hafit people returned through the mountains with a new technology that transformed their society: copper.

The emergence of trade networks

As the sea level of the Gulf stabilised,[12] around 3000 BCE, so too did the urban centres that were developing in Mesopotamia at Ur, Eridu and Uruk. Long used to the encroaching sea, the people of the Gulf Oasis had become mariners and maritime transport would have brought food and other resources to the Sumerian cities.[13] One Sumerian inscription of a later period, about 2500 BCE, asserts that the king Ur Namshe, 'King of Lagas, had boats of Dilmun from the mountains produce loads of timber' and, in fact, Sargon of Akkad boasted of his trade links to the far-flung lands of Magan and Meluhha. Trade was to help establish the urban centres of Sumer and then consolidate the power of its great kings.

Travelling over 1,000 kilometres to the southern Gulf, the traders of Sumer operated a formal network of consistent contacts with their cousins along the shore.[14]

That trade took place via Dilmun as early Sumerian reed boats hugged the coast of the Gulf to find their way to the far-flung reaches of the land they would come to call Magan. What they offered other than the Jemdet Nasr era pottery we have found, we do not know – archaeologists have guessed at trade in pearls, shell beads, livestock and fish. What they got in return, however, was a most valuable metal indeed. They came to the far-away land of Magan for the copper buried deep in its dry, forbidding mountains.

Copper Culture

The first use of metals in Southeastern Arabia took place in the middle to late fourth millennium BCE. We know that the Sumerians referred to 'copper from Dilmun' as early as 3200–3000 BCE[15] and we have direct archaeological evidence from Hafit Period burials of the use of copper as a worked metal, which would date the material's use in the area to before 3200 BCE.[16] Dilmun, of course, produced no copper but its merchants brought ingots of the prized metal from the Hajar Mountains, where it is still mined today.

There is evidence that Anatolia was the site of earlier discoveries of copper – did the technology travel south via Sumeria and become recognised by those people as they travelled to the Hajar Mountains? Or was the discovery made in isolation by the people who had fled the inhospitable west coast?

In either case, news of the abundance of this valuable ore would have travelled fast. And it would have travelled north, to the sprawling civilisation of Sumer.

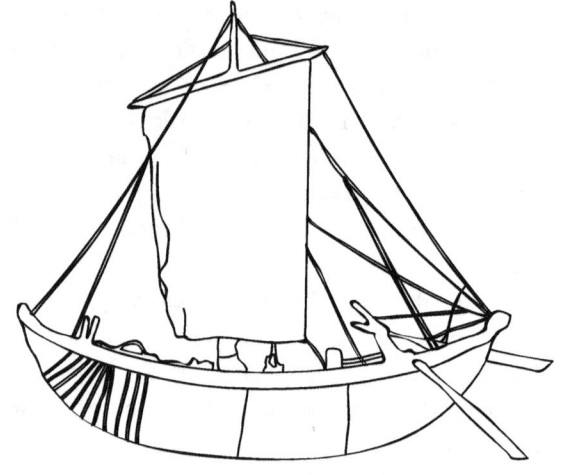

Chapter 3

THE LORDS OF MAGAN

"Let the lands of Meluhha, Magan and Dilmun look upon me, upon Enki. Let the Dilmun boats be loaded with timber. Let the Magan boats be loaded sky-high."

– Enki and the World Order

Marking the end of the 'Dark Millennium', the Hafit people settled the west coast of what is today the Emirates. Whether they were settlers from further north or the returning ancestors of those who had fled over the mountains to escape the great drought, they buried their dead in 'beehive' tombs, a domed construction with a stepped outer wall to seal the entrance. They were small-scale collective burials, and grave goods found in these tombs include Jemdet Nasr pottery from Sumer and, significantly, weapons and trinkets made from copper. The pottery attests to continued links between the peoples of the southern coast of the Gulf and the Sumerian communities coalescing in what we call Iraq today – Ubaid era pottery finds told us of these links between the Neolithic people of the Arabian Bifacial era. Similarly, Jemdet Nasr pottery finds in Hafit tombs link the two communities and speak of a continuity to those links. Another link between the two was the trade in copper.

The discovery of copper by the Hafit people could have been influenced by earlier finds and working of copper from Anatolia, it could have been an independent discovery of the properties of this green metal during the diaspora triggered by the Dark Millennium. What we do know is that this new material was highly prized in Sumer and was imported to the Sumerian cities via Dilmun – from a faraway land the Sumerians called Magan. For decades, archaeologists played an academic version of 'pin the tail on the donkey' as they tried to locate this 'Magan' or 'Makkan' from Sumerian writings. Was it in Iran? India? Further afield?

Slowly, wiser heads prevailed and the emerging picture being painted by the modern archaeological exploration of the UAE and Oman started to narrow down the field. Magan was mentioned time and again in Sumerian writing as a source of copper. References to copper being brought in from Dilmun seemed to point to the source being elsewhere (there are no copper deposits in Bahrain or eastern Saudi Arabia). High in the Hajar Mountains even today, tumbles of green-coloured rock point to the rich veins and deposits that lace the crags and ridges. Modern copper mines in Oman have frequently obliterated their millennia-old forebears in the hunt for new deposits or buried them under mounds of spoil. But a number of ancient workings survive and have been investigated by archaeologists, yielding some remarkable results. We have evidence of mining and smelting and even of communities grown up around the exploitation of this precious metal, so easily worked and yet so much more effective as a weapon than flint-tipped arrows and spears. As an ornamental metal, as a material to form beakers, jugs and pans, copper was at the core of the Bronze Age industrial revolution in Arabia. And at the heart of that revolution was the mysterious land of Magan – the land of the Emirates.

A New Era – Umm Al Nar

A few hundred years after the beginning of the age we associate with the Hafit people came a new age, one marked by a larger, more sophisticated version of the Hafit burials. It was attested by hard evidence of innovations in metallurgy, ceramics and the manufacture of soft-stone vessels from chlorite and steatite.[1] This was the Umm Al Nar era, named after the first discovery of burials from this time by Glob and Bibby on the island of Umm Al Nar in Abu Dhabi.

It is difficult to visit Umm Al Nar today: you can just about make out the graves on Google Earth, but you'd be hard put to find a more sensitive area – the island is home to military installations and oil production facilities and it's most definitely a 'no go' area. Luckily there are other Umm Al Nar era sites around the UAE and Oman. Once the first find had established this was a culture with a specific and unique identity, Glob and Bibby's discovery led other archaeologists onto the Umm Al Nar trail. Key sites opened up, including Hili (the Hili Archaeological Park today features a beautifully rebuilt Umm Al Nar tomb), Mleiha (once again, a rebuilt tomb is the centre-piece of the Mleiha Archaeological Centre), Al Sufouh, Tell Abraq (not accessible to the public, the dig at Tell Abraq is both a work in progress and, tragically, left entirely open to the elements) and Bidya on the east coast, where the Umm Al Nar tomb was cannibalised by the Portuguese to build their fort, thousands of years later.

The Umm Al Nar settlements feature fortifications, often constructed around wells and built from mudbricks and stone and compared by archaeologist Daniel Potts to Martello Towers. These great towers speak of an age when communities had to prepare against aggressive grabs for resources by others – the age, for instance, when the Kings of Sumer made war against the Lords of Magan.

The largest of these Umm Al Nar sites yet discovered lies to the right of the Umm Al Quwain junction on the Sharjah/Ras Al Khaimah highway. Turning towards Falaj Al Mualla, you'll see a rounded white water tower on the left of the road. Opposite this is a hill capped with a concrete pillar. This is the archaeological site of Tell Abraq and under the sand here lies an enormous defensive tower fully forty metres in diameter, made of mud bricks faced with stone.[2] The tower stood at least 7.5 metres high. At the time, it would have been an awe-inspiring sight. At the heart of the tower is a deep well, which would have been both protected by the fortification and would have offered those in the fort resistance against siege.

Excavated by Potts, his team and colleagues from other universities (including Peter Magee, who would go on to become director of archaeology for the Abu Dhabi Department of Culture and Tourism), the tower at Tell Abraq and its associated buildings and tombs have yielded a number of outstanding finds that have given us new insights into the Bronze Age of the United Arab Emirates. These range from the first recorded case of polio in human history through to gold and bronze ornaments including toe rings and combs, hair pins and a seashell containing atacamite (copper hydroxychloride), a copper-based pigment used as eye makeup.[3] This use of shells to store cosmetics was well documented in excavations at the Sumerian city of Ur by Leonard Woolley in the 1920s: these finds attested to the rarity and value of the pigments and subsequent analysis of the similar green cosmetics found at Ur has confirmed that they came from the Hajar Mountains – Magan.[4]

One fascinating discovery made by Potts and his team at Tell Abraq was a pendant depicting a boat, dated to between 1000 and 500 BCE – which sports a mast from which hangs a lateen sail, the first depiction we have in human history of an innovation that was to revolutionise maritime exploration but which also attests to a history of maritime trade.[5]

The various items of personal adornment, from gold jewellery through bone hairpins and combs to the cosmetic pigment in its polished shell speak to a society that has moved beyond subsistence and has the leisure and wealth to indulge in fine decorations. But people still lived short lives and infant mortality was high: of the remains of 300 individuals found at the tomb at Tell Abraq, something like half were children. Analysis of these remains helps us to paint a similar picture to that emerging from the tombs at Hili in Al Ain – anaemia, arthritis and bacterial infections are common, tooth decay and loss ubiquitous. Few of the interred individuals appear to have died violent deaths. Life, it seems, was brutal enough.

Potts, who would spend over a decade digging and cataloguing the site at Tell Abraq, first started to explore the site on a whim, having felt constrained by the limited time sequence of the work he was conducting at the nearby pre-Islamic city of Ed-Dur. Though some excavations had been undertaken at Tell Abraq much earlier by an Iraqi team, it was never properly published. In Tell Abraq, he found a site that spanned millennia, with occupation from the Neolithic, across the Umm Al Nar period and subsequent Wadi Suq era and even finding evidence of occupation as late as the first century CE.[6]

Other Umm Al Nar era towers can be found at Bidya in Fujairah and in Hili in Al Ain as well as Kalba and Sufouh in Dubai. The other towers are generally smaller than that at Tell Abraq. In all, over fifty Umm Al Nar settlements, forts and tombs have been identified across the Emirates and Oman.

The pottery and other artefacts of the Umm Al Nar period show evidence of widespread trade links. Pottery imported from Iran and locally made wares inspired by Iranian patterns are found. There are linkages to the wider world – to trade with the Levant (in olive wood), Bactria in modern-day Afghanistan (ivory) and the Indus Valley in Pakistan (carnelian beads, weights, seals and ceramics) as well as our old friends the Sumerians. Of the famed links to Dilmun, we not only see constant reminders in terms of ceramic finds, we also see at Tell Abraq evidence of continuity even as other signs of trade with Sumer and Akkad die off.[7]

We can date the Umm Al Nar period to 2600–2000 BCE. Uniquely, our observations come not just from archaeology and examinations of necropolises and settlements but from a written record: the Sumerian innovation of the written word leaves us records from which we can stitch together a picture of this land of Magan and its newly emerging trading centres, communities and innovations. Many of these are hammered into tablets or stelae of a hard, granite-like rock sourced uniquely from the Hajar Mountains and highly prized by the Sumerians – diorite.

This flourishing was not only to draw the attention of the Great Lords of Sumer. It was to draw their envy and, finally, their greed.

Sargon and the Akkadians
The Akkadian monarch Sargon boasted that his port was 'visited by ships of Dilmun, Magan and Meluhha'. Clearly, the growing trade between the Sumerians and Magan had grown into a regular route that extended both east and west – from the Indus Valley (in modern Pakistan, home to the Harappan Culture) to the east coast of the Emirates and Oman overland to the Umm Al Nar ports on the west coast and from there on to Dilmun. While it is possible there were direct links between Sumer and Harappa, it is unlikely – the Straits of Hormuz would not have been easy sailing for boats of the type that we have seen the Sumerians built.

This sophisticated trade network had its intermediaries and middlemen – there is a celebrated complaint, written in 1750 BCE by a Babylonian buyer named Nanni to a merchant called Ea-Nasir, complaining that Nasir had supplied sub-standard copper ingots from Dilmun. It might date from a thousand years after the Umm Al Nar period, but then trade is perennial. Dilmun traded copper from Magan, it had no copper of its own. And it brought wood from mountainous countries because, beyond date palm groves, Dilmun had no forests.

Trade with Magan also took place directly: a merchant called LuEnlilla traded during the end of the third millennium BC and there is mention of cloth being traded for copper and ivory – which

Magan middlemen would have traded on from Bactria or India, also from the Indus Valley trade which gave them their source of carnelian.[8] Sumerian writings have talked of a trade in garments, wool, silver, perfumed oil and leather.[9]

The Sumerian civilisation developed and expanded, eventually transforming into what we now recognise as the world's first empire, that of the Akkadians. Many of the writings the Sumerians have left behind them celebrate their rulers and the great achievements and victories they boasted of. None was to match the first Akkadian emperor, Sargon the Great, who unified the Sumerian city-states and boasted of the ships from far-flung places that rode at anchor in his great port of Akkad between 2300 and 2400 BCE.

Empires have a nasty habit of establishing trading ties and then cementing these with conquest and the Akkadians, first among empires, set a fine precedent. Sargon left his newly unified empire to his sons and they inherited not only his power and his lands, but the ties to the riches of the 'lower sea' (the Gulf).

No wonder, then, that following on from Sargon boasting of these trading ships gracing his ports, a symbol of his power and reach, his sons would cast a covetous eye at the very source of all this wealth. Sargon's son Manishtushu left behind him an obelisk of black diorite, itself sourced uniquely from the Hajar Mountains, carved with the legend that he navigated the Gulf Sea to subjugate the thirty-two Lords of Magan.

Following Manishtushu's reign, Naram-Sin also claimed victory over Magan's king, or malek (a word that persists today in Arabic, meaning King). The Umm Al Nar towers may have been constructed against local rivalries or even this very threat from across the sea – but they clearly proved to be unequal to the forces that fell on them from further up the Gulf. And history, by no means for the first time, but in this case perhaps more unfairly because the vanquished lacked even the skill, was written by the victor.

This is by no means the only use of diorite from the Hajar Mountains we see: the material was highly popular with the Sumerians. The Code of Hammurabi, dated back to 1750 BCE, is a black diorite stele. One of the most significant deciphered pieces of early writing we know, it lays out, literally, the law – including the principle we would recognise today as 'an eye for an eye'.

The society of Magan was different to those emerging in Iran and Sumeria: it was arguably less concentric and strongly kin-based.[10] Umm Al Nar burials are collective and give no sense of being monuments to kings or elites (rather, they speak of short and brutal lives with high infant mortality and commonplace malnutrition and disease). Its settled communities consisted of strongholds built around its towers, guarding water resources and the agriculture and husbandry those resources nourished. Alongside these communities, nomads travelled between the coast and interior, herding their animals to make the most of seasonal grazing. Indeed, we are seeing the establishment of a pattern of life that was to persist in Arabia, almost unchanged, for the coming four millennia: coastal urban trading centres, oasis settlements and nomadic tribes travelling, often seasonally, between the two and roaming the land between. The camel, it is perhaps worth noting, had not been domesticated at this time.

The Akkadians may well have written of their conquest of the Lords of Magan, but there is no evidence that their conquest endured to become a settlement of the land. Perhaps, as the administrators of the British Empire were later to conclude, they won a war on the coast and then realised the interior was a vast, inhospitable and ungovernable territory. The interior trading networks that brought copper and diorite down from the mountains and carried goods imported from the Indus Valley through the passes were by now well established and it is likely the Akkadians, confronted by the reality of a harsh and unknown land, accepted some form of tribute or fealty from Magan rather than interrupting these valuable links. Even as late as the Sumerian Third Dynasty, the ruler Ur-Nammu (who ruled Ur from 2047–2030 BCE and was responsible for the construction of the great Ziggurat of Ur) records putting down a rebellion from Magan. If the Akkadians did not settle Magan, they certainly seem to have imposed enough authority – perhaps 'informal empire' – to have invited rebellion.

Rich in trade goods, carnelian from the Indus Valley; wood from the Levant; ivory from Bactria – all of this wealth flowed through Southeastern Arabia. But this all-too-brief flourishing of trade would be brought swiftly to an end when Magan's trading partners collapsed.

In the final years of the second millennium BCE, the great Sumerian/Akkadian cities of Mesopotamia appear to have ceased to focus on the East and turned their gaze Westward and, arguably, inward. Assailed by the rebellious Elamites of western Iran and invaded by the Kassites, a foreign power that appears to have arisen north of Elam, the Akkadians entered into their slow decline. Dilmun ceased to be an entrepôt port serving the wealthy overlords of Sumeria and itself became a Kassite vassal state.

To the east, the Indus Valley was rocked by earthquakes and plunged into drought as climate change tore into the heart of the flowering of this elaborate civilisation. The Harappan people, too, focused inwards. With the loss of their two greatest trading partners, the Umm Al Nar people also pulled back from exploring the seas of commerce and retrenched, focusing on the land they lived in to sustain them. The period of their decline and eclipse would be called the Wadi Suq period, after the outstanding funerary fields in the wadi of that name, which snakes inland of the port city of Sohar, in north-eastern Oman, to join with the Wadi Jizzi and carve through the mountains to the ancient oasis of Buraimi – these days mostly located in Al Ain.

Chapter 4

DEATH IN THE MOUNTAINS

"I destroyed, I devastated, I burned with fire. 1,200 chariots, 1,200 cavalry, 20,000 soldiers of Hadad-ezer, of Aram; 1,000 camels of Gindibu, the Arabian."

– *Shalmaneser III of Assyria*

Under the shadow of the red and white telecommunications tower that stands above the village of Bithnah on the Fujairah/Masafi road, is an ancient burial site. For years following its discovery and excavation by the Swiss-Liechtenstein Foundation for Archaeological Research Abroad in 1987–1991, the grave stood open to the elements, the heavy winter rains of the mountains washing away its walls and swirls of blue plastic bags and other rubbish blowing to settle into the deep stone-lined trough in the summer months.

Although nowadays there is a fence around the site and a corrugated iron roof provides a basic level of protection, it is little enough to preserve – let alone mark or celebrate – such an important site.

The grave was originally dug something like 4,000 years ago. It not only points to the importance of the Wadi Ham route which snakes through the Hajar Mountains from Fujairah to Masafi and then tumbles down, via the Wadi Siji, to the plains of the interior and out to the west coast, but it shows that this route has been in use – and settled – by humankind over the millennia.

The Bithnah burial was typical of the Wadi Suq era, which ran roughly from 2000 BCE to 1300 BCE – from the 'end' of the Umm Al Nar period to the beginning of the UAE's Iron Age. It was a longitudinal pit, lined with stones and was a communal burial. Other Wadi Suq burials litter the landscape of the UAE and Oman, from Shimal and Dhayah in Ras Al Khaimah to the vast necropolis of Jebel Buhais inland of Sharjah, just south of Mleiha and its famous 'Fossil Rock'. The Bithnah tomb is unique, however, in that it is T-shaped – a number of Wadi Suq grave designs have been unearthed, from cloverleaf to barrow – but only at Bithnah do we see this particular T-shape. Most, however, are simply straight, stone-lined pits.

Another pass, which cuts through the Hajar Mountains away to the south of the Wadi Ham is the Wadi Jizzi. This leads from the Omani port city of Sohar to the inland oasis of Buraimi. The hills to the left and right along the road inland of Sohar are littered with tumuli and it is here, in a tributary wadi, the Wadi Suq, that the distinctive burials that gave us a name for this cultural epoch were first discovered.

Yet again, it was the Danes.

The University of Aarhus' Karen Frifelt, who had made the original linkage between the Hafit Culture and Sumeria via the distinctive Jemdet Nasr pottery found in the Hafit beehive graves, found the first evidence of Wadi Suq burials inland of Sohar. A field of some 400 graves was mapped out, still there today across the road from the Crowne Plaza, Sohar.

A large number of Wadi Suq burials have been examined in the foothills of the Hajar mountains around Ras Al Khaimah, from Khatt and Seih Al Harf up to Shimal to the north of the city and burial sites during this era certainly seem to favour inland areas rich in water resources, including Al Ain and the nearby Bidaa bint Saud. There have also been major Wadi Suq finds in Fujairah, Qusais in Dubai, Tell Abraq and Ed Dur in Umm Al Quwain, as well as Kalba on Sharjah's east coast.

The end of Umm Al Nar

It is tempting to look at the end of one era and the start of another as a collapse or cataclysm and this is certainly the case when we try and explain the passing of the vibrant trading culture of Umm Al Nar and its great fortifications and carefully constructed communal graves. However, the burials of the Wadi Suq period which followed show a long transition, from complex communal burials to the distinctive stone-lined pits of the later Wadi Suq period that abound in the region, especially to the north.

Archaeologists have focused on the population centres that emerged with the Umm Al Nar era, but there was also a widespread settled population inland, small communities of pastoralists and subsistence farmers. The transition from trade to subsistence would have largely passed these communities by – nothing much would have changed for them if the trade with Sumer and Harappa failed.[1]

And although there's a tendency to see the Umm Al Nar era as sophisticated and that of Wadi Suq as inward-looking and somehow a period of decline, we see a refinement of jewellery, pottery and metallurgical production through the transition from Umm Al Nar to Wadi Suq.

The weapons and adornments produced by the Wadi Suq people are decidedly more sophisticated, with double-edged, hilted bronze swords and bronze-tipped arrows supplemented by throwing spears. The metallurgical prowess now emerging included experiments with alloys and jewellery of the period includes pieces worked in both gold and electrum – a naturally occurring alloy of silver and gold, mostly found in Anatolia. Jewellery pieces from the period include electrum brooches portraying back-to-back animals. The pottery we find in Wadi Suq era burials shows a great liking for soft-stone vessels, carved with lined patterns which contrast with the dotted circles used by the Umm Al Nar people to decorate many of their vessels.[2]

In short, it is not as simple as it looks.

Certainly, there is a focus away from the ports of the Gulf coast. The port of Umm Al Nar itself becomes deserted, and so, too, Tell Abraq declines. At Tell Abraq and also at Kalba, we see Wadi Suq construction layered on top of Umm Al Nar era fortifications.[3] One interesting characteristic of the Wadi Suq era is that we find widespread evidence of burials, but little built infrastructure. It is this remarkable delta between the legacy of the dead and the living that has led us to think of Wadi Suq as a period of decline rather than as a period of transition and growth. Yet, despite the decline of trade with the outside world, we still see evidence of links to 'Tilmun', with pottery finds in Bahrain pointing to Wadi Suq era trade still taking place between the two former Sumerian centres. At the same time, we see the collapse of trade with the Harappan civilisation to the east, a trade we think persisted at Tell Abraq and Kalba until the second millennium.[4]

So what changed for the Wadi Suq people? Perhaps the biggest change was the passing of the threat from the West. Umm Al Nar fortifications are no longer necessary – as the trade links fade away, so do the demands and threats of foreign emperors. Defence becomes secondary to survival, not an absolute requirement. But with the decrease in the threat of subjugation came the lack of trade and the passing of the wealth that it brought.

Umm Al Nar centres of occupation continued to house Wadi Suq communities, but there is no further development of urban centres.

Climate may well have had a part to play in these changes in human behaviour and settlement, with evidence that a more arid climate prevailed towards the end of the third millennium. There are signs that the water table at the time dropped.[5] This would have forced the human population once again towards the mountains, to the north and east, where wetter conditions could be found and that is, indeed, what we see in terms of Wadi Suq burials – the mountains to the north, in Ras Al Khaimah and the east in Fujairah and Oman, dominate our records of Wadi Suq interment. This movement to the mountains and coast to the east was not as absolute as that which took place during the 'Dark Millennium', but it was a migration, nonetheless.

It would appear that key Umm Al Nar urban centres continued to host a settled population, but equally finds at sites such as Jebel Buhais, between Madam and Mleiha in Sharjah's interior, show us a picture of a nomadic, pastoral community emerging. Once again, as the weather changed, the people moved to meet the new conditions, seeking pasture for their herds and water resources for their crops. The pattern of settled coastal and oasis communities and nomadic tribes roaming the interior persists to this day and the basic rule of existence remains, as always, the same: follow the water.

The transition between Umm Al Nar and Wadi Suq is by no means sudden. Each of the causative factors behind the evolution of the new era has its part to play, but none is transformational in itself. Continuity of settlement at key locations such as Tell Abraq shows a shift of some 200 years' duration and the response of a people to changing environmental, trade and societal factors,[6] while even burials reflected an evolutionary change, with one tomb in particular, found at Qarn Al Harf in Ras Al Khaimah, clearly showing signs of both Umm Al Nar and Wadi Suq influence.

The iron-free Iron Age

There are three defined Iron Ages in the UAE, Iron Age I spanned 1300–1000 BCE, Iron Age II ran from 1000–600 BCE, and Iron Age III takes us from 600–300 BCE. If they have one, rather ironic, feature in common, it is that through none of these three 'Iron Ages' do we find much evidence of the production of any actual iron.

Major Iron Age I finds are centred around Shimal in northern Ras Al Khaimah, Tell Abraq in Umm Al Quwain and, to the south of it, Hamriyah in Sharjah, as well as on the east coast area at Kalba. They speak of a continuity from the Wadi Suq era, with the emergence of large and coarse locally-made ceramic ware, but the nature and behaviour of the human population appears to change – the Wadi Suq period was a time of introspection following the collapse of trade with Sumeria and Harappa and the population would appear to have declined through the intervening period so that, with the emergence of the Iron Age I period, a significant reduction in human settlements had taken place, with a broad range of resources being relied upon to sustain communities, including fishing, hunting and husbandry. Each settlement appears to have been creating its own ceramics and there is some evidence of seasonal movement among populations,[7] but overall there appears to have been a decline in population, settlement and development throughout the Wadi Suq and Iron Age I periods, even if handicrafts surviving from these eras demonstrates significantly enhanced sophistication.

The Iron Age II period not only saw rapid settlement growth throughout the region (in coastal as well as inland areas), but also the emergence of a more structured society. Interior settlements, such as the Iron Age town of Muweilah in Sharjah, start to appear as important regional centres. This is believed to be at least in part due to the domestication of the camel, which allowed easier movement and carriage of trade throughout the interior and opened up new settlements where before they may not have been viable.

In fact, it is Muweilah which gives us one of the few examples of iron artefacts to be recovered from 'Iron Age' sites in the Emirates. Even the twenty-odd objects, including an iron sword, unearthed at Muweilah are thought to have been Persian in origin. The Iron Age settlement of Muweilah, today located in the packed residential suburb of Juraina, east of Sharjah's University City (just off the road between Sharjah International Airport and the '06' shopping mall, as you ask) is now just a big, fenced-off sandy lot nestled in an area of densely-packed housing. And yet in its prime, around 850 BCE, Muweilah was a busy major inland settlement, with copper-smelting and casting taking place, as well as widespread production of flour from barley and wheat. Artefacts recovered from Muweilah are contiguous to those found from the same period at Tell Abraq and other Iron Age settlements, evidence of an emerging uniform material culture that interconnects the settled areas of the time.[8]

One key factor in the growth of settled populations and communities is that of the advancement of techniques of irrigation. Ever since the monsoons departed the Gulf, the arid summer season would have been problematic for farming and animal husbandry. Nomadism, the idea that you would abandon the coast and plains for the oases and mountains as the season turned hot, was a constant feature of the human economy of Southeastern Arabia. The earliest finds at Tell Abraq and Jebel Buhais pointed to the seasonal movement of populations in the fourth and fifth millennium BCE and now, with camels available to heft baggage, a combination of settled and semi-settled populations emerges. Irrigation was to transform human existence in the area – and that was to lead to the development of increasingly complicated *falaj* systems and the concept of *bustan* agriculture.

The Arabic word *falaj* means water channel, and its plural is *aflaj*. These channels at first would have been simple mud ditches connecting water sources such as springs to planted areas, with these expanding both with the water channels feeding them and date palms shading them. Communities would have learned to share water resources, as they in fact do in the present day, 'time sharing' the flow of water from its source and diverting it to irrigate crops throughout the oasis. In Masafi, for instance, evidence is clear of an increasingly sophisticated system of water management being employed to organise the irrigation of crops, including wells, canals and subsidiary waterways to feed stepped plantations.[9]

More and more complex systems of irrigation evolved and, in the Iron Age II era, we start to see the emergence of centralised authority imposed over the most precious resource known to man at the time. With that communal approach came more efficient resource utilisation and increasingly complex communities grew around water sources and their associated irrigation systems. In important Iron Age sites such as Rumeila and Bidaa Bint Saud as well as, most recently, in Al Thuqaibah, Muweilah and Masafi, we find buildings and ceramics associated with the distribution of water and with rituals, including the burning of incense and communal banqueting.[10]

One major innovation in this emerging capability to harness water resources was the development of intricate irrigation systems, including extensive underground waterways – and it is only recently that we have both come to realise – and been prepared to admit – that this technology *originated* in Southeastern Arabia. Classical historians over the past century have attributed the technology, the *falaj* or *qanat*, to an Iranian origin and it has been a somewhat jealously guarded attribution. Our modern, archaeologically based, understanding not only questions that attribution – it knocks it out of the park.

The problem with Qanats

The *qanat* problem originated with academics in the 1970s, who took to citing the Greek historian Polybius to derive an Iranian origin for the innovation of underground waterways that tapped deep aquifers in higher ground and channelled the water from these down to irrigate oasis areas. The problem was that these accounts were not backed by any hard evidence and so, in 2002, with the publication of a paper by UAE-based archaeologist Walid Yasin Al Tikriti, *The Southeast Arabian Origin of the Falaj System*, something of an academic controversy developed.

Al Tikriti provided the first counterpoint to the long-accepted narrative that the *qanat* originated in Persia in the time of the Assyrian King, Sargon II, in 714 BCE. Al Tikriti based his work on the excavation of seven Iron-Age *aflaj* in Al Ain, as well as work in Al Madam, Sharjah and in Oman – these finds provide reliable carbon-dated provenance of *aflaj* to Iron Age II dates of 1000 BCE and older. With modern archaeology and carbon dating set against unreliable textual references that had been interpreted by scholars in the 1970s and earlier, the accepted narrative was effectively challenged. An academic consensus slowly emerged that the *qanat* of Persia could not be reliably attributed to an early pre-Islamic date and that, in fact, the innovation would have been taken back to Persia by the Sasanians, who invaded Southeastern Arabia in the third century CE. Tikriti's work was incontrovertible – the *qanat* was not a Persian innovation – it originated in Iron Age Southeastern Arabia. Over a dozen sites have now been investigated in the Emirates and Oman that offer reliable, carbon-dated evidence of the Arabian origin of the *falaj*.[11]

Challenging the traditional consensus, despite the existence of incontrovertible, carbon-dated evidence set against narrative sources with no backing in actual finding, has been oddly difficult – and yet this is not the only area where our emerging understanding of the archaeology of the Emirates is finding itself at odds with long-accepted ideas.

The innovation of the *falaj* during the Iron Age II period only added to the development of oasis agriculture, already thought to have emerged around the need to cluster agricultural production around sources of water. Wells had been core resources for communities since the Umm Al Nar period and even Hafit burials tend to be clustered around or near known oasis locations. As water management techniques developed and new crops were introduced, it is thought that the *bustan* oasis we know today became established. In this system, water channels support palm groves, which give much-needed shade to less hardy crops. This multi-layered form of agriculture brought collectivism to communities and the need to sustain and support the *aflaj* would have been critical to maintaining the viability of the plantation. This in turn meant settlement and a sedentary population with an agreed system of water management,[12] distribution and sharing. It also brought a new cohesiveness to the idea of *community*. Agreeing to share resources, a system of dispute resolution and even of the concept of rule of law would have developed in these pre-Islamic societies.

The stabilisation of populations around improved water management and formalised systems of community and agriculture is therefore the key innovation we can attribute to Southeastern Arabia in the Iron Age II period.

It is also during this period that evidence emerges of domesticated camels – both the burial of camels and the appearance of their images in cultural artefacts. Carbon dated remains from Tell Abraq and artefacts from Muweilah (including the famous camel figurine found in Building 1 at Muweilah, which now graces the entrance to the Sharjah Archaeological Centre) give Iron Age I and II dates.[13] Whether the camel was locally domesticated from wild populations or imported to the region from Egypt or elsewhere is still being debated by archaeologists, with recent research suggesting native Arabian origins for the wild camel but the introduction of such a rich source both of protein (as many camel bones as cow bones were found at Muweilah) and reliable long-distance transport brought a revolutionary capability.

We have records from Assyria at this time of camels in use to mount warriors, notably by Shalmaneser III, the warlike Assyrian king who campaigned against pretty much all of his neighbours in the eighth century BCE – as well as his predecessor Tukulti-Ninurta II, who conquered the Zagros Mountains, which line the northern coast of the Gulf. Shalmaneser tells us, in no uncertain terms, 'I destroyed, I devastated, I burned with fire. 1,200 chariots, 1,200 cavalry, 20,000 soldiers of Hadad-ezer, of Aram; 1,000 camels of Gindibu, the Arabian.'[14]

Gindibu the Arabian (it's tempting to think of the name as being a corruption of Bu Kindi), passes into and out of history with that single mention, but his camels mark a moment in the human development of Arabia. Facing a line of camel-riders would have been a fearsome prospect at the time, one only matched perhaps by the sight of elephant riders. And so we see the third use for the newly domesticated camel in Southeastern Arabia – as an instrument of war.[15]

Chapter 5

THE IMPOSSIBLE DESERT FORGE

"This land connected ancient civilisations and we will continue to be a hub that connects the world."

- Mohammed bin Rashid Al Maktoum

To the south of Marmoom, in Dubai, the deep desert sands roll on to join up with the Rub Al Khali, the Empty Quarter, one of the world's great desert wildernesses. Flying over the golden sands in his helicopter in 2002, Sheikh Mohammed bin Rashid Al Maktoum, then Crown Prince of Dubai, noticed something unusual on the undulating ground down below and went around to investigate.

A keen aviator, Mohammed originally trained in the 1960s on Aermacchi jets in Italy. He often flew over this area – Marmoom has long been a favoured location for the Maktoum family at leisure and in fact Marmoom today is the location of Dubai's Endurance Racing track as well as the luxurious Bab Al Shams desert resort and is home both to Godolphin's Marmoom Stables and Mohammed's beloved Arabian Horse Stud.

Back in 2002, it was a place where Mohammed could relax in the desert he had been brought up to love by his father. He thought he knew the area like the back of his hand and yet this strange dark shape below him had never caught his eye before. He circled, viewing the odd, crescent-shaped field of what appeared to be dark stones. He waymarked the site using his GPS and resumed his flight.

At the time he thought no more about it, distracted by other affairs. But some time later, he called Hussein Qandil, the director of the Department of Archaeology at Dubai Municipality. He had seen something strange in the desert, something that looked oddly man-made and yet appeared to be a rock field of some sort. Here was the location. Could they investigate?

Qandil and his team ventured into the desert in four-wheel drives to the area marked by the GPS location. They pulled up and jumped out, surveying the swathe of black deposits splayed out before them. Bending down to pick up one of the strangely-shaped 'rocks', he realised this was a field of slag, the by-product of smelting. Here, in the middle of the deep desert, was a major metallurgical production centre, presumably of some antiquity. Yet, its location was highly unusual, miles away from the three things you'd need to smelt and work with metals: water, ore and wood for the fires. The site was, literally, in the middle of nowhere.

Qandil's team returned with equipment to survey the site and trial excavations were carried out on the sand beneath the 1.5-hectare field of copper slag. The site was named Saruq Al Hadid, which means The Iron Path. In 2003, excavations started in earnest, with a team from the Jordanian Department of Antiquities from 2003-2008, followed by a series of small-scale excavations in 2008-2009 by the Dubai Desert Survey, a joint effort between American researchers and the Dubai Department of Tourism and Commerce Marketing (DTCM). A three-year programme of excavations by the University of New England, Australia followed in September 2014.

The results right from day one were spectacular. Qandil's first trial soundings yielded a huge inventory of finds, including copper and bronze arrowheads, tweezers, axe heads, knives, bracelets, pins, rings and tiny effigies of snakes. This trove established that there was something special below the surface covering of dark slag and dated finds back to the first millennium BCE – the UAE's Iron Age II era.[1]

The whole area of Saruq Al Hadid is desert sand laid on a gypsum base, evidence of a much earlier abundance of water (the first layer of sand to cover the gypsum layer has been dated to around 3,800 BCE). Today, the sand covering the gypsum floor is up to seven metres deep. The water table is lower today, but only about two metres below the surface in places. This abundance of ground water is seen down the road from Saruq Al Hadid at Al Ashoosh, where several wells have long provided relief to camel trains travelling through the desert and, coincidentally, where an Umm Al Nar settlement has been found.

It was to the Umm Al Nar era that further digs pointed, layers of time lurking below Qandil's initial finding of Iron Age II provenance. Saruq Al Hadid's gypsum layer showed signs of Umm Al Nar era settlement, including hearths, ash-pits and post-holes dug into the gypsum itself. Above this layer, Wadi Suq and late Bronze Age middens were found, with extensive bone deposits. Higher up in the timeline, life becomes a great deal more interesting – scattered throughout the site are evidence of mud-brick platforms, smelting furnaces and thousands of objects, from weapons to earrings, and soft-stone, copper and ceramic vessels.[2]

A picture emerges from the excavations at Saruq Al Hadid of continuous habitation at the site from 3,200 BCE and earlier (some evidence points to Hafit era occupation) right through to 800 BCE, the middle of the UAE's Iron Age II and arguably the flowering of the site, when it was a major metallurgical centre producing weapons, ornaments, utensils and – arguably – objects of devotion. Its inhabitants ate dried fish brought from the coast, although extensive finds of animal bones suggest that the settlement was a centre for processing hides rather than slaughtering animals for meat. A number of small animal and bird bones is thought to indicate the area was home to much more vegetation than it is now.

But Saruq Al Hadid was, above all, an Iron Age metallurgical centre of tremendous significance. The smelting that took place there was sophisticated, likely using multi-stage processes and included the production of bronze, an alloy of copper and tin. Tin is not found naturally in south-east Arabia, so must have been traded from elsewhere, possibly Afghanistan or the Indus Valley.

But what really sets Saruq Al Hadid apart are two very special metals: gold and iron.

Metals of note

Something like 200 kilograms of iron artefacts and remains have been recovered from Saruq Al Hadid, an amazing trove given that nowhere else in Iron Age Southeastern Arabia do we find any evidence of iron implements, except at Muweilah, where we believe the relics were Persian imports. The iron artefacts of Saruq Al Hadid mainly date back to the latter part of the Iron Age II (1000–600 BCE) and were recovered in a bad state of corrosion – most were weapons or fragments which suggest they were once weapons. And although a lot of iron articles have been found, there's been no find so far of furnaces or slag associated with iron production. Despite its name, Saruq Al Hadid was a major centre of copper and bronze production but not, as far as we know, iron.

Some of the most beautiful objects recovered from Saruq Al Hadid have been worked in silver and gold, including the ornate ring that was to inspire the Dubai Expo 2020 logo (and indeed, provide the cover for this book). And the site has yielded up huge finds of beads and other ornamental goods made from seashell, eggshell, pearl, stone (including carnelian) and other materials.

Apart from the enigma of Saruq Al Hadid's location (deep in the desert, 120 kilometres from the sea or known sources of water, wood or ore), there is another mystery which forms part of a wider enigma when we examine the Iron Age in the Emirates. Snakes.

The mystery of the snakes

There is an element of cultural uniformity that emerges during the Iron Age II in Southeastern Arabia that speaks to either a centralised system of governance or possibly of belief and certainly a sharing of common behaviours and styles of artefact. Nowhere is this so clearly the case than the snake symbolism we see emerging at the same time at Saruq Al Hadid, Muweilah, Masafi, Bithnah, Ed-Dur, Tell Abraq, Rumailah, Bidya and Qusais. In each of these places, we have seen snake figures portrayed either in ceramics or in representations worked in bronze. They curl into mandalas; they slither around pots and they wriggle and writhe their way in waves across slipware and metal alike. The emergence of certain types of ceramics, larger pots and censers, columned buildings and *aflaj* all date to this time and although we can support the innovations in buildings and ceramics as being part of normal human development, we have no idea of why the snake suddenly emerges as such a powerful cultural symbol at this time.

The first find of a site with this strong snake symbolism in the Emirates took place in 1982, with the uncovering of what became known as the 'Mound of Snakes' at Qusais in Dubai, a site that was thought to be a dedicated temple and which shared certain characteristics (including walled buildings which were left open to the northern side) with a temple complex unearthed in Bithnah, in Fujairah.

We know of other snake cults: what we do not know is whether the snake symbol that appears so strongly across so many sites in the Southeastern Arabian Iron Age II is a religious icon or a symbol of central authority. In a number of sites, both seem to sit together – buildings and structures that appear to have a religious function, together with finds of snake-decorated ceramics and incense burners, with columned halls and signs of a water distribution strategy tied to centralised authority.[3] The link between snakes and water is strong at all of these sites.

Certainly, there is evidence of the dispersal of ideas and ways of life that are similar across the region at this time – and we have evidence of Sumerian snake imagery, although by now the Sumerians have been left far behind. The cult of the snake, the iconography, are found in Elam and Susa, in south-western Iran and in Mesopotamia, associated with worship of fertility, healing and the Earth – the snake changes its skin and emerges smooth and youthful, sinuous and reminiscent of the sweet water of underground springs.[4]

A change of ages

As we enter the first millennium BCE, we see tremendous change in the area, evidence of a great series of conflicts and movements of humanity. A number of towers and other fortifications have been dated back to this time, offering protection to *aflaj* and their crops, as well as the communities around them and fulfilling much the same function as the Umm Al Nar round towers. Forts at Hili in Al Ain; Madhab and Awhala in Fujairah; Jebel Buhais near Madam in Sharjah and Rafaq in the Wadi Qawr in Ras Al Khaimah all date to this time,[5] leading us to assume that these communities were forced to protect themselves against some outside force.

Saruq Al Hadid goes quiet a little after 800 BCE. So does another important Iron Age metallurgical site, Muweilah, destroyed in a cataclysmic conflagration 200 years later. The thriving mountain oasis of Masafi and the settlements around it were silenced around 600 BCE[6] and Bithnah is also abandoned.

For the first time in a while, we start to see the region recorded in the annals of outside forces – the Achaemenid King Darius links the land of Qade to the Akkadian Makkan and Elamite Makkash. It is clear from the inscriptions and from texts from Persepolis that there is now a satrapy of Maka.[7] The Achaemenids arrived in Southeastern Arabia: and they didn't come in peace.

The Persian Achaemenid Empire stretched from the Indus Valley to the Balkans and North Africa and Maka not only fell under its sway, according to Herodotus' Histories, Maka supplied troops to fight with Xerxes' army in 480 BCE. We have unearthed Iron Age short swords with distinctive crescent pommels from finds at Qusais in Dubai; Buhais in Sharjah and Rumailah and Qattara in Al Ain that are identical in form to that borne by the figure of a native of Maka carved in Darius II's grave relief at Persepolis.[8]

Established by the sword with remarkable rapidity, Achaemenid rule resulted in a series of satrapies, sub-kingdoms, and an effective bureaucracy to administer their enormous empire, including a postal system. This was an age of great empires and their clashes would rock the ancient world. The Achaemenids were to flower and dominate a huge area, and yet their empire would endure only two hundred years before their nemesis fell upon them and all but wiped them out. This was Alexander the Great – the Macedonian king who conquered Persia but who died before he could invade the little satrapy of Maka across the Arabian Gulf. Alexander's empire was divided following his death and the area from Persia to Syria fell under the Seleucid Empire. Although the Seleucids' conquests took them as far as present-day Kuwait on the Gulf, they left Southeastern Arabia alone and so a Hellenistic era society was able to thrive in an age of political independence from 300 BCE onwards. Two key centres were to emerge during this time: one on the coast of what today is Umm Al Quwain. And one near a place where the human history of the region first started, 125,000 years ago: Mleiha.

Chapter 6

THE RISE OF MLEIHA

"As we follow the history of man, we shall find the centres of interest, the fresh growing points, swinging from continent to continent. Often after a period of such eminence or initiative, the region may lapse into relative unimportance, only to come to the fore at a later time."

– *Leonard Woolley*

Fossil Rock or, to give its proper name, Jebel Mleiha has long been a popular day out destination for off-road enthusiasts: the sand has piled up against the rocky ridge from the surrounding red desert, creating a pass through the 'head' of the rock high above the vast dunefields which, when breasted, gives a satisfyingly gut-lurching descent down to join the undulating, shifting land below. Its popular name comes from the many little fossils which can be found embedded in the foothills of the great spur that traverses the dune fields of inland Sharjah.

It is here, at Mleiha, that the desert of Sharjah's interior gives way to the huge inland Jiri plain, a gravelly flat expanse dotted with ghaf trees, which stretches out towards the foothills of the Hajar Mountains. Water from the mountains runs off and gathers in the wadis, barrelling down narrow waterways in a breakneck rush that will easily (and has often) pick up a car and dash it against the walls of the canyon until it is reduced to a twisted ball like a crumpled-up piece of aluminium foil.

The waters peter out as they meet the plains, forming alluvial fans with tree-like branches. Seeping down into the gravel, underground rocky layers trap the waters and channel them away from the mountains, forming a network of aquifers which will eventually reach the coast.

At Mleiha, those waters wash up against the rocky outcrop of Jebel Mleiha, Jebel Faya and Jebel Buhais. The rock wall forms a natural barrier, creating a fertile strip that runs from Dhaid down to Madam. It is no wonder that humans have settled here over the millennia, sometimes fleeing during periods of exceptional aridity but always returning to the welcoming shadow of the winding ridge that snakes its way through the interior desert.

By about 300 BCE, Mleiha was a substantial settlement, dominated by *areesh* (palm-frond) dwellings. It stands out as a key settlement of its time because of the sheer size of the place (just under 300 hectares of built-up area) and because of the strange, ornamented mud-brick graves with towers that characterise the period. Nowhere else in the area are these types of burials found, although they seem to echo Nabatean forms. It is to the Nabateans that we owe the towering stone monuments of Petra in Jordan and Mada'in Saleh (now known as Al Ula) in Saudi Arabia – a proto-Arab culture which flourished in the late Iron Age, migrating northwards from Arabia sometime after 600 BCE. The tantalising link between Mleiha and Nabataea is so tenuous as to be purely coincidental without further evidence. As is so often the case, there is more to be found before we can make the connection.

The fertile area was used to grow wheat and barley, as well as to cultivate the ubiquitous date palms. The grains were then ground into flour. Farming, by now, had become a sophisticated pastime and an Iron Age farmhouse is preserved at Mleiha with its rooms reconstructed to show the complex as it once stood.

Mleiha shows signs of two distinct cultural influences. As well as home-made production of ceramics, we find Greek amphorae at the site dating back to between 100 and 300 BCE. At the same time, we find engraved bronze bowls and alabaster-ware, which is distinctively southern Arabian, inscribed both in Aramaic and Hasaitic. Inscriptions found here mention the 'King of Oman', one particularly rich find which has been dated between 214–222 BCE reads, in Aramaic, 'This is the memorial of Amud, son of Gurr, which built over him his son Amud, son of Amud, year 90 (or 97)' and then, in Hasaitic, 'Memorial and tomb of Amud, son of Gurr, son of Ali, inspector of the King of Oman, which built over him his son Amud, son of Amud, son of Gurr, inspector of the King of Oman.' That inscription fits in with a wealth of other discoveries from Mleiha which place it as an important regional centre and a locus for linguistic and cultural influences as well as trading relationships linked to Seleucid Persia, the Parthians, Sasanians and the peoples of southern Arabia.[1]

It is at Mleiha that we find evidence of the widespread late pre-Islamic era production of iron implements, from nails through to weapons.[2] Sources of iron ore are to be found close by but it has been suggested that the influence of surrounding iron-using empires finally weaned the people of the region away from their long-standing dependence on bronze and copper and started them on a path to using the harder, more durable material.

Discovering Mleiha

The Danish teams from Aarhus University had been digging in the UAE for something like ten years when, in 1968, the Ruler of Sharjah at the time, Sheikh Khalid bin Mohammed Al Qasimi, contacted Karen Frifelt, who was leading the team. He had found some interesting-looking objects during a hunting trip; would she care to take a look at them?

Clearly there was something going on at Mleiha and, in 1974, an Iraqi team performed an exploratory dig. It was not to be until 1986 when the French archaeologists Remy Boucharlat and later Michel Mouton headed digs across successive seasons that Mleiha would start to be truly appreciated as the huge site that it is. Excavations there have been taking place ever since.

In January 2016, Mleiha became home to the UAE's first archaeological visitor centre, with displays showing the rich history of the region and presenting some of the huge trove of finds made throughout the work that has taken place across the extensive site.

Equal and perhaps even greater in splendour to Mleiha was Ed-Dur, a city at its peak between 300 and 100 BCE and sprawled across some 800 hectares. In the pre-Islamic era, it would have been an impressive sight indeed, sitting overlooking the coast of Umm Al Quwain's Khor Al Beida (it is a few hundred metres inland these days, thanks to the silting of the creek and changing water levels over the past two millennia) and home to a vast variety of mud-brick constructions, from fortifications to houses and temples. It is here that we see alabaster sheets used for the first time in recorded history as glass in windows and it is here that we find ceramics from Mesopotamia, Iran and India as well as Roman glass, all dated to the first century BCE. Ed-Dur has been put forward as Pliny's 'Omana',[3] 'a harbour of great importance in Carmania'.[4] Carmania was a Persian province under Alexander the Great which stretched along the coast from Bandar Lengeh to Bandar Jask.

Mleiha and the coastal city of Ed-Dur were contemporaneous and formed part of an extensive trading network during the time of the Seleucids, with links to Greece, Egypt, Rome and Persia reflected in an enormous trove of objects recovered from the graveyards and buildings of the ancient city. Mleiha was undoubtedly wealthy, as attested by the finery its citizens left behind. Coin moulds found at Mleiha were used to mint coins found at Ed-Dur and animal burials at both sites follow the same distinctive positioning, with their heads turned to face behind them. Mleiha sits equidistant between the Wadi Siji/Wadi Ham crossing of the Hajar Mountains and the Hatta crossing. And following the wadi from Dhaid takes you through Falaj Al Mualla down to the coast just north of Ed-Dur. No wonder, then, that the two ancient cities were so interlinked.

Another series of links to be found at Mleiha are with the interior of the Gulf – alabaster vessels and coins alike testify to southern Arabian contacts, while Aramaic inscriptions found on stone stelae and bowls at the site provide evidence of cultural links to the Levant. These provide some of the early links we see to the 'two tribes' who would populate the area – the southern tribes including Al Azd, who would be instrumental in bringing Islam to the area, and those who came to the area from central and northern Arabia. We would come to group the southerners together under the 'Hinawi' banner and the northerners under the 'Ghafiri'.

For all the graves found at Mleiha, no burial from the period of the city's existence as a pre-Islamic regional centre so far has been found with human remains.[5] In fact, one of the fortresses uncovered at Mleiha shows every sign of having been sacked and there is every chance that the graves were pillaged as an act of war likely, given the timing, to have marked the conquest of the area under the first Sasanian King, Ardashir I, who reigned from 224–240 CE.

The Sasanians invade

If the evidence of Mleiha is to be believed and if, indeed, it was by their swords and arrows that Mleiha fell, the Sasanian invasion was swift and brutal. Mleiha was reduced and its population scattered.

The Sasanians had bigger fish to fry – on the Western borders of their empire was Byzantium, the centre of the eastern Roman Empire and the two expanding waves of the competing empires crashed against each other with devastating effect in the battle for the domination of the

Near East. To the Sasanians, Southeastern Arabia was – to borrow T. E. Lawrence's description of his part in the Arab Revolt of 1916–18, 'a sideshow to a sideshow'.[6]

By the time these new invaders arrived, the area had declined in economic importance, population and cultural significance. The people of Magan, that great former centre of trade between East and West had lost their markets and had instead turned to a mixture of nomadism and *bustan* oasis agriculture for survival. Fishing and limited trading sustained the coastal communities. Mleiha and Ed-Dur stand out as centres of power and wealth, cities of considerable size but which appear to have suffered a long and slow decline, Mleiha first. In the early years of the Common Era, by about 200 CE, both cities had shrunk and human occupation appears to have been concentrated around central fortified areas, testament to a long series of attacks, whether by local forces or foreign ones we will likely never be quite sure.

One thing we can be sure about is that the Sasanians came. Equally surely, they conquered. We would be safe in assuming that in between these two events, they saw. But the area they conquered was no economic powerhouse and offered very little to the hungry expanders of an ambitious empire. Even the copper in the mountains was not quite as desirable as it used to be in the good old days – iron was the metal of choice for weaponry.

Sasanian records tell us that campaigns were launched against Arabia, but they were limited and there was no attempt to impose direct rule – northern Arabia was ruled in their name by their clients, the Lakhmids. Although we find evidence of Sasanian period artefacts, particularly at Kush, Khatt, Hulayla and Mleiha, there is little to no evidence of an enduring Sasanian occupation of Southeastern Arabia.[7] One rare exception to this is a late Sasanian era fort at Al Fulayj in Oman, which stands as the only securely dated such fortification in the area.[8]

Christianity in the Gulf

The Sasanians gave sanctuary to the Church of the East after its doctrine was declared heretical (the Church, often incorrectly referred to as Nestorians, believed that the mortal and divine Christ were two different things) and Christianity thrived in many areas throughout the Sasanian empire. Perhaps strangely, some of the most enduring monuments left behind in the wake of the Sasanian presence in Southeastern Arabia are churches.

The Eastern Christian church and monastery on the Abu Dhabi island of Sir Bani Yas opened to the public in December 2010. They are an eerie memory of a community who lived a life on the island dominated by its ore-smeared hill, that must have been grinding and debilitating. Life in the dreary, arid climate was relieved by fresh water from their cistern and fine wines taken out of blown glass vessels. The community, active in the pearl trade of the time and connected by trading routes between the Gulf and India, would therefore would likely have been relatively wealthy. First unearthed in the 1990s by a team from the Abu Dhabi Islands Archaeological Survey (ADIAS), the church complex was one of a number found along the shores of the Gulf: in Kuwait, Bahrain and Saudi Arabia. Another, larger, church, with an associated settlement, was found on Umm Al Quwain's island in Siniyah in 2021, not far from Ed-Dur. The Siniyah monastic complex has been dated between 534 and 656 CE and included a kitchen, storerooms, a water cistern and an oven, thought to have been used to bake communion wafers. A large house forms part of the complex and has been called a 'Bishop's Palace'. Finds at the site include an altar and a cistern that could been used for baptisms. Large glass chalices found at the site are thought to have been used to celebrate the Eucharist. Led by archaeologist Tim Power, the team working on Siniyah announced in 2024 the discovery of the oldest known pearl fishing town in the Persian Gulf on the island, identifying a major settlement of some 12 hectares, comprising a number of houses built of rock and lime mortar. Thought to be one of the largest such settlements of its time, it has been compared in importance to the city of Julfar in Ras Al Khaimah.

This period is a fascinating time because by now you would expect recorded human history and archaeology to come together in some focus. We have long enjoyed the written records of the Sumerians and their inheritors in both Mesopotamia and Persia, the effigies of Kings and Queens and their stelae carrying accounts of their conquests and constructions, and we have been able in a number of cases to match these to actual places and monuments.

Now we have the Romans, the Greeks and others. Herodotus, Pliny, Ptolemy and unknown authors join to give us recorded accounts of events and places and so we could perhaps expect history and archaeology to match by now, giving us reliable dates and locations of events on the record which match the geographical facts on the ground.

Nowhere is this less so than in the Christian Eastern Churches of the Gulf, in particular on Sir Bani Yas. The churches were confidently dated by their discoverers because the record is so clear as to the time of their existence. Church records tell us that churches were established in the Arabian Gulf sometime after the year 300 but archaeology tells us that every one of the communities we have discovered dates between 650 to 750, which means they must have been in use during the Islamic era.[9] Academics are still arguing – at times bitterly – about the exact date of the foundation of the church at Sir Bani Yas.

This does not mean the history is wrong. Churches may well have existed, predating these more sophisticated communities and there is evidence from elsewhere of a rebuilding programme instituted at the time we see these new churches emerging. But these early Christian communities existed at the time when Islam came to the Gulf and were clearly co-existent with their Muslim neighbours. This may be, as Robert Carter, an archaeologist at University College London, has speculated, that the Christian communities were economically active in the fishing and pearl trades – documents attest to the latter – and were accepted by the community leaders of the time as beneficial sources of revenue and commerce. Whether it is this pragmatic approach, or the well-documented Islamic practice of encouraging co-existence among other branches of the Abrahamic faiths, the Church complexes on Sir Bani Yas and on Siniyah endured well into the Islamic age.

But while the Christians were free to worship and hunt for their pearls, the Sasanians were about to get an invitation they couldn't refuse.

Chapter 7

HERE LIE 10,000 MEN

"The repentance of those who reject Faith after accepting it and who then persist in denying it will never be accepted, for they have gone astray."

- The Holy Quran, 3:90

The Sasanians ruled Arabia at a remove, employing their Lakhmid clients to manage affairs in north-eastern Arabia from their cities at Al Hira and Thaj and building significant fortified defences against the troublesome Arabs of the interior. Their forays against the tribes – particularly Al Kindi, the Ruler of the great central Arabian tribe which was to give us the root of the Emirati and Omani Kunud tribe, were brief and without gain, but must have sown the seeds of an enduring enmity.

In Southeastern Arabia we have evidence that a similar arrangement was made with the Julanda, a local Arab dynasty. That arrangement would divide the territory and areas of military and civil administration between the Sasanian governors and their Arab associates. With the cities of Ed-Dur and Mleiha now effectively abandoned (in Mleiha, likely the result of the first wave of Sasanian invasion followed by vicious reprisals), it would appear that Southeastern Arabia under the Sasanians was locked in a period of prolonged and enervating decline.[1]

Movement of the people

Since the rise of Mleiha and Ed-Dur, we have historical and archaeological evidence that cultural encounters were taking place across the landmass of the Arabian peninsula and being forged into more enduring links, whether through trade and cooperation or conflict. Aramaic inscriptions appear at Mleiha, ceramics are dotted around sites that attest to a variety of origins. Artefacts from the West are found alongside those from the East. A gold coin of the Roman Emperor Tiberius, found on Siniyah Island off Umm Al Quwain, connects Rome to Ed-Dur.[2]

As south-east Arabia enters its long, slow decline under the Sasanians, the tribes of central Arabia are roiling, clashing with the Sasanian invaders and their client despots. Moving up the coast from Yemen, finding their way along the Gulf, the tribes of Arabia repeat the pattern of ancient settlement and start to expand their area of influence and explore the under-populated lands to either side of the forbidding Hajar mountains and the life-giving sources of water – and wealth-creating sources of metals – that they brought. Other tribes arrived from the north-west and interior. Over time, these would become identified as Hinawi, while the tribes from Yemen and the east coast would become associated with the term Ghafiri.

One of those Ghafiri tribes was the Al Azd, who became subsidiary to Oman's Julanda rulers. They were mariners: seamen, fishermen, merchants and they slowly progressed northwards, populating the Indian Ocean coast and establishing themselves on the islands dotting the Straits of Hormuz and the southern coast of Persia. Their principal ports were at Sohar and Dibba.

A Prophet

About the year 571 a child was born to a woman of the Quraysh tribe of Mecca, who died when her son, Muhammad, was yet six years old. He was brought up by his grandfather and, following his grandfather's death, his uncle.[3]

We know little of his upbringing, but we know he travelled to Syria with his Uncle and we know that, aged twenty-five, he married a noble widow, Khadijah. And we know that, given to contemplation and solitary meditation, he received the word of God through His messenger, the angel Gabriel. The series of revelations commenced while he was reflecting in a cave called *Ghar Hira*, and first took place on a night Muslims now celebrate as *Laylat Al Qadr*, the night of power.

Muhammad's message was powerful and started to attract followers, particularly amongst the poor and marginalised. The Quraysh, who controlled the lucrative business of pilgrimage to the pagan shrine at Mecca, at first ridiculed Muhammad and then turned to persecution. A number of his followers fled, taking refuge with the Christian Negus of Abyssinia. Muhammad continued to preach fearlessly, transported in a vision from Mecca to Jerusalem and up to the celestial spheres and the seventh heaven. This miraculous journey is known as *Isra Wa Al Miraj* (the journey and ascent), resulting in the veneration of the city of Jerusalem by Muslims.

Inspired by his message, representatives of the people of Madinah invited him to make their city his home and he travelled there, arriving on 24 September in the Gregorian year 622. It is from this day that the Islamic calendar commences – the day of the flight to Medina, the Hijra.

Muhammad's message spread and tribes came to Madinah to hear him. A brief conflict with soldiers from Mecca took place, resulting in a decisive victory for Muhammad's growing legions of followers. By 628, Muhammad returned to Mecca with some 1,400 followers and negotiated a peace between the people of the city and his adherents.

Now, attracted by his message of faith in one God, the tribes of Arabia came to Mecca to find out about this God and his Prophet. Muhammad's message, delivered in divine language that moved the Bedouin deeply, coursed through Arabia like wildfire. Southeastern Arabia heard his call and responded: even the tribes of Oman and Yemen rallied to the new belief.

'There is a tradition' that an Omani man, Mazin bin Ghadhubah, embraced Islam, visited the Prophet in Mecca, asking that Muhammad pray for him and the people of Oman (at the time, Oman referred to all of Southeastern Arabia, including the land of the Emirates). Muhammad's response was to send letters to the people inviting them to embrace Islam and also to the two sons of Al Julanda, Abd and Jaffar, telling them that if they would accept Islam he would confirm them as the Governors of Oman, otherwise they would be deposed.[4]

Muhammad sent this message with a trusted messenger, Amr bin Al As, a member of the Quraysh who had converted to Islam after seeking protection and restitution from the Prophet's wife following a robbery in which he had been the victim. Al As landed at a place called Damsetjerd, near Sohar, 'which had been built by the Persians' (it was the seat of the Sasanian governor, Maskan) and took his sealed message to the two Al Julanda brothers.

It is tempting to identify Damsetjerd 'which had been built by the Persians' (a place no longer recognised in the area) with the recently discovered Fulayj Fort, a late Sasanian fort thirty kilometres from Sohar and the only Sasanian fort found anywhere on the Batinah Coast. Fulayj was abandoned at the beginning of the Islamic era – and, as we'll see, so indeed was the Damsetjerd of historical record.

The Julanda ruled the Al Azd, an uneasy relationship as the tribe was powerful and numerous on the Omani coast and the islands of the Straits of Hormuz. The Julanda had another uneasy relationship – with the Persian Sasanians, who had entered into a treaty with them to cede the interior to the Julanda while the Sasanians dominated the coast and its trade.

The Julanda was having a hard time maintaining these two juggling acts, particularly in view of a powerful member of the Al Azd who was governing Dibba for the Sasanians. This was Laqit bin Malik Al Azdi (also known as *Dhu Al Taj*, 'the crowned one') and his rising power was often at the expense of that of the Julanda. There is a school of thought that the Julanda turned to Mecca in an act of desperation, trying to find an ally against their powerful subjects and their uneasy Sasanian bedfellows.

The Julanda brothers called the Al Azd to a convocation and read the Prophet's message, which had brought by Al As, to them. Fired by the new faith, they agreed to follow Islam and the Julanda sent messengers to other Al Azd branches, including Laqit bin Malik in Dibba. They also called on the Sasanian governor, Maskan, to embrace Islam. Perhaps unsurprisingly, Maskan refused.

Already on bad terms with the Sasanians, the Al Julanda and Al Azd now had a cause to rally around: the Sasanian rejection of the message of Islam was their *casus belli* and they promptly went to war, killing Maskan and, following the siege of Damsetjerd, taking the Sasanian surrender and expelling them all from the land of Oman and retaining the Sasanian hoard of gold, silver and other property.

With that expulsion, Southeastern Arabia, 'Oman', became Muslim and was ruled entirely by the Al Julanda as Governors for Mecca. The brothers visited Mecca at the head of a substantial Al Azd delegation and were duly confirmed in their roles by the Caliph Abu Bakr.[5]

The great apostasy

By the time of his death, in the tenth Muslim (Hijri) year, the Gregorian year 632, Muhammad's message had transformed into an ardent faith. And it had reached every corner of Arabia, from Mecca and Medina to the tip of the Straits of Hormuz.

The period following Muhammad's death led to a period of uncertainty and the emergence of the first Caliph, Abu Bakr, as the leader of the faithful. A pious man, Abu Bakr was one of the first people to have believed in Muhammad and his message and he had been a steadfast companion throughout the difficult days of persecution and flight, as well as witness to the triumph of the young Prophet.

The death of Muhammad was taken by many among the far-flung tribes of Arabia as the end of Islam. They stopped paying *zakat*, the tax collected to benefit the poor, and went back to their old ways. Islam faltered as many of its new adherents turned their backs on the central authority located so far away in Mecca, the city in Al Hijaz, the west of Arabia. In Oman, the Julanda found themselves facing an old rival, the former governor of Dibba under the Sasanians, Laqit bin Malik Al Azdi. Now Laqit fought back against the two brothers and their Islamic rule in the name of the Prophet from far-flung Mecca and, according to the historian Abu Jaffar Tabari, writing in the 800s (He was the author of *The History of Prophets and Kings*), 'seized Oman as an apostate and forced Jaffar and Abd to take refuge in the mountains and sea.' The Julanda sent a messenger to the Caliph Abu Bakr in Mecca, begging for help.

Abu Bakr responded, sending an army to Oman under two commanders: an Omani and a Yemeni. The army would first suppress the insurrection in Oman under the Omani commander and then proceed to Yemen to restore order there, under the Yemeni commander. They were joined by a second army from Yamama, the central region of Arabia, whose commander had failed in his original assignment and who was sent to Oman to redeem himself.[6]

Laqit heard of the approach of the army from Mecca and set himself up at Dibba to await their arrival. The two Meccan armies met in Buraimi and marched through the Wadi Al Jizzi to meet the Julanda at Sohar. There, they refreshed themselves after their long march and gathered the tribes to them.

And then the combined force marched north to fall upon Laqit and his followers.

The battle of Dibba

Dibba is a pleasant, sleepy town facing east from the Emirates to the Gulf of Oman. Today it is a town of three parts, the northern section is Omani, the central Dibba Al Hisn (Dibba of the Fort) is part of Sharjah and the southern section is part of Fujairah. If you turn north at the roundabout from the Masafi Road, you will enter Oman and perhaps make your way to the luxurious Zighi Bay Hotel or maybe explore the breath-taking canyons and glorious heights of the Wadi Bih track. To do that these days, you will need to be a GCC national or have an Omani visa. Most visitors pull a right at the roundabout, hurrying on their way to the Al Aqah hotels – a development of big-name east coast beach hotels which started with the construction of the Le Meridien Al Aqah in 2003.

In the year 633, Dibba was an important market town and port, home to a lively and thriving trade with the Indies and Far East, landing goods from Alexandria and Rome as well as other markets as far afield as China. It was wealthy and arguably influential – Laqit bin Malik would have been a leader backed by considerable resources.

The armies met in the dusty plain behind the town, Seih Dibba, and the clash would have been mighty indeed. This was a time of raw power and savage weaponry, bronze and iron-tipped arrows, heavy swords and cavalry. Whether there were camels or horses in the battle, we will likely never know. But that there was a great force of men, there is no doubt. Under the fierce sun, they sweated and cried in fear, battering each other with every last ounce of energy and trying to keep on their feet in the vicious, swirling melees.

Laqit was clearly taking no prisoners: he had the families of Dibba placed behind the line of battle so their menfolk would fight all the harder. His desperate gambit almost succeeded, a collapse of the Muslim army seemed inevitable but then reinforcements arrived, seemingly miraculously. The Banu Najiyah and Abd Al Qays joined the battle and turned it into a rout.[7]

The Muslim army pursued Laqit's fleeing troops and a huge slaughter took place as they hacked down their vanquished foes, the fine, choking dust clouds kicked up by the battle blinding the fighters. It is said that 10,000 men died in the conflict. Although the number is temptingly huge and often repeated locally, it is worth noting that historians of the time were quite fond of the number 10,000 when recounting the death tolls of great battles.

Their graves are said to be found standing today, in the Omani part of Seih Dibba, the town's extensive hinterland plain. Each one is a standing stone, a cairn, in a field of such stones to be found on the northern reaches of the great wasteland that stretched out behind the coastal port and town.

The victory was absolute. The Muslim army collected their trophies, divided the spoils and sent one fifth of the booty to Abu Bakr in Mecca. The market of Dibba was plundered and the Omani commander, Hudhayfah, stayed to consolidate the Muslim hold on the territory of Oman while his fellow commander proceeded, in accordance with their original instructions, to pacify Yemen. Their colleague, Ikramah, who had failed in Yamama and been censured by Abu Bakr, was sent back to the Caliph with the booty to redeem himself – a generous gesture on the part of his co-commanders.

This great battle marked the end of the Ridda Wars, the conquest of the tribes and territories of Arabia against the wave of apostasy that followed the death of Muhammad. Few people appreciate that drowsy Dibba, in its time, marked a turning point in the history of Arabia and, in fact, the modern world.

It was at Dibba that the future of Islam in the Gulf was finally sealed.

Chapter 8

SCHISM, RIFT AND WAR

"If your enemy stretches his hand out to you,
cut it off if you can. Otherwise, kiss it."

– Caliph Mansur

The religion established by the Prophet Muhammad would not only shake the ancient world, it would shape it, too. The very evolution of Western Christianity was to be defined not only by the clashes between forces driven by their beliefs, but by the interplay between the two cultures that these systems of belief represented. Innovations travelled in both directions, between West and East and the Muslim world was to become a crucible in which the ideas and records of the Greeks and Romans would be forged into a new flowering of science and discovery, resulting in a flow of knowledge, and the means to attain and store that knowledge, throughout Europe.

The new religion faltered following Muhammad's death, but its adherents united and the Ridda Wars brought Arabia once more under Mecca. Now the Caliphs following in Muhammad's footsteps would conquer new territories, their armies victorious against the Sasanians of Persia and the armies of the eastern Roman Empire – the Byzantines.

The first caliphate, established by Abu Bakr, was the Rashidun Caliphate. Four Rashidun caliphs ruled, the fourth being the husband of Muhammad's daughter, as well as Muhammad's cousin, Ali. His caliphate was contested, leading to a civil war which established the second caliphate, the Umayyad Caliphate. The first Umayyad Caliph was Muawiya and his reign started a long period of both expansion of the Muslim sphere and internal wars and conflicts which threatened to tear the heart out of the caliphate. Following the short-lived rule of several caliphs, the Umayyad Caliphate finally collapsed in 750 after a third civil war. This saw the commencement of the third caliphate, the Abbasid Caliphs of whom the first only lived four years. Mansur, the second Abbasid Caliph, established the city of Baghdad. This great city and its caliphate endured for centuries, battling – and falling to – the great Mongol invasions and seeing the emergence of the Mamluks of Egypt, until the birth of the fourth caliphate, the Ottomans, in 1517.

Throughout this long, and often violent, history, the territorial conquests and rivalries of the Caliphs and their would-be challengers and feuding regional governors would have their impacts on Southeastern Arabia, the whole area of which (including the modern-day Emirates) was then commonly known as Oman. Time and time again, great armies would be sent by the Caliphs to bring the serially secessionist territory under control.

The first caliphate – the Rashidun

The Ridda Wars had cemented the Julanda as governors of Oman at the head of the Al Azd and so they remained while the Rashidun Caliphate presided over Arabia and the wider empire. The Muslim expansion continued westward and also northwards to Mesopotamia and Iraq – the Sasanian Empire fell in 651 to the Caliph Uthman Ibn Affan, the third of the Rashidun Caliphs. An army sailed from Julfar (a fast-growing Islamic era port city situated to the North of what is now the city of Ras Al Khaimah) to Iran in support of that effort.

The news of the fall of their old Sasanian enemies must have been cause for celebration among the Julanda and Al Azd of Oman, who were now enjoying virtual independence under the protection of their new religion. Quite how assiduously that religion was practiced among the people was questionable, as indeed was the case when Christianity came to the pagan lands of Europe. Islam took some of the practices of the old to be its own, subsumed festivals and celebrations and supplanted 'old gods' with 'new'. And yet this seeming syncretism masked a yearning back to old ways that sometimes meant animistic practices survived even among those professing to have taken to new ways. The Julanda's conversion – whether passionate or pragmatic – would have been shared by the Al Azd but old traditions would also have been followed, particularly by the older country folk.

At the same time, the politics and machinations of Mecca and Medina, although in every way distant to Oman, were about to have a devastating effect on the far-flung province. The fourth Rashidun Caliph, Ali, fought the first civil war of the new Muslim Empire. Muslim cut down Muslim and the very words of the Prophet – words of peace and unity – were ignored by men now caught up in the ambition and desire for power that mastery of an empire demanded. At the end of the conflict, a new caliphate emerged triumphant and determined to stamp the seal of its authority on all of the newly forged lands of Islam.

The Umayyads had arrived.

The Umayyads – new kids on the block

The Umayyads sought to consolidate their new primacy and one particular thorn in their side was the Khawarij, a sect who believed that the selection of the Caliph should be by the will of God, rather than from any particular popular selection process – especially derived from a given tribe or lineage (for instance the Quraysh, from whom the Umayyad Caliph was by practice selected).

The Khawarij had risen against the Caliph Ali when he attempted to broker a peace with the Umayyads and they rose frequently against the Umayyads. Fleeing to Oman, the Khawarij found sanctuary among the Al Julanda and Al Azd – and their ideas took root among the independently-minded leaders of this backwater of Empire, so early converted and consolidated and yet so seditious in its seclusion. It was from these Kharijite 'heresies' against the 'mainstream' of Umayyad policy that the tenets emerged that were to form the basis of the unique Ibadi school of Islam which persists in Oman today.[1]

This divergence from the path was not to be tolerated by the Umayyads and Al Hajji bin Yusuf Al Thaqifi, the Umayyad governor of Iraq, sent an army to invest this independently minded former vassal state. The first force to reach Oman landed from a large flotilla near Muscat and was resoundingly beaten off by the Azdi forces with some reports citing the loss of all hands. Furious at this unexpected setback, Thaqifi threw an army of 40,000 men into the fray against the Julanda and Al Azd – half embarked by sea and the other half travelled down the coast of the Gulf on land. The land army was met by the Al Azd forces with a force of 3,000 horsemen and 3,500 camel riders, somewhere near the west coast – likely in the area to the west of Abu Dhabi we now know as Baynuna.[2] Whichever location the meeting took place at, the result was an overwhelming rout of the Umayyad forces. Gleefully pursuing their vanquished foes for a great distance across the sands, the Al Azd ran into the seaborne force which had landed at Julfar. Realising they were 'to that of the enemy as a white spot on the body of black bull', the Al Azd retreated and took shelter in the mountainous region of Jebel Akhdar.[3] Their enemies pursued them and they found themselves besieged on the peak of the mountain by the Umayyad army which, unable to pursue them into the heights, camped in the Wadi Maskal.

The Julanda fired the boats of the Umayyad fleet in anchor at Muscat: over fifty boats were lost of an armada of 300 vessels before the Umayyad force fled the harbour and made for Julfar, lifting the siege of the Azdi force in Jebel Akhdar. There the Umayyad army licked its wounds and their commander sent messengers to the Caliph asking for help.[4] The Al Azd were, in the main, coming over to the Caliph's side, he said, it just required a final push to get rid of the insurgent faction. The Caliph responded munificently: 5,000 Bedouin marched overland to Julfar and joined the Umayyad forces, readying a hammer-blow against the Julanda. An Al Azdi spy among the newcomers dashed across the desert and informed the Julanda leaders of this new force and they immediately decided on flight rather than fight. The Julanda embarked for Zanzibar – Al Zenj – and the Umayyad army entered into Oman unopposed and commenced 'a great plunder'.[5]

This war against Oman would be one of the last acts of the Caliph Abdel Malek bin Marwan, who died in the year 705. His four sons would succeed him, but ruled in a period of great instability and internecine strife, at one time resulting in three caliphs being appointed in a single year. Nevertheless, the Islamic Empire blossomed, reaching its zenith under the Umayyads to stretch from the French towns of Arles and Avignon in the west to the Indian subcontinent in the east.

Abdel Malik's half-brother Marwan bin Muhammed bin Marwan would eventually preside over the third great civil war (*fitna*) to tear apart the Muslim empire. On his death, the Umayyad dynasty and its capital Damascus fell to the Abbasids, with a great slaughter of the Umayyads by the Abbasids almost wiping out the whole dynasty. A notable escapee from this terrible purge was the Umayyad prince Abdulrahman, who escaped and fled to Cordoba in Spain, where he founded the splendid and enduring Caliphate of Cordoba.

The Abbasids – conquest and purge

The Abbasids lost no time in consolidating their rule throughout the region and the first Abbasid Caliph, Abu Abbas Al Saffah, resolved to quell the followers of the new sect that had sprung up in the wake of the Kharijites' flight to their remote home in Southeastern Arabia – the Ibadis of Oman.

The Ibadis elected their first Imam to rule over them, a member of the Al Julanda.[6] Another group of Kharijites under Shaiban bin Abdulaziz Al Yashkuri had settled the island of Qeshm, off the Persian coast on the mouth of the Straits of Hormuz. Qeshm was the greatest of the islands of the Gulf, a long islet that was all shallows and mangroves to the north and deep sea ports to the south.

Meanwhile Al Saffah, the Abbasid Caliph, was facing a humiliating situation. One of his military commanders was Khazim bin Khuzayma, originally of a Christian tribe from Najran, the fertile, mountainous area to the west of Yemen. Riding past a group of lesser relatives of the Caliph, Khazim had failed to offer the traditional greeting of 'Salaam' and they 'reviled him' in turn. He wheeled about, picked a quarrel with them and then had all thirty-two beheaded and their property demolished and plundered.[7]

This was a mortal insult to the Caliph and he was about to have Khazim executed when two of his most trusted advisors begged for the man's life, citing his long service and faultless obedience. Instead, they suggested, send him on an insanely dangerous mission where if he is killed, his blood will not be on your hands but if he is victorious, the victory will be yours.

This was adjudged a fine solution indeed and Khazim was sent on what at the time was seen as something of a mad mission – to put down the Ibadis and their Azdi allies in Oman and Qeshm, to earn glory in victory or – perhaps better – a glorious death. Almost everyone who had gone before had been trounced – Khazim had received his 'hospital pass'.

Embarking from Basra with a force of 700 men and more, Khazim invaded Qeshm and drove out the leader of the Qeshm Sufris, Shaiban, and his followers. They fled by boat to the mainland. There, they encountered the Ibadi Julanda and Azdi forces, (being Sufris, Shaiban's followers were competitors to the Ibadis), and a bloody battle ensued in which Shaiban and his followers were comprehensively slaughtered, the Ibadis rather conveniently doing Khazim's work for him.

Khazim landed on the west coast of Oman and encountered the Julanda forces in the desert. In the following day's battle, Khazim lost almost a hundred men. On the second day of fighting, he rallied and his foes, the Julanda, lost something like a thousand men. A week later, Khazim's forces attacked the Julanda settlement (this has been speculated to have been the coastal township of Julfar) and fired arrows tipped with burning flax soaked in naphtha at the settlement's *areesh* houses, essentially shanties constructed from woven palm fronds. Tinder-dry, they would have provided a splendid – and deadly – conflagration.

As the Julanda battled to save their families from the inferno, Khazim's forces fell on them, slaughtering men, women and children indiscriminately. The historian Al Tabari says ten thousand died – we can perhaps remember this as the figure given for the dead at the Battle of Dibba. It was a popular number to attribute to big battles.

Khazim sent a grim memento to Basra for the Caliph, the heads of the slain.[8]

Shortly afterwards, Khazim received his recall from Oman (presumably having now been recognised as having achieved a victorious deed on behalf of the Caliph) and the country fell into a dark period of tyrannical governance, leading to the plunder of the inland capital of Nizwa, before a second Imam was appointed in 783.[9]

There is mention of a force sent against the troublesome people of Oman by the Abbasid Caliph Harun Al Rashid, consisting of 1,000 cavalry and 5,000 infantry, which met a comprehensive defeat at the hands of the Ibadi forces in the Wadi Hatta, fleeing to their ships and being pursued by the Imam's forces. The leader of the army was captured and taken to Sohar where he was imprisoned. Whilst awaiting his fate, local rowdies broke into his prison and killed him 'without the knowledge of the Imam'.

We are told that Harun Al Rashid resolved to send another army, but died before he could carry out his resolution.

It is worth noting that the Ibadi faith of Oman was by no means accepted by all of the communities of Southeastern Arabia and even by all of the Al Azd, even if it was enthusiastically embraced by the ruling Al Julanda faction. As the Abbasids' focus was directed elsewhere in their expanding and often fractious empire, Oman was allowed to default to a state of independence but fell into a period of internecine squabbling and warring. Most of the intercessions by the Caliphs in the affairs of the area can be traced back to appeals sent from opposing factions and that of 891 was no different.

The faction fighting and rivalries in the region reached the point where, within a single year, sixteen imams were elevated to the leadership and then subsequently deposed. A complaint was raised in the year 891 to the Caliph's representative in Bahrain, Mohammed bin Nur, who sent the complainants onto Baghdad to place their case before the Caliph himself. With the Caliph's support, an army of 25,000 men (including 3,500 cavalry) was raised from the tribes of Arabia and headed by Mohammed bin Nur himself.

The Caliph's army under Mohammed bin Nur took Julfar and then marched south to Buraimi, with a number of skirmishes in the desert failing to even slow his progress. The people of Sohar – a short march away down the Wadi Al Jizzi – fled at the rumour of this great force, emigrating to Shiraz and Basra. The army took Sohar and Nizwa unopposed and Oman finally fell to the Abbasids.[10]

Mohammed bin Nur established himself at Nizwa, sending the severed head of the Imam to Baghdad.

Mohammed was not to enjoy his leisure for long. The tribes rose up against him and raised an army, which marched on Nizwa. He took to his heels and, once again, the Omani forces were fast in pursuing the retreating enemy and found themselves engaging with their fleeing foes, who turned and gave them battle at Dibba. Mohammed bin Nur would have lost the action but for the fortuitous arrival of a force sent to relieve him, the hurriedly raised relief force riding two men to a camel. A great slaughter ensued and he triumphed – a strange re-enactment of the great battle at Dibba that ended the Ridda Wars..

A vengeful Mohammed bin Nur returned to Nizwa and set about ensuring that the message to anyone thinking about rebellion was sent loud and clear. He had the *aflaj* blocked, burned books, and tortured the terrified populace indiscriminately. When he judged the Omanis sufficiently cowed, he placed a governor at Nizwa and returned to Bahrain.

The governor was overthrown soon after, killed and his body was dragged through the streets.[11] The Abbasids, their minds elsewhere as their great empire began to implode, didn't return – but Mohammed bin Nur had laid waste to the whole country and it was to take decades to recover.

Chapter 9

LORDS OF THE SEVEN SEAS

"Their merchant vessel is without nails. The only material they use to set the parts of the ship together is coconut fibre."

- Chinese official, c. late 700s CE

In early 1980 the British explorer, adventurer and historian Tim Severin arrived in Muscat to put together his latest spectacular voyage. He wanted to recreate Sindbad the Sailor's journey to China by building a traditional Arab dhow based on documented evidence and then sailing it on the eight-month, 6,000-mile journey to China. He might have seemed mad to any reasonable person, but then he had previous form.

Severin shot to fame in 1977 when he set out on the Brendan Voyage, a recreation of the epic seven-year transatlantic voyage of St Brendan. The voyage, which took place in the 500s but was only recorded two hundred years later in the 700s, was always seen as the stuff of legend and considered impossible for a vessel of that time to actually have achieved. Severin set out to prove the doubters wrong. Constructing an historically accurate replica of a boat of the time, a thirty-six-foot currach, made from oak and ash wood, tarred hide and leather rope, Severin and his crew set out on the arduous 4,500-mile journey and not only survived, but proved a number of the locations mentioned in the original manuscript had their basis in reality – and that the boats of the time were indeed capable of the voyage. Severin's account of the Brendan Voyage became an overnight sensation and an international bestseller.[1] The boat he built is preserved today and displayed at the Craggaunowen Folk Park in County Clare, Ireland.

Severin had shown the documentary of the Brendan Voyage to Oman's Minister of Information, who had secured the blessing of Sultan Qaboos for the Sindbad Voyage and, indeed, his sponsorship. Severin, in an early meeting with the Minister, had not understood what 'sponsorship' meant until the Minister took out a blank piece of Ministry letterhead and slid it across the desk to him, suggesting he might like to draft the letter of agreement himself for the Minister to sign – a *tabula rasa* indeed. Severin staggered out of the meeting with the assurance that he would have everything he would ever need to build his ship – accompanied by a deadline of fifteen months to build and launch the boat in time for Oman's tenth National Day.

Building the boat would prove to consist of a series of seemingly insurmountable challenges. Severin had found accounts of early shipbuilders and their work which suggested the original dhows were built without nails, their planking lashed together with coir rope, which is made from coconut fibre. He travelled to the Laccadive Islands off the Malabar (Kerala) coast, a region of India which even today preserves close links with the UAE and Oman, and there found traditional rope makers who could create the lengths of coir rope he would need – something like 400 miles of it.

He also bought Indian aini wood, his journeys to India taking him to Calicut, long a centre of Arab trade and a source of spices, timber and other goods. Aini was a traditional wood for dhow building, cheaper than teak and with a very high alkalinity which prevents attack from the dreaded *Teredo navalis*, the naval shipworm, a seaborne pest that can reduce a wooden boat's hull to a crumbling mess within a year.

Basing his operation on the beach at Sur, Severin brought together Laccadivian, Keralite and Omani craftsmen and set about creating his eighty-seven-foot replica of an Arab dhow from the 700s. Succeeding in his task, the *Sohar*, as his dhow had been named, was launched on time on 21 November 1980 and took its crew on the perilous journey east.

Once again, Severin was proved right when, on 6 July 1981, *Sohar* made port in Canton, China. The Arab dhows, as documented, were not only capable of the journey to China but were adapted brilliantly to the task. And the men who sailed them were traders, astronomers and navigators of exceptional skill who defined global trade at a time before the Vikings had even set sail for Britain. They sailed, literally, the seven seas – the phrase to sail the seven seas itself derives from the voyage across the seven seas between Arabia and China.

A tale of two ports

Even before the reed boats of the Sumerians had first explored the warm shallows off Failaka and Bahrain, the exploration of the sea had been in the bones and blood of the coastal communities of Southeastern Arabia. The trade with Dilmun and Harappa, with Sumer and Persia had been woven in the lives of people and provided them with luxuries when times were good and essentials to ease life's harshness when times were bad. Cloth, oil, rope, wood, pearls and, of course, copper and bronze were ferried between ports by sailors who were constantly pushing the boundaries and setting out for new markets to explore.

We have seen from Tell Abraq that lateen sail boats were known from the Iron Age, pre-dating any other evidence of the innovation elsewhere in the world.[2] That sail alone would have given the mariners of Iron Age Arabia (the pendant with the sail on it found at Tell Abraq was dated to between 1000–500 BCE) a huge advantage in being able to harness the wind. Almost a millennium later, the conflict between expansionist Islam and the Eastern Roman Empire not only saw innovations percolate between the Islamic and Christian world (very much a two-way traffic), it drove innovation. Arab navigational skills were enhanced by the scientific miracles of the Umayyad golden age, the Bait Al Hikmah of Baghdad saw astronomy and navigation become synergistic avenues of exploration and discovery. Even today, some 60 per cent of the stars in our night sky bear Arabic names and Arabic gives us the names of innovations in science and mathematics from alcohol to zenith, algorithm and mantissa to algebra and so on.

It would be only natural, then, that the ports either side of the Straits of Hormuz would come to be known as maritime centres as the long decline following the Iron Age and the Sasanian invasion of the area was reversed and the maritime communities of the area emerged to become an Islamic era centre for trade on the route from Baghdad to the Eastern world – and back again.

Although there are Chinese traditions that a messenger arrived in China sent from the Prophet Muhammad, one Sa'd Ibn Abi Waqqas, the earliest textual references maintain that Arabs arrived from the Caliph Uthman, the third of the Rashidun Caliphs, to Tang China in 655 CE. A large trading community was in place by a century later and a conflict erupted across the land routes between the flowering Abbasid Empire and Tang China, the two forces colliding in 751 at the battle of Talas, resulting in the defeat of the Chinese. Actions taken against the traders at Canton were answered with the sack of that city in 758.[3] Conflict and trade appear to have been bedfellows and we have a large number of documentary sources describing the trade routes between India and China.

In 851, 'Sulaiman the Merchant' wrote *Akhbar Al Sind Wa'l Hind* (*News of Sind and Hindustan*) while Ibn Khurdadhbih in 850 gave us a guide to the stages in the journey from the Gulf to China. By the tenth century, traders from Southeastern Arabia were flourishing across India, China and the east coast of Africa and their cargoes ranged from fine porcelain china through spices and ambergris to ivory and slaves.[4]

Writing in the middle of the tenth century, the historian Al Masudi opines extensively on Europe, India and East Africa. 'I have seen in the country of Serendib (Sri Lanka), which is an island of the sea, that when a king dies he is laid upon a car with small wheels and made for the purpose.'[5] He writes of the island of Thule, part of Britannia in the north, and of China – as well as of the Moon, Mercury, Venus, Mars, Jupiter and Saturn, which he asserts 'are all spheres revolving around the spherical Earth'. The geographic and astronomical information displayed form an amazing assemblage of early knowledge and theory, including anecdotes from Al Masudi's own travels as well as those collected from travellers to distant lands. He writes of the Omani sailors who plied the route to East Africa (Zenj) and who were 'Arabs of the tribe Azd' as well as the sewn boats made by the Azd from wood lashed together with rope made 'from the islands that produce the coconut'.

Despite being at the centre of these explorations of the world, Julfar and Sohar offered what must have at times been a precarious existence to their curious citizens. This was by no means a time of stability for the area – the Qaramatians, a puritanical Muslim sect, one of many to emerge as different belief systems flourished in the fragmentation of the Abbasid empire, invaded – as did the Buwayhids and the Seljuks. The Buwayhids landed at Julfar, just north of present-day Ras Al Khaimah, and established a mint at Buraimi.[6] By now a pattern is emerging whereby regional instability meant Rulers came and went, but trade became a constant. Even for conquerors, maintaining the lucrative trade routes and keeping them open would be in everyone's interests.

As the second millennium progresses, Sohar on the east coast and Julfar on the west start to emerge as ports of significance, linked by inland trade routes through the Wadis Ham, Hatta and Jizzi from the east to the interior. These and more southerly routes through the mountains provided inland access and avoided the hazards of the Straits of Hormuz, even if they sometimes encountered the hazard of inland raids by wandering tribes.

Kush abandoned

Julfar, at least in its early incarnations, was – as we have seen from the wars between the Abbasids and the Julanda – wholly or almost entirely constructed from *areesh* buildings, *khaimas*. This type of structure, seen throughout the UAE interior until at least the 1970s, likely gave Ras Al Khaimah its modern name (Ras Al Khaimah is Arabic for 'headland of the hut' or also 'headland of the tent').

However, as it grew in significance as a port and trading centre, Julfar would have evolved more sophisticated infrastructure – including defences. Our earliest evidence of this type of evolution comes from Kush, which has been put forward as an early location of Julfar's northern port.[7]

Excavations at Kush, vying with Tell Abraq for the title of largest archaeological tell in the Emirates, have unearthed a citadel, abandoned in the early Islamic period and then reoccupied in the 800s, after which the town was constantly occupied until it is abandoned – seemingly in an orderly rather than, as is more usually the case, a disorderly fashion. This event is roughly contemporaneous with the rise of the site we now know as Julfar.

Chinese pottery has been found at Kush dating back to the 700s and 800s, earlier than any find elsewhere in the area, while Indian pottery at Kush dates back to the earliest period of occupation. These finds point to Julfar's early incarnation being an important locus on the Umayyad and Abbasid trade route through the Gulf to India and the Far East. Julfar, Buraimi and Sohar seem to have converged as both ports and routes to the interior caravans that would have taken goods to the Arabian interior as well as to Egypt, Damascus and other routes to the burgeoning markets of the Mediterranean Sea.

Apart from Kush, the area around Julfar is rich in Islamic era settlements, spanning the 900s and first millennium settlement at Jazirat Al Hulayla, the fortress of Shimal, dating to the 1100s (known today as Sheba's Palace) and farms in the Wadi Haqil. This development of agricultural resources inland of the port town is mirrored at Sohar, where at around the same time we see extensive development taking place along the Wadi Al Jizi, the route from Sohar inland to Buraimi.[8]

Other ports on the coast thrived at this time, including Dibba and Khor Fakkan. However, both Kush and Sohar appear to have declined in the period between 1000 and 1200, at a time when the island of Qeshm across the Straits of Hormuz, blossomed. Populated by a tribe from the Arabian peninsula, the Bani Abdul Qais, Qeshm rose between the 1100s to the 1300s to become a locus for trade between the merchants of Mesopotamia, Iran and India. But it was to be eclipsed by the brilliance of its neighbouring island – Hormuz.

A gem on a pillar of salt

The history of the Kingdom of Hormuz, which would come to completely dominate the trade of the Gulf and the routes east to span the seven seas, is a tale of two cities. 'Old Hormuz' was located on the Persian shore, on the north eastern side of the Straits of Hormuz, in the area of the Minab Delta. Founded by Arab tribes who had crossed over from Southeastern Arabia,[9] the city competed for the Gulf's trade, first with the northern port city of Siraf, then with Kish island in the 1200s. It came to dominate that trade by the end of the century under its leader, Mahmud Qalhati.[10] Persia fell to the Mongols under the Generalship of Hulagu, Genghis Khan's grandson, in 1259 and it was decided to, literally move the capital of the Kingdom of Hormuz to the island of Jarun, a strategic location that was to reward Qalhati and his people with the dominance of this critical seaway, at the beginning of the 1300s. Jarun would come to be known itself as Hormuz.

The Island of Hormuz grew to become like something out of a science fiction or fantasy novel: a wealthy, great and cosmopolitan city, the centre of a kingdom, with rich rich houses, fountains, sun-dappled walkways and gardens of fruit trees filled with birdsong – yet all situated on a desolate, waterless island of strange beauty formed from rock of brilliantly coloured minerals, all surmounted by a great central mountain made of salt.

Hormuz was barren in the extreme, but it was safe from the Mongol armies and perfectly situated to act as a locus for the trade between Mesopotamia and Persia on the one hand and Africa, India and Asia on the other. Its business model would be immediately recognised by the management at Emirates or Etihad today – 'feeder' trade came from the region's markets and was consolidated at Hormuz to take to the great routes east to Sind and Hind, Serendib and China, while Chinese and Indian shipments were broken down to serve smaller regional markets or to send on to the trade routes to Europe through Baghdad, Alexandria and, latterly, Istanbul.

To the north, Hormuz not only had access to Iran and thriving central Persian cities of the time such as Shiraz and Tabriz, but also to the interior trade opened up by the Mongol expansion. It sat on a maritime silk road and had access to the interior one, too.

Hormuz was in many ways a 'duty-free' or 'free-trade' zone and its influence extended to the southern coast, where the newly established city of Julfar was starting to take hold as Kush was abandoned. The decline of Kush is likely a result of changes in the shoreline, with its lagoon/harbour silting up as new sandbanks appeared on the coast. It was on one of these newly emerged features that a new port would be built and the maritime city of Julfar would emerge in the 1300s.[11] Julfar, Dibba, Khor Fakkan and Muscat all fell under the sway of the great trading nation and became part of Hormuz' massive mercantile network, which grew to span the world. Maps of the time show the area from Bahrain to Muscat as 'The Kingdom of Hormuz'.

The city was tolerant and open to all – traders from Iran, India and Asia assembled there, Hindus, Jews, Muslims and Christians rubbed shoulders in the city's shaded streets and busy souqs. An early Portuguese visitor, Tomé Pires, wrote, "This city has beautiful walls and houses with terraces and beautiful towers and a citadel and is one of the four largest cities of Asia. The trade revenues of its neighbours are not comparable with its revenues. If something is needed for eating, be it bought in France or Flanders, it is brought to this island."[12]

Hormuz was visited by Abd-al Razzaq Samarqandi in 1442 during his journey to the Indian city of Calicut. Samarqandi, an ambassador for Shah Rukh, the son of Tamerlane, the founder of the Timurid Empire, recorded his impressions of the island in his book, *Matla-us-Sadain wa Majma-ul-Bahrain* (*The Rise of the Two Auspicious Constellations and the Confluence of the Two Oceans* – book titles of the time were generally a great deal more fun than they are these days).

Samarqandi emphasises the importance of Hormuz as a trading centre: 'Ormuz, which is also called Djerrun (Jarun), is a port situated in the middle of the sea, and which has not its equal on the surface of the globe. The merchants of seven climates, from Egypt, Syria, the country of Roum (Anatolia), Azerbijan, Irak-Arabi, and Irak-Adjemi (Iran), the province of Fars, Khorassan, Ma-wara-amahar (literally 'what lies beyond the river', lands under Muslim control in Central Asia lying north of the Oxus or Amu Darya river, such as Tajikistan, Turkmenistan and Kazakhstan), Turkistan (Central Asia), the kingdom of Deschti-Kaptchack (the Central Asian Kipchak people), the countries inhabited by the Kalmucks (a branch of the Mongols, present from eastern China to Central Asia), the whole of the kingdoms of Tchin (China) and Matchin (southern ports of China), and the city of Khanbalik (Beijing), all make their way to this port.

The inhabitants of the sea coasts arrive here from the countries of Tchin, Java, Bengal, the cities of Zirbad (south-east India), Tenasserim (southeast Myanmar), Sokotora (Socotra), Schahrinou (possibly Shahnoor or Sivanur, in Karnataka, India), the islands of Diwah-Mahall (The Maldives), the countries of Malabar, Abyssinia, Zangeubar (Zanzibar), the ports of Bidjanagar (Bijanagur, once capital of an empire in southern India), Kalbergah (near Hyderabad), Gudjerat, Kambait (Cambay, India) the coasts of Arabia, which extend as far as Aden, Jiddah, and Yembo (Yanbu); they bring hither those rare and precious articles which the sun, the moon, and the rains have combined to bring to perfection, and which are capable of being transported by sea. Travellers from all countries resort hither, and, in exchange for the commodities which they bring, they can without trouble or difficulty obtain all that they desire. Bargains are made either by money or exchange. For all objects, with the exception of gold and silver, a tenth of their value is paid by way of duty... This city is also named Daralaman (Dar Al Aman – the abode of security).'[13]

Sitting at the locus of this great Arab global trade network, the tiny island of Hormuz, in its heyday, was home to some 50,000 people and a bazaar that retailed the world's finest luxuries, rarities and trade goods. Marco Polo recorded the trade commodities of Hormuz as including pearls, spices, gemstones, silk, gold, ivory and horses. The Portuguese historian João de Barros would write in the early 1500s, *Si terrarum orbis, qauqua patet annulus esset. Ilius Ormisum gemma, dequsque foret.* 'If all the world wore a ring, Hormuz would be its gemstone.'

Hormuz had a partner across the Gulf, another centre of trade and maritime derring-do. And it, too, would thrive on the back of the new artery of global wealth being opened up by the Arab traders voyaging to trade with the wonderful lands of Africa, India and Asia. The port of Julfar.

Julfar

Julfar was a Hormuzi possession, and the new maritime city thrived under the influence of the trading links Hormuz now enjoyed. Hormuz itself was wealthy beyond belief, importing its water in daily shipments of enormous quantity from nearby Qeshm and also from rivers on the mainland to top up cavernous underground cisterns, linked by a series of *aflaj*.

The movement from Kush to the newly emergent sandbanks off the coast saw a city of two halves developing: Al Mataf and Al Nudood, the northern and southern parts of Julfar, which dominated access to the safe shelter of the new lagoon. These two place names persist today as suburbs to the north of modern Ras Al Khaimah. Between the 1300s and 1600s, Julfar was transformed from a settlement of *areesh* shacks to a town of mudbrick and coral houses arranged in streets, with mosques and other public buildings springing up.

It was at this time, too, that the fertile interior was developed, both feeding the appetites of the burgeoning city and providing goods for trade across to Hormuz for consumption there or possibly export. The inland settlements and some 85 per cent of the arable land farmed by Julfar were protected by a defensive wall which also gave the port of Julfar security from raiders heading from the interior – the Wadi Sur wall was a 7-kilometre barrier with towers placed every 150 metres or so, which stretched from the coast at present day Al Uraibi to Shimal at the foothills of the forbidding barrier of the Hajar Mountains. The Umm Al Quwain Wall, the fortification which completely barred the way to the old town and which still stands today, is a similar concept, albeit spanning a mere three towers rather than the forty-five-odd which would form the Wadi Sur wall.

Straddling the Straits of Hormuz, this confederation of Arabian trading centres created a powerful economic force. Julfar and Hormuz grew and prospered, with Hormuz playing host in the 1400s to the Chinese Admiral and Court Eunuch Zheng He, visiting from Ming era China with his fleets of treasure ships, junks and support vessels.

Zheng He's first visit to Hormuz took place in 1413 and established a remarkable record of formal trade between the two centres. Zheng He was by birth a Muslim, a product of the outward migrations of people resulting from the expansion of the Mongol empires. He was originally from Yunnan and was trading with the Gulf at a time when international commerce with China was officially banned – Zheng He effectively enjoyed the Emperor's monopoly.[14]

Hormuz sent embassies to China from 1414 onwards, with a first cargo including a gold leaf covered tablet and horses (Hormuz did a lively trade in horses with India, its dependency Khor Fakkan maintained extensive stables for that very purpose). Several embassies followed, laden with gifts for the emperor, including pearls, gemstones and live animals – lions, leopards, Arabian warhorses and giraffes. In turn, Zheng He brought to Hormuz jewellery, precious metals, silks and porcelain.[15] It is this latter commodity we see appearing in the archaeological record of Julfar in enormous abundance. Given the value of these precious pots, each sherd found represents a terrible cost – and that speaks to what must have been huge volumes of trade passing through Hormuz and Julfar. Other Asian ceramic markets were represented, too: Burma, Thailand and Vietnam all contribute to the shattered record we can find today.

It is worth noting that the traces of ceramics found at Julfar precede Zheng He – the trade with China had been lively for centuries and finds from Julfar include sherds dated from the Yuan Dynasty of the 1300s.[16] The original trade links between Arabia and China, as we have seen, dated back at least to Haroun Al Rashid and likely earlier into the pre-Islamic era – Baghdad's potters had even tried to emulate the brilliant porcelain of China's making. But it was Zheng He, breaking the Ming era embargo with Imperial consent, who established that valuable link and virtual monopoly for Hormuz. The wealth it generated was enormous.

Lots of pots

The fine porcelain being imported from China must have been a wonder to the people of Arabia, much as it was to the Europeans when they first encountered the delicate bone china and exquisite patterned glazes and vivid illustrations that blazed their way across the milky-white surfaces of the fine ceramics packed in their straw-lined wooden crates, likely packed as they would be today as they are unloaded by pallet trucks at Dubai's Dragon Mart: wooden crates lined with straw, densely stacked with their fragile cargoes.

Zheng He made a total of seven journeys across the world between China and Hormuz, staying for two months each time. Each voyage took some five months, actually a remarkably fast passage for the time. Hormuz was at first counted as a key trading partner and given precedence over the other embassies to the Emperor, but contacts between the two partners reduced in the period 1425–1431 and by the time of Zheng He's last visit to Hormuz in 1433 and the embassy to Canton that followed it, Hormuz had fallen to last on the list of foreign powers received by China.

By 1436, two further embassies had arrived from Hormuz, but Zheng He was dead and his ships stood by at harbour. From the great trading expeditions to Hormuz and breathless accounts of their size and wealth, we now appear to enter a period of relative silence.

But China was not the only trading partner keeping Hormuz and Julfar busy – there were spices to trade from India, slaves from Africa, frankincense from Oman, cloth and jewels, gold and medicinal herbs. There was precious amber, the hardened sap of trees from the icy north of Europe through to ambergris, found on the beaches of Zanzibar. Ambergris, a treasured component in the manufacture of perfumes, is a highly odiferous substance thrown up in lumps by sperm whales. For all that, it has long been (and remains!) a rare, prized and fabulously expensive substance.

By 1506, Hormuz was exporting three thousand head of horses to India each year. That trade was to increase to ten thousand head by 1567, carried in triple-decked 'horse ships'.[17]

The rise of the Ottoman Empire provided new markets for the Arab traders of the Gulf, formalising an East/West locus that would create immense wealth and trigger jealousy in its turn.

The dark spectre of disintermediation was soon to come knocking – the process of cutting out the middle man. If our greatest example of disintermediation in the 2000s is amazon.com, the version to emerge from the 1500s was Portugal. Trade from the whole of the mysterious, fabulous East into Europe was channelled through the eastern Mediterranean Arab ports of Alexandria, Beirut or Istanbul. That this lucrative monopoly was dominated by Muslims was a source of infuriation to the evangelical Catholics of Portugal, whose entire state had been born in the flames of the battle against the expansion of the Umayyad Caliphate in Spain – originally established by that fortunate survivor of the Abbasid purge of the Umayyads, the prince Abdulrahman, and one of a number of emerging Islamic dynasties.

The Kingdom of Portugal was forged in the crucible of resistance against the Muslims, founded into the core of the Reconquista, the re-establishment of Christian rule in Spain. For the Portuguese, this was personal – and, faced with an effective Arab monopoly over Chinese ceramics, Indian and Eastern spices and Asian finery, traded with eager Western markets by the Genoese and Venetians, the Portuguese would seek another way.

The battle for Africa

The Portuguese won back their Kingdom from the declining Nasrid Caliphs, the inheritors of the great Umayyad caliphate of Cordoba, and set about taking the fight to the enemy. Geographically a maritime nation, they sent ships against North Africa in an expansionist gambit triggered by a trinity, appropriately enough, of needs. Economic expansion was desperately needed to address Portugal's penury in the face of a paucity of natural resources, religious evangelism was a way of not only asserting a belief system but showing Rome that Portugal was a good client and trustworthy ally and fighting the good fight drove the need to combat the Muslims who had been such an existential threat to these die-hard Christian hold-outs against the Umayyad incursions and depredations in Spain and France.

It was a heady combination of drivers – the Portuguese set out against North Africa at first, then found their way down the west coast of the huge continent of Africa. Exploration after exploration not only unveiled new lands, but reaped rewards in trade goods – including human cargoes of slaves.

It was the brilliance of Vasco Da Gama that was to conclusively break the Arab monopoly on the markets of the scintillating East. Sailing around the Cape of Good Hope, a voyage that took place in 1497 and cost, by the time it returned, the lives of half the embarking company, Da Gama reached Calicut in India. His achievement was to change the face of the world for ever.

Chapter 10

THE PORTUGUESE SWORD AND CROSS

"As for the old Moors who were of no use for work, we had their noses and ears cut off and then let them go, so that all who had their lives spared were marked in this manner."

– *The Commentaries of the Great Alfonso Dalboquerque*

Vasco da Gama was a Portuguese noble who followed in the tradition of exploration and aggressive commercial expansion established by the Christian nation that emerged from the long anarchy of the 'Reconquista' of Muslim Spain in the 1400s. His King, John II of Portugal, had sent him on a mission against the French, in which he had excelled. Now, the new King, Manuel I, was to entrust an altogether greater enterprise to da Gama – a voyage around the Cape of Good Hope to trade with the glittering markets of Asia.[1]

At the time, trade from Asia was routed through the Eastern Mediterranean to Venice which, together with Genoa, enjoyed a virtual monopoly over the commerce in spice, aromatics and other goods from the Middle East, India, Asia and China – and had done so for centuries, having made its peace with the Mongol Empire in the 1200s. With the fall of the Eastern Roman city of Byzantium to the Ottomans, the Asian trade fell entirely into Muslim hands. Venice and Genoa had no qualms doing business with Muslims, but Portugal's King wanted to both smash this 'dirty money' duopoly and take it over in the name of Christianity – messianism and mercantilism were rolled into one mission to civilise and profit. Inevitably, death trailed in the wake of these two 'noble' missions.

King Manuel had sent men to explore the origins of the Arab trade and they travelled dressed as Muslim merchants overland to Aden and India and visited the vital emporium of Hormuz. Others had taken to the seas, hugged the coast of West Africa and finally breasted the Cape of Good Hope to start the exploration of East Africa. Da Gama was sent to build on these explorations and find the route to India that the Arabs were using so effectively.

Da Gama set out with four ships and rounded the Cape of Good Hope as others had before him. He led his fleet along the East African coast, making contact with native tribes and marvelling at the wealth of some of the cities he encountered on the way – to which he would return to comprehensively plunder at his later convenience.[2]

After bombarding the coast of what we know now as Mozambique and looting Arab vessels at Mombasa, da Gama and his captains reached

Malindi (now in Kenya) on the East African coast, encountering Indian traders but finding himself frustrated in his efforts to find a reliable guide to cross the great ocean and reach India. This is where we are told by most contemporary sources that he met an Arab navigator by the name of Ibn Majid, who showed da Gama the way.

It was a lie, very much born of its time.

The innocent lion

Ahmad Ibn Majid, the 'Lion of the Seas', was a native of Julfar and an Arab seafarer and navigator of tremendous reputation. He authored a number of influential treatises on navigation and seamanship, including *The Benefits of the Principles of Seamanship and Lessons on the Foundation of the Sea and Navigation* (remember, book titles in those days were altogether more wonderful). Three of Ibn Majid's rutters, or navigational manuals, are preserved at the Institute of Oriental Manuscripts of the Russian Academy of Sciences, St Petersburg. The navigational directions contained in these books are exquisitely rendered in Arabic poetry.

The story has long been told of how one of da Gama's men befriended Ibn Majid and got him drunk, obtaining the directions he needed from the inebriated navigator. The story does not go well for Ibn Majid, a drunk Muslim who blunders into giving the key to India over to the Portuguese, who would in their turn use the knowledge not only to break the Arab monopoly on Asian trade, but would also go on to create havoc and carnage among the Muslim communities of the East. Da Gama would massacre a boatload of pilgrims on the way to Hajj, sack the Muslim quarter of Calicut and open the door for a wave of religious persecution and commercial predation that would blaze a trail of blood across Asia. The Portuguese had arrived – and we are told Ibn Majid was to blame for it all.

Researchers, including the highly respected historian His Highness Dr Sheikh Sultan bin Mohammed Al Qasimi, have used the three rutters of Ibn Majid, particularly the 'Sofala Rutter', to debunk the entire story of Ibn Majid and da Gama. A rutter was basically a navigator's book of directions. The evidence in these, as well as letters written by da Gama himself and Ibn Majid's age (he considered himself too old to navigate – in 1498, when da Gama arrived in Malindi, Ibn Majid would have been 77), all provide a strong refutation of the entire story and it is now accepted as highly unlikely that Ibn Majid had ever even met da Gama, let alone given him the route to India. In fact, we now have solid evidence that it was a Gujarati pilot who led da Gama across the Arabian Sea from Malindi to Calicut – and who was then taken back to Lisbon with da Gama. Ibn Majid, the Julfari and greatest of Arab navigators, has been vindicated by modern research and his name comprehensively cleared. As with so much of the history of the Emirates, contemporary research has revealed a very different narrative to the 'accepted facts'.[3]

Fire and the sword
Da Gama returned from Calicut with relatively little to show for his voyage in terms of trade goods – the merchants of Calicut had been reluctant to do business with this threatening interloper, whose rough manners had triggered instant distrust. On the return voyage to Malindi, da Gama lost half his ships and only fifty-four of his 170 embarking men survived the devastating monsoons – a weather event the Arabs and Indians had long known to avoid. But he had blazed a path and others were set to follow it with messianic zeal and materialistic avarice.

King Manuel sent another expedition to Calicut under Pedro Alvares Cabral. Cabral managed to miss Africa totally and discover Brazil instead, by sailing clean across the Atlantic. He then proceeded to Calicut, where the Ruler, the Zamorin, had previously been upset and insulted by da Gama.

As a result, Cabral found his reception not only cool, but actively antipathetic – clashes broke out and several of Cabral's men were killed. He seized a dozen Muslim boats and fired them, taking their cargoes and killing hundreds of men. At daybreak the next day, Cabral bombarded the city wharf killing hundreds more. Sailing further up the coast in search of more compliant trading partners, Cabral encountered the city of Cochin, whose Raja (or king) was opposed to Calicut and who consequently allowed the Portuguese stranger to open a trading post in his territory. Returning to Portugal in 1501, Cabral's ships were heavily laden with precious aromatic spices, but he left the stench of death behind him.

Da Gama now mounted a second expedition, heavily armed and prepared for war against the recalcitrant Zamorin of Calicut, as well as the wealthy coastal settlements of Africa. They plundered Africa's East Coast and set up trading posts there before embarking on the crossing to India. It was here that da Gama's fleet came across a large dhow carrying hundreds of pilgrims returning from Mecca. Da Gama captured the dhow and had the pilgrims deliver up all their wealth to him. Then he fired the boat and watched them burn, the women holding out their children for mercy as the flaming hulk and its desperate passengers were finally extinguished by the waters closing over them.

Da Gama went on to revisit Calicut, where he plundered some twenty large dhows in the harbour and had the hands, ears and noses of 800 captured Arab sailors cut off. Da Gama sent a boat to the Zamorin, containing the pieces he had lopped from his victims along with a message suggesting the Zamorin make himself a curry from the meat.

Da Gama then bombarded Calicut for three days, razing the city before making for Goa, where Jesuit priests would embark on a campaign of forced baptisms. He returned in triumph to Lisbon.[4]

Now it was to be Arabia's turn

Death in the Gulf

Like Vasco da Gama before him, Afonso de Albuquerque was landed gentry turned military man and a conqueror of new lands in the style of the 'Renaissance' men of the Portuguese Empire. Following on from his two illustrious predecessors, he embarked on a mission around the Cape of Good Hope to bring the choice of the cross or the sword to the heathen. De Albuquerque had a strategy, a grand design of throttling the Arab trade routes by establishing fortified 'choke points', particularly at Socotra and Hormuz to control the Red Sea and Arabian Gulf routes.

Having blocked the main routes west, he would then set up competing establishments throughout the Arab trade network spanning the Indian Ocean and all points east. Forts at Aden, Hormuz, Goa and Malacca would be supported by a fleet of ships and a powerful military, cutting the Arab Muslims entirely out of the eastern trade.[5]

De Albuquerque left Lisbon for this, his second mission to India, in 1506. The expedition consisted of two fleets, one of which split off at Mozambique to head for India and the other, under de Albuquerque himself, headed towards the Gulf and the prize it harboured – Hormuz. First, de Albuquerque established a fort on the island of Socotra with the aim of controlling the trade to Aden and then headed up the Omani coast to Muscat. The fort on Socotra, the island that sits between Yemen and Somalia in the mouth of the Gulf of Aden, was plagued by disease and supply issues and was consequently abandoned four short years later.

The invasion of the Hormuzi dependency of Muscat was messy: de Albuquerque's commanders lost their heads and disobeyed orders, pursuing their enemies into the densely packed streets and alleys of the town, where their long lances were rendered useless and many of their men were killed. However, they fought furiously and soon were chasing fleeing men, women and children and hacking them to death indiscriminately.[6] The dead included the eunuch who governed Muscat on behalf of the King of Hormuz.

De Albuquerque then proceeded to round up all the survivors and put them to the sword. By the time his men commenced the sack of the town, eight days after they had invaded, they not surprisingly found that little of value was left. However, one of de Albuquerque's men by chance made a hole in a wall with his lance and found a store of treasure hiding there. The townspeople, it seems, had taken measures to hide their treasure and now de Albuquerque's men ransacked and smashed every building in search of the hidden loot. They left few structures standing.

The sack of Muscat was finished off by raids on all the water tanks and vessels the Portuguese came across, siphoning off the liquid and smashing the receptacles, before snatching every weapon or good they could find. They fired the remains, as well as thirty-four ships and the fishing vessels and barques in the harbour.

De Albuquerque then proceeded to lash ropes around the minarets of the mosques and pull them to the ground. His last act before embarking was to free the prisoners taken during the bloody purge of the town. Before doing so, he had their ears and noses cut off.

Sohar was de Albuquerque's next port of call. The fleet moored offshore of the 'large and beautiful town' and an exchange of messages took place resulting in the capitulation of Sohar and its acceptance of the sovereignty of the King of Portugal.

Unusually for de Albuquerque, this involved nobody dying or losing their extremities. The fleet proceeded up the coast, leaving behind it the fortress of Sohar merrily flying a Portuguese flag.[7]

North of Khor Fakkan
De Albuquerque's little fleet hove to off the port town of Khor Fakkan and anchored for the night. His boats chased a small Arab vessel, which eluded them and escaped the harbour to warn Hormuz of the impending Portuguese storm.

Khor Fakkan's numerous contingent of Gujarati traders had already judiciously left, but the local population tried (as they had, initially, at Sohar) to frighten the foreigners away. A great display of strength took place on the beach, where men riding camels paraded and threatened the invaders with a great show of ballyhoo.

At 2 a.m., de Albuquerque gave the signal to his captains to prepare and at daybreak they sailed for the beach in their landing craft, firing mortars. The gunfire cleared the beach and a landing took place without incident, followed by a concerted attack on the town.

A great deal of skirmishing ensued in the hinterland and date palm groves of Khor Fakkan, with the Portuguese crossbows and arquebusiers easily outgunning the Arabs' arrows. The patchy outbreaks of fighting quickly became a rout and a triumph of martial technology over stone-throwing and arrows. Even in close quarters fighting, swords were no match for the long lances of the Portuguese. The town fell quickly to de Albuquerque's forces and he wasted no time in plundering the remains.

Following the sack of Khor Fakkan, de Albuquerque found himself burdened with a number of old and infirm people and so had their noses and ears cut off. He spared one elder of the town, who amused him with a display of learning and who provided details about Hormuz and its disposition. He freed his maimed prisoners, before firing the remains of the town, including the extensive stables. Khor Fakkan had been a key embarkation point for the thousands of Arabian horses that found their way from Hormuz to India each year.[8]

De Albuquerque set off for Hormuz in high spirits, leaving a black pall rising above the remains of Khor Fakkan behind him.

The Portuguese fleet reached Hormuz at daybreak three days later, having weathered a storm north of Khor Fakkan. His captains were aghast at what they saw as the ships rounded the point, revealing the great city with its densely packed fleet of well-manned ships and a great force of mounted soldiery displayed defiantly on the harbour. De Albuquerque argued with his captains, who all counselled caution until he eventually refused to listen to them anymore. The Portuguese fired a salute at the city and hove to, waiting until the sunset. The demonstrations onshore continued. 'The shouting of the Moors, and the sounding of kettledrums and trumpets was so great that there was not a man who could hear what any other said to him.'[9]

Warned by the little boat that had escaped Khor Fakkan, the King of Hormuz had prepared for the arrival of the Portuguese and had massed sixty large vessels (of 600–1,000 tons) as well as some 200 rowed gunboats armed with mortars. There were many shore-boats (used to load and unload cargoes) with small guns and archers on board. The Hormuzi land force consisted of some 15,000–20,000 armed men.

De Albuquerque, surrounded, consulted his captains. Messengers were exchanged, the King of Hormuz enquiring what the strangers wanted and de Albuquerque placing himself at the King of Hormuz' service if he, in turn, would but submit to the King of Portugal. However, de Albuquerque told the King's messenger, 'if he be unwilling, let him know that I will surely destroy all this fleet wherein he placeth his trust and take his city by force of arms.'

De Albuquerque's captains were less than pleased at the prospect of throwing themselves at such a superior force of arms, but their commander was implacable. The King's messenger dissembled, playing for time while more reinforcements were brought from the mainland (asking, not unreasonably, if de Albuquerque was come to parlay, why had he sacked the towns of the coast on his way to Hormuz?). De Albuquerque was having none of it and laid down an ultimatum.

On the fourth day after their arrival, on the expiry of de Albuquerque's ultimatum, the Portuguese artillery fired into the great Hormuzi fleet packed closely around them. The damage was enormous, sowing instant panic among the defenders of the city and sending many of the great boats to the bottom of the warm, shallow (just five fathoms deep) Gulf.

Confusion reigned, boats colliding and men fleeing, jumping ship in their hundreds as de Albuquerque's sharks remorselessly fell on their prey. They flung themselves at the greatest ship of the Hormuzi fleet, the thousand-ton *Meri*, which capitulated following vicious hand-to-hand fighting on decks slippery with blood. Sixty Hormuzi men died on the *Meri* before it was taken and then turned against the rest of the Hormuz fleet.

The water thrashed with the sheer weight of panicked men trying to escape the attack and the Portuguese wasted no time in slaughtering the swimmers, plunging their lances into the sea time and again until they simply could kill no more. Even the cabin boys and servants joined in to lash at the men in the water with whatever weapons they could find, including grappling hooks. One cabin boy alone claimed eighty men killed in the foaming sea below. The blue-green waters ran carmine with the blood of the defenders. By three in the afternoon, the Hormuzi fleet was in a state of total disarray and de Albuquerque's captains landed and pressed their attack on the fort.

By sunset, Hormuz had put up a white flag and sent out messengers to sue for peace. De Albuquerque demanded ten hostages, to be selected from the elders of the city, to be sent to him at dawn.

The Portuguese rested and, as dawn broke, they busied themselves cutting loose the abandoned remains of the Hormuzi fleet and setting the boats on fire to drift in the hot breeze that blew from landward. Hostages were delivered up to de Albuquerque – but only four instead of ten. Protracted negotiations followed, eventually ending up with de Albuquerque demanding a tribute of 30,000 Xerafins[10] yearly and the grant of land to build a fortress over the city. The King of Hormuz replied that, as his kingdom was ruined, he could only afford 6,000. In true souk bargaining style, de Albuquerque settled for fifteen.

On 10 October 1507, Hormuz hoisted the Portuguese flag. It was over.

Construction of the fortress began. Named 'Our Lady of the Victory', it still stands today. Its doorway is built around three anchor stones taken from the great ship *Meri*.

Following his victory at Hormuz, a messenger arrived from Ismail, the Persian Shah, demanding the payment of Hormuz' annual tribute. De Albuquerque sent him back with a load of cannon balls, shot, arrows and muskets along with a message that Hormuz now belonged to the Portuguese and any tribute the Shah could expect to receive was in the form of the cargo delivered to him.

De Albuquerque's fortress became the subject of disagreement with his captains, who wanted to press on to India without delay, and the disagreement spread among the men and became a full-blown mutiny. Learning of this dissension in his ranks, the Hormuzis rose against the Portuguese and de Albuquerque reciprocated by blockading the island and fouling its water tanks. This action almost brought Hormuz back to its knees, but de Albuquerque was deprived of a final victory by the dissent among his men.

At this point, a fleet of some sixty boats arrived from Julfar to relieve Hormuz and stationed itself at the island of Larak, just to the east of Qeshm. De Albuquerque called his captains to rally together at Hormuz but found that three of them had taken on fresh water from Qeshm and set sail for India before the Julfari fleet could cut off the wells, leaving de Albuquerque with three ships to both blockade Hormuz and see off the relieving fleet, reportedly carrying some 4,000 men.

De Albuquerque knew the game was up. His fortress at Socotra had sent word that it was in desperate need of supplies, the fresh fleet from Julfar now blockaded the water supplies of Qeshm while giving the people of Hormuz access to the wells denied to the Portuguese – and he had three ships to face off the Julfari force as well as the entire Hormuzi fleet which, albeit reduced, was still a major threat.

Afonso de Albuquerque left Hormuz, but not without leaving behind a chilling message for the island's defiant – even triumphant – king. Boiled down and stripped of its courtly language, it said simply: 'I'll be back.'

Many unhappy returns

De Albuquerque was indeed to return. The captains who had deserted him in 1507 had promptly made for Goa, where they had laid charges against him with the Portuguese Viceroy of India. These had to be answered and de Albuquerque found himself called away to India, much to his frustration (and not before he'd managed to kill a few more people). He sent his nephew back to Hormuz in 1514 to collect the overdue tribute and recommence building the fort there, but the young man failed in both objectives. De Albuquerque proved as brilliant a navigator of politics as he was of the seas and not only managed to outflank his accusers, but elevate himself to the very post of Portuguese Viceroy of India. It was now that he took matters into his own hands and returned to Hormuz in 1515, forging a new treaty recognising Portugal's supremacy and finishing the construction of his beloved project, the fort that would subdue the locus of the Arab eastern trade.

By now, Portuguese adventurers had followed the Arab traders throughout their great eastern network, building fortresses and trading establishments, 'factories', to eclipse those of the Arabs. Although de Albuquerque died before he could construct his second choke point – the fortress at Aden – the Portuguese now effectively dominated the trade between Europe, the Indian Ocean and the East. In 1543, they took over the customs at Hormuz, turning the Ruler there from a payer of tribute to Portugal to a recipient of a stipend from Portugal – in other words, a Portuguese vassal.

Conquest

The Ottomans loomed, taking Yemen and Basra (an extension of de Albuquerque's choke point strategy), threatening the Gulf and particularly the Hormuzi dependency of Bahrain, but the Portuguese beat them back and from 1565 treaty relations existed which effectively ended any Ottoman intentions for the pursuit of power in the Arabian Gulf, allowing the Sublime Porte[11] to focus on its western ambitions.[12]

The Persian coast of the Gulf was to cause the Portuguese more problems than the Ottomans, when Safavid Iran conquered Bahrain in 1602, initiating a state of war between the Safavids and the Portuguese Estado da Índia (State of India) which persisted until 1604. Played out against a background of constant raids by the Nakhilus, an Arab maritime tribe whose people had migrated from the Gulf coast to Larak Island in 1564 under their leader Ali Kamal, the structures of Portuguese presence in the region started to totter. Sohar emerged as a port independent of Hormuz in 1610. The Portuguese moved against Rams (north of Ras Al Khaimah), captured two Arab Sheikhs and then sacked Julfar and reduced its fortress in 1621, but the growing threat from the resurgent Arabs was nothing compared to that of the English. It was an entente between the English and the Persian Shah Abbas that was to see Hormuz fall to the Persians, supported by English forces, in 1623. A newly emergent dynasty in Oman, the Yaaruba, took Muscat in 1650 and a naval war broke out which saw fighting taking place from Muscat to Kenya. The cost of maintaining Portuguese supremacy was rising and the returns falling. Worse, the Dutch and English started to become not only active and interested in the area, but aggressively so.[13]

The Portuguese built and garrisoned forts around Southeastern Arabia, at Julfar, Dibba, Bidya, Khor Fakkan, Kalba and along the Batinah Coast of Oman. The fort at Julfar was constructed following the Portuguese expulsion from Hormuz, but fell two short years later following an invasion from Oman, under the first Imam, Nasir bin Murshid. It is likely this invasion that led to the abandonment of Al Mataf and Al Nudood in favour of the southern development of Ras Al Khaimah, which forms the centre of the city we know today.[14] Al Mataf and Al Nudood were enveloped in the northwards development of the city from the 1970s onwards and now much of 'historical' Julfar and its lagoon sits beneath modern construction. Although Julfar and Ras Al Khaimah are often conflated, they are two different settlements with distinctive histories. Much as Kush was a precursor settlement to Julfar, but was not 'ancient Julfar', Julfar was a precursor to Ras Al Khaimah, but was not 'ancient Ras Al Khaimah'.

With the fall of Julfar, for something like a century there was no dominant force in the Gulf as the Portuguese, Dutch, English, French, Persians and Arabs negotiated, skirmished and established various points of presence in the region with varying degrees of success. Gone was the great global trading network of the Arabs, channelled through Hormuz, Julfar and Aden. Now the East India companies of the expanding European powers were to emerge as dominant commercial and military forces in the Gulf and all the seas to the east – the Dutch and the English in particular.

Into this power vacuum, a new class of maritime force and mercantile competitor was born, and it was the natural successor to the maritime town of Julfar on the Arabian coast. Its rise would come alongside that of a number of coastal and inland communities established as the human tectonics of the Arabian Peninsula shifted and the tribes spread out in search of new lands and resources.

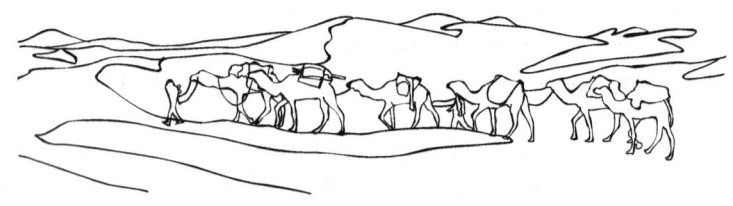

Chapter 11

THE COMPANY AND THE PROPHET

"Arabia Felix! Strange that the epithet 'Happy' should grace a part of the Earth's surface, most of it barren wilderness where, since the dawn of history, man has ever been at war with his environment and his neighbour."

– Bertram Thomas

The Portuguese adventure in the Indian Ocean and beyond defined the period from Vasco da Gama's first voyage to India in 1498 through to the 1600s. This tiny European kingdom, founded out of the Reconquista (the reconquest of the Muslim-dominated Iberian Peninsula by Christian forces), was to straddle the world with its ships and trading outposts following the strategy essentially defined by Afonso de Albuquerque. They set about superseding the Arab sea routes and trading outposts, ensuring the wealth of trade was either directly in Portuguese hands or controlled by Portuguese nominees.

The Arab presence across the maritime Silk Road has been enduring: its legacy exists today in a number of, sometimes surprising, forms. For example, the Sri Lankan port town of Galle today is home to the Dutch Fort, a UNESCO World Heritage Site, as well as Portuguese cathedrals and, by the sea, a Muslim community that has persisted despite the domination imposed by its colonial neighbours. Malaysia and Indonesia are Muslim nations and China has a significant Muslim community dating back not only to the Mongol invasions but also far earlier to the merchants who traded in spices, silk and ceramics through the centuries.

Today in Thailand (or any Thai restaurant in the world) you can enjoy a Massaman curry – a rich lamb, potato and cashew nut curry which combines Thai ingredients with distinctly Indian flavours, including tamarind. Its name derives from its origin, India and the 'Mussulman' (Muslim) merchants who travelled from there via the Strait of Malacca, which divides Malaysia and Indonesia.

The new-found wealth of Portugal attracted attention from others, notably the Dutch who were to follow in the globalising footsteps of their adversaries as a result of their struggle for independence and ensuing colonial rivalry. That struggle was to become known as the Eighty Years' War – a conflict that took place between Holland and its northern European allies and the alliance of Spain and Portugal, from 1568–1648. Fighting the Portuguese, the Dutch naturally aimed to supplant their adversaries' lucrative trade network.

Coming late to the party, the English founded the East India Company on 31 December 1600 under a charter from Queen Elizabeth I (it originated a year earlier in September 1599 as 'an association of Merchant Adventurers'). Decades later, the 'old enemy' threw its hat into the ring: the French followed the Dutch model and also founded an East India Company – as, indeed, did Denmark.

If the Portuguese had three aims in their expansion throughout Asia – put down Islam, promote Christianity and dominate the Eastern Arab trade network – those who followed them had perhaps simpler goals. For the Dutch, the English and the French, it was all about the money rather than any ideological goal. The race was on to control trade and it took the shape of a scramble to build preferential relationships with local rulers and gain better access to the rich resources of the mysterious orient. Soon enough, cooperation turned into coercion and trade routes started to be hammered into what would emerge as empires.

The Gulf was inevitably drawn into this great European expansion. Most activity in the 1600s focused on the Strait of Hormuz, the islands of Hormuz and Qeshm and the port of Bandar Abbas on the Persian shore, then known as 'Gombroon'. The companies vied to establish 'factories', not manufacturing facilities but agencies or trading posts, from the French word facteur, or agent.[1] In this, they competed with the Arab traders of the area, in particular the Huwala – the Arabs who had settled the islands and the Persian coast around Hormuz. The Europeans strove against each other to establish relationships with the dominant powers of Persia in order to set up and manage these factories.

The English allied with Persia against the Portuguese; an early success that was to be compounded with their alliance with the Omani Seyyids.

The first factory established by the English East India Company (EIC) in 1609 was in Surat, under the Mughal Emperor Jahangir.[2] It was barely months later that English vessels were plying a somewhat forceful trade around Yemen, coming up against Dutch resistance in Japan and fighting the Portuguese in India. The trading company was soon to form the 'Indian Marine' in 1613, essentially a naval force. The conflict with Portugal that followed was a war in everything but name.

In 1618, an English trading vessel was despatched from Surat to Jask (a port on the Persian coast, off the Gulf of Oman in a location approximately opposite to Dibba) and, its journey being pronounced a success, a regular trade route was established. This broke the Portuguese monopoly of trade with the Gulf, which had been in place since de Albuquerque.

King James of Great Britain sent a letter to Shah Abbas requesting permission to establish a factory at Jask. The port was blockaded by the Portuguese in November 1620, resulting in two English ships being turned away and returning from Surat with reinforcements. The ensuing action was won by the English, news of which travelled quickly along the Gulf and was received with joy by those who had endured Portuguese oppression.

The English participation in action against the islands of Qeshm and Hormuz of 1622 was at the insistence of the Shah of Shiraz, who refused English trade unless they agreed to help him against the Portuguese. The invitation was clearly one the English found hard to resist. The combination of a Persian army (of some 13,000 men, although some estimates go as high as 40,000–50,000) and English ships 'struck a fatal blow against the Portuguese ascendancy in the East.'[3] The conquest of Hormuz was to win the English a half share of the revenue of Gombroon. It also led, in one of those odd moments that history throws up, to the death of the man who gave his name to Baffin Bay in the Arctic, William Baffin.

The invasion was also to result in an episode of shameful pillage on the part of both the English and Persian forces. Squabbling broke out between the two allies as they engaged in looting, rape and vandalism. Hormuz, once a prized jewel of the East and a great and serene trading city of 50,000 souls with its bustling bazaar and fragrant courtyards, was reduced, once again, to a waterless, barren island with its salt mountain and deposits of red oxide mud, home to some 200 salt traders. The beautiful gardens and whispering alleyways of Hormuz were lost forever.

The English expectation of half the income from Hormuz and the port of Gombroon, the port to the landward of Hormuz, was to be dashed. Shah Abbas renamed Gombroon as Bandar Abbas and proceeded to ignore the East India Company and its intentions to establish a factory at Bandar Abbas. Eventually, the English were granted the right to ship Persian silks from Isfahan without incurring duties and were paid their half of the customs duties levied at Bandar Abbas (in 1632, this amounted to 1,650 pounds, a tidy enough sum). They were only allowed to occupy two houses at Bandar Abbas, for fear they would start building a fortified facility.[4]

The paucity of the loot from the taking of Hormuz was to result in a major upset in Britain. The King himself was dismayed at how little the venture had returned from the considerable outlay it had incurred. Yes, the Portuguese hold on the Gulf had been broken, but the aim of the adventure had not been the consolidation of power, but pecuniary gain. The East India Company's ships were held at Tilbury until it paid 10,000 pounds respectively to its principal (and most powerful) investors – the King and Lord Buckingham. This was an even more tidy sum and it was to mark the beginning of a period of decline for the Company, which was losing out to the Dutch in the East Indies and facing a period of great civil unrest in India following the death of the Mughal Emperor Jahangir. Forced to close two of its Indian factories, the Company also found itself struggling with its relationship and trade with Persia.

A resurgence in Portuguese trading and raiding in the Indian Ocean (and a Portuguese plan to retake Hormuz) resulted in the reinforcement of the forces from England and a number of actions at sea, which the English resoundingly won. With relations now well-established between the Company and the new Persian monarch, reinforcements were sent by the Persian army to protect the English trading houses at Bandar Abbas against the Portuguese. Soon after, a treaty of peace was signed between Britain and Spain which, at the time, included Portugal. Hostilities ceased, but further developments on the home front were to weaken the Company significantly as the English Civil War broke out and home market demand plummeted. The Dutch seized the opportunity and soon rendered the English position in the Gulf untenable, almost bringing the Company's factory at Gombroon to its knees. Inheriting much of the Portuguese network of trading posts and relationships, the Dutch dominated global maritime trade by the mid-1600s.

In 1652, war was declared between England and Holland, arguably as a result of English envy of the Dutch maritime pre-eminence of the time. The Dutch, rather than incur the wrath of the Mughal Emperor by attacking the English in India, headed for the Gulf and launched a successful series of attacks against English shipping. An English rout was only narrowly avoided by the outbreak of peace between the two nations and the Company once again set about rebuilding its factories and recommencing its trading.

The long-rumbling conflict between England and Portugal was eventually settled by a marriage, to the great delight of the English East India Company – Catherine of Braganza, the Infanta of Portugal, married Charles II and part of her dowry was the Indian port and island of Bombay. Charles transferred the ownership of Bombay to the Company for an annual ten-pound 'farm free rent' – an instrument of land ownership long lost to antiquity everywhere in the UK except in Northern Ireland, where it persists as a common arrangement today.

The acquisition of Bombay revolutionised the company's fortunes and it asserted itself throughout the region, sending an expedition to Bandar Abbas to recover the long-overdue payments against its share of the customs revenue there. It is also at this time, in 1675, that we see the first mention of pirates in Company records. A Malabari boat is involved in a brisk exchange with a Company boat, narrowly won by the English vessel. These pirates from Malabar had their counterparts with boats from Surat, who cruised the Indian Ocean between Surat and the Gulf: 'Sindian pirates wreak their malice on the unarmed merchants who, not being able to resist their unbounded lust, become tame slaves to their lawless rage. These are alike cruel and equally savage as the Malabars.'[5]

By 1683, the Malabaris had company. Pirates attacked the large Company ship, *the President*, with a force of two ships and six 'grabs' and were beaten off. Prisoners taken from the attacking force revealed them not to have been from Malabar, but Muscat. At the same time, the Company sent a force to Bandar Abbas once again, demanding its share of the customs revenue and seizing a number of ships there in lieu of payment.

In 1695, an Arab rebellion against Persia took place when a force of five large ships carrying 1,500 men and twelve cruisers was reported to have formed and the Company, not beyond seizing local ships to offset its debts, sent its ship *Nassau* to assist in the defence of Bandar Abbas against the local forces. The Arab forces overran Portuguese positions on the Omani coast and also in East Africa, as far as Mozambique. This is the first mention we see in British records of 'Arab pirates'[6] and it is perhaps notable that there is no incidence of piracy noted against them, but of rebellion against their former invaders, the Persians (who invaded the Arab port of Bandar Abbas and then took Hormuz with English assistance) and the Portuguese (who did pretty much the same thing).

Rebellion and piracy

The Arab rebellion against the Portuguese saw the taking of the port of Versova, just to the north of Bombay, by a significant force from Muscat in 1690. The Portuguese fort fell to the Arabs and the population fled south to Bombay in a panic. The action was a Godsend to the English of Bombay, who were in a dispute with the Portuguese governor of Versova and in fact were bracing for a Portuguese attack. In a strange reversal of the situation, the Portuguese appealed to the English for help and the Arab force prudently left, taking with them 1,400 captured slaves.[7]

It was at this time that the rich community of pirates in the Indian Ocean was joined by a merry new band: English privateers. The 'notorious rover named Avory' captured a number of merchant ships from Surat, including pilgrim ships, which so incensed the local popular feeling against the English that the trading community at Surat and Swally were thrown into jail by the Nawab to save them from the mob.

The English pirates now arrived in force, attracted by the ease and wealth of Henry (Avory) Every's plunder. They unconsciously mirrored de Albuquerque's stratagem of choking the routes to the West, establishing themselves on the island of Perim, in the Bab Al Mandab Strait between Djibouti and Yemen – even today, an area synonymous with modern piracy. With the Company controlling the Strait of Hormuz from Jask and the English pirates dominating the Red Sea, the chokehold on trade was repeated. Large, well-armed and manned by European crews, the privateers' ships were a fearsome force. They not only cruised the Red Sea into the Indian Ocean but were seen in the Gulf. By 1698, the infamous Scottish pirate, Captain Kidd, sailed the shores of India and plundered ships from Rajahpore to the Laccadives. Having failed to find water on Perim Island, the privateers established a new base off Udupi in Karnataka, India. Kidd, Chivers and others were eventually defeated and hanged at Tilbury. The notorious Henry Every was never apprehended and his disappearance and subsequent life were a source of controversy and speculation, and remain a perennial mystery.

It seems odd that, with pirates from Malabar and Surat and a force of well-armed English pirates operating against the Company ships, it was 'Arab piracy' that attracted the attention of English officials. In 1702 we see Company official Sir John Gayer writing of the 'insolence of the Arabs, who grown confident by their successes, were only deterred from making attacks on the company's ships by an impression that they were too strong to become easy prizes'.[8]

Accusations and counter-accusations of piracy flew and a picture emerges of opportunism on all sides: the English accused the Portuguese of piracy, the English privateers sacked Malabar and all stations north while the Arabs cruised the Gulf but also took their fight against the Portuguese to towns on the Indian coast.

The Arabs knew little peace, though. Quite apart from conflicts with the foreign powers plying their seas, they were also at war with themselves.

War in Oman

Not for the first time, the Imamate of Oman was in dispute. In 1719, a schism emerged between the tribal and the religious leaders over who should succeed the Imam Sultan bin Saif II. The religious leaders (the Ulama – or, as Omani historian Salil bin Razik had it 'the intelligent and pious') favoured Muhanna bin Sultan Al Yarubi, whereas tribal leaders ('the illiterate') favoured the former Imam's son, Saif bin Sultan, who was, however, still a minor. Saif having been pronounced the new Imam, in May 1718 the Ulama's preferred candidate, Muhanna, was taken by them to the fort at Rustaq in secret and there pronounced Imam.[9]

The move triggered an uprising of the tribes and calls to arms echoed across both the east and west coasts and throughout the interior. These were to bring tribal affiliations and differences into stark contrast. The tribes of the area had long been characterised by their origins: the Ghafiri tribes had moved from northern and central Arabia to settle the coast and interior oases such as Buraimi, where they found themselves washing up against the Hinawi, tribes who had come to the region through the northward expansion of the Al Azd from Yemen, tracing their origins to Malik bin Fahm.[10]

The Ghafiri included tribes such as the Na'im and Daramikeh, the Bani Ka'ab and Bani Qitab and the dominant northern force, the Al Qawasim. The Hinawi tribes settled in the areas around Buraimi and Liwa as well as the south-east coast – the Batinah – and included the Bani Yas, the Awamir and the Dhawahir as well as the Sharqiyin of the north-east coast, the Shamaliyah. There was some fluidity involved in these alliances and tributary relationships, particularly in the densely populated area around the oasis of Buraimi. The competition between the two groups (Ghafiri and Hinawi) for resources had often resulted in conflict in the past, but now the whole area was to be plunged into a complex and bloody struggle as the two candidates' backers sought to forge alliances to press their case.

Muhanna's Imamate lasted about a year before Yarub bin Bil Arub, the grandson of the former Imam Sultan bin Saif I, and his backers besieged Muhanna at Rustaq and took his surrender. Despite their assurances regarding his safety, on his capitulation Muhanna was bound, flogged and eventually murdered. Yarub proclaimed his eternal sadness at the loss of the Imam, shed many crocodile tears and promptly declared himself Imam in Muhanna's place, moving to Nizwa where he set up his Imamate, with the hapless young Saif bin Sultan, the former Imam's son, in tow. This move split the tribes, who had up until now supported Yarub. They continued to believe that Saif was the rightful Imam and a rebellion soon broke out against Yarub, led by yet another member of the same Yaarubi tribe, Bil Urub.

Bil Urub turned to the Hinawi tribes and, with their backing, set himself up at the fort of Rustaq, which had been fired with the loss of 150 lives. The ranks of the rebellion swelled and soon Bil Urub was effectively in control of the east coast and the routes to the interior. Yarub, recognising he was losing, stood aside and the young Saif bin Sultan was finally declared Imam. Bil Urub lost no time in declaring himself Regent and in doing so, alienated the head of the Ghafiri faction.

The Ghafiri united behind the former Imam, Yarub, and called on the tribes of the north and west to support them. They raised a force made up of the Bedouins of Dhafra, the Na'im of Buraimi and the Bani Qitab, whose *dar* or area of influence, comprised Dhaid and much of the interior of what we know as Sharjah today.

This combined force marched on Nizwa and attacked Bil Urub's forces, taking his surrender and proclaiming Saif bin Sultan as Imam. The conflict had raised tensions across the interior and fighting broke out as tribes faithful to both factions clashed. The whole populace lived in constant fear – in 1723, a group of women and children fled Rustaq and the threat of enslavement only to die of thirst in hiding in their cave in the mountains, their bodies being found later.[11]

Yarub passed away (his death was concealed for a full fifty days by the populace, fearful of an attack being prompted by the news) and his place at the head of the Hinawi faction was taken by Khalaf Al Hinai, who bore the nickname 'the dwarf'. While the Ghafiri were consolidating their hold over the interior of Oman, Khalaf marched on the coast and took Muscat. Meanwhile, the other Ghafiri forces went on to take Rustaq. They were joined there by a force of some 6,500 men made up of members of the tribes of the coast and interior led by Rahmah bin Mattar Al Huwala of Ras Al Khaimah,[12] the leader who would emerge as the founder of the Al Qasimi dynasty.

It was Rahmah bin Mattar who offered battle to the Hinawi force under Kaza Al Darmaki, with whom Rahmah had a feud. Rahmah rode ahead of his men and defeated the Hinawis, before taking his wheeled cannon ('guns which were drawn over the ground', according to Ibn Razik) and meeting up with the rest of the Ghafiri forces. They used the cannon to bombard Khalaf's fleet at sea.[13]

A Ghafiri force totalling 15,000 men marched to the east coast, meeting Khalaf's forces at Barka (between Muscat and Sohar), where they defeated the Hinawi forces. They laid siege to the fort at Barka, which they were eventually forced to raise when they were no longer able to feed their huge army. The coalition melted away and the Ghafiri returned to the interior town of Rustaq, allowing Khalaf to break out and take Sohar as well as laying siege to Rustaq itself. Khalaf and the Hinawi effectively controlled the coast and the passes to the interior. The Ghafiri, able to draw on the significant fighting resources of the Bedouin of the interior, took the Shamaliyah, the north-eastern coast, with the help of the Bani Yas and Na'im, after a number of skirmishes with Khalaf and his forces.[14] These battles saw great confederations put together to take forts and towns, water systems destroyed and date groves cut down as the armies forced populations to capitulate. The whole area lived in a state of perpetual fear and instability.

A mildly improbable story is told of Khalaf using a trick (involving an aggrieved farmer whose field of crops had been trampled by the coalition army) to incite the head of the Ghafiri faction to have the Sheikhs of the Bani Yas, Bani Qitab and Na'im flogged. Whether or not this took place as it is recounted or for other reasons, the interior and western tribes at this point withdrew from the Ghafiri coalition, fatally weakening it. Khalaf promptly attacked the remaining Ghafiri and was himself killed – alongside the Ghafiri leader – in the great reckoning that took place.

In March 1728, Saif bin Sultan was once again declared Imam, but five short years later found himself challenged by one of the Yaaruba, who counter-declared an imamate. While Saif controlled the coast and Rustaq, his Yaarubi opponent controlled Nizwa and much of the interior, including the Dhahirah (the extensive desert and mountain area south of Buraimi) and the Shamaliyah (the east coast of the Emirates today).

The rise of the Qawasim

Saif bin Sultan cast about him for alliances to break the great tribal coalition drawn up against him, at first recruiting Baluchi mercenaries (these were mostly wiped out in a battle against the Yaruba, which Saif lost decisively) and then making overtures to Nadir Shah of Persia. This potential alliance played into Nadir Shah's hands. He had been involved in a campaign of subjugation against the powerful and resurgent Arab Huwala, under Rahmah bin Mattar Al Huwala, who had taken possession of much of the former territories ruled over by the Kingdom of Hormuz. The Huwala held Bahrain, Ras Al Khaimah (or Julfar), Khor Fakkan and Bandar Abbas as well as the Gulf islands. They were to become known as the Al Qawasim, the singular being Al Qasimi.

Having taken Bahrain in 1736, now Nadir Shah enrolled Dutch assistance (the British being too scrupulous to get involved) to transport an army across the Gulf, landing 5,000 men and 1,580 horses at Khor Fakkan and another force at Ras Al Khaimah. At the time, Khor Fakkan was a town of some 400 souls.[15]

Joined there by Saif's mercenaries and other forces, Nadir Shah's army took the town and defeated the Yaaruba and Hinawi forces, taking Buraimi, the Dhahirah and the coast down to Muscat. Saif had by now realised he had created something of a Frankenstein's monster, but the dawning had come too late.

The Imam Saif bin Sultan and his Yaarubi opponent met and decided to throw in their lot together against the Persians, organising a counterstrike which saw the Persian forces in the interior routed, sailing the remnants of their forces from Ras Al Khaimah in 1738. The following year, Saif planned a killing blow against Ras Al Khaimah by land and sea, but was stopped in his tracks by the loss of his admiral's ship, *Al Malik*. The army turned back at Khatt, leaving Ras Al Khaimah in the hands of the Al Qasimi-led Huwala, who were now considered as his subjects by Nadir Khan of Persia. They endured this sovereignty for a short time but eventually rose up against their Persian overlords, seizing the fleet and taking back control of Khor Fakkan and laying siege to Bahrain. An abortive Persian expedition against Muscat took place even as Sohar, further north on the Batinah coast, resisted a Persian siege. Struggling to wrest victory from the jaws of defeat, the Persian forces managed to take Muscat, Sohar and Julfar but their rule was tenuous and short-lived: the new Imam (Saif had died by then, his struggle to claim his inheritance as Imam ultimately fruitless), Ahmed bin Saeed, the former Wali of Sohar and the founder of the dynasty that rules Oman today, led an uprising against Persian rule which saw the Persian forces smashed with great loss of life. The rebellion was marked by a great three-day banquet, given to the Persians by Ahmed bin Saeed. At the end of the feast, Ahmed bin Saeed called on anyone with a grudge against the invaders to rise alongside him against the Persians. The slaughter was considerable and Ahmed bin Saeed chased the last remnants of the Persian forces to Ras Al Khaimah.

This left two men standing: the Al Qawasim Huwala of Ras Al Khaimah and the Gulf islands under their powerful Sheikh, Rahmah bin Mattar Al Huwala and the new Imam, Ahmed bin Saeed. They went to war, fighting the Battle of Bithnah in 1745, when the Al Qawasim together with the Na'im of Buraimi attempted to fight their way through the Wadi Ham to take the east coast and its great prize, the port of Sohar. This was to mark a new era in the history of the area: the drawn-out battle between the Al Busaidi Omanis against the Al Qawasim of Ras Al Khaimah and Sharjah, and other tribes of the west coast and interior.

In 1762, Ahmed bin Saeed blockaded Julfar, while the Al Qawasim moved against Rustaq. These raids across the mountains continued until 1792, when a great raid took place by the Na'im of Buraimi against Sohar, resulting in the fall of the city to the raiders. Reinforced by the Bani Yas of Dubai (under their Headman, Hazza) and the Bani Qitab, the Na'im faced an army raised by the Imam Sultan bin Ahmed, including the Dhawahir of Buraimi, neighbours to the Na'im.

The battle was decisively fought and the Na'im were routed, escaping with the loss of some 300 men to the Wadi Jizzi, the great wadi which connects Sohar to Buraimi through the Hajar Mountains. There, the remnants of the Na'im force waited to ambush the Dhawahir returning home to Buraimi from the battlefield. The Na'im fell on the unsuspecting Dhawahir, with great loss of life. This action was to result in an enduring enmity between the two tribes. The Na'im were eventually pushed back to Buraimi by the Imam, whose forces also sacked Dibba by sea, killing many members of the Naqbiyin and Sharqiyin tribes.[16]

The message

It is against this backdrop of uncertainty, civil war and general fear in the time around the year 1800, that 'a book' arrived from Nejd, sent to the Sheikhs of the area by the Saudi Ruler, Abdulaziz bin Muhammad Al Saud. The book of 'the Solution of Difficulties' and the call it contained was initially rejected by the leaders. It consisted of – in the arch tones of Omani historian Salil ibn Razik – 'a mass of incoherent sentences quite inconsistent with the truth and no-one took any notice of it'.

Abdulaziz sent a force of 700 cavalry under one of his slaves, El Harik, and they fell on the Bani Yas, Na'im and Bani Qitab, who eventually submitted, as did the other tribes of the area, including the Dhawahir and Al Shamis. El Harik set himself up in Buraimi and from there, collected taxes, Zakat, on behalf of the Saudis, as well as undertaking incursions through the Wadi Jizzi to the Batinah coast.

The Saudi influence was to polarise the rumbling conflict that had been taking place throughout the passes criss-crossing the Hajar Mountains. It was also to make itself felt at sea as El Harik encouraged the taking of passing ships. And it was to give the Al Qawasim an ally in their increasingly bitter conflict with the Omanis, an ally only too happy to encourage the powerful maritime federation to take to the seas not in the pursuit of peaceful trade, but with an aggression which was to draw the Persians and the Omanis into conflict. Eventually, as a result of the alliance they formed with the Omanis, the British were also pitched into the fray.

The Portuguese had long suspected the British of encouraging the Omanis and, whether their suspicions were founded or not, the British certainly had found they could 'do business' with the Imams of Muscat. British relations with Persia had disintegrated and the Omanis provided a convenient foil against the expansionist Persians. By 1798, on 12 August, the British East India Company had entered into a formal treaty with the Sultan of Oman.

The founding of the Emirate of Diriyah

The Emirate of Diriyah or the first Saudi State are rather grand titles for the first wave of conquests made by the followers of the House of Saud under the inspiration of the religious leader Muhammad ibn Abd Al Wahhab and the pact he made with the Ruler of the Saudis, Muhammad bin Saud, in 1744. Diriyah, today a suburb of Western Riyadh located around the Wadi Hanifa, was the original home of the Al Saud family, who occupied the extensive mud-brick citadel of Al Turaif (much of which still stands as a Saudi national monument today).

Abd Al Wahhab seemed to come from nowhere. Brought up in Nejd, taught in the most basic of Koranic schools, or madrasas, he fell under the influence of scholars who professed a return to a more stripped down, ascetic version of Islam. Known today as Wahhabism, this school of Muslim thought could perhaps be equated to early English Puritanism or European Lutheranism. Fired by his belief in the purity of this new form of Islam, Abd Al Wahhab was quick to castigate idolatry of any kind and bring harsh punishments down on those who transgressed or otherwise failed the most strict adherence to his austere version of the Muslim faith. He was expelled by the exasperated population of Nejd, but found comfort in the Al Saud ruler's company, sealing a compact whereby the Al Saud would take care of the daily lives of the people, but Abd Al Wahhab would take responsibility for their immortal souls.

The combination would prove to be electric. Not for the last time, the Al Saud were borne on a wave of evangelistic zeal and found themselves conquerors not only of hearts and minds, but of new territories. The Wahhabi Saudis swept through the Gulf, from modern-day Kuwait, through Bahrain to Southeastern Arabia. They left few untouched – either by acceptance of this radical new interpretation of Islamic thought, or by the sword.

As they had in the days of the Prophet, many of the tribes took to this new ideology. It suited them: they lived harsh, hand to mouth existences; travelled the arid desert sands and relied on their very wits for their existence. The difference between life and death in the desert was a hair's breadth, a swing in the weather and a hasty decision could combine to bring ruin on a family and its flocks. They subsisted for the most part on a diet of camel milk, dates and bread baked on brushwood fires, a diet occasionally enlivened by the killing of an animal. Water was precious and all too often brackish. They had a name for every water hole, their desert travels marked by journeys from one to the other. Finding an unfriendly tribe already camped at a watering spot would all too often result in conflict as the desperate newcomers tried to get to the water already muddied and disturbed by the incumbents' camels.

In the winter, the desert and mountains would be transformed, the wadis green and running with fresh, cool water after the rains. So, too, would the oases of Liwa, Buraimi (part of which comes under modern-day Al Ain) and Dhaid. The ease of winter, however, was all too brief.

Little wonder, then, that a strict, frugal reading of Islam found favour among the Bedouin of the interior and the coastal tribes and the fishermen and mariners who had found themselves caught in conflict with the zealous Portuguese and their vicious version of Christianity. The Saudis' preaching often found fertile soil – but it also encountered resistance. Conflicts between adherents to the new flavour of Islam and those who rejected the creed broke out, with the Hinawi Bani Yas and Ibadi Omanis often ranged against the pro-Wahhabi Ghafiri tribes to the north.

In any case, throughout much of the 1700s, the whole area was in a turbulent state. The British, Dutch and the Portuguese were consolidating and defending their trading posts and squabbling for ascendancy. In this, they each tried to knit together favourable relationships with local rulers, often backed with the threat of force. The British alliance with the Persians had changed the game in the Gulf while the Arabs' implacable hatred of the Portuguese found its outlet in their increasingly capable maritime forces and their successful ventures against the Portuguese on both the Indian and African coasts. The Portuguese claimed the Omanis had British support but in any case were so stung by the many attacks on their factories (particularly the factory at Versova in India and their last remaining, and somewhat tenuous, holding in the Gulf at Bandar Kong on the Persian shore) and shipping that they sailed a squadron into the Gulf in 1719, attacking the Arab fleet and driving it back to seek the solace of the shallow waters of Ras Al Khaimah.[17]

Fired by the bitter memory of Portuguese conquest and rule, together with the many depredations of de Albuquerque and his antecedents, the Arabs didn't follow European rules and fly under the flag of their nation, principally because they didn't have a nation: each followed a Ruler, brought together in a series of tribal alliances and federations that was as informal and fluid as it was effective in concert. Smashed by the Portuguese, belittled by Dutch, British and French ambitions allied with Persian oversight, the Arabs of the Gulf had once dominated the trade between East and West. They had been superseded and sidelined.

Now, learning new technologies and approaches from the Europeans, they combined these with traditional structures. Impelled both by need and opportunity and enabled by a long heritage of maritime capability, they started to assert themselves.

They went to war.

Chapter 12

THE ARRIVAL OF ALBION

"Every misfortune that befell a British ship inside the Gulf – and sometimes outside it – was attributed to the 'piracy' of the Qawasim."

– Dr Sultan bin Muhammad Al Qasimi

The local maritime force in the Gulf throughout the 1700s was the Huwala, the Arabs who had settled the southern Persian coast and islands of the Gulf. At times their influence had extended as far as Bahrain and Muscat and their ships roamed the Gulf, Arabian Sea and the trading routes to the east. By this time, the maritime centre of Julfar had been largely abandoned and its southernmost suburb had emerged to become Ras Al Khaimah – the capital of the Huwala Federation. South of this, a second town had developed, to become called Ash Shariqa or Sharjah. This was also to become part of the traditional Al Qasimi holding.

The inland oasis town of Dhaid was the gateway to the Wadi Siji, which snaked up into the Hajar mountains to the village of Masafi and then to the east coast – either through the Wadi Abadilah to Dibba or the Wadi Ham to Fujairah.

The Qawasim of Ras Al Khaimah and its subsidiary town Sharjah were united under one Sheikh, from 1727–1760, the fearsome Rahmah bin Mattar Al Huwala, also known as Al Qasimi. He held sway over both sides of the Gulf, and the Al Qawasim of the time were to be found at Bandar Lingeh and Bandar Abbas on the Persian side of the Gulf as well as on the islands of the Gulf – particularly Qeshm and Larak. They were a considerable maritime force with trading links that extended throughout the Gulf and beyond and they had fought against both the Portuguese and the Persians, Ras Al Khaimah being heir to the long maritime prowess and heritage of its northern neighbour, Julfar.

One of the first mentions of the Qawasim (also known to the British as 'Joasmees', a term they were to apply to all of the Arab sailors of the Gulf) in British records was in 1727, when a naval expedition 'extracted compensation' from Rahmah bin Mattar Al Huwala for having the cheek to set up a rival port to the British factory at Bandar Abbas. The Al Qasimi port, established at Basidu (at the Western end of the island of Qeshm) had competed with, and triggered a loss for, the East India Company, which was clearly unconscionable for the Company and this unwelcome competition was to be punished rather than endured.[1] Sailing the frigate Britannia, the galley Bengal and two *trankis*[2] under the British agent, Draper, the British gained satisfaction and the Al Qasimi factory's trade was suppressed.³

It is not recorded what opinion the Al Qawasim took away regarding British attitudes to competitive trade from this engagement, but it can only be imagined that it was not a favourable one. The coming years were to lay the foundation for a series of misunderstandings, actions and counteractions that would have an inevitable, and terrible, end. But this very first action by the British against the Qawasim is very clearly, even in the account of the Empire's favourite historian, John Gordon Lorimer, not a military expedition undertaken against pirates or raiders, unlawful murderers or brigands (such as the English privateers who cruised the Indian Ocean, Red Sea and Arabian Gulf) but an attempt to suppress a trading rival – as, indeed, the British had moved against the Portuguese, Dutch and even French. The Qawasim were simply fair game.

However, the British estimation of this nuisance to their trade was disastrously wrong. The Qawasim were not only a powerful maritime force, but an instrument of leverage at a time when rival interests and petty faction fighting defined the whole area of the Gulf. Initially the Qawasim submitted to overwhelming Persian force under Nadir Shah, when the latter invaded Oman in 1737, but the Omani rout of the Persians set the new Omani Imam, Ahmed bin Saeed, on a path to conflict with the people of Ras Al Khaimah. The culmination of the long-standing civil war in Oman's interior, the conflict between the Qawasim and the Imam – who believed they should acknowledge his suzerainty – certainly found its signature moment in the 1745 Battle of Bithnah – the conflict between them raged on throughout and beyond the 1760s.

Ten years later Rahmah bin Mattar Al Qasimi had forged an alliance with the Persian Mullah Ali Shah, the governor of Bandar Abbas. Rahmah knew a dynastic move when he saw one and by 1758, he had overseen a marriage between his family and that of Ali Shah, giving his daughter in marriage to the Persian. That move was to restore the Al Qasimi presence at Qeshm in 1763, giving them a third of the revenues from the island. It was also to see the Qawasim and Ali Shah moving in concert as a force in the complex regional conflicts of the time.

The year after the marriage between Rahmah bin Mattar's daughter to Ali Shah saw the Qawasim embarking on a mission, together with the Arabs of Bandar Charak (the port inland of Kish Island on the Persian coast), against the Sheikh of Bandar Rig (north-west of Bushire), Mir Muhanna. Again, this is an interesting development reported by Lorimer, because he took great care to paint Mir Muhanna as a desperate and venal pirate responsible for vice, depredation and carnality – yet we see the Qawasim acting to quell the forces of chaos in the region. It is an odd role for a people who were to be accused of being common pirates to take – regional policemen in coalition.

In 1761, the Qawasim again moved in concert with Ali Shah after his family had been imprisoned on Hormuz by the Arabs of the Bani Ma'in. During this conflict a Muscat boat was taken by the Qawasim, carrying 2,400 bags of rice and a 'Leaguer of Arrack'. The boat appears to have been sailing for the British factory and the Muslim Ali Shah made restitution for the rice but notably not for the alcoholic Arrack. A peace was brokered in the conflict between the Bani Ma'in, Qawasim and Ali Shah, resulting in the division of the revenues from Qeshm, but also awarding the Qawasim ownership of the great ship, *the Rahmani*.

Again, we see an Omani ship (the Qawasim and Omanis being at war) taken as an act of war during a conflict which was eventually to lead to a negotiated peace, and for which restitution was made. The Qawasim, a major maritime force in the region, not only acted to keep the peace against the piratical Mir Muhanna, but fought honourable wars and negotiated subsequent peace. It hardly fits the profile of opportunistic privateers that British historians of the time are keen to highlight.

Not for the first time, we are invited to look back on the record and ask, *Quis custodiet ipsos custodes* (who guards the guardian)?

Who was guarding the guardians?

In 1986, the Ruler of Sharjah, His Highness Sheikh Dr Sultan bin Muhammad Al Qasimi, published a book titled *The Myth of Arab Piracy in the Gulf*. The book made some startling claims and flew in the face of a narrative that had, until then, been almost universally accepted – that

THE EMIRATES THROUGH THE YEARS

It is here, at Faya-1, that archaeologists unearthed hard evidence of human occupation in the area during the period of humankind's emergence from Africa to populate the world. The site can be freely visited today.

The dig at Faya-1 unearthed layers dating back to some 125–130,000 years BCE. It was at this point that the dig yielded up its collection of Neolithic tools, left behind by our distant ancestors in their journey out of Africa.

The rocky overhang at Faya provided shelter from the elements for early humans. After their passing, the archaeological record of the Emirates goes quiet, yielding very little evidence of any human activity for the 100 millennia to follow. It is during this time we believe that mankind flourished in the wide, rich valley that is today filled by the waters of the Arabian Gulf.

Jebel Faya, part of an extensive spur of rocky outcrop in the desert inland at Sharjah, which links the northern archaeological sites at Mleiha and Faya with the huge burial grounds of Jebel Buhais and the Iron Age community of Thuqeibah.

THE EMIRATES THROUGH THE YEARS

The extensive tell at Bidaa Bint Saud, outside Al Ain, contains a number of Hafit-era burials as well as evidence of Iron Age occupation and an important early *falaj*, one of many discovered in the Al Ain era which pre-date the supposed Persian origin of the irrigation technology and show it to have originated in south-eastern Arabia – the land of the Emirates and Oman today.

The oldest surviving mosque still in use in the Emirates today is in the east coast village of Bidya, also home to an Umm Al Nar tomb and tower, and a Portuguese Fort.

The Hafit Period beehive tombs at the foothills of Jebel Hafit, Al Ain. Hundreds of these can be found in this area in particular. The image on the left is the entrance to one of the tombs.

THE EMIRATES THROUGH THE YEARS

The entrance to a Hafit Era 'beehive' tomb, found near Jebel Hafit in Al Ain. These distinctive tombs are the principle evidence we have of the flourishing of this early Bronze Age culture in the land of the Emirates.

This Wadi Suq burial is typical of the extensive sites linked to that period to be found throughout northern Ras Al Khaimah.

A Wadi Suq burial from the extensive necropolis at Jebel Buhais, Sharjah. The period takes its name from a wadi inland of Sohar, in Oman.

The Iron Age Fort at Jebel Buhais was first discovered by Iraqi archaeologists in 1974. It overlooks the most extensive and oldest inland necropolis in the Emirates.

THE EMIRATES THROUGH THE YEARS

The Pre-Islamic temple uncovered by archaeologists at Ed Dur is linked to the worship of the Sun Deity Shams. It has been dated to the same era of the Great Temple of Hetra in Iraq, also a temple dedicated to Sun worship.

The Mleiha Archaeological Centre and site. Mleiha is one of the most important such centres in the Emirates today and provides a rich source of information on the area's splendid past.

The distinctive T-shaped Wadi Suq tomb at Bithnah is unique in the Emirates – some Wadi Suq graves have complex shapes, including one with a clover leaf pattern found at Jebel Buhais, while most follow a single line formation.

The Wadi Suq grave at Bithnah was discovered and excavated by the Swiss-Liechtenstein Foundation for Archaeological Research Abroad in 1987–1991.

Al Dayah Fort in Ras Al Khaimah. It was here, in December 1819, that the last of the Al Qasimi forces fell to the British, following three days of sporadic bombardment. Of the 400 men, women and children blockaded here without food or water, only some 177 were eventually found to be 'fighting men' – most were farmers from the date groves around the fort.

Dhayah Fort as seen from the plain around the hilltop fortification. It was from this plain that the British eventually fired on the fort with two 24-pound cannon: powerful guns which quickly brought the siege of Dhayah to an end.

The short and brutal seige of Dhayah Fort saw 400 men, women and children penned into the tiny adobe and mud-brick building for three days under bombardment. Their surrender was never less than inevitable as they had no water source.

THE EMIRATES THROUGH THE YEARS

The frontage of Al Hisn Sharjah. The cannon were known as 'the dancer' because the recoil from firing them would make them bounce on their wheeled carriage.

Al Hisn Sharjah – Sharjah Fort. Destroyed by the Ruler of Sharjah, Khalid bin Sultan Al Qasimi in the late 1960s, the remains of the fort were saved by his brother, Dr Mohammad bin Sultan who used the preserved woodwork alongside and old plans and images of the original fort to faithfully restore it in the 1990s.

The Al Ali Fort in Umm Al Quwain. Together with the defensive wall which runs across the isthmus, the fort preserved the safety of the community against marauding Bedouin, but also in times of conflict with neighbouring emirates!

THE EMIRATES THROUGH THE YEARS

Ajman Fort, the seat of the Ruling Family of Ajman up until 1967, when it was given over for use as the police headquarters. The Fort fell briefly to Abdrulahman Al Shamsi and his forces from Al Heera in 1920, but was restored to its Ruler within the day.

Fujairah Fort today. In the period up to the 1990s, the fort had lapsed into a state of ruin but has now been restored and preserved. It was frequently at the centre of the long struggle of the Sharqiyin to assert Fujairah's independence. Although recognised by the other Emirates in the early 1900s, its independence was truly established when the British recognised it as a Trucial State.

Masfout Fort guards the tiny enclave of Ajman high in the Hajar Mountains, adjacent to the small Dubai town of Hatta. The two communities were often at loggerheads in the past.

Masafi Fort is a small but sympathetically restored fort at the head of the confluence of Wadi Ham and Wadi Jizzi. It is constructed around a well-preserved *falaj* waterway, part of the extensive irrigation systems established around the mountain settlement of Masafi, with fortifications and agriculture in the area found to date back to the Iron Age and before.

the British East India Company had fought bravely against Arab pirates in the seas of the Gulf, particularly the Qawasim, and had prevailed. The area was given the name 'the Pirate Coast' and it wasn't until well into the 1800s that the label 'the Trucial Coast' began to be applied.

Al Qasimi's book rejected the charge of piracy, detailing each of the incidents leading up to the British sack of Ras Al Khaimah and other coastal ports in 1819 and providing documentary evidence that outlined a pattern of at best ignorance and at worst wilful deceit on the part of Company officers. Although the book was received by some Western readers with a reaction which could be summed up as 'Well, he would say that, wouldn't he?', Al Qasimi's reputation as a diligent historian has, in the three and more decades that followed, been well established. Perhaps, then, there is an alternative reading to this history that up until recently was most certainly written by the victor?

We have already seen that the four great European powers clashed over the Gulf and its eastern trade, jockeying for position and establishing their factories, or agencies, to prosecute a profitable trade with the region and the markets it served. The tremendous, opulent city of Hormuz controlled the Arab commerce with Asia and funnelled goods inland through Persia and Mesopotamia alike to reach the Eastern Mediterranean where the Byzantines, Genoese and Venetians monopolised the trade with Europe. The wealth at stake was fabulous, spices, silks, ceramics and myriad other valuable cargoes sailed the seven seas and reached Europe through the great Arab trading networks that criss-crossed the East.

The Portuguese were the first to realise they could break this monopoly but the English, French and Dutch were to follow and eventually the greatest maritime power of the time prevailed: perfidious Albion.

In vying with the other powers for the domination of the Gulf, the Arabian Sea and Indian Ocean, the great continent of India and the markets beyond to the East, the British established trading outposts under treaty with and at least under the sufferance of, local rulers. This 'informal empire' established by the British East India Company was soon to become all too formal and the Indian Maharajahs (as well as Nawabs, Mirs and Rajahs)[4] found themselves one by one sidelined and compelled to reconcile themselves to English suzerainty and then British (England was brought together into union with Scotland in 1707 to form Great Britain) rule. This was often achieved by the use of coercion, a mixture of soft and hard power that very quickly saw the use of untrammelled military force normalised as an instrument of state.

The British allied variously with Persia and Oman in their bid to dominate the Gulf but appear to have simply under-estimated the powerful maritime force represented by Ras Al Khaimah and the other Qawasim ports of the region. By a trick of fate, they managed to ensure that they were seen by the Qawasim as unfair aggressors. Having established themselves on first encounter in this role, as early as 1727, the East India Company's officers did very little indeed to question their strategy. They did what they had done so often in the past century of creeping conquest – they brought in force.

At the start of 1763, under pressure from the Persians, the British relocated their principal Agency from Bandar Abbas to Basra, the Ottoman Iraqi port at the northernmost tip of the Arabian Gulf. This was to influence British policy and thinking regarding the Gulf and gave it a distinctly 'Turkish flavour' which was hostile to the Persians and their allies.[5] In March 1763, a series of British attacks took place against the islands of Larak and Qeshm in an attempt to gain reparations for their loss when the Bandar Abbas factory was closed. The British, their force damaged by repeated actions, held off from a proposed attack against the Persian admiral Mullah Ali Shah at Qeshm partly because they no longer had the armaments to prosecute such an attack and partly because Mullah Ali Shah had paid out so much in tribute to the Qawasim that his treasure wasn't worth the game. The British decided instead to seize the ship of Mullah Ali's Al Qasimi allies (and, by now, marital relations), *the Rahmani*, which was moored at the island of Luft. On arriving at Luft, the British Captain Court decided to withdraw from the attempt, 'representing the risk and dangers to be very great.'[6]

From the Al Qasimi point of view, this incident would have seemed very different to the British 'righteous attempt to retrieve reparations'. Out of nowhere, a British force had arrived at Luft and threatened one of the principal ships, probably the pearl of the Qawasim fleet for no apparent reason. The British force had been scared off, which would have resulted in the Qawasim being both angered and emboldened.

With relations between the British and Persians at best fractious (the Persian Karim Khan had taken two British officers as hostage and was attempting to negotiate using them as an asset), those between Persia and Oman broke down completely when Karim Khan demanded the restoration of Oman's tribute to Persia. Given that the Imam, Ahmed bin Said, had thrown the Persians out of Oman in a tremendous rout, his answer was predictable and hostilities broke out. The British, finding themselves caught between two desirable alliances, 'held strictly aloof'.

Unusually, the Imam Ahmed bin Said found his forces buoyed by those of an old enemy: the Qawasim. Rahmah bin Mattar having passed away in 1760, it was his successor, Rashid bin Mattar who joined with the Sheikh of Hormuz and Ahmed bin Said against the Persians in 1773.

Qawasim power

By this time the Qawasim fleet was considerable, buoyed by a number of significant vessels captured from the fleets of the Persians and other foes and consisted of some sixty-three large ships and 669 small vessels, backed by a force of some 18,000 men.[7]

One of the reasons the Qawasim would have been keen to capture ships from others was that the technology of maritime warfare had moved on, driven by the innovations introduced by the Portuguese and other European powers. Although we are used to seeing great ships of the main in naval paintings of the period, the truth of maritime power in the Gulf was altogether a more mixed bunch of capabilities, ranging from gunboats mounting a single gun on their prow through to the fearsome British frigates, their sides lined with batteries of cannon.

While the traditional Arab sewn ship (called *trankis* by the British at the time) had served admirably for centuries as a vehicle for trade, it turned out to be a disastrous gunboat. Tied together with, literally, hundreds of miles of coir rope made from battering and spinning coconut husk, these ships did not involve a single nail in their construction.

Pliable and flexible, they served as trading vessels across incredible distances and the boatbuilders of the area constructed sewn ships large enough to transport hundreds of horses from Khor Fakkan and other ports to serve a healthy trade with India and even China. The sewn ship tapered from its bow to its stern, a shape still seen among booms trading in the Gulf today. But the sewn ship proved to have one huge drawback when it was used as a warship.

Using a sewn ship as a platform for firing cannon literally tore the boat apart. The ropes, which managed to withstand the pull and punishment of years of sailing the seven seas, couldn't handle the explosive force of cannon recoil.[8]

By the latter part of the 1700s, the sewn ship had become something of a rarity in the Gulf. Grabs, gallivats, ketches, booms, brigs, bagarahs, batils, baggalas, snows and pattamars, however, abounded.

Of the larger boats, batils were twin-masted sailing boats about twenty metres in length and about four metres wide. The bagarah was a similar-sized boat, with a single mast and a deck-house, while the lateen-sailed baggala was a much larger boat, typically of 200–300 tons. Round-sterned, these large boats would accommodate several cannon. The 'Arab dhow' or boom, still seen motoring throughout the Gulf today, was then a ship of one lateen sail of some 150–250 tons with a poop deck and gun ports. The twenty-metre pattamar was a cargo ship, typically of Indian origin.[9] Grabs, a Malabari innovation, shipped anything up to 500 tons and mounted twenty-four to thirty-two nine-pound guns, while brigs were twin-masted ships of up to 500 tons and carrying up to twenty guns – snows were closely related and similar in size.

A gallivat was a small gunboat with sails and oars, typically mounting five to eight guns of six pounds and less, while a ketch was a small, twin-masted boat. In addition, various shapes and sizes of boat were pressed into service, from mortar boats (with one or two mortars mounted at their prow) to jollyboats, effectively dinghies often used to unload vessels. This name has passed into local Arabic, where a small boat is referred to as a *jalboot* to this day.

The sheer variety of boats and the anarchy of battle at sea with any combination of these being pressed into service on either side, can hardly be imagined. The Qawasim fleet at sail could range from a few warlike dhows to an invasion force supported by large gunboats and a flotilla of smaller craft packed with men, bristling with muskets and small guns. Sailing the shallow waters of the Gulf, intimately aware of every salty khor and shallow inlet, the Qawasim at sea would have been a potent and capable force.

Not only were there a number of Arab, Persian and Omani forces sailing the Gulf as well as other foreign powers, but the British presence in the region was stepped up in the late 1700s, when the East India Company's 'Bombay Marine' force of warships was supplemented by the direct presence of the British Navy. This move followed the re-establishment of the British agency at Bushire in 1770.[10]

Persia fights back

The Qawasim decision to support Oman against the Persians speaks to the fluidity and inconstancy that were characteristic of the era. Not only were the European powers fighting each other and forging alliances (through trade, friendship or threat, as best suited the situation) in the Gulf, but the local powers – including the Persians, Omanis and Gulf Arabs – were also clashing and allying. By now the most powerful of these local forces, the Qawasim, came together with the ruler of Hormuz to support their former foe, Muscat, against the Persians. Given that the Qawasim and Na'im had tried to take the coastal Omani city of Sohar with an incursion through the Wadi Ham at Bithnah in 1745 and had in turn fought off several Omani attempts at incursions into Ras Al Khaimah, it might seem odd that they had suddenly thrown in their lot with Oman. The explanation lies with the Persian Karim Khan, who appointed a member of the Ma'in tribe as Ruler over Bandar Abbas, Hormuz and Qeshm in an attempt to consolidate his rule over the coast of Persia. This resulted in the expulsion of the Al Qasimi Huwala and other Arab tribes from the three territories in 1765.[11] Having fought a long war against Muscat to assert their independence from an Omani suzerainty they had never recognised, the Qawasim now found themselves threatened by Persia. Karim Khan's move effectively pushed the Qawasim into an alliance with the Omani Imam, Ahmed bin Said.

The Persian strategy against Oman was odd, to say the least. In 1775 the Persian fleet sailed against Ottoman-held Basra, hoping to reduce the Omanis by investing the principal port with which they traded. Faced with the Persian threat to their Factory at Basra, the British failed to stay 'strictly aloof' and sailed against the Persians' Arab allies, the Ka'ab. The British then abandoned Basra for Bushire, leaving the Omani fleet to engage with the Persians. The Omanis broke the Persian blockade of Basra but the city eventually fell to the Persians. This resulted in the British being handed back their factory, in the migration of a number of Persian merchants to Kuwait and in the termination of the alliance between the Qawasim, Hormuz and the Omanis. Once again, their enmity came to the surface and the Qawasim and the Imam of Oman were soon at loggerheads.

Lorimer, at this stage, makes the strange assertion that the Qawasim had begun, by 1778-1780, 'to indulge in those indiscriminate piracies, by which a few years later, they were to acquire great notoriety' but he fails to make any mention of precisely what piracies took place in those years. Strangely enough, nobody else reporting on this period mentions any piracies attributed to the Qawasim. They don't seem to have happened at all.

An incident which did take place in 1778 is the taking of a ship flying the colours of Oman by an Al Qasimi force. The Omanis had taken a number of vessels sailing from Bushire on the grounds that their cargoes rightfully belonged to the Imam. Rashid bin Mattar Al Qasimi had resigned his Rule over the Qawasim in 1777, his son Saqr bin Rashid Al Qasimi acceding to rule in his place. The Omani ship taken by the Qawasim, on being overwhelmed, ran up British colours. A correspondence between Rashid bin Mattar and the British Resident at Bushire followed the incident, in which Rashid made it clear the ship had been sailing under an enemy flag, while the Resident claimed the ship as belonging to the East India Company. A discussion then arose regarding payments to be made to restore the ship. Despite Lorimer's lurid language

('The Qasimi fleet, manned by ruffians who depended on piracy for their livelihood, scoured the seas plundering all indiscriminately'),[12] there are few proofs offered for these claims of widespread depredations.

In fact, the next incident doesn't take place until almost twenty years later, in 1797. And as piracies go, it's not really very, well, piratical.

The dodgy roger

The Bassein was a snow, a small ship not dissimilar to a brig,[13] that was used for both trade and as a light military ship. Sailing past Rams on 18 May 1797, she was taken by a force of twenty-two dhows and escorted to Ras Al Khaimah. At this time, the Qawasim were at war with Oman and Oman was at war with Persia. The waters of the Gulf, usually unstable enough, were truly a war zone. The Bassein and its crew were released two days later on the order of Saqr bin Rashid Al Qasimi, who subsequently responded to a query from the British Resident at Basra, 'God forbid I should think of capturing your vessels,' he said. 'I must however observe on the subject of the detention of your vessel by my cruisers near the Island of Qeshm...When my cruiser meets the vessel of my friends such as those belonging to you, to the Arabs in alliance with me and to the Basra Government, they behave to them with amity, but when they meet the vessels of my enemies they attack and destroy them, placing confidence in God.'[14]

Lorimer comments, archly: 'No reparation seems to have been exacted for this insult to the British flag.'[15]

No goods or lives had been lost, no plunder or injury had taken place. The Bassein was let go on its way with all hands once the Ruler had directed its release. Even with the benefit of over 200 years' hindsight, it seems an odd sort of 'piracy', let alone an 'insult to the British flag.'

On 15 September of the same year, the British fourteen-gun brig Viper was at Bushire as were a number of Qawasim dhows under the command of Saleh, the estranged nephew of Saqr bin Rashid. Saleh approached the resident of Bushire and outlined his intention to pursue a number of dhows from Sur in Oman who were at the port and requesting that the British not intervene. He asked for supplies of powder and shot and was granted forty three-pound cannon balls but no powder. The resulting action is a confusion. The Viper was shot at and immediately cast off and prepared for war, directing a fusillade of shot herself at the dhows surrounding her at port.

Who fired the first shot? Sheikh Saqr, in a subsequent correspondence, said that the Omani dhows were the first to open fire. The Viper's captain says 'two of the dhows' fired on the ship. Saqr bin Rashid Al Qasimi made many protestations of friendship towards the British and assured the Resident at Basra that he would investigate the incident further with Saleh.[16]

The Viper lost thirty-two of its crew of sixty-five, including the young Lieutenant Carruthers, who had taken charge of the vessel as the fighting broke out (its captain was ashore).[17] Was she the victim of piracy or caught between two warring local forces while at harbour? Out of a slew of confused accounts, it seems unlikely that the Qawasim would explain they were pursuing the Omani ships and ask the British for a supply of shot and then use that shot to fire on their benefactor's ship. The level of treachery required almost beggars belief, but it is only by accepting the existence of that treacherous intent can we believe the Viper was the victim of Al Qasimi piracy rather than being caught in the crossfire of the war between the Qawasim and Oman.

In fact, a member of the Council of the British Government of Bombay, Francis Warden, reached the conclusion that a number of incidents throughout the Gulf could be attributed to the unsettled state of the government in Oman, where the Imam Seyyid Ahmed's death had resulted in yet another of the battles for succession that had marked Omani history, with the usurpation of his successor, Seyyid Sultan bin Ahmed. As a result, Omani ships from both sides cruised the Gulf and those allied to the deposed Imam felt free to attack the ships of their enemy's ally: the British, who had signed a treaty with the Sultan in August 1798

In fact, it was Warden, in his 1819 *Historical Sketch of the Joasmee Arabs*, who stated that up until the close of 1804, the Qawasim 'committed no act of piracy but, with the exception of the attacks on the Bassein and Viper cruisers, manifested every respect to the British flag'.[18]

The new influence

Like the other tribes of the area, on or around the turn of the century, the Qawasim had accepted the call from faraway Nejd of Wahhabism. They and others would have paid the Islamic Zakat tax to the Wahhabi agent, at the time sitting in Buraimi. Quite when a Wahhabi agent arrived with the Qawasim in Ras Al Khaimah is not known, but it was likely sometime around 1798–1800. As a consequence, Wahhabi influence among the family grew. Some of the many incidents that followed the attacks on the Bassein and the Viper are clearly a result of the war between the Qawasim and Oman – and can be laid at the doorstep of the British relationship with the Omanis resulting in their own interests being caught up in the regional conflict. Others could be viewed as the result of something of a power struggle between the Wahhabi agent and the head of the Al Qawasim. This increasing conflict within the family and wider tribe was eventually to lead to the deposition of the Al Qasimi Ruler, Saqr bin Rashid Al Qasimi.

More enlightened and insightful British voices of the time can be heard pointing to the 'Wahhabi influence' at work within the Qawasim. The dialogue between these 'moderates' and the hard-line officers of the company was an odd mirror to that which must have been taking place in Ras Al Khaimah at the time, with the Al Qasimi Rulers counselling moderation and restraint when it came to the British and the firebrand Wahhabi agent pointing out that all of the *kaffirs* (unbelievers) deserved no mercy and no quarter.

It is now, as we enter the 1800s, that three factors come together; the Al Qasimi war with Oman that followed the long and fruitless civil war over the successions to the Omani Imamate and the uncertainty this caused throughout the interior; the growing influence of the Wahhabis and the rising role of the British and their East India Company in the Gulf. These forces were to collide to create a perfect storm.

The clouds on the horizon loomed, heavy and portentous. The stench of death was in the air.

Chapter 13

EXILE AND THE KINGDOM

"Armed Arabs, once afloat, invariably give way to the temptation to indulge in indiscriminate plunder."

– John Gordon Lorimer

The British narrative of Qawasim piracy in the Gulf was that they contented themselves with depredations against native vessels until 1804, when they suddenly turned on British shipping in a joyous spree of maritime anarchy.[1]

The truth, as usual, is perhaps a little more nuanced. Saqr bin Rashid Al Qasimi died in 1803 and his son, Sultan bin Saqr Al Qasimi, acceded to become Ruler of Ras Al Khaimah and Sharjah.

Sultan bin Saqr had three brothers and seven sons and was to grow to become a grand and patriarchal figure, friendly to the British and yet constant and implacable in his enmity towards the Imam of Oman, Seyyid Sultan bin Ahmed. It was Sultan bin Saqr's father who allied with the Bani Utub in 1801 to retake Bahrain from the Omani Seyyid Sultan bin Ahmed but it was during Sultan bin Saqr's rule that the Omani Seyyid Sultan lost his life to an attack carried out by a combined Al Qasimi and Utubi force off the Al Qasimi held town of Bandar Lingeh, where three Qawasim dhows attacked Seyyid Sultan bin Ahmed's ship and he died of a musket shot to the face.[2] The crew was spared.[3]

Another celebrated incident was the taking of the *Fly* by the French thirty-eight-gun privateer *La Fortune* in 1804. The French had been reasonably successful in taking their war against the British into the Gulf and Indian Ocean, harrying British traders and military alike. Having captured the *Fly*, running it ashore at Kish Island, the French let the British and Indian passengers off at Bushire. These, taking a passage among other passengers to Bombay in an unflagged local ship, found themselves taken by an Al Qasimi force and imprisoned in Ras Al Khaimah. Buying their release by offering to show the Al Qasimi where they had buried the treasure the *Fly* had been carrying, the passengers found themselves marooned on Kish. Two survived to reach Bombay, presenting the despatches they had preserved and telling their tale of piracy on the high seas.[4]

The blame for the fate of the Fly was not to be borne by the French, who had committed a piracy against a British flagged boat, but the Qawasim, who had captured a local vessel.

In 1805, the British merchant brigs *Shannon* and *Trimmer*, the personal property of the British Resident at Basra (referred to by the British as Bussorah), were attacked and boarded by Qawasim vessels. The 'native' crew were put to the sword and the captain of the *Shannon* lost his arm to a sword-stroke as he tried to fire a musket at the attackers. The European crew was put ashore, however, and the two boats – one of which shipped twenty guns – were taken as prizes to reinforce the Al Qasimi fleet.[5]

Tribal coalitions and influences raged around the Gulf, an often kaleidoscopic set of alliances that sometimes appeared to be little more than brief dalliances, while enmities tended to be longer lasting. The Qawasim were allied with Mulla Hussein of Qeshm against Bandar Abbas, while their Utubi allies from the action to take Bahrain were now involved with the Omanis in a bid to counter the Qawasim. An Omani action against Qeshm with British support resulted in the defeat of an Al Qasimi force.[6]

The next report of a piracy against British shipping is the affair of the *Mornington*, a twenty-two-gun cruiser. *The History of the Indian Navy* reports the incident as an unprovoked attack by the Qawasim, encouraged by the impunity which they had enjoyed following the raids against the *Shannon* and *Trimmer*.

The facts are a little more interesting. In 1805, the British Resident at Muscat, Captain Seton, suggested to Bombay that he might assist the 'Sultan of Oman' in chastising the Qawasim and Bombay assented, with a number of codicils – many of which Seton happily ignored. At the time, Oman's Imamate had, as was often the case, by no means a clear succession: the young Seyyids Salim bin Sultan and Saeed bin Sultan ruled together under a regent, Badr bin Saif, who, although he was the effective Ruler of Oman, was not the Sultan.

Badr bin Saif sailed with Seton and his ship the *Mornington* and together they retook the former Omani-ruled Bandar Abbas from Persia, resulting in Persian howls of outrage directed at Bombay (Seton having exceeded his orders, if not ignored them completely, in attacking the Persian-held port; 'he was not a careful reader of his instructions',

Lorimer notes on recording Seton's death in 1809).[7] Only then did their fleet proceed to blockade Qeshm and the Al Qasimi fleet stationed there, but Badr – who was, as it turns out, pro-Wahhabi – proved to be lukewarm to the idea of completely reducing the Qawasim.[8]

In a breath-taking revision of the facts, Lorimer recounts the 'attack on the *Mornington*' as an instance of Qawasim piracy. 'A fleet of forty Qasimi vessels surround the HEI [Honourable East India] Company's cruiser *Mornington*, of twenty-two guns, and tried to capture her.'[9] Although the incident is presented as being separate and prior to the blockading of the Qawasim fleet at port by the *Mornington* on 5 July, no date is given for the previous encounter. In fact, Seton himself was to say that the Qawasim 'never attacked our vessels' since he had been in the Gulf.[10]

Given the Qawasim were at war with Oman, the British turning up in the company of an Omani fleet, with an Omani Seyyid in command and blockading their fleet at anchor would appear to be more than provocation and certainly hardly fits the narrative of Arab piracy against an innocent ship of the East India Company.

The upshot of this blockade of their fleet was that the Qawasim agreed a truce, part of which involved the return of the Trimmer and Shannon. These boats were duly given up to Seton, although stripped to their planks.

By October, Seton had received his instructions from Bombay. He was to negotiate a peace with all of the parties in the region and also require indemnities against British losses. These orders being nigh on impossible, Seton once again exceeded his authority in negotiating a peace with the Qawasim alone and an agreement was duly made, on 6 February 1806, which bound the Qawasim to a peace with the British. Tellingly, it was not negotiated with the knowledge or consent of the Wahhabis.[11]

Peace, at least between the Qawasim and the British, then reigned briefly in the Gulf. However, not all was well in Ras Al Khaimah.

An Al Qasimi ruler overthrown

We can only presume that Sultan bin Saqr Al Qasimi fought constantly against the authority of his Wahhabi agent in maintaining his Rule in the face of this manifestation of far away and yet very real authority. The Wahhabi agent in place would have wielded significant power and his instructions and demands would have flown in the face of any moderate view of the world – the Wahhabi way was one of absolutes and there would have been little toleration of foolishness like negotiation or parley – and especially not with idolatrous *kaffirs* such as the British or their Hindu subjects.

The Wahhabis leveraged the twin threats of their forces in Buraimi and the authority over religious affairs that their flavour of the Islamic faith gave them. It was a powerful combination and the moderate Sultan bin Saqr, the man who had signed a peace with the British, was soon to feel its full force.

In the meantime, Sultan bin Saqr contented himself with marching against his traditional enemy, the Omanis, and in fighting alongside the Omani Seyyid, Badr, against the Seyyid's potential usurpers. As a result, the Qawasim took Khor Fakkan to their own. To this day, the east coast holiday town and port of Khor Fakkan remains part of Sharjah, the only emirate to face both the west and east coasts of the Emirates.

Sultan bin Saqr's actions against Oman, British ally though it was, did not contradict his treaty with the British. Seton, the British resident in Muscat, was already conflicted as regards the contested rule of Oman, and was given strict instructions from Bombay which of the candidates to support and was provided with numerous letters to present to the 'Sultan of Oman', each one to be presented to whichever of the claimants might finally turn out to be the Sultan!

Sultan bin Saqr Al Qasimi's mission of conquest against Muscat was short-lived. By 1808, his rule over the Qawasim was in question, the Wahhabi agent overruling him and encouraging Ras Al Khaimah boats to take to the seas and harry shipping. A similar fate befell the Al Qasimi chief Qadhib of Lingeh, on the Persian coast, who found his trading links cut off and his subjects taking to piracy to survive – and egged on by the Wahhabi agent in place.[12]

Sultan bin Saqr Al Qasimi was stripped, on orders from Diriyah (then the Saudi capital, now a suburb of Riyadh), of his headship of the Qawasim and his rule was effectively confined to Ras Al Khaimah. A year later, in 1809, the Saudi emir, Saud bin Abdulaziz, appointed the Sheikh of Rams – Hussein bin Ali – as the Wahhabi governor of Sirr, the west coast of Oman. Rams, at the time a port and community independent of Ras Al Khaimah, although under Al Qasimi rule, is today to be found on the coast to the north of the city.

Control over the forts of Fujairah, Bithnah and Khor Fakkan was in the hands of Wahhabi-backed forces and the Wahhabis appointed Walis, or officers, over the whole Al Qasimi territory.

Sultan bin Saqr was given an invitation he couldn't refuse, to visit Diriyah and present himself to the Saudi ruler, Abdulaziz. To nobody's surprise, least of all his own one would suspect, Sultan bin Saqr was imprisoned when he arrived there.

Hussein bin Ali of Rams then led an aggressive campaign against shipping in the Gulf under Wahhabi influence, attacking the *Minerva* and ritually slaughtering most of its crew (an Armenian lady, wife to the Assistant Resident at Bushire, was ransomed) before capturing the cruiser Sylph which was soon retaken by the Nereid.[13]

However, under the stronger Wahhabi influence, the Qawasim now flexed their muscles, fighting actions across the Gulf at Lingeh, Basidu (called 'Bassadore' by the British at the time) and Qeshm. The British fourteen-gun brig *Nautilus* was attacked off Hengam Island (to the south of Qeshm) and it wasn't until the attackers were within earshot that the captain of the *Nautilus* hoisted the British colours, fired two warning shots and then commenced firing broadsides. What colours the *Nautilus* was flying beforehand, we are not told.[14]

Sultan bin Saqr managed, somehow, to escape his prison in the centre of the Saudi desert and make his way to Mocha, in Yemen. From there he travelled to Muscat, where he was received by the Omani Sultan, Said bin Sultan.

It does not take much of a leap of faith to imagine how delighted the Sultan would have been to receive his former foe in such reduced circumstances. It was Sultan bin Saqr Al Qasimi who had allied with Badr, the regent who had effectively usurped Saeed's birthright. And it was Said himself who had tired of Badr's close ties to the Saudis and their Wahhabi faith and struck the first blow against the man, a sword-stroke that broke Badr's arm before Badr fled the scene on horseback, only to have his wound overcome him and fall from his horse. Said and his followers killed Badr with their lances, as he lay on the ground.[15]

Here, in the shape of Sultan bin Saqr Al Qasimi, Said bin Sultan had a *casus belli* against the Qawasim. Oman was already threatened by the Wahhabi forces in Buraimi (under the Saudi general Mutlaq), a short ride along the great pass through the mountains, Wadi Jizzi, from Sohar. The Wahhabi-backed forces of the Qawasim had taken much of the north-eastern coast, the Shamaliyah – Fujairah, Khor Fakkan and the inland fort at Bithnah.

Said bin Sultan would have shared his new find with the British Resident. And Sultan bin Saqr's presence in Muscat must have formed part of the thinking on the part of the East India Company's officials in Bombay when they sanctioned an expedition against the Qawasim, aiming to reduce the Wahhabi influence over the important gateway to the Gulf, the Straits of Hormuz and its islands as well as to restore their ally, the Sultan of Muscat.

Restoring some of the Sultan's territorial losses may not have been at the core of the campaign plan as much as the destruction of the Qawasim and other aggressive Arab fleets, but it was viewed as a benefit of the action.

Another reason for the British expedition was the message from the Wahhabi-backed Wali of Ras Al Khaimah, Hussein bin Ali, to Bombay telling them that British shipping would be left unmolested in the Gulf if they paid tribute to the Qawasim. This last was intolerable and, faced by a public outcry at the piracies committed under the 'blood red Al Qasimi flag', the Company resolved to act.[16]

The Qawasim fleet at this time consisted of some sixty-three large ships and 813 smaller, altogether manned by 19,000 men. Expeditions of some seventeen ships at a time were mounted from Ras Al Khaimah and Rams, cruising the Gulf in search of prizes. A fleet to match it was assembled in Bombay.

The Company goes to war
Commodore John Wainwright was to head the fleet for the 1809 punitive expedition, which consisted of the thirty-six-gun *HM Chiffone*, the thirty-six-gun *HM Caroline* and the Company's cruisers, the twenty-two-gun *Mornington*; sixteen-gun *Ternate*; fourteen-gun *Aurora*; fourteen-gun *Mercury*; fourteen-gun *Nautilus*; fourteen-gun *Prince of Wales*; ten-gun *Vestal*; ten-gun *Vestal* and the eight-gun *Fury* and the *Stromboli*, a bomb-ketch (mortar boat). Four troop transports shipped the Sixty-fifth Regiment, companies from the Forty-seventh Regiment, a detachment of Bombay Artillery and some 1,000 sepoys under their commander, Colonel Lionel Smith of the Sixty-fifth Regiment.[17]

The ageing *Stromboli* didn't make it out of the harbour at Bombay, but foundered. Nevertheless, reaching Muscat to refresh its stores, the expedition was shipping almost 200 cannon – despite this considerable firepower, the Sultan of Muscat believed the force was too small to engage with the Qawasim. The British demurred and, on 11 November 1809, the force reached Ras Al Khaimah. The two frigates could not approach closer than four miles to the town because of the shallowness of the Gulf coast. The smaller HEI (Honourable East India) Company cruisers could reach two miles from the coast.

As the British settled at anchor, the captured twenty-gun cruiser *Minerva* crewed by Qawasim sailors set sail from Ras Al Khaimah and got a nasty surprise when it saw the British Squadron offshore. The ship turned tail and fled back to the safety of its harbour but, missing the tide it had sailed on, the *Minerva* beached and was immediately attacked by the British in their smaller boats and taken, but abandoned and set ablaze when the Qawasim counter-attacked, laying down an accurate and sustained fire.[18]

Commodore Wainwright's account of the action notes, 'We had to deal with an enemy on whom we had not set sufficient value.'

With the frigates and cruisers unable to approach within firing range of Ras Al Khaimah – and their only shallow-bottomed mortar boat lying at the bottom of the sea off Bombay – the British were forced to depend on their smaller boats to try and approach the town and these again met a sustained and accurate fire from the earthworks that had been thrown up to protect the harbour and town. The high protective southern wall, running across the isthmus, with its four towers precluded an easy approach by landing south of the town and advancing by land, a seaward approach was clearly meeting dangerous resistance. The town's mud-brick buildings and narrow alleys weren't an inviting prospect for a head-on landing force in any case. British estimates put the fighting force they faced at some 5,000 men. It appeared as if the Sultan of Muscat had been right: Ras Al Khaimah was to be no easy prize.

After much deliberation, the British forces split with a feint to the harbour made by two gunboats and a number of ships' boats, laying down a heavy fire as they approached the harbour and the northern part of the town as dawn broke on 13 November 1809. Believing the main attack was taking place here, Ras Al Khaimah's defenders rushed to meet the challenge. Meanwhile, the troops, who had been loaded onto boats under the cover of darkness in the early hours, landed to the south of the town and attempted the southern wall. The defenders, realising the danger, dashed along the beach to meet the embarking force. With their glittering swords and hoarse cries, they were on the point of falling on the first company of Marines to land when the gunboats, which had been reserving their fire, let loose with a devastating fusillade of grapeshot.

Of the many dirty weapons conceived by man over the ages, some novel uses for the cannon had been devised. Heated cannonballs was one, red-hot shot landing against wooden targets such as ships wreaking double the havoc. And another was 'grape', the cluster bomb of its time. Grapeshot consisted of smaller cannonballs wrapped together in a canvas bag and tied with rope, resembling a bunch of grapes, hence the name. The shot left the muzzle of the cannon and spread in a wide parabola to produce the same effect as a shotgun, but on a far wider scale – a deadly hail of shot cutting men down in swathes.

The defenders were halted in their charge as the barrage of shot slammed into their ranks, giving the landing troops precious seconds to form up and mount a desperate counter-charge. Leaving their dead and wounded littering the sands, the Qawasim defenders were pushed back and the British took the wall and its fortifications.

With a new-found respect for their foes, the British commanders didn't press the charge, but waited for men and materials to be brought up, including field pieces, stores and ammunition and scaling ladders. Only then did they start to move against the town and its collection of flat-roofed mud-brick houses, their walls dotted with gun-holes which were used effectively as sniper positions, and the small *areesh* (palm-frond) houses that lay packed closely between the larger buildings.

Noticing the prevailing wind ran to the north, the British set fire to the *areesh* houses, the dry palm fronds catching instantly. It was an eerie repetition of the very strategy that had been used by the Abbasid commander Khazim bin Khuzayma against Julfar a millennium before. The houses blazed, sending flames licking through the alleyways and a cloud of choking black smoke billowing throughout the town. Under cover of the smoke, their way paved by the flames, the British fought house to house, scaling to the rooftops and dropping grenades into the buildings from above. By two in the afternoon, the British forces reached the fort and brought their artillery to bear on the thick walls and high tower. The building was hardly contested by this point: the defence of Ras Al Khaimah had become a rout and the defenders took to their boats, escaping from the northern side of the harbour.

Two hours later, the Qawasim fleet was burning fiercely: the troops set fire to some fifty boats, of which thirty were large, heavily armed dhows carrying guns and ammunition. Together with stores of gunpowder in the burning town, these stockpiles exploded and Ras Al Khaimah lit up the sky at dusk, the town entirely consumed by flames.

The British 'had come to inflict vengeance and not acquire gain' and so no looting was allowed by the troops. Warehouses and stockpiles of trade goods were set afire. But Ras Al Khaimah was a wealthy town that had many 'little treasures' and many troops enriched themselves with finds of gold bullion, jewellery and other portable valuables.

Wainwright estimated the Al Qasimi losses at 300 men. The town itself was reduced to rubble and ashes, its once-proud fleet turned into a mass of burning spars and charcoal ribs poking out of the warm shallows. As dawn broke on the morning of 14 November, the devastation of Ras Al Khaimah was complete and yet the British victory had by no means been as easy as their commanders had anticipated and it was perhaps because of this that a rumour, reaching the commander of the troops, Colonel Smith, of reinforcements on the way from the interior led to the British quitting the ruined town and embarking their troops.

This brought the Qawasim down from their retreats in the date groves and wadis towards the interior, lining the shores of their ruined town, firing at the departing boats and crying defiance against the British. It was to become a source of considerable British regret that the troops had left before finishing the job: a formal submission or surrender hadn't been received and, from the boldness of the colourful ranks of townsmen brandishing their muskets and lances under fluttering flags, submission was the last thing on their minds.

The British fleet now moved to the Qawasim port and town of Lingeh on the Persian side of the Gulf. Lingeh was a bustling trading port, home to some 10,000 townsfolk and, like Ras Al Khaimah, a wealthy town with warehouses, wharfage and boats at dock. The townspeople of Lingeh had ample warning of the approach of the squadron and had used the time wisely. They fled for the interior and on 17 November, the town was taken without resistance by the Marines.

The thriving port and town of Lingeh was burned to the ground and all of the ships at anchor, including twenty-nine larger dhows (likely baggalas), were fired at anchor. Once again, a pillar of dark smoke rose into the blue skies of the Gulf.

The British squadron split up, supply missions and policing actions taking place before it reassembled on noon of 26 November 1809 at Luft, the Al Qasimi port to the north of Qeshm Island. There, Mulla Hussein and his people took refuge in the fort and refused to respond to British demands for their surrender. On the morning of 27 November, Colonel Smith and his troops landed, rolling a howitzer up to face the great doors of the sturdy fort. The concentrated fire from the loopholes around the fort was deadly accurate and the soldiers abandoned their gun and retreated. An Irish officer, Lieutenant S. Weld, refused to be cowed and ran for the gun, calling for his men to follow him. He was cut down in an instant, while other incautious souls peered above their makeshift shelters and were picked off by the snipers from within the fort.[19] The troops were embarked once again, but the *Fury* and the gunboats of the squadron were brought up and bombarded the fort.

By dawn the next day, a Union Jack flew above the fort, a soldier having ventured up to the gate in the night to find the place abandoned. The eleven dhows in the harbour were burned, while the rest of the town and its 20,000 pounds worth of property were handed over to the Sultan of Muscat, 'as Luft had been taken by the Joasmees from the Sultan of Muscat'.

Twenty-seven British soldiers were killed at Luft, the heaviest casualties the squadron had faced so far in its punitive expedition. The squadron then visited Rams, Jazirat Al Hamra and Sharjah where they destroyed any shipping they found at harbour. Having completed its sweep of the West coast, the force sailed around Musandam and met with the Sultan of Oman and his forces preparatory to attacking Shinas, which, together with Khor Fakkan had fallen to the Qawasim.

The combined force arrived at Shinas on 31 December and called for the town under its Al Qasimi commander to surrender, which it refused to do. A bombardment of the town and its fort commenced, the town being put to fire and the people fleeing to safety within the walls of the fort. This building was then subjected to a sustained and deadly barrage of fire from both the warships and batteries of guns which were landed under Colonel Smith. The barrage started on the evening of 2 January 1810, expending some 4,000 'shot and shell' and continued through the night and following day, with the defenders refusing repeated exhortations to surrender until the fort had been reduced to rubble. Accepting the final surrender of the survivors – a death toll of some 1,000 men was estimated – the Sultan of Oman didn't bother taking possession of the fort as there was so little left of it to possess.

The defence of Shinas had been so vigorous that the Sultan and the British worried about trying to take Khor Fakkan. Eventually, it was agreed that an attempt on the Al Qasimi-held town wasn't worth the salt and the Squadron broke up, the troops returning to Bombay and the cruisers returning to patrol the Gulf.

The dust settles
Was the 1809 punitive expedition a success? It had certainly inflicted damage on the towns of the coast and reduced the Qawasim fleet, but in retrospect, its commanders were to accept that the expedition had not gone far enough in prosecuting its aims. Ras Al Khaimah hadn't surrendered and the British had not only failed to make friends with their actions against the coastal towns and islands, they had demonstrated once again that they were in cahoots with the Omani Sultan, having handed Bandar Abbas and Luft over to him, as well as Shinas. Wainwright's account of the expedition mentions the firing of a number of vessels at harbour, but of the significant destruction of the fleets of the coast, we see a total of thirty-nine baggalas or large boats and forty-two other vessels claimed as destroyed by the expedition. Contrast that with the estimated strength of the Qawasim fleet at the time – sixty-three large and 813 smaller vessels, and it would seem that a significant armada remained in Qawasim hands.

A movement now took place in Bombay to prohibit the export of any teak or other hardwood to the Gulf, in order to dissuade the reconstruction of Qawasim ships, but the prohibition was not enforced.

If the aims of the expedition were to reduce the 'questionable pirates', the Qawasim, to submission and smash their fleet, it had been an expensive and remarkable failure. If it had been to restore the Sultan of Oman to a dominant role in the area and cement – even celebrate – the relationship between the British and Muscat, it had been a notable success. The abiding question is which of these were truly the British 'war aims'?

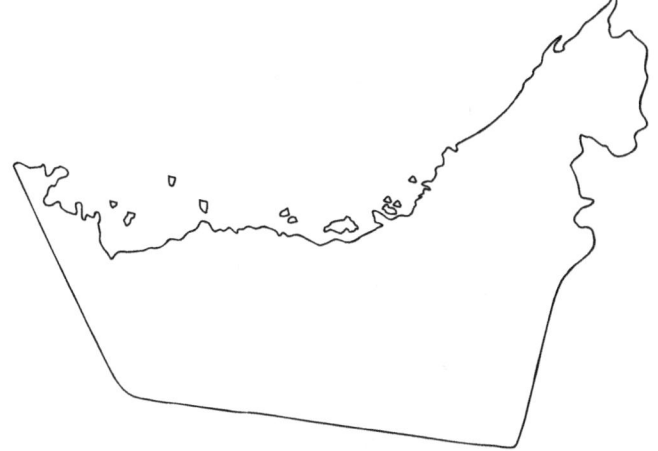

Chapter 14
THE TRUCIAL COAST

"From the period of their establishment in Oman until the year 1796, I have been unable to trace a single act of aggression, even on the part of the Joasmees, against the British flag."

- Frances Warden

In the aftermath of the British action of 1809, the coastal communities of the region knitted together, trading, fishing and sailing out to the pearl banks in the season, which ran from May to September. The Bani Yas had long established themselves as a coastal community on the island of Abu Dhabi, and on other islands along the coast, such as Dalma, as well as coastal settlements like Mirfa. They also settled and farmed the inland areas of Liwa, a crescent-shaped series of desert oases to the south of Abu Dhabi, and the fertile oases of Buraimi, watered by the run-off from the adjacent Hajar Mountains. Further north, the Bani Yas town of Dubai grew up on the south side of a natural khor or creek, a community of mostly *areesh* houses clustered in the seaside area of Shindagha and protected by the Fahidi Fort, which overlooked the harbour located to the other side of the tidal inlet of Ghubaiba.

Crossing the creek to Deira and then travelling north into Al Qawasim country, you would encounter the tiny seasonal village of Abu Hail, then the larger villages of Al Khan and Layyah before reaching the Al Qasimi town of Sharjah. North of Sharjah, the small coastal town of Ajman was settled by members of the Na'im from Buraimi, displacing a number of Al Bu Shams, themselves a subset of the larger Na'im, many of whom settled slightly south of Ajman in the coastal community of Al Heera (and Fisht) and also to the north of Ajman, at Al Hamriyah. Past Hamriyah, Umm Al Quwain (and its inland oasis town of Falaj Al Ali, known today as Falaj Al Mualla) was home to the Al Ali tribe, while between here and Ras Al Khaimah was the village of Jazirat Al Hamra, home in the main to the Al Zaab tribe. Inland were two communities tending their oases and date palms, at Khatt and Falaya. North of Ras Al Khaimah lay the coastal port of Rams and the inland oasis of Dhayah and north again from there, up in the remote, barren mountains of the Rus Al Jibal, were the plantations and homes of the strange and mysterious Shihuh, a warrior tribe who spoke an odd and unique language unknown to the coastal Arabs.

The east coast was home to the Shamaliyah – the area from the northern port and town of Dibba down to Khor Fakkan, which by 1809 was firmly in the hands of the Qawasim, and then onward to Fujairah, which was peopled by members of the Sharqiyin tribe, and then through the coastal settlement of Kalba. South of this, the town of Shinas had fallen to Oman with the help of the British and the Omani port of Sohar sat at the mouth of the Wadi Jizzi, which snaked inland to Buraimi (mainly Al Ain today). North of Buraimi was the inland oasis town of Dhaid and to the east of this, in the mountains, Masafi.

We see in these tribes, settlements and communities, much of the shape of what would emerge to become the modern United Arab Emirates. Coastal societies traded, fished and took part in the seasonal pearl fisheries, while tribes of nomadic Bedouin roamed the interior. The oases and mountain wadis were centres for settlement and people would move seasonally: the Shihuh would come down from the mountains in the summer and tribes such as the Rumaithat would move from Abu Dhabi to the oases of Liwa and Buraimi for the hot months. Often, the pearl fisheries would provide seasonal employment, attracting men from the interior to the coast, while each coastal emirate had an inland oasis town which provided relief from the intense heat and humidity of the coast in late summer. Abu Dhabi had the lush oases of Liwa and Buraimi (today forming the Omani town of Buraimi and the Emirati city of Al Ain); Dubai had Awir, Lahbab and, in the dry heat of the mountains, Hatta; Sharjah had Dhaid; Umm Al Quwain had Falaj Al Ali (today Falaj Al Mualla); Ajman had both Masfout and Manama and Ras Al Khaimah had Khatt and Adhen. Dibba, Khor Fakkan, Fujairah and Kalba, on the east coast, had no need for an oasis for those uninvolved in the pearl fisheries to escape to in the summer. They were located in a relatively temperate zone, watered by the convection currents running down to the coast from the Hajar Mountains.

The desert was majestic and beautiful in the winter, deadly in the summer when the mountains and oases offered blessed shade and relief. The east coast, as well as the higher mountain areas, enjoyed more rainfall and more temperate climates, the mountain and wadi towns of the west coast thrived with water resources skilfully channelled by the man-made *aflaj* waterways to nurture the *bustan* agriculture of towns like Buraimi / Al Ain, Dhaid and Masafi.

The Wahhabi influence remained strong over the Qawasim and their northern neighbours, but the tribes of the interior remained largely independent in thought and action from the ideas and influences emanating from central Arabia.

Now the British patrolled the waters of the Gulf; both the *Benares* and *Prince of Wales* remained behind after the punitive expedition of 1809 to cruise the troubled waters of the hot and shallow sea and try to suppress the mercantile thrust of the volatile Arab traders. By 1812 and the following year, the Qawasim were once again asserting themselves at sea. From the Al Qasimi point of view, any shipping that wasn't crewed by British crews was likely Omani – and their quarrel with Oman was arguably felt more fiercely after the loss of Bandar Abbas, Luft and Shinas to the Omanis with the assistance of their British allies. The British flags flown by 'native' vessels, largely out of convenience, were ignored.

The Sultan of Muscat mounted an expedition to Ras Al Khaimah in 1813 to restore the deposed Sultan bin Saqr Al Qasimi to the head of the tribe, it being understood that Sultan bin Saqr would then acknowledge Muscat as his overlord. The British fell in with this scheme, which despite the assistance of the Bani Yas of Abu Dhabi, was defeated by the Wahhabi Wali in Ras Al Khaimah, Hussain bin Ali. By the following year, a further attempt was made – again with the help of the Bani Yas – and this time Sultan bin Saqr was restored to become Ruler of Sharjah and Lingeh. His nephew, Hassan bin Rahmah Al Qasimi, had eclipsed Hussain bin Ali as Ruler of Ras Al Khaimah and, in 1814, entered into a treaty with the British following a long correspondence in which he protested his innocence of various piracies, pointing out that a number of regional conflicts were raging and requesting clarification from the British of what precisely constituted 'British shipping'. He eventually agreed that the Qawasim should fly a red and white flag which would distinguish them from other interests sailing in the Gulf and Indian Ocean, such as the piratical Qatari, Rahmah bin Jabir. As a result of the agreement, British ports would be opened to Qawasim shipping.

Sultan bin Saqr Al Qasimi took up residence in Lingeh and, in August 1814, made friendly overtures to Persia, which were reciprocated. In that same month, a British envoy was despatched to both Sultan bin Saqr and Hassan bin Rahmah of Ras Al Khaimah, remonstrating with them at the capture of a number of British flagged vessels. The man returned 'in a most wretched plight', accusing Sultan bin Saqr of robbing him and Hassan bin Rahmah of stealing his boat.[1]

Directly following this incident, a baggala belonging to the Sultan of Muscat was taken by the Qawasim. Laden with horses destined for the Seventeenth Dragoons in India and a large cargo of sulphur belonging to British traders, the taking of the boat was – to the Qawasim – a perfectly fair and understandable act of war against Oman. To the British it was an unforgivable piracy. The Qawasim now, in the words of Lorimer, 'now indulged in a carnival of maritime lawlessness, to which even their previous record presented no parallel.'[2]

Six other vessels were taken by the Qawasim off the coast of the Indian province of Sind and, in 1815, a Bombay ship sailing under British colours was taken by them off Muscat and many of its crew killed. The remainder were ransomed. Barely able to believe their luck, soon after that raid, a Qawasim fleet fell in with a squadron of ships which included the *Caroline* and the Sultan of Muscat's own ship, which the Qawasim sailors boarded but were unable to capture. The Sultan's ship ran for Muscat and he was wounded in the action, but survived to tell the tale.

Early in 1816, the vengeful Sultan mounted an expedition to blockade Ras Al Khaimah which was largely ineffectual. At around this time, the Qawasim found themselves in possession of an armed pattamar manned by native sailors, the *Deriah Dawlut*. In a sharp action at sea, they killed seventeen of its thirty-eight Indian crew. A number of other actions against native and other shipping took place, particularly off Muscat. This resulted in protests from Bombay to Ras Al Khaimah and a visit by British representatives with an ultimatum for the Qawasim, on 26 November 1816.

An eyewitness at the time estimated the Qawasim fleet at a hundred significant vessels mounting 400 cannons and some 8,000 fighting men. It hardly seemed like a fleet that had been reduced to ashes and penury just a few years before. The British demanded reparations and the delivery to them of two of Hassan bin Rahmah's children to be taken as hostages against his good behaviour. Perhaps unsurprisingly, he refused. He also pointed out that the Qawasim didn't regard the British as the owners of India beyond Bombay and Mangalore and that while they would respect the rights of Christians, they saw no reason to extend that to the idolatrous Hindus and other 'unbelievers' of India.[3]

The British opened fire on a number of dhows anchored at Ras Al Khaimah, but found their fire returned, with cannonades from the fort and towers onshore. They left, crowds of men crying defiance at them from the beach, dancing victory under their fluttering banners and flags. It was 1809 all over again, only this time Ras Al Khaimah wasn't burning and the British had retreated with their ultimata thrown back in their faces.[4]

A number of events now took place throughout the Gulf and Indian Ocean that saw British warships arrayed against Qawasim ships and squadrons, not infrequently involving shipping moving to and from Muscat and India. Omani actions against the Qawasim were now actively assisted by the British. At one stage, a treasure ship belonging to the Sultan of Muscat was being escorted by a British cruiser, which fought off an attack by the Qawasim. And in an incident in harbour at Bahrain, a British commander – informed that a group of dhows belonged to the Qawasim – moved against them, capturing them and killing a number of their crew who tried, in vain, to fight off the unprovoked attack. They turned out to belong to the Bani Yas of Abu Dhabi and Bombay was forced to pay blood money for the loss of the boats and the lives of their crew.

And so, allied to the Omanis, British vessels were constantly sandwiched between the Omani and Al Qasimi powers and the latter, being at odds with British policy in the region, were dubbed as pirates with each act of war they prosecuted against Oman – the regional power that threatened to overrun them and demand their submission to its sovereignty. Having placed themselves in this position between two warring local nations, the British found the waters of the Gulf becoming a little warmer, even more than the hot and humid weather usually made them.

It all became too much: Bombay resolved on action. The Qawasim had to go.

Dissent in Bombay

The decision to act against the 'Pirate Coast' was by no means consensual. One strong voice of opposition was Francis Warden, Chief Secretary and a board member of the Bombay Board of the East India Company. Warden questioned the track record of piratical acts laid at the Qawasim door and blamed British ignorant involvement in native affairs for a great deal of the trouble. Warden also contended that piracy was alien to the Gulf locals, who were commercially inclined, but that they had been effectively forced into an antagonistic position by their Wahhabi overlords. At a time when Bombay was considering placing the Sultan of Oman in overall control of the whole Arabian coast as far as Bahrain, Warden counselled against putting such an unsuitable figure in such a strong position and argued that any such attempt would result in insurrection and ongoing strife. Warden's cautionary voice was not without influence and his stamp can be found in many of the subsequent actions taken by the British that stopped short of the absolute destruction of the coastal communities.

By now, the Wahhabi influence was waning. The Saudis found themselves facing the Ottomans to their northern border and the fall of the Saudi Emirate of Diriyah took place in 1818, resulting in the death of Abdullah bin Saud and the destruction of the Saudi capital. Although the Saudi state fell, its outlying regions and dependencies continued to feel its influence. The Qawasim weren't, in any case, embarked on a war of faith – they were fighting Oman, a conflict that put them in virtually constant opposition with Oman's impossibly strong ally, the British.

In February 1819, Hassan bin Rahmah Al Qasimi of Ras Al Khaimah tried to open a communication with the British, suggesting a return to their agreement of 1814 but it was too late. His overtures were rebuffed and Francis Warden's protestations were swept aside. The die was cast.

The 1819 punitive expedition

Preparations were set underway and a punitive expeditionary force was raised. A letter was sent by the British to Persia, explaining their war aims and requesting cooperation as they acted against the Al Qasimi ports on the Gulf coast. An envoy had already been sent to the Ottoman Egyptians, who had by now successfully wrapped up the 1811–1818 Egyptian-Saudi War and taken the Saudi capital at Diriyah (today a suburb of Riyadh).

The British punitive expedition of 1819 consisted of a body of troops under their commander, Major-General Sir William Grant Keir, including a company of artillery, the Forty-seventh and Sixty-fifth Regiments, the First Battalion of the Second Infantry Regiment, the flank companies of the First Battalion Third Infantry Regiment, the Marine Battalion and a body of Pioneers, amounting to half a company. In all, this amounted to a fighting force of over 3,000 men.

The naval expedition was under Captain Collier of the fifty-gun HMS *Liverpool*, with the twenty-six-gun *Eden* and eighteen-gun *Curlew*. The East India Company's Bombay Marine contributed the sixteen-gun *Teignmouth* and *Benares*, the fourteen-gun *Aurora* and *Nautilus*, and the ten-gun *Ariel* and *Vestal*. Although they didn't take part in the expedition, the Company had three ships cruising the Gulf at the time, the *Ternate*, *Mercury* and *Psyche*.

On 30 October 1819, crowds lined the docks and beaches of Bombay to cheer the troop transports carrying the British Regiments as they left port and the following day the scenes of public jubilation were repeated for the departing Indian Regiments. The troop transports alone amounted to a considerable fleet of eighteen boats.

Over the next few days, the various marine elements of the fleet sailed for Qeshm where they were to rendezvous. Grant Keir himself sailed on the *Liverpool* for Muscat, where an audience with the Sultan resulted in an offer of 4,000 men and three ships to support the action against the Qawasim. The Sultan, it can't help but be noted, must have been in raptures over this force being arrayed against his belligerent enemy and putative subjects.

Grant Keir and Collier sailed to Ras Al Khaimah on the *Liverpool*, with the *Benares* accompanying them and carried out a reconnaissance on 26 and 27 November. *Benares* was sent to Qeshm to summon the fleet, which arrived on 2 December along with the marine force despatched from Muscat, 600 men and two frigates in all – more men would come from Muscat by land.

The British repeated their strategy of ten years previously, landing the troops two miles south of Ras Al Khaimah town ('the large boats of the Imam being great service, while his people worked with energy bringing up the guns and ammunition to the batteries') while the *Aurora* and *Nautilus* entered the mouth of the creek and commenced a heavy fire to distract the townspeople.

Ras Al Khaimah rebuilt was a heavily fortified town, with a sea wall nine feet high and two thick with twenty-foot high towers along its length. Other towers and gun emplacements stretched around the town and its harbour, back into the date plantations in the hinterland. Between 4,000 and 7,000 men defended the town, their women and children having been sent inland to the protection of the date groves.

At this stage, the 2,000 troops from Oman joined the British, having journeyed overland from Muscat. Skirmishing broke out and the landed British guns were pressed into action. On the morning of 5 December, the ships stood to outside the town and opened fire as the land forces also bombarded the town from their entrenched positions on the south side. The bombardment carried on through the next day, although return fire was sparse. The defenders were clearly short of ammunition, sending out foraging parties to pick up landed shot at night and forced into using stones as shot.

On the night of the 6th, an attack was made on the British trenches. Swift and silent, their torsos slathered in oil to make them hard to grab, they slashed at the British soldiers with their swords and stabbing knives. The Arab forces poured into the trenches, briefly capturing a howitzer before a bayonet charge ended the attack, leaving ninety of the town's defenders dead in the dugouts.

Realising that their twelve and eighteen-pound shot was having little effect on the fortified town but was providing the defenders with useful ammunition to shoot back at their considerably more vulnerable boats and men, the British brought two twenty-four-pound guns from HMS *Liverpool* and dragged them through the sandy beach to mount them overlooking the town. These huge cannon commenced fire on the morning of 8 December and by the evening flags of truce were sent from the town, its fort crumbling under the pounding from the big guns. The request for a truce was ignored. The next morning, the twenty-four-pounders once again opened fire, significantly breaching the fortified walls of the town and allowing the British storming party to stream into the deserted settlement.

Estimates of the losses to the defenders were 300 dead and 700 wounded, while sixty-two guns were captured (along with a large number of goats, to the delight of the ever-hungry sailors and soldiers). Many of the guns the British found were unserviceable. About eighty boats, ranging from forty to 250 tons, were captured but there was little plunder for the troops, the town having been emptied of people and goods alike. The British themselves lost five men.

The Ruler of Ras Al Khaimah, Hassan bin Rahmah Al Qasimi, and his followers surrendered themselves to the British.

The *Curlew*, *Aurora* and *Nautilus* were sent north to blockade the port of Rams, which was abandoned, but it appeared that some 400 local people under the local chief and former Wahhabi Wali Hussein bin Ali had taken shelter in the fort of Dhayah, situated high on a hill some two miles inland.

A sizeable body of British troops was landed, fighting their way through the date groves between 18 and 22 December and dragging two of *Liverpool's* twenty-four-pounders though the muddy, rough terrain. Mortar fire against the fort commenced on 19 December and it was completely surrounded by the morning of the 21st, with a number of field pieces firing on the adobe walls set high above the date plantations.

The two cannon from the *Liverpool* were set up and started firing on the morning of the 22nd, breaching the walls of the fort almost immediately. The fort had held out for three days, surrounded by British troops firing mortars and smaller cannon but surrendered within two hours of the big cannon opening fire.

Most of the occupants of Dhayah Fort were found to be women and children and workers who had fled the British onslaught on the date groves – many were members of the Al Tanaij tribe. Of the 400 people who had holed up in the tiny fort, only 177 were fighting men.

In effect, the British effort was gratuitous; they merely had to wait. Dhayah Fort has no spring and the terrified families huddled together as shrapnel sizzled and shrieked around them for days had no access to fresh supplies of food or water. Their surrender was as inevitable as their suffering under days of sustained bombardment was unnecessary.

The troops blew up the fort at Dhayah and returned to Ras Al Khaimah, where the occupying army had busied themselves by blowing up the walls, fort and other towers of the town. On 28 December, the British announced 'mission accomplished'.

In January 1820, the expeditionary force sailed down the coast, bombarding Jazirat Al Hamra, Umm Al Quwain, Ajman, Fisht, Sharjah, Abu Hail and Dubai and destroying any boats they found.[5] The towns of the coast burned, sending black pillars of smoke rippling into the blue December skies.

Ras Al Khaimah was turned into a garrison town, with companies of Indian soldiers billeted there among the rubble, stationed under British commanders. These remained in post until April of that year, and the British garrison was finally disbanded on 18 July 1820.

The Trucial States

A treaty was now prepared and the Sheikhs of the coast were invited (having been given a sharp taste of the alternative) to sign it. Prior to acceding to the treaty, each was required to enter into a 'preliminary agreement'. Hassan bin Rahmah Al Qasimi, formerly the Ruler of Ras Al Khaimah, was invited to sign a preliminary agreement, which included surrendering the town of Ras Al Khaimah as a British garrison and taking up the title of 'Sheikh of Khatt and Falaya'. He was to rule Ras Al Khaimah no more.

Grant Keir's original instructions from Bombay were that Sultan bin Saqr Al Qasimi was on no account to be anointed Ruler of Ras Al Khaimah, but this was later revised. The preliminary agreement removing Hassan bin Rahmah left open the question of who was to rule in his place, but Hassan bin Rahmah was not to find out who had been picked to succeed him until after he had signed not only the preliminary agreement, but the treaty itself.

The answer was, as Grant Keir well knew, Sultan bin Saqr Al Qasimi. He was to sign the treaty as Ruler of Sharjah. His signature to the Preliminary Agreement was also to bind Ajman and Umm Al Quwain. In Sultan bin Saqr, the British (and their ally, the Sultan of Muscat) clearly thought they had a man with whom they could do business.

The preliminary agreements were signed on 6 January 1820 by Sultan bin Saqr, on 8 January by Hassan bin Rahmah, 'Sheikh of Khatt and Falayah', on 9 January by the Sheikh of Dubai, on 11 January by the Sheikh of Abu Dhabi and on 5 February, the Sheikh of Bahrain. Now came the real deal: the General Treaty for the Cessation of Plunder and Piracy by Land and Sea, Dated February 5, 1820. The treaty was signed by each of the 'pacificated Arabs' in turn. Tragically, history – so often frustratingly incomplete in the recording of the minutiae of the past – does not tell us how the Sheikhs reacted to see themselves referred to as such.

The first to sign, presumably still unaware that he was signing away his status as Ruler of Ras Al Khaimah, was Hassan bin Rahmah Al Qasimi, 'Sheikh of Khatt and Falayah' and Qadhib bin Ahmad of Jazirat Al Hamra, both signing at Falayah Fort on 8 January 1820. Sheikh Shakhbut bin Dhiyab Al Nahyan of Abu Dhabi signed at Ras Al Khaimah on 11 January on behalf of his son, Sheikh Tahnun bin Shakhbut, and Hussein bin Ali of Rams and Dhayah on 15 January, coincidentally the day of his release by the British from captivity. Zaid bin Saif signed on behalf of the Ruler of Dubai, who was still in his minority, on 28 January. Sultan bin Saqr Al Qasimi of Sharjah signed the treaty in Sharjah town on 4 February and, on 5 February, the treaty was signed in Sharjah on behalf of the Sheikhs of Bahrain (who themselves ratified it in Bahrain later that month).

Two more signatures were added to the treaty: Rashid bin Humaid Al Nuaimi signed on behalf of Ajman and Abdullah bin Rashid Al Mualla on behalf of Umm Al Quwain. Despite Sultan bin Saqr's entering into a preliminary agreement on their behalf, it would appear both Sheikhs had managed to assert themselves and convince the British commander, Grant Keir, that they were independent of Sultan.

The treaty bound its signatories to peaceful co-existence, to abstain from plunder and piracy by sea and land (the acts of plunder and piracy are nicely defined, in case of any misunderstanding) and to fly distinctive flags which would mark boats as belonging to each Sheikh. The Treaty also gave its signatories leave to appoint an agent at the British Residency as well as having a British envoy and bound them to keep the peace jointly and severally and forbade both the execution of captives and trading in slaves.

Bombay disappointed

Grant Keir had clearly come under the influence of Francis Warden and others of a like mind and moderate disposition in Bombay who had counselled caution and understanding be employed in building relationships with the Sheikhs of the Gulf. It was generally considered back in Bombay that, while his management of the military side of things had been exemplary, he had 'gone soft' on the political negotiations. Bombay regretted Grant Keir's leniency and wondered, if it were not too late, if he could renegotiate a more stringent treaty. Ideally, the Company wanted the removal (and ideally detention) of any 'guilty' Sheikh, a ban on ship building and the import of hardwood, the handing over of goods and land to the Sultan of Muscat and to forbid the construction of fortifications of any sort. Grant Keir stood his ground: the treaty was in the best interests of peace, to have forced more on the Sheikhs would have involved becoming ensnared in local politics and conflict with the interior as the British defended their nominees.[6]

Grant Keir's treaty stood – and, as it happens, formed the basis for British policy towards the emirates which rapidly became known as first 'Trucial Oman' and then, as it was belatedly realised that Oman's claim to these areas was actively resisted by the local people, the 'Trucial States'.

The troops stayed stationed at Ras Al Khaimah, with the harbour guarded by the brig *Psyche*, positioned so as to have a clear shot of any aggressive vessel attempting to approach the garrison town. Grant Keir reconnoitred Qeshm Island as a permanent base for a British force, with Bombay keen to remove the Residency from Bushire to Qeshm (Bushire, it was eventually decided, would remain the Residency). With the consent of the Sultan of Muscat, who claimed Qeshm as his territory, the decision was made to move the garrison from Ras Al Khaimah to the island.

An attempt was made to get Sultan bin Saqr Al Qasimi to agree to the additional stipulations to the treaty in return for British recognition of his role as Ruler of Ras Al Khaimah, but he refused. The officer in charge, Captain Thompson, had no authority to prevent Sultan taking over the town when the troops left and no other way of forcing him to agree to the additional codicils so, in the face of Sultan bin Saqr's insistence that he not destroy the town, he blew up the sad remains of Ras Al Khaimah's buildings, effectively slamming the door on his way out.

On 18 July, the British forces embarked for their new billet on the island of Qeshm and left behind them a darkness lit by the blaze of the last few Al Qasimi boats and the woodwork of the temporary barracks they had built. Every other building and fortification in the town was utterly smashed.

Sultan bin Saqr Al Qasimi, restored to the headship of the Al Qasimi family and its domains, was free to reclaim the shattered and smoking remains of the town of Ras Al Khaimah.

Treaty relations

Qeshm was found to be as unsatisfactory as Ras Al Khaimah for the health of the troops (they had been riddled with dysentery and scurvy) and was abandoned in 1821 in favour of a system of regular patrols by four cruisers, supported by a depot on Kish Island which was later moved to Basidu on Qeshm.

The new British Resident at Bushire toured the coast in 1823 to interview the Rulers and clear up any misunderstandings regarding the interpretation of the 1820 General Treaty. He tried to convince Sultan bin Saqr Al Qasimi to finally conclude a peace with Muscat and also tried to have the Ruler of Abu Dhabi, Tahnun bin Shakhbut Al Nahyan, rein in the wild head of the Maharibah tribe, Suwaidan bin Za'al, who, together with his followers, continued to enjoy a colourful career on the high seas. Following his trip, the Resident recommended that a native agent be set up at Sharjah to represent British interests and this recommendation was followed.

The establishment of a permanent British Residency ('native') Agent on the Trucial Coast merely formalised a situation that was all too clear on the ground. The debate in Bombay as to whether to simply hand over the whole coast to Muscat had finally concluded that this was unwise. In place of that arrangement, the British had taken the effective role of suzerain over the Trucial States, although they would have strenuously denied it at the time.

Chapter 15

THE FATHER OF THE GAZELLE

"No man can live this life and emerge unchanged. He will carry, however faint, the imprint of the desert, the brand which marks the nomad; and he will have within him the yearning to return. For this cruel land can cast a spell which no temperate clime can match."

- Wilfred Thesiger

Raised in the deep desert, hospitable in the extreme yet quick to anger and proud of bearing, the Bedouin Bani Yas and their allies lived their lives roaming the sands between the desert oasis crescent of Liwa and the lush oasis at the foot of the Hajar Mountains, Buraimi. They settled the coast as far north as Dubai and roamed the plains and dunes to the south and east. The nature of the tribe was a constantly shifting patchwork of families, subsections and alliances but the Sheikhs of the tribe generally came from the Al Bu Falah, the Al Nahyan family. Other sections of the tribe and its federated allies included the Al Bu Mahair, the Al Bu Falasah, the Rumaithat, the Qubaisat, the Mazari, the Hawamil, the Maharibah, the Al Mishaghin and the Sudan. Long allied to the Bani Yas, in some eyes part of the tribe and in some independent, were the great Bedouin tribes of the Manasir and Awamir. Settled tribes such as the Dhawahir of Buraimi (now Al Ain) also formed part of the wider Bani Yas Federation and its alliances. These tribes and families recognised their Sheikh – as did every tribe of Arabia – as their authority, a judge and jury to whom disputes were taken for resolution and whose decisions were generally recognised as paramount. A Sheikh ruled with the consent of his people, a trust that was earned and retained only by constantly maintaining the respect and support of the tribe.

The movement of the Bani Yas to the island of Abu Dhabi is said to have taken place at the behest of Sheikh Dhiyab bin Isa Al Nahyan, who was based in Liwa, after a hunting party had pursued a gazelle to a brackish spring near the coast in 1761. The settlement grew to consist of a fort and a village of some twenty houses.[1] The fort still stands today in the centre of Abu Dhabi, the Qasr Al Hosn.

A slightly less prosaic version of the story has it that the Bani Yas settled the area 'between Biddah and Brymee' and the coast but not the island on which Abu Dhabi now stands, which they used as a base to fish from. A fisherman one day dug a hole and found the pit filling with 'tolerable' water, which caused some to take up permanent residence there, with an initial population of twenty-one houses quickly growing within two years to 400 houses.[2]

Dhiyab was murdered in 1793 by his cousin, Hazza, while visiting Abu Dhabi. His son, the young Shakhbut bin Dhiyab, lost no time in exacting his revenge and duly killed everyone he could find who had been present at his father's murder. By 1795 Shakhbut had put ten of them to death and Hazza fled the country with his remaining followers

Shakhbut bin Dhiyab was the sole Ruler of the Bani Yas until 1816, but he then co-ruled with his sons Mohammed, Tahnun and Khalifa. There is evidence that his giving way to Mohammed's rule was not quite without coercion, but Shakhbut eventually prevailed over his quarrelsome sons.

Having deposed his father, Mohammed bin Shakhbut ruled for two years from 1816–1818 but was expelled from Abu Dhabi by his brother Tahnun with the support of both the Bani Yas and the Sultan of Muscat. Mohammed left for Qatar. Tahnun ruled from 1818–1833, although it was his father who signed the 1820 General Treaty with the British. In seeking Muscat's support for his accession, Tahnun forged an alliance (potentially a recognition of sovereignty) with Muscat, a move that alienated the northern Ghafiri tribes, particularly the Qawasim and the Na'im, who had long fought Muscat and its long arm.

Tahnun's rule was to be marked by constant conflict. In the aftermath of the British bombardment of the coast and the subsequent 1820 General Treaty, the head of the Maharibah section of the Bani Yas, Suwaidan bin Za'al, left Abu Dhabi to avoid paying his debts, taking to the seas with a number of followers and entering into a short-lived piratical career from a base in Qatar, as well as the island of Sir Bani Yas. Tahnun captured a number of Suwaidan's boats in part payment of his debt but Tahnun's action was itself seen as piratical by the British, who were at the time highly sensitive to any maritime misdemeanour and Tahnun was forced, under threat of a visit from a British cruiser, to give the boats up. Suwaidan bin Za'al was eventually reconciled with Tahnun and returned to Abu Dhabi in 1828.[3]

In 1823 the deposed Sheikh, Tahnun's brother Mohammed, returned to Abu Dhabi from his exile in Qatar supported by a number of warriors from the Manasir tribe. Tahnun was travelling in the interior at the time and received a message that Mohammed was on the march. Raising a force of men and racing to the coast, he was too late to stop the sack of Abu Dhabi by Mohammed and his forces, who plundered the town. Tahnun's men fell on the intruders and they were driven out with the loss of thirty-five men, fleeing northwards to Sharjah. Tahnun gave chase and demanded the Ruler of Sharjah, Sultan bin Saqr Al Qasimi, give Mohammed up.

Sultan bin Saqr was saved having to make the difficult decision whether to hand Mohammed over and therefore break his duty as a host, when Mohammed took to the sea and fled back to Qatar.

However, Sultan bin Saqr was soon to find himself in conflict with Tahnun over another affair entirely. The oasis of Buraimi was fast becoming a flashpoint, a confluence of tribal leaders vying for influence and the inevitable consequent tribal conflict. The Wahhabis had established a force there, which had melted away as the Ottoman Egyptians had whittled away at the edges of the lands claimed by the Saudi Ruler, his capital at Diriyah in the arid centre of the Gulf peninsula, but Muscat claimed sovereignty over the oasis and enjoyed the loyalty of some of the tribes, while the Bani Yas and their allies also maintained a presence in the town.

Sultan bin Saqr now asserted himself in the oasis by building a number of towers. Sultan, dynastically inclined, had already constructed a thirty-foot high tower in Ras Al Khaimah, which was destroyed, unfairly, as it turns out, by an over-enthusiastic British cruiser captain. Bombay had ruled that the Trucial Sheikhs had the right to construct fortifications and Sultan had also, in 1820, built Sharjah Fort. Sultan pressed on with extending his area of influence and, with Ras Al Khaimah and Sharjah under his Rule and Umm Al Quwain recognising his sovereignty, only the Al Nuaimi coastal town of Ajman in the north considered itself independent.

Tahnun of Abu Dhabi, in turn, encouraged a dissident Sharjah faction of the Sudan tribe to construct a fort in Deira, across the creek from the Bani Yas town of Dubai. The move infuriated Sultan bin

Saqr and the British Residency agent stepped in to arbitrate between the two Sheikhs in 1824, ruling that Sharjah should quit its towers in Buraimi and that Abu Dhabi should take in the Sudan immigrants and demolish the Deira fort. An attempt by the Agent to oversee the destruction of the Buraimi forts failed when Sultan sent a force against the Deira fort, repulsing the force Tahnun had established there.[4]

The escalating conflict between Abu Dhabi and Sharjah meant that neither community could send a fleet to the pearl fisheries during the 1825 season, an economic blow that both felt keenly, leading to a rapprochement, finally brokered by the Sultan of Muscat, in October 1825.

There was to be plenty more trouble to come.

Sharjah on the warpath
Despite British attempts to convince Sultan bin Saqr to give up his fight with Muscat, he was clearly in an expansionist mood. As well as his foray into Buraimi, he was to look to his former prizes on the East coast. First, he had to clear up the mess the British had left behind – politically and structurally. The British Resident's visit to the coast of 1823 had proven something of an eye-opener, with insight into the state of political and tribal affairs being gathered arguably for the first time by the envoy from Bombay. The British Resident in the Gulf at the time found Sultan bin Saqr to be a 'turbulent and ambitious man, but superior in ability'.[5]

Following the General Treaty of 1820, Sultan bin Saqr removed the Wahhabi Sheikh of Rams and Dhayah, Hussein bin Ali, to Sharjah and replaced him with a trusted Wali. He set his own brother Mohammad over Ras Al Khaimah and attempted to argue with the British that Ajman was rightfully subservient to him – an argument the British refused to be drawn into. Nevertheless, fate played into Sultan's hands and the Ruler of Jazirat Al Hamra, Qadhib bin Ahmad – a signatory to the 1820 treaty and therefore recognised by the British as a Trucial Sheikh – died. Sultan bin Saqr lost no time in placing his nominee in charge of the town. Ajman now acknowledged Sultan's suzerainty and Dubai, linked to Sultan bin Saqr by a marriage conducted between himself and the sister of the young ruler of the town, Mohammed bin Hazza bin Zaal, looked set to accept the influence of its powerful neighbour.[6]

Sultan rebuilt Ras Al Khaimah from the stones and rubble littering the ground, house by house and wall by wall. The southern defence wall was reconstructed and, despite his setback at losing his first tower to an over-zealous British action, his subsequent fortifications were allowed to develop. Sultan's power and influence were by now at their height and straddled the east and west coasts of Southeastern Arabia.

The alliance that had grown between Tahnun of Abu Dhabi and the Sultan of Muscat irked Sultan bin Saqr. In 1828, the Bani Yas joined with Muscat to invade Bahrain. The affair was a fiasco and resulted in a resounding defeat for the invading forces.[7]

Sultan bin Saqr had already come to blows with Tahnun over the Deira tower and Buraimi affairs and he now took advantage of the weakened state of the Bani Yas following the disaster in Bahrain. In February 1829, Sultan bin Saqr declared war on Abu Dhabi and blockaded the town. The action was to bring the British ship *Sunbury* briefly into the spotlight, when it docked in Sharjah carrying a cargo bound for Abu Dhabi. The agent agreed to sell the boat's cargo to Sultan bin Saqr, but neglected to inform the captain of the *Sunbury* of the deal. As a result, when local boats approached to unload the cargo, the crew attempted to repel them, resulting in the mate of the ship being injured and the British flag being hauled down. Sultan bin Saqr had the first boat that had boarded the *Sunbury* against its captain's pleasure burned and the man who had hauled down the British colours was flogged. Honour, it would seem, was duly (if unfairly) restored.

By April, the increasingly likely prospect of losing the pearling season brought both towns to the negotiating table and the siege of Abu Dhabi was lifted. However, the die was cast and relations between Abu Dhabi and Sharjah were far from cordial. The two forces were once again pitched into conflict in 1831, when Sheikh Rashid bin Humaid Al Nuaimi of Ajman joined with the Sultan of Muscat against the rebellious port of Sohar.

Sultan Said of Muscat was increasingly to become preoccupied with the conquest of East Africa, particularly the old Arab holding of 'Zanj' or Zanzibar. Leaving on a journey of conquest in 1829, Sultan Said left himself wide open to a general (and, wearyingly, almost inevitable) rebellion which took place across his territories. The beleaguered Sultan called upon the aid of two old foes, the Rulers of Ras Al Khaimah, Sultan bin Saqr Al Qasimi, and Ajman, Rashid bin Humaid Al Nuaimi – effectively as mercenary forces. Sultan bin Saqr demanded the restitution of Khor Fakkan or at least Dibba in turn for his help but the Omani gambit was to be unsuccessful. Ras Al Khaimah's forces were kept at home by a move against the interior made by Abu Dhabi, while the Na'im of Ajman turned against their employer[8] and took the opportunity to use their boats not only against Sohar but to waylay any passing trade they could loot. Sultan bin Saqr denied all knowledge of, or responsibility for, the boats from Ajman and two British warships were duly called out to put a stop to the affair. Ajman's Ruler, Rashid bin Humaid Al Nuaimi, was forced to make reparation for the damage his boats had caused.[9]

Returning to Ajman after their adventure off Oman, the Na'im under Sheikh Rashid found that the Bani Yas and their close allies, the Bedouin Manasir, had been busy in their absence and had sacked and plundered the town of Ajman and helped themselves from the town's livestock.

This prompted Ajman, supported by Ras Al Khaimah, to declare war on Abu Dhabi.

As usual, the affair was patched up in time for the pearling season, but the protagonists could barely wait until the season was over before they once again flew at one another – in September Sharjah boats attacked two Bani Yas boats off the coast of Bahrain and Tahnun of Abu Dhabi in turn seized fourteen Al Qasimi boats which had attempted to load provisions in Abu Dhabi.

Tahnun mistrusted his brothers Khalifa and Sultan and kept them away from Abu Dhabi, by now the seat of Bani Yas power. His father prevailed upon him to reconcile with the two and he allowed them into the city, but soon found they were plotting against him. Rounding up a number of conspirators in April 1833, Tahnun found himself attacked by his brothers and fell to a ball from Khalifa's matchlock pistol and the blade of Sultan's dagger.

Although the two brothers set out in joint rule under the watchful eye of their father, Khalifa was the stronger of the two and Sultan was soon effectively sidelined. Khalifa pledged allegiance to the Wahhabi Amir, paying Zakat in tribute and was recognised by the Ruler in Nejd, who cautioned Sharjah from meddling in Abu Dhabi's succession. The move was to gain Khalifa's good standing in the eyes of the newly re-emergent Wahhabi state of Nejd and its agent, once again installed in Buraimi.

A plot to overthrow Khalifa and install a cousin in his place came to light when the cousin confessed to Khalifa. The three ringleaders were immediately killed and Khalifa was only stopped from meting out similar justice to two powerful merchants by a popular outcry and the intercession of his brother, Sultan. One of the merchants was nevertheless beaten up, stripped of his property and expelled to Lingeh.

Khalifa's violence was widely deplored, particularly by the mercantile-minded Al Bu Falasah section of the Bani Yas.

Flight to Dubai

Appalled by Khalifa's attacks on the merchant community of Abu Dhabi, the Al Bu Falasah resolved to leave the town and, through the course of the 1833 pearling season they decamped and moved to the coastal town of Dubai under the leadership of Obeid bin Saeed Al Rashid and his younger associate Maktoum bin Butti Al Maktoum.

By the time of the Al Bu Falasah exodus, Dubai was a Bani Yas town of some 250 houses in the coastal area of Shindaga, protected by the Al Fahidi Fort, situated across the tidal inlet of Ghubaiba. Its headman was Mohammed bin Hazza bin Zaal, whose uncle Saeed bin Saif Al Zaal had signed the 1820 General Treaty with the British on his behalf. Now, aged 23, Mohammed stepped aside and allowed the Al Bu Falasah to make Dubai their home.[10] In all, some 800 members of the tribe moved to live in Dubai.

Sheikh Khalifa of Abu Dhabi would have been livid to not only lose 800 subjects and their pearling boats, a significant part of the fleet, but also control over the town of Dubai. Sultan bin Saqr Al Qasimi of Sharjah had already been jostling for influence over the town, including arranging a dynastic marriage with the sister of the headman, Mohammed bin Hazza bin Zaal. The Sultan of Muscat had also expressed a desire to possess Dubai for himself. Obeid and Maktoum were, quite literally, surrounded by envious eyes and, with their newly settled town, were virtually powerless to resist military force. And yet they and their people took root in their new home and started to trade from their naturally protected little creek.

Obeid bin Saeed was an old man and the exodus to Dubai was an arduous undertaking. By 1836, he succumbed to old age and Maktoum bin Butti became the sole Ruler of the town and the founder of the Al Maktoum dynasty that continues to rule Dubai today.

The Al Bu Falasah had left Abu Dhabi just in time: two short years later, the cost of reparations that Khalifa had to pay the British (for 'acts of piracy' committed by Abu Dhabi) were so great that a number of merchants and other prominent figures fled the town to avoid being pressed into paying contributions. The flight was on such a large scale that the British asked the other Trucial Sheikhs not to afford asylum to Abu Dhabi run-aways.

The entire Qubaisat sub-section of the Bani Yas fled, sailing across to Khor Al Odaid on the border with Qatar. Here, 200 miles from their former home, they set up under their leader and considered themselves apart from the authority of both Khalifa and the British and their treaty. Once again posing a threat to shipping, the Qubaisat fell in with bad company such as the predatory pirate Jasim bin Jabir, who was based at Khor Al Odaid.

The British Residency Agent gave Khalifa carte blanche to rein in his unruly subjects. This Khalifa proceeded to do, massing an army and smashing the Khor Al Odaid settlement, killing fifty of the Qubaisat, flattening their houses and filling the wells of the town with the bodies of the slain. The tribe was broken up, fleeing to seek asylum from other Trucial Rulers, but gradually they returned to Abu Dhabi when it became clear their brethren who had chosen to return to Khalifa's rule were being well treated.[11]

War on the pearl banks

The flight of the Al Bu Falasah to Dubai in the 1833 pearling season was a gift to Sharjah's confident and ambitious Sultan bin Saqr. By now in his early 50s, he was at the height of his considerable powers, having bounced back from losing everything (very nearly his life) and being flung into captivity by the Wahhabis, to escaping and restoring not only his role at the head of the Al Qasimi, but his rule over much of what we now know as the Emirates. Ajman and Umm Al Quwain accepted his suzerainty: he had taken back Khor Fakkan, lost to him after his removal as Ruler by the Wahhabis in 1809 and he was Ruler of Ras Al Khaimah and Sharjah. With the eclipse of the young headman of Dubai, Mohammed bin Hazza bin Zaal, by the arrival of the Al Bu Falasah and their leaders, Sultan bin Saqr lost the influence over the town he had gained when he had married Mohammed's sister, but it was a passing setback – Sultan resolved to use the Al Bu Falasah to help him deliver a hammer blow to the Bani Yas, the ally of his great foe the Sultan of Muscat.[12]

Sultan bin Saqr recalled the boats of Sharjah and Ras Al Khaimah from the pearl banks (amid much grumbling – the move meant considerable losses for the men, the captains and for the town's pearl traders) and brought together a fleet of over 100 boats and a thousand men drawn from Dubai as well as the Al Qasimi towns of Ras Al Khaimah and Sharjah. The fleet sailed on 10 September 1833, reaching a landing point north of Abu Dhabi town where they planned to overnight before undertaking the assault of the town. However, word had got out of the planned invasion and, waking at sunrise, the putative conquerors found themselves surrounded by a huge force of Bani Yas and Manasir. In a panic, the invaders fled for their boats but the tide was out and most of the larger boats were beached. The Abu Dhabi men attacked, slashing at the trapped intruders desperately trying to push their boats back off the cloying sands. The losses for Dubai and the Al Qasimi were disastrous – sixty of the eighty Dubai boats in the fleet were captured, while thirty Al Qasimi men were cut down. Sultan bin Saqr got away, having almost drowned when a small boat he tried to use sank. 235 of the Dubai men were taken prisoner and forced to return to Abu Dhabi and their old homes. Another fifteen died on the sandbank.

The adventure had been a catastrophe for the fledgling town of Dubai and yet it was to host a second fleet two months later, when a flotilla of Al Qasimi boats together with boats from Ajman and Lingeh sailed for Abu Dhabi on 9 November. The force attacked Abu Dhabi from the sea, finding itself assailed by a squadron of seven batils at anchor within the harbour, whose cannonade not only threw back the invaders but damaged Sultan bin Saqr's own baggala.

The fleet withdrew out of range of the large boats and their guns and set up a blockade which was quickly effective and brought the town to its knees. Appeals to Muscat for help were useless, the Sultan was once again away in East Africa chasing past glories. The blockade by sea and land held firm. The Dubai force killed ten Abu Dhabi men, the Al Qasimi captured thirty Abu Dhabi boats trying to make harbour and a relieving caravan of fifty camels from Buraimi was taken, despite the Wahhabi agent in Buraimi attempting to intercede on Abu Dhabi's side.[13]

A desperate sally was made by Abu Dhabi, sending three batils with 500 men to run the blockade by night. Chased up the coast by twenty of the blockading boats, the Abu Dhabi boats managed to lose their pursuers and attack an Ajman baggala, putting most of its crew to death. Coming upon a baggala from Muscat, they killed the crew and took the guns, cash and the boat's cargo of dates and returned to Abu Dhabi in triumph.

Sheikh Khalifa was later forced by the British to make full restitution to Muscat for this breach of the Maritime Treaty.

Things looked bad for Abu Dhabi, but all was not as bleak as it may have seemed. The blockading fleet was barely better supplied than the town they surrounded, having to bring in food and fresh water from Dubai, Lingeh and Ras Al Khaimah. Eventually, with the approach of the 1834 pearling season, a peace was brokered by the Sheikh of Lingeh and Sultan bin Saqr's blockade was withdrawn in return for the restitution of all the vessels that had been lost, including the original fleet of sixty boats captured from Dubai.

The peace did not last. During that pearling season, while the men were at sea, the Manasir Bedouin raided Sharjah. Sultan bin Saqr took his revenge against the Bani Yas pearling fleet, seizing ten boats with their crews and 4,000 rupees worth of pearls. The move sent a shudder through the whole pearling community, forcing the recall of both fleets and resulting in a second year of disruption to coastal economies that were dependent on pearling.

It could be argued that Khalifa had inherited this long and festering conflict with Sultan bin Saqr from his brother, Tahnun, but, by killing him, any inheritance Khalifa had acquired he brought upon his own head. He was already unpopular because of the means of his accession and his action against the merchants, let alone the loss of the Al Bu Falasah and their pearling boats – now he had presided over two years of disrupted pearl diving, which would have brought his whole city to the brink of penury. Khalifa, if he wanted to keep his position, had to act.

He sent his father, Shakhbut, to parley with Sultan bin Saqr at Sharjah and, after prolonged negotiations, a treaty was arrived at. Part of the settlement was that Abu Dhabi would consider the secessionist Al Bu Falasah who had settled Dubai to be subjects of Sharjah.

The newly independent little town of Dubai had, it seems, gained a breathing space.

Piracy suppressed

In 1835, in the wake of the war of attrition between Sultan bin Saqr and the Bani Yas, Abu Dhabi boats took to plundering passing trading vessels. This was likely an act of desperation in view of the huge economic losses sustained by Abu Dhabi's seafarers, merchants and traders.

Two figures in particular are associated with these forays, Muhammad bin Saqr and Muhammad bin Majid. Following a brief but successful season of piracy, the pair found themselves facing significantly more capable British vessels than those which had been deployed in 1819, in particular the *Elphinstone*, which carried eighteen thirty-two-pound cannon. In a decisive action, the *Elphinstone* blew apart the pirates' baggalas with its powerful broadsides at close quarters. Huge reparations were exacted from Khalifa, including a number of vessels and thousands of Maria Theresa thalers (or dollars).[14] Muhammad bin Saqr was tried in Bombay for piracy and sentenced to transportation for life, while the case against Muhammad bin Majid couldn't be made satisfactorily and he was to be released to Sultan bin Saqr. Eventually he escaped by jumping ship off Sharjah and swimming the four miles to shore.[15]

Peace for pearls
The attempt to pacify the shores of the Gulf represented by the 1819 punitive expedition and 1820 General Treaty had clearly borne fruit in that it had effectively reduced the impact of the ongoing maritime trade war with Oman and forced a reconsideration of what was acceptable to the dominant maritime force, the British.

At some level, there was a certain understanding between the Trucial Rulers and the British – the British, especially those governing India, were comfortable with the roles of Sheikhs in their society, mirroring in many ways those of the Maharajas and Rajas of India (if perhaps lacking the same degree of fabulous wealth). To some degree enchanted by the 'noble savage' Bedouin and feeling they could understand the social structures of the Trucial Coast (as we have seen from the 'eye opening' 1823 tour of the British Resident, very little was truly understood of the society, culture and politics of the area), the British fulfilled at turns a sternly paternalistic and broadly supportive role in their relationship with the Rulers. For their part, the Rulers were getting used to this odd suzerainty, where no tribute was exacted, but where the relations governed by the all-encompassing treaty were policed relatively effectively.

The Treaty itself clearly didn't cover all the bases – the enduring and enervating conflict between the Al Qasimi and Muscat and also the wearying war between Sultan bin Saqr and the Bani Yas showed that acts of war at sea were not dissimilar to piracy (which, in hindsight, is what the Al Qasimi should have been arguing, perhaps even were arguing, albeit to deaf British ears). Blockades, trade wars, opportunistic plunder of enemy shipping and seaborne invasions had all taken place 'legally' under the very nose of the 1820 'General Treaty for the Cessation of Plunder and Piracy by Land and Sea', all of them being actions that took place under the banner of declared war.

The Trucial Rulers themselves seemed to see the sense in maintaining the maritime peace – both the Rulers of Sharjah and Bahrain had argued that the British were bound to prevent all maritime incidents and yet the Company in Bombay had no desire whatsoever to assume a formal protectorate – in 1834, the Court of Directors ruled this out, 'even at the invitation of the petty Arab states'.[16] The pearl merchants of Sharjah had even offered to buy British protection during the season and were prepared to advance twenty dollars per annum for each boat so protected. Not for the last time in the history of the Trucial States, the British refused to be treated as 'mercenaries'.

And yet disruption to the lucrative pearl trade was to be avoided, even to the point of considering any aggressive act that interrupted that trade as 'piracy'. Finagling the Treaty in this way wasn't a long-term solution – could a more comprehensive peace be envisaged? One, for instance, which would ensure the peaceful prosecution of the pearling season?

In 1835, the Acting Resident in the Arabian Gulf, Captain Samuel Hennell, an unusually perspicacious and sensitive administrator whose understanding of the ways of the Trucial Coast was quite extraordinary for his time, assembled the Sheikhs at Basidu, on Qeshm island, in the light of the peace concluded between the Bani Yas and the Al Qasimi, to discuss a peace that would prevail over the coming pearling season. Having endured the grinding poverty resulting from two interrupted seasons, Abu Dhabi, Dubai, Ajman and Sharjah saw the sense in it and on 21 August 1835, they signed a truce to bind them to pursue a peaceful pearling season and, in the case of any infraction of that peace, to refer it to the British. Hennell was careful to explain that any such reported case would have to be treated as a piracy (allowing him, therefore, to act within his remit from Bombay) and that the treaty would stand regardless of any conflict taking place on land. In other words, no act of war at sea whatsoever would be tolerated under this new treaty of peace.

The pearling season peace ran from 21 May to 21 November 1835. It was a resounding success and Hennell's gambit was to be repeated year after year, in 1838 becoming a year-long treaty rather than just covering the pearling season. The period was almost entirely free of incidents, the only major relapse being in 1840, when Sultan bin Saqr managed to squeeze a quick maritime raid on a mildly fractious Umm Al Quwain to bring it into line before the 1841 treaty was negotiated.

Another innovation brought in by Hennell in 1846 was the 'restrictive line', which defined an area of the Gulf where everyone agreed not to undertake acts of war with or without a truce, to the Persian side of the islands of Sirri and Abu Musa. This was later extended to the Sharjah-owned island of Sir Bu Nair.

Apart from a couple of notable criminal actions, the peace held. In one 1841 incident, a pair of robbers fled with their considerable cargo of pearls to Dubai, which was reluctant to give up such a prize and had to be reminded, with a couple of eight-inch shells fired over the town by the steamship *Sesostris*, of its treaty obligations. By 1844, Sheikh Maktoum bin Butti had reaped the rewards of peace and, when a spat erupted between Al Qasimi and Ka'abi pearling boats, he stepped in and punished the miscreants, having them lodge a bond with the British Residency Agent in Sharjah against their good behaviour.

By 1843, the brilliant Samuel Hennell (appointed British Resident in 1838, a post he was to hold until 1852) concluded a ten-year treaty to run until 1853. The peace held and the waters of the Gulf, once so turbulent, became a glittering sea of calm.

Chapter 16

WAR IN THE SANDS

"Men have looked upon the desert as a barren land, the free holding of whoever chose; but in fact every hill and valley in it had a man who was its acknowledged owner and would quickly assert the right of his family or clan to it, against aggression. Even the wells and trees had their masters."

– T. E. Lawrence

The first British Residency ('native') Agent in Sharjah, a post established in 1823, was Mulla Hussain and his relations with the Trucial Sheikhs, particularly the governor of Sharjah, Sheikh Salih bin Saqr (brother to Sultan bin Saqr), were critical in building trust between the British Political Resident in Bushire and the rulers of the Trucial States. He was followed by Haji Yaqub, whose relations with Sharjah were rather less cordial.

The British Residency Agent was not the only representative of a foreign power on the Trucial Coast. The Wahhabis maintained an on-and-off presence with an agent in Buraimi and, in 1839, an Egyptian agent appeared, to the great alarm of the British.

The Mamluk Caliphate of Egypt had fallen in 1798 to the conquest of Napoleon Bonaparte, who was in turn defeated by a coalition led by the British. Bonaparte had allied with the Ottomans and they lost no time in taking control of Egypt, placing Muhammad Ali Pasha, an Albanian mercenary, as Viceroy of Egypt. Muhammad Ali's rule over Egypt was only nominally Ottoman, he embarked on a campaign of expansion and conquest, allied with civil works and a wide-ranging reform of the Egyptian government. Throughout the first three decades of the 1800s, Muhammad Ali built a sizeable industrial base, much of it dedicated to military manufacturing, supporting in its turn, his conquests of Saudi Arabia and Sudan and his repression of the Greek rebellion on the behalf of his Ottoman masters.

Ambitious above all else, by 1838, Muhammad Ali had declared himself independent of the Ottomans. He gave a pledge to the British representative in Cairo not to extend his earlier conquests of the Hejaz and Nejd (including the Saudi capital of Diriyah) to the coast of the Arabian Gulf. However, his forces appeared set to take Bahrain and, with the despatch of an agent to the Trucial States, his ambition appeared to extend even further.

The British Resident at Bushire was instructed to use his influence to stop the Egyptians from extending their sphere to the Gulf and the British Naval Commander in Chief in the East visited the Trucial Sheikhs together with the Assistant Political Resident, gaining an undertaking from them that they would hold not friendly relations with – indeed, that they would actively oppose – the Egyptian Resident when he, inevitably, would arrive.

The arrival of this much-anticipated gentleman was something of an event, as it turned out he was none other than the former Wahhabi agent in Buraimi, Saad bin Mutlaq, the son of the Saudi general who had been an active participant in many of the conflicts of the interior and was a much-respected military commander. In March 1839, Saad arrived at Sharjah and was presented by Sultan bin Saqr with a handsome, and suitably fortified, house and tower to use as his residence.

Muhammad Ali's choice of Agent was inspired: Saad immediately got to work and conspired with Sultan bin Saqr to approach the Na'im of Buraimi, old friends, and arrange to have the oasis occupied by a Wahhabi garrison which Saad just happened to have brought along with him.

The Na'im opposed the approach and were backed in their opposition to Saad, perversely, given they had in the past tried to invade the place, by the headman of Sohar, who sent his brother up the Wadi Jizzi from the east coast with a force of 200 men to back them up.

Saad also approached Khalifa bin Shakhbut of Abu Dhabi, who proved more amenable (to the consternation of the British, who had expected he would be staunchly opposed to such an approach and who would have rightly expected the Na'im to have been more than open to it).

On 1 July 1839, Samuel Hennell arrived to try and manage the worrying situation. Carried along the coast in the *Hugh Lindsay*, a steamer with an eleven-foot draught which could navigate its way up the shallow creeks of the coast, previously barred to the Company's old frigates and brigs, Hennell found that Dubai and Umm Al Quwain were against the Egyptians but that Sultan bin Saqr and Khalifa bin Shakhbut were vying with each other to win Saad's approval and backing. Hennell collected written agreements to oppose Egypt's influence from all concerned, taking care to add an additional codicil to Sultan bin Saqr's agreement, that he would have no truck with Muhammad Ali, his representative Saad bin Mutlaq or indeed any foreign power without British consent – a precursor to the treaty that all of the Trucial Sheikhs would sign in 1892, confirming the Trucial States as independent states in treaty relations with Great Britain.[1]

Hennell assured Sultan bin Saqr that any military backing needed to defend him against Saad bin Mutlaq and the Saudi force would be furnished by the British. At the same time, having received a request for help from the alarmed Na'im of Buraimi (to which he rather disingenuously replied offering them ammunition and hinting that a British Agent could be appointed to Buraimi), Hennell wrote to the Wahhabi agent, Saad bin Mutlaq, and told him to leave, asserting that Buraimi was under British protection.

There is little doubt that Samuel Hennell was one of the most outstanding British officers to have come into contact with the Trucial Coast, and his influence with, and clear understanding of, the Trucial Sheikhs was exceptional. Saad bin Mutlaq did, indeed, depart and Bombay was quick to express its delight with Hennell and his remarkable achievement. They were also very quick indeed to deprecate his involvement with the interior, it being very much a pillar of British policy not to get involved in the wild desert areas and their constantly warring tribes. The British protectorate of the broad area of Buraimi was put very much on the back burner but was, in an odd presentiment of the future, eventually to come to fruit over 100 years later.

Saad bin Mutlaq having quit Sharjah to the relief of all but perhaps Sultan bin Saqr and Khalifa bin Shakhbut, the latter wasted little time in mounting his own attack on Buraimi, hoping perhaps in this way to win a gift for the Egyptian viceroy Muhammad Ali which would ensure his undying gratitude and favour. He sent a force to Buraimi to subjugate the Na'im who responded with a gallant and fierce defence which saw the Abu Dhabi force sustain such losses that Khalifa sued for peace. Hennell stepped in and demanded Khalifa pay 1,000 silver dollars in compensation to the Na'im or be considered an enemy of the British. Having a keen idea of the consequences of defying the British, Khalifa bin Shakhbut paid up.

Hennell now held meetings at Ajman with the Sheikhs of Buraimi and was able to forge an alliance between two former foes, the Na'im and the Dhawahir. A further attempt at an alliance with the Bani Qitab was beyond even Hennell's powers, but he liberally distributed gifts of rice, silver dollars and ammunition.

While his involvement in the interior may have been contrary to Bombay's policy, it was a typically inspired initiative on Hennell's part and was to pay dividends in the future because Saad bin Mutlaq was by no means a spent force, despite the collapse of Muhammad Ali's brief attempt to extend his empire to the Gulf. Saad bin Mutlaq would be back.

The Shihuh of the mountains

Sultan bin Saqr Al Qasimi's considerable ambitions were not only directed south and east, but also upwards. The mountains behind the coastal littoral of Ras Al Khaimah were inhabited by a different people, the Shihuh (singular Al Shehhi).

Speaking a distinctive language understood only by themselves, rumours abounded that they were descendants of the Portuguese, of Iranians or of a number of other origins. People pointed to red-headed members of the Shihuh, to their language which was certainly not Arabic (which many Shihuh only spoke haltingly) and to their strange axes, called *jerz* – long-handled with small, curved heads, which each Shehhi carried proudly. They were a law unto themselves and fearsome warriors. When the Sultan of Muscat ceded the mountains (Rus Al Jibal) behind Ras Al Khaimah to Sultan bin Saqr in 1836 – just one of a number of territorial and tribal changes triggered by the long-running conflict between Muscat and the Qawasim – he forgot to inform the Shihuh, and Sultan bin Saqr found himself with a very troublesome bunch indeed on his hands. A conflict broke out between him and the Shihuh following the taking and subsequent demolition of a fort belonging to the tribe in Dibba, on the east coast. Sultan bin Saqr sent a force against them, but the mountains, wadis and deep passes were the Shihuh's domain and Sultan's fighters were easily defeated. Setting out against the Shihuh towns of Khasab and Kumzar, far up on the Musandam Peninsula, Saqr realised his attempts to bring the fierce men of the mountains to heel was doomed to failure and resolved on a blockade by sea. Distracted by his conflict with the Wahhabi state, in 1839, Sultan concluded an uneasy peace with his troublesome subjects, but the Shihuh remained fiercely independent in their mountain villages and stepped pastures.[2]

Of slaves and successions

Although the 1820 General Treaty had included a reference to the suppression of the slave trade, it had been something of a hobby horse on the part of the 1819 British punitive expedition's translator, did not reflect a concern of Bombay's and therefore was not enforced with any rigour. However, attitudes in Britain towards slavery had hardened and, in 1833, the British government passed the Slavery Abolition Act, which gave the East India Company responsibility for the abolition of slavery in its territories. Consequently, a treaty was signed with the Trucial Sheikhs (with the exception of Umm Al Quwain, which Sultan bin Saqr of Sharjah considered to be subject to his rule, the British presumably agreeing at this time) in 1838 which gave the British the right to stop and seize any boat suspected of carrying slaves. A further treaty of 1839 expanded the area of concern to the Indian Ocean and expressly defines Somalis as 'free men' and made their sale illegal. A third treaty, dated 1847, prohibited the taking of slaves from Africa and elsewhere on any boat belonging to the Sheikhs or their subjects.

Despite these treaties, slavery in the Trucial States persisted until well into the mid-1900s, both domestically and in the pearl trade, where many divers were slaves.[3] In fact, the governor of Kalba in the 1930s, and the figure at the centre of the disputed succession of the emirate at the time, was a slave by the name of Barut.

Disputed successions were very much the norm in the Trucial States, few of them having been more sanguinary than those of the Al Nahyan ruling family of Abu Dhabi and few being more complex than those of the Qawasim.

When Sultan bin Saqr acceded as head of the Qawasim on the second occasion in 1820, he appointed his brothers as governors, or Walis, of Ras Al Khaimah and Sharjah. Muhammad bin Saqr governed Ras

Al Khaimah until his death in 1845 or shortly before, while Salih bin Saqr governed Sharjah. He went on to enjoy the respect of the British and a close working relationship with the first British Residency Agent, the Sharjah-based Mulla Hussein. In 1838, Sultan bin Saqr replaced his brother with his son Saqr bin Sultan. Two years later, in 1840, Saqr declared himself independent of his father, gaining popular support by promising to reduce the annual tax on pearl divers, which Sultan bin Saqr had levied at seven (Marie Therese) dollars per head. Sultan bin Saqr prepared for war, but eventually was prevailed upon to accept tribute from his wayward son in return for letting Saqr hold Sharjah.

Saqr bin Sultan had been encouraged in his quest for independence by Maktoum bin Butti of Dubai, who must have been delighted at thus creating a friendly buffer state between himself and the towering, dominant figure of Sultan bin Saqr in Ras Al Khaimah. However, Maktoum's ongoing influence over the young Saqr was resented by some of the elders of Sharjah and they supported the return of Salih, capturing Saqr in his sleep one night and handing him over to his father.

Sultan bin Saqr sent his son into exile in Ras Al Khaimah, but Saqr slipped away from his captors and took refuge in Dubai.

It was not uncommon for people to seek refuge in Dubai – debtors from both Abu Dhabi and Sharjah had done so, as had others fleeing for one reason and another. Khalifa bin Shakhbut of Abu Dhabi had never quite forgiven Dubai for its secession and in May 1838, when the Dubai fleet had embarked for the pearl banks at the start of that year's season, Khalifa led a raid from Abu Dhabi against the independently-minded town, captured a tower and garrisoned it. Returning from the pearl banks, the Dubai men assaulted the tower. Three days of fighting saw the Abu Dhabi garrison removed, but resulted in the destruction of the tower.

Sultan bin Saqr, infuriated by Saqr's desertion to Dubai, enlisted the help of his old enemy, Khalifa bin Shakhbut of Abu Dhabi. The two agreed on the destruction of the town of Dubai, following which they would force the Al Bu Falasah and others living in Dubai to choose to move to Abu Dhabi or Sharjah. Sultan then recruited Abdulla bin

Rashid Al Mualla of Umm Al Quwain to the cause. A feud the year before, in 1839, between Dubai and Umm Al Quwain had led to Saqr intervening on Dubai's behalf, so Abdulla bin Rashid would have been pleased to join in the alliance against Dubai.

Having put together his coalition, Sultan bin Saqr suddenly accepted a gift of 1,000 dollars and the submission of Maktoum bin Butti in return for withdrawing from his plan. Lacking the man who had been the impelling force behind the agreement to pulverise Dubai, the coalition dissipated like a dust devil and Saqr was brought back to Sharjah by his father, where he was allowed to rule until his death.

Dubai, not for the first or last time, breathed a sigh of relief and had cause to celebrate its leader, who was, in general, making a fine job of charting the difficult course between his powerful and ambitious neighbours.

Disaster strikes Dubai

1841 saw an exodus from Dubai of some 500 members of the Al Bu Muhair tribe who, dissatisfied with Maktoum's rule, decamped and settled in Sharjah. Hot on the heels of their exit, during the pearling season, a violent epidemic of fever broke out and many of the people of the town fled to Deira, across the creek from Bur Dubai. Saqr bin Sultan of Sharjah gave his permission for the temporary settlement (Deira being part of Sharjah at that time).[4]

Khalifa bin Shakhbut seized his opportunity. The town of Dubai was virtually undefended and he paused only to secure assurances of neutrality from the Bani Qitab and other tribes of the interior before falling on Dubai with a force of 150 men. They plundered the deserted town, destroying stores, smashing the date plantations and burning any boats not out at sea for the pearling season, including a *batil*, with the two men on the big boat being put to death.

The invaders occupied Jumeirah and, when Maktoum raised a force of 200 men from Saqr bin Sultan to bulk out his own forces, Khalifa outflanked him with a lighting raid and looted Al Khan, taking fifteen slaves and re-joining the main force, which returned to Abu Dhabi jubilant. Soon after, Khalifa sent another force north, aiming to take Dubai, Sharjah and even Ras Al Khaimah, but he found the towns ready for him and was knocked back, his own riding camel shot out from under him in the clashes that followed.

In the following two years, despite the considerable damage his forces had wrought in Dubai, a reconciliation between Khalifa bin Shakhbut and Maktoum bin Butti took place which by 1843 had warmed into friendship. Maktoum was the only friend Khalifa made in the north at that time – the interior was to be pitched into a series of tremendous tribal conflicts and the man behind the whole descent into anarchy was none other than Khalifa bin Shakhbut.

Perhaps emboldened by his friendship with Maktoum, certainly egged on by the wily Ruler of Dubai once things started heating up, Khalifa went to war. One hundred and fifty Bani Yas riders under Khalifa's brother Sultan rode north against the Bani Qitab, allies of Sharjah. Killing three men and taking seventy camels, the raiding party came across a Na'im caravan making from Buraimi to Sharjah and killed three of the Na'im. In August, the Bani Yas rode out again, raiding the Bani Qitab, Ghafalah and Na'im and falling upon the inland oasis town of Dhaid. There they looted the town, taking a number of camels.

The Ghafalah themselves attacked a Dubai caravan in November 1843, triggering a response from Maktoum who rode against them and also attacked the Na'im, who were allied to Sultan bin Saqr. Sultan tried to maintain the peace with Maktoum, despite Dubai's assault on two of his key allies. The tribes themselves, infuriated by his lack of support in the face of Maktoum's attacks, threatened to rise against Sultan and transfer their allegiance to Khalifa bin Shakhbut. However, Maktoum wasn't to be placated and, with his relationship with Sultan bin Saqr stretched to breaking point, he led his forces into battle with the Ghafalah once again and put them to flight. Maktoum, victorious, lost an eye in gaining his victory.

The interior was in a state of turmoil and fear as tribal alliances ebbed and flowed and the people scattered throughout the area's oasis villages trembled in dread as raiding parties swept across the land.

Sultan bin Saqr's vacillation in the face of Maktoum's raids against the tribes damaged his standing and he found himself vying with Khalifa bin Shakhbut, who lost no time in making a tour of the interior and gathering the tribes to himself. Khalifa's mastery of Bedouin statecraft culminated in a great meeting in Buraimi in the summer of 1844 at which the Walis of Sohar and Shinas both (today in Oman) presented themselves, along with other tribal leaders. Maktoum was invited in a bid to settle his differences with the Ghafalah but he rightly feared for his safety in the face of so many recent enmities and sent his brother, Saeed bin Butti, in his place.

The Saudis return to Buraimi

Adding to the volatility created by the squabbles and ambitions of the Rulers and tribal leaders, the Saudis now embarked on a fresh attempt to suborn the area. Influence in Buraimi and indeed the whole area of the Trucial States remained an ambition for the Saudi Amir Faisal, who had been removed by the Egyptians in 1838 and sent to Cairo where they could keep an eye on him. He managed to escape and, in 1843, re-established his rule over Riyadh and the Nejd. A resurgent Saudi state under Faisal now embarked on a move to re-establish its presence in Buraimi and letters were despatched to the Sheikhs from Riyadh which presaged the return of the Wahhabi agent, Saad bin Mutlaq, to Buraimi at the end of the summer.[5]

The Na'im were greatly alarmed at this fresh overture, particularly following the interception, in 1841, of a letter from Sultan bin Saqr of Sharjah to Saad bin Mutlaq which indicated that Sharjah's Ruler was keen on bringing the Saudis back into play. Meanwhile, the Saudi succession entered a period of messy dispute and Saad bin Mutlaq found himself professing his allegiance to a slew of new Rulers. His ability to survive these quick successions and his ambition to return to Buraimi were undimmed and Faisal, once returned from Cairo, wasted no time in harnessing Saad bin Mutlaq's connections.

An expression of intent by Faisal was worth taking seriously. The Na'im promptly sent to the British for help, remembering Samuel

Hennell, his generous gifts and assurances of friendship and support and buoyed by the British intervention of 1841. Hennell had, however, been a little too enthusiastic in his involvement in the interior and Bombay had disavowed his support for the Rulers of the area – reminding him that British policy remained not to become embroiled in the interior and that British interests remained purely maritime and mercantile. Besides, Bushire and Riyadh were by now exchanging friendly letters. The Na'im were told that the British, now that the Egyptian cloud had passed, had no interest in their concerns. They had no alternative but to accept their fate and when Saad bin Mutlaq arrived, early in 1845, both the Na'im and Dhawahir welcomed him and offered up the forts of Buraimi to his forces.

Delighted by his reception (having expected resistance), Saad bin Mutlaq now set out to collect submissions to Wahhabi rule as well as taxes and extended his influence over the coastal town of Sohar as well as Dhank and the area of origin of the settled Dhawahir, the Dhahirah.[6] By October 1845, he was ready to embark on a seizure of Dhaid and the establishment of a coastal fortification at Al Zorah – today a part of Ajman and home to a fine Marriott hotel, golf course and residential development. The leaders both to the east (the Na'im, despite their acquiescence, remained resentful of their new overlord and both Sohar and Muscat found Saad's taxation onerous) and west of Buraimi found themselves united against Saad's ambitions, only Umm Al Quwain – with an eye on the prize of Dhaid, the desert oasis adjacent to their own oasis town of Falaj Al Ali – supported him. Unable to rise against the power of the Wahhabis, they instead conspired to accuse Saad bin Mutlaq of embezzlement. Riyadh called on Saad to send payment and, with the help of Sultan bin Saqr, he promptly despatched a boatload of treasure to his master in Riyadh. Saad, for now, at least, was safe.

However, Saudi rule was at best nominal (probably better considered as a Saudi 'presence') and it was the coastal Rulers whose scuffles for influence and territory who were to plunge the area into instability as Sultan bin Saqr of Sharjah sought to re-establish his primacy, setting out to bring Umm Al Quwain and Ajman back under his control and reduce the threat from Dubai and the influence of Abu Dhabi over the tribes. The killing of Khalifa bin Shakhbut in 1845 proved to be timely for Sultan bin Saqr, as it plunged Abu Dhabi once again into a familiar pattern of internecine strife and at the same time saw Khalifa's influence over the tribes fade even as Saad bin Mutlaq's sun rose over the interior.

Umm Al Quwain under attack

The small town of Umm Al Quwain had managed to lead a mostly quiet life, having proclaimed its independence from Sultan bin Saqr in 1832. However, Sultan kept a baleful eye on the little port and its people and when a dispute broke out with Dubai in 1839, he gladly gave permission for a Dubai force to raid Umm Al Quwain in response to the murder of two Dubai men who had been mistaken for members of the Manasir tribe from Abu Dhabi. The raid was a disaster and six of the Dubai men were taken prisoner.[7]

Saqr bin Sultan of Sharjah and Maktoum bin Butti of Dubai now raised a joint force from their two towns against Umm Al Quwain. The fighting that followed saw twenty men dead and a large number of wounded, but Umm Al Quwain capitulated and the Dubai prisoners were released and blood money paid.

However, Sultan bin Saqr wasn't satisfied and, in 1840, he led a force, assisted by men from Dubai, intended to reduce Umm Al Quwain, with 700 camel riders attacking from the landward side, while three baggalas and sixty smaller boats with a force of 1,500 men attempted to blockade the port. Sultan's army met with spirited resistance from the defenders and his fleet was beaten back by fighters based in a tower overlooking the harbour which was defended with the loss of eight killed and forty wounded from the Al Qasimi force. Meanwhile, Khalifa bin Shakhbut of Abu Dhabi attempted to relieve Umm Al Quwain by attacking Dubai. With the towns of the coast on the verge of being pitched in all-out battle, an attempt by the British Residency Agent to mediate in the dispute was met with relief all round and a peace was eventually concluded.

Perhaps understandably, Abdullah bin Rashid Al Mualla of Umm Al Quwain was left feeling vulnerable and, despite having undertaken not to resume construction of his fortifications of the town as a condition of the peace, in 1841 he started work on shoring up the town's defences. Sultan bin Saqr went to the British Residency Agent and a ruling against Umm Al Quwain was sought. The case was referred to government and eventually, in May of 1843, Abdullah bin Rashid was compelled to destroy his new towers. At this time, the annual Maritime Treaty was being replaced by the new ten-year treaty and the threat of more violence lay heavy over the forthcoming pearling season. After one tower had been reduced, honour was proclaimed satisfied and Sultan bin Saqr withdrew his objections. Umm Al Quwain kept its forts.

Ajman, meanwhile, was concerned at this time with its own affairs. Sheikh Rashid bin Humaid Al Nuaimi, signatory to the 1820 General Treaty, passed away in 1838 and was succeeded by his younger son, Humaid bin Rashid Al Nuaimi, whose elder brother Ali had no interest in becoming Ruler. Humaid married into the Al Qasimi of Sharjah, taking a daughter of Sultan bin Saqr Al Qasimi as his wife. Humaid was deposed in 1841 by his brother Abdelaziz bin Rashid, who took Ajman fort and declared himself Ruler. In doing so, Abdelaziz made himself a powerful enemy and Humaid's father-in-law now plotted to restore his young ally to Ajman.

Death in Abu Dhabi

Shakhbut bin Dhiyab passed away, leaving his third son as absolute Ruler of Abu Dhabi and the Bani Yas. Khalifa bin Shakhbut was to enjoy his primacy for a short period only, because five years later he accepted a fateful – and fatal – invitation to dine on the beach at Abu Dhabi in July 1845. Almost unthinkably, his hosts breached one of the most revered tenets of Bedouin hospitality and at the end of the meal a man by the name of Isa bin Khalid, who had long held designs on Khalifa's life, rose up and killed both Khalifa and his brother, Sultan. The usurper took advantage of the absence of most of the townsfolk, either embarked on the annual pearling season or tending their herds in Liwa and Buraimi, and declared himself Ruler over the sparsely populated town. His tenure was to be short-lived; Isa bin Khalid was in turn killed within two months of asserting his rule over Abu Dhabi. His murderer was then slain by Isa's son, who travelled from Sharjah in search of revenge and who promptly returned there, leaving the Al Nahyan family to continue their domestic disputes over the succession. The Bani Yas supported Khalifa's nephew, Saeed bin Tahnun Al Nahyan and, with British acquiescence, Saeed acceded as Ruler of Abu Dhabi.

Sultan bin Saqr Al Qasimi was quick to forge a link with Abu Dhabi's new ruler. Undoubtedly aware of the brooding Saudi threat from Buraimi, barely confirmed in his position, Saeed bin Tahnun accepted the overtures from his Uncle's old adversary from Ras Al Khaimah.

Meanwhile, Sultan bin Saqr was set on cutting the brash new town of Dubai and its Ruler, Maktoum, down to size. His actions were to lead to a new outbreak of war on the coast.

Effectively ceding much of his former territory of Deira, Sultan set about constructing a line of towers inland of the coastal village of Abu Hail, hoping to halt Dubai's northward expansion. Maktoum bin Butti, with the backing of Abdullah bin Rashid of Umm Al Quwain, sallied forth and fighting had only just broken out when British ships arrived and their commander brokered a truce pending a hearing by the British Residency Agent in Sharjah. No sooner had the British ships sailed away than Sultan bin Saqr recommenced his construction works and Maktoum once again threw his forces against his northern neighbour. The British Agent had barely started negotiations between the warring factions when Sultan bin Saqr's son – Saqr bin Sultan, the governor of Sharjah – was killed in fighting with Umm Al Quwain.[8]

Saqr bin Sultan had led a force, including a mounted force of raiders from the Bani Qitab, against Umm Al Quwain. Meeting fierce resistance, the raiding party was beaten back and put to flight, but the young man was cut down.

Sultan bin Saqr called for a six-month truce in order to mourn his son and this was brokered by the British and promptly broken by Sultan, who started building his very own Maginot line of fortifications against Dubai once again. Sultan threw any Dubai people he could find out of Sharjah and brought Abu Dhabi into play against Umm Al Quwain. Twenty men of the Ghafalah tribe were killed in the ensuing warfare.

Not surprisingly, widespread fighting broke out. Sultan bin Saqr allied with Abu Dhabi against Dubai but then moved against Umm Al Quwain instead, while Maktoum of Dubai made his peace with Sultan bin Saqr in March 1847 when Sultan promised to destroy his line of fortifications at Abu Hail. Umm Al Quwain was also party to the 1847 truce, but Abdullah bin Rashid kept a wary eye on his volatile and ambitious neighbour – Sultan bin Saqr could be expected to seek revenge for the death of his son.

Dubai remained at war with Abu Dhabi and its allies, the Bani Qitab Bedouin. Sultan bin Saqr broke his promise and kept the forts, but the uneasy truce between Dubai and Sharjah held.

The fine sand of the coastal pathways was constantly thrown up in clouds against the blue skies as riders raced across the tracks snaking across salt flats and low dunes carrying messages between rulers. This intent was matched to that action, this tribe was a tributary and answerable for that act of despoliation. The rulers balanced their interests and calculated their potential losses and gains.

Sultan bin Saqr's restless ambitions were limitless and his son, Abdullah bin Sultan – the new governor of Sharjah – led a disastrous foray against Ajman in January 1848, attempting to seize the town's fort and restore Sultan's deposed son-in-law, Humaid bin Rashid Al Nuaimi, to his position. The failure of this expedition led to a general outcry among the Trucial Sheikhs, but no tangible retaliation took place as a consequence. Alliance and counter-alliance were forged and the tapestry of fast-changing allegiances became almost impossible to follow. Dubai allied against Buraimi with Sharjah and Ajman (oddly enough, in support of the Saudi agent), although to little effect,[9] and then Dubai, Abu Dhabi and Umm Al Quwain closed ranks against Sharjah.

Ajman went to war with Hamriyah in September 1848, Abdelaziz bin Rashid Al Nuaimi of Ajman leading a force of 400 men against the town, which was then subject to the rule of Sharjah. They were beaten back by the people of Hamriyah with huge loss of life. Among the dead was Abdelaziz himself. His brother, Humaid bin Rashid, was himself wounded but overcame his injuries to take his position once again as the ruler of Ajman – having originally been deposed by Abdelaziz in 1841.[10]

The whole patchwork became a mishmash, the colours of the Trucial States mixed and mingled until, to the outsider, it all became a strange purple/brown, like old classroom plasticine. The one quality lacking in the whole mad and, ultimately, murderous imbroglio was trust. And rightly so.

There was nobody at all, it seemed, to be trusted.

Chapter 17

OF PERPETUAL PEACE

"Petty theft is rare and looked on as immoral: but robbery with violence a manly act and the raid, with murder and looting, as unquestionably honourable as military prowess in Europe."

– Bertram Thomas

The British presence in Sharjah was by now generally accepted amongst the Rulers and people of the Trucial Coast and the Residency Agent was increasingly frequently called in to mediate in disputes, of which there were a great many.

The annual treaties of maritime peace had led to a ten-year peace treaty brokered by the British Political Resident, Samuel Hennell, in 1843. With the expiry of that treaty in 1852, it was time to reflect and take stock.

The Sheikhs of the Trucial Coast were in a state of almost perpetual conflict, but the maritime treaties had generally held and there was broad recognition that the pearling season was virtually sacrosanct – even to the point where landward disputes had been settled – or at least patched up – in time to allow the fleets to take to the pearl banks in peace.

Captain Arnold Burrowes Kemball, the British Resident at Bushire, was Assistant Political Resident under Hennell and was appointed to the post of Political Resident in 1852 (a year after his promotion to Captain)[1] when Hennell gave up the residency, at the age of 52, to return to Bombay with his wife Ann and their two young sons, both born in Bushire.[2] Kemball's career in the Gulf had spanned the ten year period of Hennell's treaty and Kemball now proposed to the Trucial Sheikhs that the ten-year treaty be replaced with a perpetual treaty of maritime peace. His overtures met with a positive reception both from the Rulers and Bombay and so, at the start of May 1853 (just before the pearling season commenced), Kemball sailed to meet the Sheikhs in the *Clive*. The treaty negotiations were straightforward, even Sultan bin Saqr – assured that the treaty wouldn't stop him from defending himself against the Sultan of Muscat – was quick to sign. Kemball collected his signatures between 4 and 9 May and the new treaty came into effect. The Perpetual Maritime Truce of 1853 was signed by Abdullah bin Rashid Al Mualla of Umm Al Quwain; Hamed bin Rashid Al Nuaimi of Ajman; Saeed bin Butti Al Maktoum of Dubai; Saeed bin Tahnun Al Nahyan of Abu Dhabi and Sultan bin Saqr Al Qasimi, 'Chief of the Joasmees'.

It is perhaps noteworthy that the Rulers travelled to meet Kemball from Buraimi, where they had all – apart only from Saeed bin

Butti – been gathered to meet with Abdullah bin Faisal Al Saud, the son of Faisal bin Turki bin Abdullah Al Saud, the Saudi Ruler.

Although a number of incidents occurred over the next decade which required the intervention of the British in one form or another, these were more often associated with the conflicts of the coast and interior spilling over rather than overt acts of maritime force, brigandage or piracy. In fact, the British reports of the time now resort to a new linguistic nicety, referring to maritime incidents as 'irregularities' rather than 'piracies'.

Sheikh Maktoum bin Butti wasn't to live to sign the 1853 treaty. He died in early 1852, of smallpox, while travelling from Muscat to Qeshm. Maktoum's brother, Saeed bin Butti, acceded in his place and although his accession was straightforward, his right to rule was challenged by Maktoum bin Butti's sons, Hasher and Suhail. Saeed travelled to Muscat to meet with his ally the Sultan (with whom Maktoum had been meeting shortly before his death) in October 1852, leaving Dubai in the hands of a governor, his uncle Saeed bin Rashid.[3]

No sooner had Saeed bin Butti left, than Maktoum's sons made their move, taking over the Al Fahidi Fort and imprisoning Saeed bin Rashid. Their triumph was short-lived, however, and Saeed bin Rashid regained control of the town and forced the brothers to flee to exile in Sharjah, even before his nephew returned from Muscat. A number of Al Bu Muhair left Dubai at this time to join their relatives in Sharjah (the majority of the tribe having previously left for Sharjah).

In December 1852, Saeed bin Butti concluded alliances with Abu Dhabi and Umm Al Quwain, in an attempt to neutralise Sultan bin Saqr Al Qasimi and the threat from Sharjah.[4] However, Sultan bin Saqr, the head of the Al Qasimi Federation and Ruler of both Ras Al Khaimah and Sharjah, had bigger fish to fry.

Trouble in Buraimi

Saeed bin Tahnun Al Nahyan of Abu Dhabi moved against Buraimi on 4 May 1848. The troublesome – and influential – Saudi agent Saad bin Mutlaq left the oasis for a time and Saeed bin Tahnun, with the assistance of the Dhawahir, captured a Saudi post in the area. The Na'im joined Saeed, as did a force from Sohar and they marched together on Buraimi and took both of the fortified Saudi encampments there. Saad bin Mutlaq returned from his travels, promptly realised the situation and fled for and fled for Sharjah. Saeed bin Tahnun lost the support of Sohar and found both Dubai and Sharjah ranged against him. Nevertheless, he maintained his hold over Buraimi until, finally, a mediation by the Sherif of Mecca restored the forts to Saad bin Mutlaq.[5]

It was late in 1849 that Abu Dhabi found itself once again handling the rebellious (and indebted) Qubaisat tribe, who again decamped to the Qatar peninsula and the inlet of Khor Al Udaid. Dubai and Sharjah both lobbied the Saudis to give the Qubaisat protection at Khor Al Udaid. Before anything could take place, the Qubaisat found instead that the long arm of Saeed bin Tahnun reached them: he invited their tribal leaders to a banquet and, while they were busy eating, their ships were stripped of mast and sail. They were compelled to return to Abu Dhabi, pay their debts and also a stiff fine.

With the Al Qasimi under Sultan bin Saqr still implacably opposed to the Sultan of Muscat and allied to the Saudis. Saeed bin Tahnun of Abu Dhabi was allied to Muscat and opposed to the Saudis. He sent a force to Muscat to support the Sultan against an Al Qasimi attack on Shinas in March 1850, consisting of some 400 Bani Yas and Manasir. At the same time, he once again raised a force against Buraimi, tearing up the *aflaj* in order to deprive the Saudi garrison of water. His position was briefly threatened by the raising of an army from Sharjah, Dubai, Ajman and Umm Al Quwain, but that force eventually (after much disagreement between the leaders) moved east to the Batinah, where it took part in fighting between the governor of Sohar and the Sultan at Muscat. The end result of this conflict was to cede Kalba and Khor Fakkan once again to Sultan bin Saqr Al Qasimi, while Dubai backed the Sultan in Muscat and recovered Sohar and Shinas for him.

Despite Saeed bin Tahnun of Abu Dhabi's continued occupation of Buraimi and the raising of a number of forces (of bewildering complexity as the alliances between the Sheikhs shifted) to annex the whole oasis, the arrival of the Saudi Ruler's son – Abdullah bin Faisal Al Saud

– in early 1853 signalled a general gathering of the Sheikhs (with the sole exception of Saeed bin Butti of Dubai) to pay tribute to the representative of the powerful Saudi state – Abdullah bin Faisal wanted to move against Sohar, supported by Sultan bin Saqr but Saeed bin Tahnun managed to arrange a negotiated peace between Sohar and the new Saudi agent, Ahmed Al Sudairi.

Dragged away by Kemball from the campfires and rich rice and meat feasts in Buraimi, the Trucial Sheikhs made their way to the coast, to sign their perpetual maritime treaty even as they plotted to undo each other inland.

The small sheikhs

Apart from the heads of the Bedouin tribes of the interior, there were a number of smaller sheikhs on the coast who had not obtained the status of 'Trucial Sheikh', a gift entirely in the hands of the British. These towns and ports were part of the landscape of shifting allegiances and occasional consolidations and break-ups of larger confederations. The northern port of Rams and its inland settlement of Dhayah were, in 1820, a sheikhdom in their own right, as indeed were the inland towns of Khatt and Falayah, although both were quickly subsumed into the greater Ras Al Khaimah under Sultan bin Saqr Al Qasimi. Jazirat Al Hamra, the traditional home to the Zaab tribe, was likewise a town under its own headman with an allegiance to Ras Al Khaimah which at times was shaky in the extreme. South of this, Umm Al Quwain fought for its independence even after its recognition as a Trucial State. Between Umm Al Quwain and Ajman lay the port and village of Hamriyah (today home to a large free trade zone on the southern side of its creek) which was claimed by Sharjah but which frequently asserted its independence. Similarly, Al Heera and Fisht to the south of Ajman and Al Khan to the south of Sharjah were claimed by Sharjah but asserted their own sovereignty at one time or another. Both Al Hamriyah and Al Heera were strongholds of the Al Bu Shams tribe (singular Al Shamsi). Abu Hail on the coast of Deira was important enough for the British to bombard in 1820 but after a brief rebellion, it subsequently passes out of history as an independent entity. Originally part of Sharjah, as was Deira itself, it slipped into the encroachment of the ever-expanding town of Dubai. The Sharjah suburbs of Al Khan and Lulayya (today the location of Sharjah's main power station) were also individual settlements, with Al Khan attempting secession from Sharjah's rule on more than one occasion.

A year after the 1853 Perpetual Maritime Peace, Hamriyah was pitched into revolt against Sharjah when 500 fighting men of the Shwaihiyin tribe arrived to live in the village. The Shwaihiyin and their families were settled there by Sultan bin Saqr of Sharjah, acting on the suggestion of the new Saudi agent in Buraimi, Ahmad Al Sudairi. Hamriyah was traditionally home to the Al Bu Shams, the group of the Na'im who had moved north from Buraimi and settled Hamriyah, Ajman and Al Heera. The Shwaihiyin had caused trouble in Sharjah town, fighting with townsfolk of the Huwala tribe, and now proceeded to cause more trouble in Hamriyah, where they talked the headman of the village, Abdulrahman bin Saif, into declaring independence from Sharjah.[6]

Kemball sallied forth from Bushire again following the pearling season in September 1854, undertaking a tour of the Trucial Coast to see how his Perpetual Maritime Truce was holding up (it was, he found, doing fairly nicely) and was promptly petitioned by Sultan bin Saqr for permission to sail against Hamriyah and bring the rebellious residents of that place back into line. Kemball, rightly concerned that Hamriyah sat between Ajman and Umm Al Quwain, asked that Sultan hold off from direct action without reference to the British Residency Agent.

Called away to Lingeh, still in Al Qasimi hands, Sultan bin Saqr left the Hamriyah affair in the hands of the Saudi Agent and Ahmad Al Sudairi lost little time, while Sultan was away, in resuming his meddling. Having precipitated the whole troublesome affair with his advice to resettle the Shwaihiyin in Hamriyah, Al Sudairi now proceeded to inflame matters with clumsy attempts at mediation and then added injury to insult when he tried to install a Saudi presence in the fort at Hamriyah.

By the time Sultan bin Saqr Al Qasimi returned, Hamriyah was at boiling point and, egged on by Al Sudairi, Sultan resolved to put an end to the rebellion. Embarking a force both by land and sea in April 1855, he enlisted the help of Ajman's Humaid bin Rashid who had acceded after his brother was killed by the people of Hamriyah and he himself was wounded. For Humaid, this was personal and he would have welcomed any excuse to move against Hamriyah, at least nominally until then under Sultan bin Saqr's protection. He threw 3,000 men into the fray – these joined Sultan's forces and also 150 levies raised from Saudi allies then in Sharjah. Sultan brought two cannon from Lingeh and two from Sharjah by sea. Humaid brought another cannon from Ajman.

The combined force mounted a siege of Hamriyah, which was defended by some 800 men. Over the next month, Sultan and his allies threw themselves at the fort but the defenders fought back heroically and the losses sustained by the attackers were something like sixty men killed to just ten of the defending force. Of those killed, Sultan bin Saqr Al Qasimi lost his own son, the governor of Sharjah, Abdullah bin Sultan Al Qasimi.

At this point, on 31 May 1855, Captain Kemball arrived on board the *Clive* to find that Sultan had ignored him entirely. Protesting that he had, indeed, sent a letter to Kemball outlining his intentions, Sultan bin Saqr appealed to the Resident to mediate in a dispute which had so far been a disastrous affair all round for the Al Qasimi Ruler – and undoubtedly a source of some glee for Dubai and Umm Al Quwain. In fact, the latter overtly supported Hamriyah's claims, a move which threatened to derail Kemball's attempt to seek a deal and forced him to eventually fall back on a strict interpretation of his Perpetual Maritime Truce and threaten to cut off Hamriyah's supply line from the sea. The rebels collapsed and agreed to submit to Sultan bin Saqr and pay 500 dollars in token of their submission. The Shwaihiyin agreed to quit Hamriyah at the end of the year's pearling season and the peace was overseen by the British Residency agent, Haji Yacoub.

The affair at Hamriyah would have been just another spat in the tumultuous history of the Trucial Coast if it had not resulted in the death of Abdullah bin Sultan Al Qasimi. When the dust had died down, the village returned to normal life and, later that year the Shwaihiyin would have made their homes once again in Sharjah town. But Sharjah had lost its governor – actually, effectively its Ruler, as Sultan bin Saqr had increasingly allowed both Sharjah, under Abdullah bin Sultan Al Qasimi, and Ras Al Khaimah, under Ibrahim bin Sultan Al Qasimi, to be ruled by his sons in his name.

By now 74 years of age – a remarkable age given the conditions of the time – Sultan bin Saqr Al Qasimi was no longer the giant he had been as a young man. Increasingly short of sight and hard of hearing, he was still titular head of the Al Qasimi, but his hold on power – once a fierce and fearsome grip – was relaxing. A grandson of Sultan's, Muhammad bin Saqr, assumed the leadership of Sharjah but his rule was contested by one of Sultan's sons, Khalid bin Sultan and the town was split between the two contestants and their supporting factions. This unstable arrangement persisted throughout 1859 and 1860, but at the turn of the year Khalid invited Mohammed to ride with him out into the desert, where he killed him.

Khalid sought British recognition of his status as Ruler of Sharjah, but the Resident refused to converse 'with one so recently and fearfully polluted'.[7] Quite apart from being shunned by British fastidiousness, Khalid would, in time, receive his come-uppance.

Rebellion in the mountains

The rebellion of Hamriyah was not the only insurrection faced by Sultan bin Saqr in 1855. The Shihuh, those fierce mountain warriors who had already made clear that they did not accept Al Qasimi suzerainty, once again rebelled against Ras Al Khaimah. Sultan's grandson Mashari bin Ibrahim Al Qasimi (the son of the Ruler of Ras Al Khaimah) was the governor of Dibba and reportedly ruled with a very heavy hand – so much so that the Shihuh, pushed beyond endurance, rose up and killed him one day as he travelled from Dibba to visit Ras Al Khaimah.[8] Sultan bin Saqr raised a force from his dependencies of Abu Hail, Al Khan, Sharjah, Al Heera and Fisht and they joined forces with men from Ras Al Khaimah and marched overland to Dibba. Sultan bin Saqr himself, meanwhile, took to the sea with a fleet of 100 boats and the men of the Zaab tribe of Jazirat Al Hamra. The army was unable to force its way through the mountain tracks (presumably trying to cross through the precipitous heights and high-walled gorges of the Wadi Bih) and was eventually embarked from Ras Al Khaimah to Dibba by sea.[9]

The battle around Dibba escalated, with the Shihuh of Musandam joining in and taking to the sea to harry the Al Qasimi boats, while the Al Qasimi attacked the Shihuh wherever they encountered them (including the killing of eight men and the seizure of a Shihuh batil at Khor Fakkan). In January 1857, the British Resident at Bushire intervened to stop what was, effectively, a huge breach of the Maritime Peace. Sultan bin Saqr argued that he was within his rights to repress his rebellious subjects, even escalating his argument to Bombay. The result of all this was a tour of the region by the British Resident, who visited Bukha, Khasab, Kumzar and other settlements in the Rus Al Jibal in 1859 in a steamship, a leviathan novelty which caused a great deal of consternation among the awed populace. The Resident secured the release of a number of Al Qasimi prisoners from the Shihuh but also came away from his tour with the firm belief that the Shihuh considered themselves to be subjects of the Sultan of Muscat and harboured an implacable and irreconcilable hatred for the Al Qasimi and their kind. As a consequence, subsequent disagreements involving the Shihuh were to be handed to the British Resident at Muscat to decide and the area remains Omani to this day – the rather odd-seeming Omani exclave of the Musandam Peninsular can trace its origin to 1855 and the conflict between Sultan bin Saqr and the Shihuh.

A sanguinary footnote to this conflict was the discovery by the British Resident of a wanted pirate who had fled Dubai to his home in Khasab and who was subsequently arrested and handed over to the Sultan of Muscat, who in May 1859 had the man 'blown from a gun'.[10]

As the 1860s progressed, Sultan bin Saqr's rule increasingly became in name only, and his sons ruled Sharjah and Ras Al Khaimah effectively independently. And, in 1866, at the ripe old age of 85, Sultan passed away quietly in his sleep.

Subsequent events were to be anything but quiet.

News of Sultan's death travelled to the east, where the headman of Fujairah, Abdullah bin Khamis, stopped paying tribute to Sharjah and the Sharqiyin of the Shamaliyah (the east coast north of Kalba through to Dibba, with the exception of the Naqbiyin at Khor Fakkan) as well as the Shihuh no longer recognised the authority of their Al Qasimi rulers.

Sultan's son and the Ruler of Sharjah, Khalid bin Sultan Al Qasimi, now considered himself to be the ruler of all the Al Qasimi towns. As Ruler of Sharjah under his father, Khalid had already made clear his ambitions towards the north. Khaled had already killed his rival for the rule of Sharjah, his cousin Mohammed. With his father in his dotage, Khalid had sallied forth in 1865 to construct a fort at Al Zorah, between Ajman and Hamriyah. This endeavour was effected with Saudi support, Khalid having accepted the guidance of the Saudi Agent, Turki bin Ahmad Al Sudairi. The move horrified Al Zorah's neighbours and the British agreed that a Saudi-backed fort to the north was a bad idea. In January 1866, HMS *Highflyer* bombarded the fort and destroyed it.[11]

Sultan bin Saqr's death would give Khalid the northern foothold he so desired, handing him control over Ras Al Khaimah as well as over Sharjah. However, Khalid's opinion of his pre-eminence was contested by Ibrahim bin Sultan Al Qasimi, the governor of Ras Al Khaimah. A son of Sultan's by a wife of the Maraziq (singular Al Marzouki) tribe – Ibrahim had ruled Ras Al Khaimah as governor in his father's name from some time before 1860.

Now he declared independence from Khalid in Sharjah, the first time that the two Al Qasimi towns were split. Khalid promptly pulled together an army and marched against Ras Al Khaimah before the 1867 pearling season, taking the town in May of that year and putting Ibrahim to flight – despite an attempt by Ibrahim to appeal to the Saudis for assistance.[12]

Now, for the first time, the Al Qasimi Federation was ruled from Sharjah, not Ras Al Khaimah.[13]

Two giants

Sultan bin Saqr Al Qasimi's passing marked the end of a remarkable life which had straddled – and shaped – much of the 1800s in the Trucial States. Relentless, ambitious and driven, Sultan bin Saqr had enjoyed a career of remarkable highs and lows – he had lost everything and been a dispossessed and penniless prisoner in Riyadh, escaping only to throw himself on the mercy of his life-long bitter enemy, the Sultan of Muscat, and then finally finding himself restored at the whim of the British, who had discovered in him a man with whom they thought they could do business, following the sack of Ras Al Khaimah in 1819.

Sultan bin Saqr established his primacy over territories formerly claimed by Oman along the east coast, including Dibba, Khor Fakkan, Fujairah and Kalba. He had warred incessantly with his neighbours and jostled for primacy among the Sheikhs of the powerful interior tribes. His influence over the affairs of the area is still felt today – it was the tumultuous rule of Sultan bin Saqr that gave shape to much of what we now recognise as the Emirate of Sharjah.

Even as Sultan was being bent double by old age, his sight and hearing fading and his faculties deserting him, another force was growing in Abu Dhabi. As so often is the case, Sultan left behind him small men who were not equal to the task he had undertaken and his realm fragmented and fell to internecine squabbling even as another star rose. The Al Qasimi Federation was never to recover the stature it achieved under Sultan bin Saqr. But the Bani Yas were already flourishing under a new giant: Zayed bin Khalifa Al Nahyan – Zayed the Great.

Chapter 18

THE RISE OF THE TRIBES AND ZAYED THE GREAT

"His name is Zayed the Great. His father Khalifa died when he was seven years old and he was young, a real horseman and a great marksman."

– *Mohammed bin Rashid Al Maktoum*

Sheikh Saeed bin Tahnun Al Nahyan ruled Abu Dhabi and its interior for ten years, from 1845 to 1855. Having inherited the allegiance of the principal tribes of Buraimi from his predecessor, Khalifa bin Shakhbut, probably Saeed's greatest achievement was to bring those tribes together to wrest the Al Ain oasis from the control of the Saudi Agent, Saad bin Mutlaq. Collecting the Dhawahir and Awamir, he took control of the two principal forts in the oasis in 1848, placing the Bani Qitab, Ghafalah, and Awamir at Khatam and gathering the Manasir and Mazari Bani Yas from Liwa at Dhafra to block Saad bin Mutlaq's relieving army. It was a decisive strategic victory.[1]

Saeed's rule and his triumph over the Saudis at Buraimi, was cut short by murder. A senior member of the Bani Yas killed his own brother, an act which appeared to have had the broad support of the family. Although Saeed had pronounced the death penalty on the murderer, his decision was clearly highly unpopular and he subsequently announced that he would forgive the killer. However, when the man was brought into Saeed's presence, the Ruler stepped forward and lunged at him, stabbing the miscreant to death.

Saeed's action was disastrously unpopular and the Bani Yas rose against him, pinning him down in his fort until, recognising that all was lost, he fled to exile on the island of Kish.[2]

The Bani Yas now selected a successor to Saeed, unanimously appointing Saeed's cousin, Zayed bin Khalifa Al Nahyan, to rule them. It was to be a momentous decision.

Zayed's first experience of the British on his accession in 1855 was to find himself being held responsible for an attack by two Abu Dhabi boats on a Bahraini boat which had taken shelter from a storm in the inlet of Khor Al Udaid, an event that had resulted in the death of one of the Bahraini sailors. This incident had taken place during Sheikh Saeed bin Tahnun's rule (Saeed had, in fact, told the British that he been deposed because he had enforced justice on the two boat's captains rather than relating the story of stabbing the family killer) and Zayed initially refused liability for it, but eventually was prevailed upon to pay 600 Maria Theresa thalers in blood money and to burn the two offending baggalas.[3]

In July 1856, Sheikh Saeed bin Tahnun Al Nahyan attempted to return to Abu Dhabi, sailing from his exile on Kish via Sharjah, at the height of the pearling season, with a force of three vessels. He landed at Abu Dhabi on 19 July and met up with a number of Bedouin allies and then proceeded to sack the town – Zayed bin Khalifa was in Dhafra at the time and his brother Dhiyab led the few townspeople to the fort, Qasr Al Hosn, where they barricaded themselves in against the violent intruders.

Zayed rode back together with a contingent of Bedouin, falling on the invaders and scattering them totally in a battle at Maqta. Saeed bin Tahnun and his brother Hamdan were both killed in the fighting.

For allowing the attack to be launched against Abu Dhabi from his territory, the Ruler of Sharjah, Sultan bin Saqr Al Qasimi, was held responsible by the British for the damage inflicted by the outrage on Abu Dhabi and was forced to pay a huge fine of 25,000 Maria Theresa thalers, the last instalment of which was finally made four years later, in May 1860.

In 1851, a peace between Bahrain and the Saudis resulted in the Ruler of Bahrain retaining Qatar (having lost Dammam to the expansionist Saudi Ruler, Faisal bin Turki Al Saud) but owing fealty to the Saudis. By the 1860s, his Qatari subjects were becoming restive and he enlisted the help of Zayed bin Khalifa of Abu Dhabi in an attack on the towns of Doha and Wakrah in October 1867. Zayed sent some 2,000 armed men in a fleet of eighty boats.[4] Both Qatari towns were effectively demolished and their populations scattered.

Part of the reason the attack on Qatar was at all successful was that the British at this time were suffering from the reform of the Bombay Marine: the Indian Navy was disbanded and responsibility for naval patrols passed to the Admiralty,[5] causing British policy in the Gulf at the time to descend into a period of near-chaos. However, the British eventually waded in to settle the dispute and seek redress from Bahrain, deposing the Bahraini Ruler in the process and imposing a large fine. Zayed was also made to pay reparations for his part in the attack.[6] The fine levied on Abu Dhabi was enforced by a British squadron under the Political Resident at Bushire, Lewis Pelly. Pelly also confiscated Zayed's three cannon, although these were restored when it was clear they would have left Abu Dhabi defenceless in the face of Bedouin raids.[7]

Not only did his action against Qatar cost Zayed dear (although the Ruler of Bahrain had indemnified him from any payment of damages the British might extract), it also heralded a new migration by the Qubaisat, who in 1869 once again fled Abu Dhabi and set themselves up at Khor Al Udaid.

Zayed's feud with Sharjah rumbled on in the background and eventually, in April 1868, Zayed found himself forced to raise an army and march to meet an attacking force moving south from Sharjah to threaten Abu Dhabi. In one of the most striking acts of his long and turbulent rule, Zayed rode out ahead of his army to face the Sharjah force and demanded that Khalid bin Sultan, the Ruler of Sharjah, meet him in single combat. Trapped by this call to his honour, arguably tainted by the killing that led to his succession, Khalid agreed to the challenge and was cut down by Zayed, dying of his wounds on 14 April 1868.[8]

Khalid arguably got his just desserts. And Zayed the Great started to write his legend.

Sharjah aflame

In the meantime, the Trucial Coast was once again in a state of flux and conflict. The whole coast and the tribes of the interior now conspired to fling mounted forces of Bedouin at each other, attacking towns and desert encampments alike. Alliances shifted, as they so often did, with bewildering speed and enmities were buried with shocking alacrity if any gain could be had as a result.

For a start, Zayed's killing of Khalid bin Sultan Al Qasimi on the battlefield left a power vacuum in both Sharjah and Ras Al Khaimah. Acceding to rule Sharjah in 1868 was Salim bin Sultan Al Qasimi, a son of Sultan bin Saqr. At the same time, Humaid bin Abdullah Al Qasimi, Salim's nephew, took over the rule of Ras Al Khaimah and promptly declared himself independent, a status he maintained from his declaration in 1869 until his death in 1900.

Humaid soon found himself in his Uncle Salim's crosshairs, likely through no fault of his own. The Saudi agent in Buraimi, Turki bin Ahmad, visited Sharjah and immediately (and unwisely, it was a Gordian knot to take on) started to involve himself in Al Qasimi politics – he attempted to instigate a plot whereby Salim bin Sultan of Sharjah would be imprisoned and his brother Ibrahim bin Sultan made Ruler of Ras Al Khaimah, over Salim's nephew Humaid.

The familial infighting that followed was a period of bewildering change, shifting alliances and an internecine battle for supremacy that marks one of the most confusing and turbulent periods in the history of the Northern Emirates. Ibrahim bin Sultan was formerly deputy Ruler of Ras Al Khaimah under his father and had got himself into hot water with the British, having been fined for petty piracies (a fine exacted after the arrival of a handy British gunboat in Ras Al Khaimah to enforce it) back in 1860. He had been removed from Ras Al Khaimah by Khalid bin Sultan in 1867 and sent into exile. Now, on Khalid's death, he clearly felt he, and not Humaid, should be Ruler of Ras Al Khaimah but was powerless to act against Humaid. The Saudi scheme would, as he would have seen it, restore him to his rightful position.[9]

Under the Saudi agent's plan, Humaid bin Abdullah would be, for his part, made Ruler of Sharjah. Whether this attempt to remove Salim for the benefit of Humaid was because of Wahhabi fastidiousness at Salim's mother's humble origins we will never know and the plot failed miserably in any case: the Saudi Agent's actions triggered a general affray in Sharjah town and the Agent was himself promptly shot and killed in the ensuing unrest. Salim bin Sultan now sought to defer the wrath of the Saudi Ruler and agreed that Sharjah would be ruled by Ibrahim in name – although this scheme was soon abandoned when it was clear that Riyadh couldn't have cared less about the fate of its Agent and any personal vendetta the man had pursued against Salim. Consequently, Salim bin Sultan once again assumed the rule of Sharjah and Humaid bin Abdullah remained Ruler of Ras Al Khaimah.

Soon after, in May 1869, Salim and Ibrahim moved together against Humaid bin Abdullah with the intention of removing him and installing Ibrahim as Ruler of Ras Al Khaimah. The two landed at Ras Al Khaimah town with a force of some 1,500 men shipped in thirty-two boats.

Humaid bin Abdullah for his part was reinforced by 500 men landed from his ally, Umm Al Quwain, and fighting took place both at Jazirat Al Hamra and in Ras Al Khaimah town proper. The British Resident, Lewis Pelly, on hearing of this breach of the Maritime Truce (the embarkation of troops by sea breached the treaty) sailed from Lingeh in the *Dalhousie* with the gunboat *Hugh Rose* accompanying. Arriving at Ras Al Khaimah on 12 May 1869, Pelly ordered Salim and Ibrahim to withdraw their forces from Ras Al Khaimah by sunset the next day.[10]

Alliances shifted quickly, however, and in 1871 Humaid bin Abdullah Al Qasimi, together with the Ruler of Umm Al Quwain, supported Salim bin Sultan Al Qasimi when Salim's brother Ibrahim, effectively sidelined by Salim and bilked by the British of his expectation of rule over Ras Al Khaimah, decided that he now wanted to assert his rights over Sharjah.

Ibrahim became increasingly troublesome and so Salim took advantage of Ibrahim's absence on a journey to Abu Dhabi and cemented his ascendancy by asserting his total control of Sharjah with the help of Humaid bin Abdullah and their mutual neighbour – and Humaid's ally – Umm Al Quwain.

At the same time, Humaid bin Abdullah took the opportunity of a general mobilisation to retake the village dependencies of Sha'am, Rams and Shimal, which had managed to sneakily secede from his rule. Humaid not only managed to retain his control over Ras Al Khaimah, but also to expand his area of influence.

The fight over Ras Al Khaimah may have been over, but it was to spark resentments and yet more shifting alliances and was to blossom into a conflagration throughout the Trucial States.

The Ruler of Umm Al Quwain at this time was Ali bin Abdullah Al Mualla, whose rule spanned the time between the Perpetual Maritime Peace (signed in 1853 by Abdullah bin Rashid, Ali's father) and his death in 1873. Following the attempt to remove Humaid from his rule of Ras Al Khaimah and the cementing of Salim bin Sultan Al Qasimi's rule in Sharjah, Ali bin Abdullah appears to have thought better of his support for Sharjah's Ruler and settled into a state of enmity with Salim bin Sultan, even while he remained allied with Humaid bin Abdullah of Ras Al Khaimah. One area of contention between Umm Al Quwain and Sharjah was the island of Abu Musa, claimed by both rulers. Ali bin Abdullah sent a number of boats to the island to seize Salim bin Sultan's herd of horses but was met by a force of Sharjah boats. The conflict continued to smoulder and Ajman joined with Sharjah, while Hamriyah (always keen to take action against Sharjah), backed Umm Al Quwain.

Abu Dhabi and Dubai were at odds at this time over disputes involving fleeing debtors, but it was Abu Dhabi who joined in the northern dispute first, backing the alliance against Salim bin Sultan of Sharjah and in 1873 Zayed bin Khalifa's forces fell upon Sharjah, killing fifty men. In a kaleidoscopic shift of alliances in 1874, Ras Al Khaimah joined with Sharjah against Ali bin Abdulla of Umm Al Quwain and Dubai threw its hat into the ring supporting Ali. It was all too much for Hamriyah, which now withdrew from its alliance with Umm Al Quwain.

Dubai attacked Ras Al Khaimah, a raiding party of some 200 men killing seven in a foray against Ras Al Khaimah town. The headman of Hamriyah, Saif bin Abdulrahman, now attempted to take a role as mediator between the warring Sheikhs. By 1875, he'd clearly given up his brief career in diplomacy and Hamriyah declared itself yet again independent from Sharjah.

The conflict between Sharjah and Dubai blazed on, however, and in May 1875, a combined force from Sharjah and Ajman together with Bedouin riders from the Na'im, attacked Dubai. By July, anarchy prevailed: Abu Dhabi threw a force of 200 riders against Hamriyah. This force then combined with a party from Dubai and raided the villages and date groves of the Sharjah dependencies of Al Heera and Fisht.

Just as suddenly as the descent into war had taken place, peace now broke out. In September 1875 Dubai and Sharjah negotiated an armistice. It was unusual that this would take place at the end of the pearling season – most peace agreements took place in time to commence the annual voyages to the pearl banks. The war had clearly cost all of the Rulers of the west coast dearly in terms of disruption to their respective pearling fleets.

A shifting mountain of debt

If it was pearling that often brought about peace between squabbling neighbours, it was also frequently the cause of conflict in the first place. Although the 1853 Perpetual Maritime Peace had all but eliminated maritime disputes escalating into violence, the pearl banks still held the power to engender quarrels that would fester and smoulder until something gave way and a dispute ensued.

Abu Dhabi and Dubai had fallen out on a number of occasions over the issue of absconding debtors and this was also the case with the other Trucial States: Abu Dhabi's Qubaisat tribe was in the habit of making for Khor Al Udaid when their debts mounted, but many individuals took to taking shelter in a neighbouring emirate when their debts became too onerous. Not infrequently, these debtors would be the captains of pearling ships who, for instance, had a bad season. The fleeing debtor, bringing one or more pearling boats (albeit with a dose of bad luck) with him, would be an economic gain for the Ruler giving him safe harbour.

The cycle would be the same each time: the debtor would abscond and seek the protection of a Ruler who was for one reason or another estranged from or competing with another Ruler. The home Ruler would, already for whatever reason aggrieved, demand restitution which the other Ruler would deny and they would then frequently come to blows or undertake other punitive actions against each other until things escalated into violence.

The British now set out to enshrine a solution to this issue with a new treaty and so, on 25 June 1879, an agreement for the 'mutual surrender of fraudulently absconding debtors' was concluded by the Trucial Rulers together with the British Residency Agent in Sharjah, Haji Abdulrahman and the Residency Munshi who had been sent from Bushire to ensure the treaty was understood and accepted by all. It imposed a fine of fifty dollars on any Ruler harbouring a debtor, which rose to 100 dollars if the debtor took to the seas for the pearling season. Any dispute would be settled by the Ruler's *majlis* and no fine would be exacted without the approval of the British Resident.[11]

This wasn't the only modification to the 1853 Perpetual Maritime Peace: in 1856 a codicil was added for the suppression of the slave trade and in 1864 an additional article provided protection for the British telegraph line and its associated outstations.

The 1864 codicil was the result of Persian intransigence. The British wanted to lay a telegraph cable to connect their empire and, in 1862, the Indo-European Telegraph Department was formed, but its scheme to lay a cable from India to connect with Europe via the Gulf was foiled when the Persians refused permission for the cable. Following a survey, it was decided to place a repeater station in the waterway of Khor Ash Sham, at the tip of the Musandam Peninsular. This would support the hop to Gwadar on the Indian coast (now part of Pakistan, but at that time a tributary of Oman) and then on to Karachi.

The cable was in use only briefly, from 1865 until the end of 1868, when it was abandoned in favour of a new line between Aden and Bombay.

'Telegraph Island' can still be visited today, sitting off Khasab in what is now known as the Elphinstone Inlet. The remains of the telegraph station are there, a memory of the brief time when this place had any use other than as a reef around which curious fish darted. Today tours take guests out to play with the dolphins and visit the island where, local guides will assure you, the phrase 'going around the bend' was derived from the pairs of British telegraph operators, who regularly went mad waiting for the next six-monthly supply vessel to 'come around the bend' past Khasab and relieve them of the sheer monotony of their isolated, boiling hot posting and the desperate monotony of each other's company.

The story is in all probability apocryphal, but it is honestly too good not to report.

However, the impact of the 1879 agreement was perhaps the most far-reaching of all of these codicils, because it established the principle of criminalising debt and making indebtedness a matter for the authorities (in those days, the Ruler, his *majlis* and the British Residency Agent) to decide, rather than a civil court. That principle persisted in the UAE beyond independence and still remains enshrined in UAE Federal Law today.

Buraimi restored

The death in Sharjah of the interfering Saudi Agent in 1869 led directly to the retaking of Buraimi by the Omani Imam, Azzan bin Qais Al Busaidi, but the area was dominated by the influence of Abu Dhabi and its tribes mostly considered themselves to be allied to the Bani Yas. A notable exception to this was the Na'im, who were in a state of almost perpetual war with the Bani Yas of Abu Dhabi with a number of raids being carried out by mounted forces of both tribes. The Na'im were generally subordinate to Muscat (itself generally allied to the Bani Yas), but then alliances in the region were always subject to shifts and the Na'im had also been known to ally with the Saudis.

Omani politics, as it had so often done in the past, now threatened to dominate the life of the Trucial States. Buraimi may well have been taken by Azzan bin Qais, but Azzan himself was involved in a fight for ascendancy over Oman with the Sultan of Muscat, Turki bin Said. The conflict between Sultan and Imam, as ever in Oman, raged throughout the interior.

Zayed bin Khalifa of Abu Dhabi supported Imam Azzan bin Qais, who paid Abu Dhabi a stipend for its defence of Buraimi, but Sultan Turki bin Said now went looking for support for his cause from other Trucial Rulers and in 1870 Turki visited Dubai with that goal in mind. However tempted the other Trucial Sheikhs may have been to support Turki against Abu Dhabi, it was not enough to support feet on the ground. Although Azzan bin Qais saw the Ghafiri northern emirates as being Wahhabi in nature and therefore supportive of his enemies the Saudis, Sharjah (presumably to his surprised delight) joined the alliance between him and Abu Dhabi against Muscat's Turki bin Said.[12]

However, in October 1870, Turki bin Said took his forces to the field in the Battle of Dhank, supported by men from Dubai, Ajman and Ras Al Khaimah, as well as riders from the Na'im and Bani Qitab.

Winning that battle, Turki cemented his ascendancy as Sultan over Muscat and Oman. Azzan bin Qais was eventually killed in battle at Mutrah in January 1871.

The Battle of Dhank resulted in Oman having a single ruler across both the interior and coast for the first time in centuries and was to cement Busaidi rule over the whole Sultanate. But it did nothing to lessen the relentless jostling of the tribes around Buraimi and Zayed bin Khalifa's ambitions to hold the fertile oasis, following on from the Saudi withdrawal from the area in 1871, only grew with time. This culminated in January 1875 in an attack made by Zayed against the Na'im town of Dhank and the area south of the town, the Dhahirah, by a mounted force of 200 Manasir and Bani Hajir Bedouins. At the same time, Zayed sent a force of Manasir and Mazari against Buraimi, an act which led to the Bani Qitab applying to Dubai for assistance and a force of riders being sent from Dubai to Buraimi. This resulted in a standoff and Zayed suspended his operations against the oasis, biding his time until, two years later, he was to act with decisive force.

The Eastern insurgency

As Zayed bin Khalifa focused on expanding his fiefdom, Sharjah's Ruler, Salim bin Sultan Al Qasimi, was trying to defend his rapidly collapsing authority. With Hamriyah effectively independent and Ras Al Khaimah now confirmed as existing entirely without recourse to Salim bin Sultan's authority, he now faced further trouble from his eastern holdings: the Sharqiyin tribe of the Shamaliyah.

Fujairah, under its Sharqiyin (singular Al Sharqi) headman Abdullah bin Khamis Al Sharqi, stopped paying tribute to Sharjah when Sultan bin Saqr, the great Al Qasimi leader, died. Sultan's son Khalid ruled for two short and turbulent years and clearly had little time to concern himself with the distant Shamaliyah, the north east coast, but his successor, Salim bin Sultan Al Qasimi, attempted to bring the area back under control, first sending an army to take Dibba.

In the meantime, the Sharqiyin had taken the trouble to form an alliance with their fierce cousins in the northern mountains, the Shihuh, who had little reason to love the Al Qasimi rulers and who considered themselves in any case to be subjects of the Sultan of Muscat.[13]

When Salim's army appeared out of the Wadi Abadilah to gallop across the great plain leading down to the sea that is Dibba's hinterland, the Seih Dibba, they had no idea they were headed for disaster but on entering the town found themselves almost instantly besieged by the Sharqiyin arrayed together with the Shihuh. Reinforcements were blocked from reaching Dibba through the mountain passes by forces of Shihuh, who were well versed in their terrain and dominated the region's wadi crossings and tracks. Suing for peace, the Al Qasimi force was lucky to emerge from the affair not only alive, but with a promise from the Sharqiyin to pay tribute to Sharjah – a victory literally wrested from the jaws of defeat.

A few years later, in 1876, the Al Qasimi governor of Dibba triggered another insurrection when he imprisoned twelve of the Sharqiyin. Again, an alliance between the tribes of the coast and mountains was made and Salim bin Sultan found himself blocked from sending men and material to relieve Dibba. Applying to the British for permission to send forces by sea, Salim was rebuffed[14] but nevertheless, he embarked a force of fifty men to relieve Dibba.[15]

The arrival of HMS *Arab* at Dibba to enforce the Maritime Treaty brought a ceasefire, but Salim had sent a force of some 800 fighting men through one of the southern mountain crossings, likely passing through the Wadi Hatta to emerge north of Shinas – a crossing of the southern Hajar Mountains that wasn't in Shihuh hands. They would have passed through the coastal villages of Kalba and Rugaylat, impressing on the local population that they were, indeed, to consider themselves Al Qasimi subjects before they took Fujairah Fort, situated inland of what was then known as Ghurfa, (today an area in central Fujairah marked by a post office, a mosque as well as lots of towers, houses and other buildings), killing thirty-six and capturing thirty of the fort's defenders.

There was now an argument over whether Salim had broken the Maritime Treaty, with the argument being made that because the action was against the east coast, it didn't count. A ruling was made, finally, in 1880, that the east coast was subject to the Treaty. Salim appears to have escaped the customary fine for breaching the treaty in recognition of the lack of precedent.

In 1879, the Shamaliyah rose again, overthrowing a slave by the name of Sarur who had been placed as Wali of Fujairah by Salim bin Sultan Al Qasimi. This rebellion was followed by sending a delegation to Sharjah to explain their actions to Salim, who responded by imprisoning the members of the delegation and sending a force overland to retake Fujairah and garrison its fort with Baluchi mercenaries.

This action sent the headman of Fujairah, Hamad bin Abdullah Al Sharqi, into exile to Muscat where he attempted to enlist the assistance of the Sultan Turki bin Saeed who, although minded to act in support of Hamad, was reminded by the British that Fujairah was recognised Al Qasimi territory and that he had signed a document, in 1871, ceding the coast from Kalba to Sharjah (but with the exception of Khasab) to the Al Qasimi.

Although Hamad gained no material aid from Turki bin Saeed, he used his time in exile to regroup and, at the end of 1879, he returned to Fujairah by sea and led a new uprising, which marched against the fort and drove out the Al Qasimi occupiers after fierce fighting in which eight of the fort's garrison were killed.

The fate of Hamad bin Abdullah Al Sharqi and his people now hung in the balance as the British, the Sultan of Muscat and the Ruler of Sharjah wrangled over the legal position, with Ras Al Khaimah being brought in to mediate. British opinion of the time was that Fujairah's independence was not desirable and so, in 1881, Hamad bin Abdullah accepted the suzerainty of Sharjah and agreed to pay tribute to Salim bin Sultan.

This was clearly little more than lip service. Hamad bin Abdullah would soon be once again fighting for independence for his people.

War with Qatar

Even as the Al Qasimi federation was coming apart at the seams, Zayed bin Khalifa's consolidation of Abu Dhabi's power and influence was now shaping the southern areas of the Trucial States. Zayed wasn't only interested in tightening his grip on Buraimi, relentlessly buying up the lush oases of the area every time an opportunity to acquire land arose, but was also committed to securing his western border, where Khor Al Udaid had sheltered a number of secessionists from Abu Dhabi over the years. The inlet sits today just astride the Qatari-Saudi border, some 100 kilometres west of Sir Bani Yas Island. Although each of the attempts to secede, mostly on the part of the Qubaisat tribe of Abu Dhabi, had eventually failed, Khor Al Udaid was definitely on Zayed bin Khalifa's radar.

The expansion of the Ottoman empire into the Gulf had resulted in the Eastern Saudi territory of Al Hasa (whose capital today is the town of Hofuf) falling into Ottoman hands and now the Bani Yas at Khor Al Udaid, mostly the remnants of the Qubaisat, found themselves offered an Ottoman flag to fly. A subsequent British investigation found that the small population at Khor Al Udaid hoisted a Trucial or Ottoman flag as the occasion demanded. However, in 1878, the British moved to punish the community at Khor Al Udaid for acts of maritime aggression and the Qubaisat moved back to Abu Dhabi in 1880, abandoning Khor Al Udaid. The Ruler of Qatar, Jasim Al Thani, considered them to be his subjects and demanded reparations for the abandonment of the town. A number of raids followed this and Zayed prepared for war with Qatar, but the Saudi Ruler mediated and the threat of conflict abated.

By 1885, however, Jasim Al Thani was continuing to press his case for reparations from the Qubaisat and he now commenced a number of raids against Abu Dhabi territory, including one particularly daring exploit against Liwa in March 1888 which saw Qatari raiders seize no fewer than 400 camels and also savagely beat twenty of the inhabitants of the oasis. Zayed retaliated with a raid against Doha itself – 250 riders under Zayed's son Khalifa killed thirty-four of the townspeople, including Jasim's son, Ali.[16]

Jasim was infuriated and cast around him for any alliance or support he could raise against Zayed, but merely obtained muted expressions of sympathy. Himself an Ottoman subject, Jasim's appeals to the Sublime Porte to invade the Trucial States on his behalf fell on deaf ears and his subsidies, offered to tribes and Trucial Rulers alike, couldn't buy him allies willing to stand against Abu Dhabi's fierce leader. In February 1889, Jasim's forces once again raided Liwa, his men cutting down date groves and killing a number of men, women and children.

Raid and counter-raid now became a constant between the two territories, developing into a slow-burning conflict of attrition.

Conflict on the coast

Following the settlement of the peace between Sharjah and Dubai, a brief period of welcome quiet descended on the area, and the 1876 pearling season saw not only peace at sea, but relative peace on land, too. However, from 1877 onwards, a number of raids took place across the Trucial States, shattering the brief harmony and often pitting the well-armed tribes of the interior against lightly defended coastal communities.

After raids by the Awamir and Duru on Dubai and the Bani Qitab on Abu Dhabi in 1877 resulted in significant loss of life on both sides, a peace was arranged. A brief period ensued where a conflict between different groups of the Na'im tribe embroiled Sharjah and Ajman, with Abu Dhabi lining up behind Sharjah and Ras Al Khaimah and Umm Al Quwain supporting Ajman. The affair petered out without conflict, but in 1882, a quarrel between Ahmad bin Abdullah Al Mualla of Umm Al Quwain and Humaid bin Abdullah Al Qasimi of Ras Al Khaimah broke out into open conflict. Umm Al Quwain's Ruler was censured by the British and forced to pay a fine after he breached the Maritime Peace with a raid against the northern port of Rams carried out by seven Umm Al Quwain boats. Fighting on land now took place, with Ajman backing Umm Al Quwain against Sharjah and members of the Na'im backing Ras Al Khaimah. Zayed bin Khalifa of Abu Dhabi mediated and the affair was eventually closed.

By this time, Zayed bin Khalifa was broadly recognised to be the principal amongst the Rulers of the Trucial States, wielding considerable influence over the tribes of the interior and commanding the loyalty of key Bedouin groupings beyond the Bani Yas core. His authority had waxed while that of Sharjah, which previously, under Sultan bin Saqr, had most certainly been the principal mover among the emirates, had waned. Sharjah's decline under first Khalid bin Sultan Al Qasimi (killed in hand to hand combat by Zayed) and then Salim bin Sultan Al Qasimi continued under its new Ruler, Saqr bin Khalid Al Qasimi, while Dubai now emerged as the principal trading port of the Trucial Coast – a role which Ras Al Khaimah had fulfilled since the heyday of Julfar, which was a key link in the chain of Arab trade from China through Hormuz and Julfar to Europe.

Saqr bin Khalid Al Qasimi of Sharjah came to power through a coup at the end of March 1883, replacing his unpopular Uncle, Salim bin Sultan Al Qasimi while the latter was on the island of Abu Musa, where he kept a herd of horses at grass – apparently the envy of other Sheikhs, as evidenced by Ali bin Abdullah Al Mualla of Umm Al Quwain's attempt to appropriate them. With Salim stranded on the island and his brother Ahmed away visiting Abu Dhabi, Saqr moved on the town of Sharjah and was quickly recognised as Ruler by the Sheikhs of the coast as well as the Na'im and Bani Qitab of the interior.[17]

Salim bin Sultan was exiled to Dubai, where an arrangement was made for him to be paid a pension by Saqr bin Khalid. However, this fell through and, in 1884, another arrangement was concluded in Ajman. Salim continued to intrigue for his restoration, but never managed to find quite enough support for his cause and, despite Saqr bin Khalid being regarded as an ineffectual ruler, Salim was eventually persuaded to be bound over to keep the peace and accept an appointment as Wali to Saqr.

The secessionist town of Hamriyah was a particular thorn in Saqr bin Khalid's side and he seized the opportunity to assert his dominance there when Mohammed bin Abdulrahman, the brother of Hamriyah's headman, Saif bin Abdulrahman, appeared to be amenable to acknowledging Saqr as his Ruler. This seemed to be too good a chance to waste and so, in April 1884, Saqr called Saif bin Abdulrahman to attend a meeting with him in Sharjah. Once Saif had left Hamriyah, Saqr sent Saif's brother to rule Hamriyah in Saif's place and in Saqr's name. The cunning plan was executed brilliantly until Saif bin Abdulrahman, returning to Hamriyah following his meeting with Saqr, promptly expelled Mohammed.

Saqr bin Khalid's attention was briefly snatched away from Hamriyah by affairs in Ras Al Khaimah. In December 1885, Saqr helped his cousin Humaid bin Abdullah Al Qasimi to reassert his control over the northern village of Sha'am (extorting, in the process, a 1,600-dollar fine from the independently minded community). They were assisted in this by boats and men sent by the Sheikh of Bukha, a town to the north of Sha'am, now part of the Omani Musandam exclave. The headman of Bukha received a rebuke from the British Resident for this breach of the Marine Treaty.[18] However, the subjugation of Sha'am was a rare victory for Saqr, who by now presided over a much-reduced Sharjah.

In 1884, after three years of relative peace had prevailed over the east coast, Hamad bin Abdullah Al Sharqi once again led his people in revolt against Sharjah's rule, taking Ghurfa (at the heart of modern Fujairah town) and also winning control of the strategic Bithnah Fort, which dominated the inland pass through the Wadi Ham to Masafi and then down the Wadi Siji to the interior, as well as the Wadi Abadilah inland route north east to Dibba. He then appealed to Humaid bin Abdullah of Ras Al Khaimah for protection against Sharjah.[19]

However, Saqr bin Khalid chose not to act against the rebels, as indeed the Sultan of Muscat, Turki bin Said, chose not to offer them protection after they appealed to him to assume suzerainty over them. British advice to the Sultan was not to get embroiled in what would ultimately lead to an inevitable clash with Sharjah. Muscat stayed away and Saqr bin Khalid lost effective control over the whole of the east coast Al Qasimi possessions, from Dibba down to Kalba. Control over the coastal town and trading post of Khor Fakkan, which could only be approached by land via Fujairah or Dibba at the time, was lost by default.

A general state of war

After a short period of stability leading into 1885, the Trucial Coast was once again pitched into a series of conflicts and shifting alliances when the son of Ahmed bin Abdullah Al Mualla of Umm Al Quwain quarrelled with his father and took refuge in Ajman. When Rashid bin Humaid Al Nuaimi of Ajman refused to hand the young man over, Sharjah and Umm Al Quwain joined together against Ajman. Ahmed bin Abdullah of Umm Al Quwain landed fifty men at Al Heera, on Ajman's southern border, transporting them there in two baggalas. He now found himself in hot water with the British for having breached the Maritime Treaty. Visited in Umm Al Quwain town by HMS *Reindeer*, Ahmed bin Abdullah was brought to book for his action, but raids continued between Umm Al Quwain and Hamriyah, Ajman's northern neighbour. In November 1885, Hasher bin Maktoum Al Maktoum of Dubai forged an alliance with Rashid bin Humaid of Ajman and the two now harried Sharjah's borders in turn. These skirmishes escalated until, on 20 January 1886, a force of 1,000 men of Dubai, Ajman and Hamriyah attacked Sharjah town, killing forty men and wounding another twenty-five.

Chaos now descended on the coast. Saqr bin Khalid Al Qasimi of Sharjah appealed to the British, who stepped in and arbitrated a deal whereby Dubai would be at peace with Sharjah if Saqr bin Khalid would renounce his alliance with Umm Al Quwain. This now left Dubai, Ajman and Hamriyah ranged against Umm Al Quwain but Ras Al Khaimah joined in on Umm Al Quwain's side. Raids took place along the coast, with Ras Al Khaimah beset by Shihuh raids from the north, instigated by Hasher bin Maktoum of Dubai. An attempt at mediation by Abu Dhabi failed, and in May 1886 Hamriyah raided Umm Al Quwain. The Hamriyah fighting men then took to the pearl banks for the season, unwisely leaving their town undefended. Umm Al Quwain lost no time in falling on the town of Hamriyah, destroying property and capturing slaves and trade goods. The headman, by barricading himself in the fort, survived the action but he managed to alienate his ally, Hasher bin Maktoum who had set off with a force against Umm Al Quwain but now threw up his hands and went home.

Raids against the north by the Bani Yas' allies, the Bedouin Manasir, now took place and these were compounded by the Shihuh who once again rose against Ras Al Khaimah, raiding the town and killing several people in the date plantations and destroying 200 palm trees in the village of Khatt.

The divide between the Hinawi (broadly encompassing those who had their origins in Central Arabia and centred around Abu Dhabi, Dubai and Muscat) factions and their allies and the mostly northern Ghafiri (those who traced their origins to Yemen), now settled into a clear north-south divide. In part polarised by Wahhabi influence, Sharjah and Ras Al Khaimah drew Ajman and Umm Al Quwain into a northern Ghafiri alliance. Dubai had hoped to preserve its alliance with Ajman and Hamriyah as a foil against Sharjah, but the two prevaricated and eventually threw in their lot with their immediate neighbours.

Further Manasir raids against the north took place in 1889 but an unsteady peace generally prevailed until March 1890 when fighting intensified between Dubai and Sharjah. Abu Dhabi sent a force north in support of its Hinawi ally and a general conflict ensued with losses sustained by both sides. Raids by Bedouin marauders loyal to both factions broke out, while the Shihuh once again threw themselves against Ras Al Khaimah.

By 1891, the combatants had exhausted themselves and the northern Trucial States settled down to a period of relative peace, disturbed only by the migration of some 400 members of the Marar tribe from Dubai to Sharjah at the end of the pearling season. The move left a considerable financial mess and resulted in a slew of claims and counterclaims which not only dragged on but often led to minor clashes between the two emirates.

There was little peace in the interior, however. The alliance between Dubai and Abu Dhabi bolstered Zayed's ambitions in Buraimi and he expanded his influence in the oasis, buying up date groves and water rights, eventually alienating his long-standing allies, the Dhawahir. Although the Dhawahir had previously sold land to Zayed, they eventually realised that bit by bit the pattern of land ownership had changed and they had effectively ceded control of the oasis. They rebelled.

Having been prevented from acting by an intercession by Dubai in 1875, Zayed laid his plans and effected a reconciliation with the Na'im, long a thorn in the side of the Bani Yas. Bolstered by his new alliance, Zayed marched against the oasis in May 1887. The Sultan of Muscat supported the Dhawahir, sending them money and ammunition, but his aid arrived too late. Zayed claimed a fast and decisive victory of arms and took the two Dhawahir Sheikhs hostage against the tribe's future good behaviour.[20]

They can't have been much use as hostages, because Zayed marched against the Dhawahir once again in 1891, this time with the support of thirty horsemen and 300 camel riders from Dubai. Zayed took the main Dhawahir settlement, 'Ain Dhawahir and built a fort there to ensure his dominance over the oasis. Appointing a Dhawahir Wali, Ahmad bin Muhammad bin Hilal Al Dhahiri, over the oasis, Zayed brought the Na'im fully onside by marrying the daughter of the Nuaimi headman of Buraimi. By now, Zayed not only dominated the oases of Buraimi and Ain Dhawahir, he also commanded the loyalty of the powerful Bani Ka'ab and Bani Qitab, who dominated the area to the north of Buraimi and who had been generally considered to be dependents of Sharjah. Saqr bin Khalid Al Qasimi saw Sharjah's influence diminished – and not for the first time – at the hands of Zayed bin Khalifa.

Ain Dhawahir is known today simply as Al Ain, the inland oasis city of Abu Dhabi.

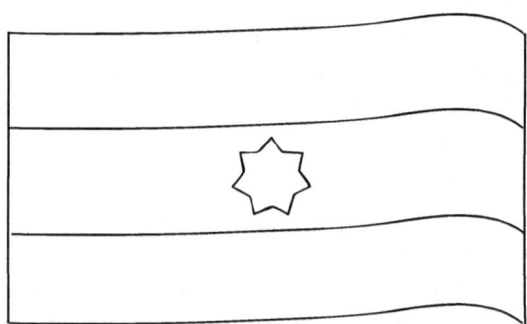

Chapter 19

THE PROTECTORATE AND THE DARBAR

"Chiefs, your fathers and grandfathers before you have doubtless told you of the history of the past. You know that a hundred years ago there was constant trouble and fighting in the Gulf; almost every man was a marauder or a pirate; kidnapping and slave-trading flourished; fighting and bloodshed went on without stint or respite; no ship could put out to sea without fear of attack; the pearl fishery was a scene of annual conflict and security of trade or peace there was none."

- Lord Curzon of Kedleston

In May 1892, the Sheikhs of the Trucial Coast signed the Exclusive Agreement with the British, 'not to enter into any agreement or correspondence with any Power other than the British Government' and that each would not, without permission from that government, 'consent to the residence within my territory of the agent of any other government'. Furthermore, they would not 'cede, sell, mortgage or otherwise give for occupation any part of my territory, save to the British Government.'[1]

It seemed like a schizophrenic kind of arrangement. Why would the British, so disinclined to become embroiled in the interior of the Trucial States, suddenly be interested in the influence of these 'other powers'? Troublesome, requiring of frequent policing visits from British warships and constantly riven by internecine squabbles and violence, the Trucial States had little enough of value to offer its imperial protector, surely?

The British telegraph station on its island in the Elphinstone Inlet had long been abandoned. It would be sixty years and more until oil would be discovered in the Trucial States and forty years until Sharjah would be useful as a stopping point for the Imperial Airways flights.

The pearl trade was a lucrative line of commerce, but the British derived little or no value from it: native merchants sold their pearls freely and without taxation wherever they wished, to Indian Maharajahs and Parisian socialites. The Sharjah-based pearl trader Obaid Al Naboodah was so wealthy he maintained houses in Paris and Mumbai as well as a teak-pillared and palatial family home, today preserved as the Bait Al Naboodah, a museum in the heritage area known as the Heart of Sharjah.

Although it could be argued that the Trucial States were a vital asset in protecting the trade and communications route from the Gulf through to India, it was Suez, the canal opened in 1869, which allowed shipping to avoid the long voyage around the Cape that the Portuguese had pioneered. The British had acquired a substantial interest in, and then complete control of, the Suez Canal by 1882. They did not need the Gulf to protect their route to India.

The British move to protect the Trucial States from foreign influence appears to have been purely instinctive. Having gained influence over a region, finding the Persians, the Turks, the French and the Germans seeking to compete, the British were resolved to keep them all at bay. The fact that there was little to gain in terms of revenues does not appear to have affected their decision.

The Persian 'pitch' to the Trucial Rulers came in 1887, when the former deputy Governor of Bushire, Sartip Haji Ahmad Khan, took off for the Trucial States in the Bombay and Persia Steam Navigation Company's ship *Calder*, landing in Abu Dhabi in the searing heat of August wearing full ceremonial uniform. The whole mission had struck the British Resident at Bushire as so very odd that he despatched the Residency steamer *Lawrence* to follow Haji Ahmad Khan. The Persian official spent a few days in Abu Dhabi, travelled up to Dubai and spent some time there before returning to Abu Dhabi and embarking to Lingeh on a native boat.[2]

A little like recalcitrant children, in British eyes, the Trucial Rulers stayed tight lipped when pressed by British officials about the colourful figure of Sartip Haji Ahmad Khan and his discussions with them. It was eventually Rashid bin Maktoum Al Maktoum, the newly acceded Ruler of Dubai (his brother, Hasher, died on 22 November 1886), who in late 1887 confided in the Sultan of Muscat, Turki bin Said, that Ahmad Khan had proposed an alliance between Persia and the Trucial Rulers with a view to ejecting the perfidious British from the Trucial States. Turki clearly lost little time in telling his British Resident in Muscat about these discussions.

The British Political Resident at Bushire, Edward Charles Ross, kept informed by the *Lawrence* and also by his resident agent in Muscat, moved with alacrity. In December 1887 he obtained the agreement of the Rulers of Abu Dhabi, Dubai, Sharjah, Ajman, Umm Al Quwain and Ras Al Khaimah that they would not have dealings with any other government than the British and not allow any other government's agent to reside in their territories.

In January 1888, Ahmad Khan hove into view once again, this time in Ras Musandam, intending to make a southwards progress along the coast, but was refused landing. Backed by an armed force from Qeshm and carrying a number of Persian flags to distribute to the liberated peoples of the Trucial Coast, he met with the Ruler of Umm Al Quwain, Ahmad bin Abdullah Al Mualla.

Ahmad bin Abdullah acceded to the Rule of Umm Al Quwain in 1873, on the peaceful death of his elder brother, Ali bin Abdullah Al Mualla. If Ali's reign had been as peaceful as his death, Ahmad was set on an altogether more turbulent career and got himself into fights with Sharjah and Ajman. He was found to be in breach of the Perpetual Maritime Peace by the British on a number of occasions during the complex internecine battles fought by the Trucial Rulers in the late 1800s. Ahmad bin Abdullah could perhaps be expected to welcome Ahmad Khan's offer of Persian influence against the British, but finding this was clearly not the case, Ahmad Khan realised he was something of a busted flush and returned to Persia with his tail between his legs and his collection of liberator's flags still on board.

The British complained to Tehran, which lost no time in diplomatically disowning Ahmad Khan and his extravagant actions. The Persian adventure was at an end.

But it wasn't the Persians who caused real concerns in Bombay, it was the French. The British could deal with the Sartip in his dress uniform, sweating and saluting away on the sandy shore at Abu Dhabi as the astonished Trucial Rulers wondered what on Earth this new apparition actually meant. But the French? That was another matter altogether!

Two French adventurers, suspected by the British of being 'agents' of the French government, now appeared on the scene, a Monsieur Tramier (AKA Thomy) and a Monsieur Chapuy were suspected of distributing French flags. They found themselves received altogether more congenially by Ahmad bin Abdullah Al Mualla of Umm Al Quwain, who found the offer of French flags a great deal more appealing than that of Persian pennants.[3]

The idea of taking two men handing out French flags seriously may seem odd today, but in 1891 it enabled a number of ships sailing from the Omani port of Sur to once again start shipping slaves from Africa without fear of British interdiction and reprisals, simply by hoisting a

French flag and therefore becoming effectively immune to British interception. The British were alarmed enough at this unwelcome activity, but when the two Frenchmen were reported to have obtained the grant of a site in Umm Al Quwain from Ahmad bin Abdullah, it was all too much. A formal agreement was drawn up along the lines of Edward Ross' agreement of 1887 and was presented to the six Trucial Rulers and the Sheikh of Bahrain for their signature by Ross' successor as Political Resident in Bushire, the fabulously named Adelbert Talbot. The last significant treaty between the Trucial Sheikhs and the British government, the Exclusive Agreement of 1892 effectively put the foreign relations of the Trucial States in the hands of the British and confirmed the Trucial States as a British protectorate in all but name. It tied the two together irrevocably, if they had not been already so tied.

Dubai, in particular, gazed wistfully at the departing French and their handy flags of convenience which would have supported some of the town's more dubious trading activities taking place away from the censorious gaze of Albion's puritanical administrators.

A new century

As the Trucial States emerged, blinking, into the twentieth century, it may be worth taking stock of where each emirate stood, particularly in light of the great change which now took place with Sharjah and Ras Al Khaimah as, on the death of Humaid bin Abdullah Al Qasimi in 1900, Saqr bin Khalid Al Qasimi assumed the leadership of Ras Al Khaimah and once again both towns were joined decisively under a single ruler.

If Saqr bin Khalid enjoyed a brief resurgence with the reunification of the two Al Qasimi towns, he still faced constant trouble from the Shihuh, lacked clear authority over the interior and was now constantly engaged with trying to bring Fujairah and its strong-minded headman, Hamad bin Abdullah Al Sharqi, back into line. Shamaliyah, the east coast, was nominally under the rule of two Al Qasimi governors, one at Dibba responsible for the northern territories and one at Kalba taking care of the south. Their authority was at best shaky, although their posts were personally lucrative.

The rumbling dispute with Fujairah threatened to bring other Rulers into the fray and the British became alarmed at the growing signs of another all-out war between the Trucial States and particularly so when it looked as if the Sultan of Muscat, Turki bin Said, was minded to also throw his hat into the ring. Failing to reach any agreement between the opposing parties, the appearance of a gunboat even having failed to bring them together, the British essentially gave up and left them all to it.[4]

Umm Al Quwain was, after decades of conflict with its neighbours, enjoying a period of peace as the century turned, its often-quarrelsome Ruler, Ahmad bin Abdullah Al Mualla, was by now in his seniority and increasingly troubled by paralysis.

Ajman also saw great change in 1900. Humaid bin Rashid Al Nuaimi acceded as Ruler of Ajman in 1891 following the death of his father, Rashid bin Humaid Al Nuaimi. A signatory to the 1892 Exclusive Agreement, Humaid bin Rashid defended Ajman against a predatory alliance between Sharjah and Umm Al Quwain in September of that year. Humaid was assisted by Rashid bin Maktoum of Dubai, who was made to pay a fine by the British for breaching the maritime truce because he sent his force by sea.[5]

Humaid was deeply unpopular with his family, however, for failing to pay various family members the traditional subsidies from the emirate's revenues. On the morning of 8 July 1900, he was killed by his uncle, Abdulaziz bin Humaid Al Nuaimi, who then became the Ruler of Ajman. Perhaps fittingly, Abdulaziz was to eventually suffer the same fate he had engineered for his nephew.

The rule of Abdulaziz bin Humaid was to be characterised by conflicts, not the least of which was a fight with Sheikh Zayed of Abu Dhabi, who had designs on Al Zorah. In 1895, Zayed had tried to build a fort there, giving him a foothold in the north, but had been frustrated in this design by a general outcry raised by the northern Ghafiri tribes and Rulers. Now, Zayed backed a move to settle Al Zorah by a section of the Sudan (singular Al Suwaidi) tribe.

Zayed's backing for the move was barely less than transparent in its aims; his mother was a Suwaidi and he was himself married to a daughter of the Sudan Sheikh Sultan bin Nasir Al Suwaidi. Any Sudan settlement at Al Zorah would be established in all but Zayed's name.

Abdulaziz bin Humaid moved immediately to build a fort blockading the landward access to Al Zorah and, simultaneously, Sheikh Saqr bin Khalid Al Qasimi, the Ruler of Sharjah, petitioned the British against the establishment of this alien community in the middle of Al Qasimi territory. The British permission to establish the settlement, previously granted, was revoked and it was eventually decided that no settlement should take place at Al Zorah without the unanimous consent of the Trucial Rulers. Zayed retired from the fray, foiled in his plan, to focus once again on consolidating his southern federation of tribes.

Dubai in 1900 was a thriving mercantile hub, becoming recognised as the principal port in the region. Its Ruler, Maktoum bin Hasher Al Maktoum, had acceded in 1894 following the death of his uncle, Rashid bin Maktoum Al Maktoum, during an outbreak of cholera in the town. Maktoum's accession was briefly disputed by Rashid's two sons, Butti and Saeed, who were imprisoned in Dubai's Al Fahidi Fort before being allowed to travel north to exile in Sharjah.[6]

While Rashid had been involved in a number of conflicts and was an active participant in the politics of the interior (he married into the Na'im tribe of Buraimi and was party to Zayed's subjugation of the oasis), Maktoum bin Hasher focused on increasing the revenue and trade from his port and it was under his rule that Dubai started its rise to prominence as a major regional trading hub. It was by no means plain sailing: outbreaks of disease were common and epidemics of cholera and infestations of locusts could bring a thriving town to its knees. In 1896, a series of fires broke out along the coast, with the majority of homes constructed of palm fronds, *areesh*. Especially in the summer months, these were tinder-dry and fires caused huge damage in Sharjah, with the loss of 400 houses and Abu Dhabi, with the loss of 170 houses. Dubai, a fast-expanding town whose streets were becoming increasingly packed, was also swept by flames that year and half of Bur Dubai was lost, as well as every house on the Deira side of the creek. Shindaga alone at that time consisted of 250 houses and the entire population of Dubai was some 10,000 souls. The fear of these conflagrations was great indeed and, in 1897, a female slave was caught starting a fire and was put to death for the crime of arson.[7]

In 1901, Maktoum bin Hasher established Dubai as a free port, with no taxation being levied on imports or exports and he also gave merchants land on which to build warehouses and other establishments. A number of traders moved to Dubai from other coastal towns, as well as from the Persian town of Lingeh, encouraged by these free trade policies and also guarantees of security and tolerance. The imposition of taxes by the Persian government added impetus to the exodus. The impact of Maktoum's policies was immediate and can be demonstrated by the movements of the steamers of the Bombay and Persia Steam Navigation Company. From 1899 to 1901, the company's steamers visited Dubai five times yearly. In 1902 they called in twenty-one times and subsequently their visits became fortnightly.[8] By 1906, these boats alone were trading 70,000 tonnes of cargo. Dubai was most certainly on the rise.

In 1900, Zayed bin Khalifa of Abu Dhabi was without doubt the pre-eminent Trucial Ruler. He held sway over a huge arc of territory, from westerly Khor Al Udaid on the Qatari peninsula to Liwa and the southern sands across to the oases of Buraimi / Al Ain to the east. The border between Abu Dhabi and Dubai, a long source of dispute in the years to come, was generally reckoned to be somewhere near to Jebel Ali.

Buraimi had not been without its conflicts in the years leading up to the turn of the century, but these were increasingly being settled through negotiation rather than open warfare. Abu Dhabi under Zayed The Great was at peace and his rule, judgement and influence, even among the tribes of the interior, was generally accepted and recognised.

The Trucial States at the turn of the century can therefore be seen to have assumed much the same shape as the modern United Arab Emirates. British rule, although it brought few practical benefits in terms of investment in healthcare, schools or any other form of development, at least was not full colonial occupation and the affairs of the

Rulers and their towns, of the tribes of the interior and their relationship with the Trucial Sheikhs, were generally left well alone. British interventions, for the most part, were the result of requests for arbitration from the Rulers themselves and generally took the form of mediation rather than the gunboat diplomacy that had characterised much of the British involvement in the area over the previous century.

Perhaps, then, this new stability deserved a celebration. And it was to get it. In 1903, the Trucial States were to be the, possibly mildly perplexed, recipients of a Viceregal Durbar.

Curzon comes to town – and goes to town

"Chiefs, your fathers and grandfathers before you have doubtless told you of the history of the past. You know that a hundred years ago there was constant trouble and fighting in the Gulf; almost every man was a marauder or a pirate; kidnapping and slave-trading flourished; fighting and bloodshed went on without stint or respite; no ship could put out to sea without fear of attack; the pearl fishery was a scene of annual conflict and security of trade or peace there was none."[9]

So George Nathaniel Curzon, the first Marquess Curzon of Kedleston and the Viceroy of India, addressed the assembled chiefs of the Trucial Coast on the *Argonaut*, moored some five miles offshore of Sharjah on account of the shallowness of the coastal waters, on 21 November 1903.

The *Argonaut* was dressed to impress, with the ship's quarter-deck hung with fine cloth hangings, gold-embroidered drapes and the flags of the world. At the centre of the whole display was a raised dais. Two great guns were elevated above the whole, just in case anyone missed the point. Great multi-gun salutes had boomed out from the *Argonaut* when the ship reached Muscat, with replies from batteries ashore. No such salutes were afforded Sharjah, which had no great cannon with which to return the compliment.

If the choppy weather was not enough to make the Rulers seasick, Curzon's speech would have certainly have agitated them. He celebrated the Pax Britannica and, at least verbally, gave them a good finger-wagging. They were to be appreciative of the peace the British had brought. They were to consider that 'the influence of the British government must remain supreme' and abide by their treaty obligations by sea and on land, although Curzon was careful to note that the British wanted no part of the internal affairs of the Trucial States.

Curzon's speech was intended to ensure that his subjects understood the greatness of the Empire which overlooked them. He lost no time in talking down to the 'pacificated Arabs', including a very pointed reference to the 'Al Joasmee' authority over the East Coast and a warning that any disputes over this should cease and the peace remain undisturbed. It was a blow as killing to Fujairah's bid for independence as the absence of Hamriyah's headman was to that town's bid for recognition. In the end, Hamriyah remained effectively independent (although eventually was to be subsumed into Sharjah) while Fujairah did not wait on Curzon's blessing to declare itself – even if its independent status would not be recognised by the British for decades.

Meanwhile, shock and awe was the order of the day. "The Sovereign of the British Empire lives so far away that none of you has ever, or ever will, see his face," Curzon rather patronisingly told the Sheikhs and dignitaries gathered on the rolling decks of the *Argonaut*. Munificent gifts of swords and rifles were presented but refreshments, it being Ramadan at the time, were not offered.

And that was that. They must have made their way home in a state of some considerable bewilderment. His Majesty's representative had spoken to them and given them fine gifts, but to these practical men, the message must have been very strange indeed.

Three years later, in 1906, the Sheikhs were all presented with a bound collection of the treaties their predecessors had entered into with the British, as a reminder of the obligations they were considered to have inherited. Printed in both Arabic and English, the collection was introduced by a transcribed copy of Curzon's 1903 Durbar address.[10]

The exclusion of Hamriyah from the Durbar would have pleased Saqr bin Khalid of Sharjah, but the town remained effectively independent. Almost a year after Curzon's departure, in September 1904 the headman of Hamriyah, Saif bin Abdulrahman, died. He was succeeded, after a great deal of internecine strife and killing, by his son, Abdulrahman bin Saif.

Hamriyah's northern neighbour was itself to see a succession take place when, on 13 June 1904, the paralysed Ruler of Umm Al Quwain, Ahmad bin Abdullah Al Mualla, quietly died. Ahmad's son, Rashid bin Ahmed, acceded in his place and set about assuring the British that he recognised his obligations under the treaties between them. Ahmad bin Abdullah had, as a younger man, been an ambitous ruler and his son Rashid bin Ahmed was to follow in his father's footsteps as a dynamic and dynastically inclined leader. He cemented an early alliance with his neighbour, Ajman, when he married his cousin, the daughter of the Ruler of Ajman, Abdulaziz bin Humaid Al Nuaimi. Rashid bin Ahmed was to find his taste for dynastic intrigue would pitch him against the greatest figure in the Trucial States at the time, the dominant force that was Zayed bin Khalifa of Abu Dhabi.

If Umm Al Quwain had found fresh zeal, Sharjah was increasingly diminished under its unpopular leader, Saqr bin Khalid Al Qasimi. In 1904, Saqr bin Khalid managed to survive yet another attempt to unseat him by his uncle, Salim bin Sultan. Salim bin Sultan became Wali of Ras Al Khaimah in 1910 and, although Saqr bin Khalid remained nominally the Ruler of the emirate, Salim consolidated his hold on power and was in all but name independent.

The growing influence of Hamad bin Abdullah Al Sharqi in Fujairah had led to a declaration of independence in 1901, although in 1903, the British once again decided not to recognise Fujairah as an independent Trucial State but to consider it a dependency of Sharjah. Despite a sally by Saqr bin Khalid against the fort of Bithnah early in the year and a rather pointed exhortation to peace by Curzon during his Viceregal Durbar, Fujairah remained a nominal dependency at best and by 1905, Saqr bin Khalid Al Qasimi had ceased to press his claims to Fujairah. In 1906, Fujairah was claimed as a dependency of Abu Dhabi, with no opposition from Sharjah.[11] As far as the Trucial Rulers were concerned, Fujairah was independent. The British would consistently refuse to recognise that status until 1952.

The fortunes of Hatta

A 1905 dispute brought the young and ambitious Ruler of Umm Al Quwain, Rashid bin Ahmad Al Mualla, to the forefront of Trucial States politics, when the mountain village of Hajarain – known today as Hatta – was embroiled in a conflict between the Bani Qitab and the Na'im. The conflict, as usual a complicated affair, was also to mark the first meeting called between all of the Trucial Sheikhs with a view to solving issues of territory and sovereignty.[12]

Hajarain lay nestled in the Hajar mountains, at the top of a sinuous path that wound up from the plains around Madam and then down again through to the town of Shinas on the east coast, one of the three main northern crossings of the Hajar mountains. Another route out of Hajarain led down to Buraimi (the once-famous Hatta Track, now sadly closed from the UAE side. It can still be explored from the Omani side, however). Located next to Hajarain, the mountain village of Masfout was subject to the Na'im and Bani Ka'ab of Buraimi. Although the people of Masfout considered themselves subject to the Na'im, Hajarain was considered to be part of Oman until around 1870, when the Omani Sultan Turki bin Said ceded the territory to the Ruler of Dubai, Hasher bin Maktoum Al Maktoum.[13]

In 1905, the Bani Qitab Bedouin moved against the Na'im, constructing a fort at the head of the Wadi Hatta at a place then known as Jabail, which controlled the mountain pass down to Shinas. The fort, apparently named Al Hauz, was constructed with the support (including financial) of Rashid bin Ahmad Al Mualla, who backed the Bani Qitab in their adventure.

Having established dominance over the trade route, the Bani Qitab proceeded to harry passing caravans, much to the annoyance not only of the Na'im, but also of Hasher bin Maktoum. In September 1905, a meeting was held in Dubai between the five Trucial Sheikhs under the leadership of Sheikh Zayed bin Khalifa and it was agreed that the fortification at Jabail should be demolished and that the Bani Qitab should restore Masfout (whose people had supported and indeed benefited from the whole enterprise) to the Na'im. Zayed bin Khalifa urged Umm Al Quwain's dynamic new leader to abstain from interfering with the

Bani Qitab, but Rashid bin Ahmad clearly had other ideas and proceeded to take the side of the Bani Qitab and reconcile them to the northern Rulers, arranging meetings in both Ajman and Sharjah between the two principal Bani Qitab Sheikhs and the two Trucial Rulers.

The Bani Qitab were also involved in a conflict further south, with a group of Baluch who had set up a fort in the village of Mazim, between Buraimi and Ibri, next to Aflaj Bani Qitab (now on the Ibri–Hafeet Road), the home to a settled portion of the tribe. The settled Bani Qitab called in the help of the Bedouin section of the tribe against the Baluch. They attacked the fort at Mazim and the Baluch appealed to Sheikh Zayed bin Khalifa.[14]

Rashid bin Ahmed's diplomacy now paid off, with Sharjah and Ajman joining with him in support of the Bani Qitab, while Zayed bin Khalifa opposed them. In February 1906, Zayed moved against the Bani Qitab in order to compel them to make restitution for the killing of a number of Baluch. Appealing first to Hasher bin Maktoum of Dubai (who backed Zayed) and then to Saqr bin Khalid Al Qasimi (who refused to get involved), the Bani Qitab finally went to Rashid bin Ahmed, who was compelled to support his allies but clearly unwilling to come to blows with the fearsome Zayed bin Khalifa.

In April 1906, a second meeting between the five rulers was held at the desert encampment of Khawaneej, East of Dubai town. A treaty was agreed, allocating responsibility for the tribes to the two Rulers – Rashid bin Ahmad was to be responsible for the Bani Qitab, Ghafalah and Bani Ka'ab, while Zayed undertook responsibility for the Na'im of Buraimi, the Dhawahir, the Sharqiyin of Fujairah and the Shihuh.

This agreement between the Rulers not only confirmed a significant voice in Bedouin tribal politics for Rashid bin Ahmad of Umm Al Quwain, but also gave Zayed bin Khalifa at least nominal control over widespread territory and resources that had previously been tributary to Sharjah and which were historically disputed by Zayed's long-standing ally, Oman.

It was not to last, however, and Zayed had clearly decided to act against the young upstart from Umm Al Quwain, Rashid bin Ahmed.

By November 1906, Zayed allied with Dubai and Sharjah and raised a force of Manasir and Bani Hajer Bedouin and prepared to attack Umm Al Quwain's inland desert town of Falaj Al Ali (known today as Falaj Al Mualla). Sharjah's support for what would otherwise have been a southern, Hinawi, alliance, can be perhaps explained by the proximity of the fertile desert oasis town of Falaj Al Ali to the Sharjah town of Dhaid. Falaj Al Ali would have made a nice addition to the Sharjah oasis.[15]

At this point, approached by Rashid bin Ahmad Al Mualla for assistance in acquiring breech-loading cannon to help defend the fort at Falaj Al Ali, the British got involved. The British resident, Major Percy Cox, declined to supply arms to Rashid bin Ahmad, but called him together with Zayed bin Khalifa to negotiate, resulting in a round of meetings between the two.

Seemingly out of the blue, in January 1907, Rashid bin Ahmad was overpowered during one of his visits to Zayed and held prisoner inland of Sharjah town (likely at Dhaid), where the Rulers of Dubai, Ajman and Sharjah had joined Khalifa bin Zayed and were preparing to move against Falaj Al Ali.

Percy Cox made his way to Sharjah on RIMS[16] *Lawrence* and embarked on a week-long round of diplomacy, with Saqr bin Khalid of Sharjah acting as a messenger. A much-abused Rashid bin Ahmad was finally released up to Cox, having been comprehensively beaten up in the interim. Two days' negotiations followed, with Saqr bin Khalid representing both himself and Abdelaziz bin Humaid Al Nuaimi of Ajman and Hasher bin Maktoum representing himself as well as Zayed bin Khalifa of Abu Dhabi. A reconciliation agreement was eventually forged and a treaty signed. Rashid bin Ahmad Al Mualla was returned by the *Lawrence* to Umm Al Quwain to general rejoicing, his feathers most thoroughly ruffled.

If Rashid bin Ahmad was now cured of political meddling with the Bedouin, Zayed bin Khalifa Al Nahyan was not to enjoy his victory over the younger Sheikh for long: on 19 May 1909, Zayed the Great died. He had ruled Abu Dhabi and the Bani Yas for fifty-four years, commanding the respect of the Bedouin and his fellow Trucial Sheikhs alike. His reign had spanned two centuries, his writ ran throughout the area from the northern Shihuh territories to the east coast, inland to Buraimi and through Liwa to Qatar. Zayed was acknowledged as the greatest of the Trucial leaders, a giant of a man whose figure straddled the whole region and whose reputation for wisdom was matched only by his ability in action. Respected by the Bedouin and townspeople alike, held in high regard by the British, Zayed the Great's passing was literally the end of an era. His passing was to see the powerful tribal alliance he had forged dissipate. One consequence was the loss of the confidence of the Na'im, who once again were to come under Saudi influence, leading inevitably to the Buraimi dispute of 1952.

The 'Hyacinth Incident'

By 1910, the Trucial Coast had settled down into a nice, easy pattern of life. The annual pearling season passed by peacefully, employing men from the coastal as well as Bedouin communities from May to September. Dubai, in particular, had emerged as a lively trading entrepôt and dhows and steamers alike called in from around the Gulf, Red Sea, East Africa, Persia and India to feed the commerce of the merchants and agents who had set up there. All sorts of commodities were traded through Dubai and the other coastal emirates and, although the trade in slaves had officially been abolished (treaties abolishing slave trading in 1856 and 1873 had both been signed by the Trucial Sheikhs), there was a very African makeup to the pearling crews and most of the larger households still had slaves – in fact, a trusted slave would often be given a position where he was a manager of free men and it was not unknown for a slave to act as a Ruler's Wali over a town or district. A particularly lucrative trade in the Gulf was gun-running and, like slaving, this was a trade the British would dearly have liked to have seen eradicated. The Sheikhs had agreed not to smuggle guns and had signed a treaty to that effect with the British in 1902, the year before Curzon's celebratory durbar.

The British had curtailed the lively maritime trade of weapons into Persia from Muscat but trade, like water, flows along the route of least resistance. Dubai's merchants had a lucrative new market to explore and, mercantile and opportunistic as ever, they pursued this new break. If the guns could not come by sea, they could travel overland. Camel trains from Mutrah in Oman made their way to Abu Dhabi, Dubai and Sharjah and from there crossed the Gulf. Boats from Qatar, in particular, were ferrying large quantities of arms, secure under French flags. And arms were making their way to Ibn Saud's forces in the interior of the peninsula, too.[17]

The British did all they could to stem the tide, and on 20 December 1910, John Noakes of the First Pinnace stationed at Dubai called on Sheikh Butti bin Suhail Al Maktoum, Ruler of Dubai, and demanded to search a house in the town for illegal weapons. Butti bin Suhail reportedly took his time in complying with this request, and it is tempting to think that he sent a messenger to the owner of the house in question to tell him that the British were on the warpath and that the owner had better get rid of whatever it was he was storing there. It is equally tempting to think that Butti bin Suhail would have known perfectly well precisely what it was his subject was storing!

Noakes was kept waiting for an agonising hour before the party left the Ruler's house and headed for the town, with further delays once they arrived. By the time the door of the house in question was opened, Noakes found the cupboard was unsurprisingly bare, but was encouraged to be told by a slave by the name of Sultan that the arms he was looking for were concealed elsewhere, in the house of a trader called Ahmed.[18]

Arriving at Dubai on 23 December, the Captain of the HMS *Hyacinth*, James Dick, was briefed by Noakes on the disappearing guns and now decided on a dawn raid. In the early morning of Saturday, 24 December 1910, Captain Dick sent John Noakes to wake the Ruler of Dubai and have him ready to meet Dick and his men. Dick himself set off from the ship at 5.30 a.m. that morning with a force of 100 men. Arriving at the Sheikh's house, Captain Dick was told by the Sheikh's father that Butti bin Suhail would not see him. Noakes, who had arrived at the house at 5 a.m., had been similarly rebuffed. Captain Dick lost no further time and went with his landing party directly to the house Noakes had inspected previously. Finding arms buried in the house, Dick left an army major in charge of further prosecuting the search for arms and proceeded with a force of men to Ahmed's house, where men on the roof fired at his soldiers. Dick's men returned the fire and forced an entrance to the house, posting sentries and searching the premises. Butti bin Suhail arrived at the house at 8 a.m. but a mob had also gathered and at around 8.20 a.m. firing broke out and the British fired volleys into the crowd, before withdrawing into Ahmed's house.

One of the detachments had been pinned down under heavy fire from the townspeople and was relieved by the *Hyacinth* firing her six-inch guns. It's perhaps worth highlighting that ships had moved on by 1910 and *Hyacinth* wasn't one of the sailing ships of the line which had bombarded Ras Al Khaimah with such devastating effect in 1819 – *Hyacinth* was an armoured steamship capable of twenty-three knots and bristling with armaments, including her six-inch quick firing guns, each firing forty-five kilo lyddite-packed high-explosive shells. Smashing into the adobe walls lining Dubai's close-packed alleys and sending buzzing clouds of razor-sharp shrapnel flying to cut down anything standing within sight, these fearsome weapons were unleashed directly – and knowingly – into a densely populated civilian area.

At 8.45 a.m., Captain Dick says he asked the Sheikh to stop the men firing at him, with which request the Sheikh complied, but sporadic firing continued until about 10 a.m. Stopping to pick up the body of an able seaman, Dick and his party took refuge in Sheikh Butti bin Suhail's house before making their way back to *Hyacinth* under the Ruler's protection, a large, heavily armed and furious mob lining the streets.

The British force sustained losses of five killed and nine wounded. Commenting on the incident, Rear-Admiral Slade, Secretary of the Admiralty, pointed out, "I must state my opinion that the conduct of both officers and men of the *Hyacinth* was extremely creditable but that the operations were somewhat hastily undertaken without paying sufficient consideration to the prejudices and ideas of an oriental people."

Thirty-seven of the townspeople of Dubai were killed, an unknown number more wounded. The 'oriental people' had paid dearly for resisting the British forces which had landed without permission and stormed their town without warning. Now their ruler was to pay more.

A set of demands was laid out that Sheikh Butti bin Suhail Al Maktoum was expected to meet, including the installation of a British Agent (a demand that India was to decide was unsupportable) and the payment of reparations. Just in case he or any of the other Rulers got any smart ideas, the Rulers of Sharjah, Umm Al Quwain and Dubai were given a tour aboard *Hyacinth*, no doubt so they could properly appreciate the ship's armaments. The ship was, they had pointed out to them, ready to set up a bombardment should Butti bin Suhail decide not to comply.

Butti bin Suhail handed over the 400 rifles demanded, as well as 50,000 rupees. He acquiesced to the setting up of a new 'tide pole' to help the British ships gauge the depth of the creek and to the setting up of a telegraph and post office – both desirable to the British and developments he had previously resisted.[19]

As a result of the incident, to the grave concern of Butti bin Suhail, who was trying to build his mercantile port and actively welcoming traders to set up their businesses in Dubai, some 150 merchants left the town, mostly Persians who had some involvement or other in the armaments trade.[20]

"The recent occurrence," noted Percy Cox, the British Political Resident, "was of course unlucky and we may have to face newspaper misrepresentation…"

Cox was on the defensive – he'd received a broadside from Bombay on 2 January 1911: "The Government of India are not satisfied with situation that has arisen in Dubai… action of Commander was hardly prudent and was likely to provoke reprisals." The Viceroy, Curzon, noted: "object originally in view was hardly worth the risk", labelled the reprisals "Onerous" and urged Cox to restore "friendly relations with the least possible delay".

Cox back-pedalled. "I think this is perhaps a case in which telegraphic brevity or faulty expression has conveyed a wrong impression." He cavilled in a telegram back to Curzon, who had balked at the very idea of installing a British agent in Dubai under threat of bombardment of the town,[21] let alone at the fine of 50,000 rupees Cox had levied against Butti bin Suhail.

Cox's presentiment of 'newspaper misrepresentation' was to prove all too true. The influential *Times of India* gleefully weighed in with a piece filed on 31 December 1910, which pointed out that the mood on the coast generally was that the British interdiction of shipping that had been taking place was viewed by the locals as an attempt to disarm the Arabs – a sentiment stoked by Egyptian newspapers and helped by the fact that the British were allowing the trade at Muscat to continue even as they captured and burned dhows in the Gulf. "They see no reason why what is sauce for the Muscat goose," sniffed the *Times*, "should not be sauce for the Dubai gander."

Curzon clearly agreed with this view of public opinion on the coast. His cable to Cox ends with an instruction to British forces in the area: "it should be clearly explained to the tribesmen at Dubai, as elsewhere, that they have no intention of weakening their independence, or of preventing their own possession of arms."

Cox, bowed down by the pressure from India, had to relinquish his idea of further bombarding Dubai and installing a British agent. "It was only intended to demolish the fort and then some of the outlying houses," he whined in a cable to Bombay.

It was left to the townsfolk of Dubai to bury their thirty-seven dead, tend to the wounded and repair the walls the *Hyacinth's* guns had brought down. No apology from the British Government has been forthcoming to this day.

Chapter 20
TROUBLED TIMES IN SHARJAH

"You cannot separate the just from the unjust and the good from the wicked, for they stand together before the face of the sun even as the black thread and the white are woven together."

– Khalil Gibran

When Cleopatra and Mark Anthony were courting, they each set out sumptuous banquets for the other, Cleopatra drawing on the huge resources of Egypt and Mark Anthony on Rome to provide displays of such outrageous finery that they are still remembered today. Cleopatra won their little game by putting on a dinner that cost more than any other in history. At the end of what was no more or less than the other dinners, Cleopatra provided her coup de grâce – she took off one of her priceless pearl earrings, placed the white orb into a glass containing a little vinegar and drank the dissolved pearl.

Of all the pearls in the world, those of the Gulf were most sought after through the centuries. Even the Sumerians, the old trading partners of the Hafit and Umm Al Nar peoples, referred to shipments from Magan of 'fish eyes'. As the 1800s drew to their close, the international trade in Gulf pearls remained vibrant. Merchants such as Sharjah's Obaid Al Naboodah rubbed shoulders with the finest jewellers, the Fabergés and Cartiers, and were feted by buyers from Parisian socialites to Indian Maharajahs. They represented the pinnacle of a complex set of relationships that effectively defined the economy of the Trucial Coast. The pullers and divers sweated through the humid summer months as they toiled daily to bring up the shells in coir rope bags, brushed by the stinging tendrils of jellyfish and their lungs bursting as they grabbed a few precious breaths before diving again. Many were slaves, some were Bedouin working seasonally. The catch would be laid out, the shells prised open and the nacreous lining displayed, carefully examined for the potential booty within. Hundreds of oysters would be shucked for each pearl found. Their calloused fingers raw and bleeding, the men would pray, eat and sleep before waking to the dawn prayer and another day's back-breaking work. The scale of the fisheries was enormous – oyster shell middens found on the coast dating from the late 1800s have been measured at as much as 200 metres wide by three kilometres long, comprising millions of shells.[1]

Their *nakhuda*, captain, would take the catch to the merchant, his hopes and those of his men contained in a little leather bag which would be presented for weighing and measuring. Haggling would be prolonged and almost ritual, involving every trick in the book as the merchants hid the gleam in their eyes when a particularly big pearl was presented, the *nakhuda* airily offering to take the prize elsewhere if the price wasn't right.

A bad season would bring gloom to the towns of the coast and hardship to the families who depended on the fisheries – including the rulers who taxed the pearling boats.

A slow decline

The accepted narrative is that the Gulf pearling industry was decimated by a double blow, the invention of the cultured pearl by the Japanese entrepreneur Mikimoto Kokichi and the Great Depression of 1929. Between them, we have been told for decades now, these two events caused the decline of the pearl fisheries, plunging the economies of the Trucial Coast into penury and extreme hardship. It turns out, sadly, that this is and always has been complete rubbish.

The truth is that the rot had set in long before either Mikimoto or the depression. The pearling industry faced a slow and merciless death from the early 1900s onwards. By the time 1929 came around, the industry was already beyond recovery. 1929 may have provided the final nail, but the coffin was already made, the corpse laid out and the lid firmly in place.

If the 1910 '*Hyacinth* incident' had caused many of the Persian merchants so successfully lured to Dubai by Suhail bin Butti Al Maktoum to remove themselves back to Bandar Abbas or to seek sanctuary in other Trucial ports, the constant conflicts in Persia drove more to settle in the busy little port on the southern shore of the Gulf. In November 1911 alone, 300 people fled from Lar, heading for Lingeh and Dubai.[2]

Against this background of instability and the movement of people, the 1911 pearling season was poor and the demand in the market was low. By the following year, the pearl market was virtually paralysed by the outbreak of the Turkish/Balkan war. The take from the 1912 season was not only poor, but the market in Bombay was so dull that there was actually a glut of pearls in Dubai and Sharjah with no takers for them.

Following a stroke on 15 October 1912, which paralysed his left hand, Butti bin Suhail Al Maktoum died on 29 November at the end of the pearling season. His cousin, Saeed bin Maktoum bin Hasher Al Maktoum, acceded – his smooth accession guaranteed by Sheikh Butti bin Rashid Al Maktoum, the son of the former Ruler Rashid bin Maktoum, who managed the transition.

Saeed bin Maktoum was to rule over a difficult time for Dubai as the pearl merchants and boat owners suffered from the constantly depressed market conditions but barely had time to set his affairs in order before a virulent outbreak of plague swept through the town. Saeed bin Maktoum removed his household to the interior, as did many of the wealthier families of Dubai. Houses left empty were looted as the townspeople grappled with despair and the narrow alleyways were filled with the wailing of mourning women: something like twenty people were dying daily and mortality in the first quarter of 1913 was estimated at 1,300.

By 1914, the plague had spread to Sharjah, with up to five people dying daily, and to Ajman. Although the outbreak subsided by May of that year, over a thousand lost their lives in Sharjah, with the death rate in Dubai still running high. Sharjah's Ruler, Khalid bin Ahmed Al Qasimi, himself fell victim to the disease, but made a full recovery. In August, Sheikh Butti bin Rashid Al Maktoum, a senior member of the family, also contracted the disease and died of it.

In 1914, the pearling season was brought to an early close by Ramadan, which started at the end of July. The season was not only short, but the catch poor and the fleets had struggled with a series of northerly shamal winds. The market was depressed by the outbreak of war in Europe and by August the French pearl buyers had left the Gulf. German traders also set off for home as Europe mobilised.

The pearl market was now plunged into crisis and wherever possible foreign pearl divers were repatriated. Receipts to the Rulers of the Gulf from pearling and general trade plummeted as spending dried up and the whole coastal economy was driven into recession. By the start of the 1915 season, the Great War led to a state of constant uncertainty and wild speculation, with some local notables backing Turkey against the European powers, while many waited to see whether Persia would join the war. German agents were active in the region, particularly in Mesopotamia and Persia, and sentiment was highly volatile.

Many of the Kuwaiti pearling fleet didn't even bother to sail, some 60 per cent of the boats at port stayed behind. The fleets of the Trucial Coast sailed in May, but the Trucial Rulers laid out lower rates of pay for pullers and divers alike. These were generally accepted; the febrile state of the market being widely recognised. Merchants speculating on pearls lost huge amounts, having taken pearls against 1914 debt payments, while others just about broke-even on 1915 purchases.

The 1915 season was again split by the Holy Month of Ramadan, the first fishing taking place from May to mid-July, then the second from mid-August. Once more, the yield was poor and the market depressed and few of the boats made a profit. Dejected, dispirited and no doubt squabbling amongst themselves, the divers made their way back to their ports and worried privately about the future. The merchants had visited the boats on the pearl banks throughout the season, and would have known that the take was bad. There were no prizes, no glorious pearls to inspire any *nakhuda* down on his luck that fortune could change in an instant.

And even if there were, the market was not interested. There were other stores of value in time of war and Europe, laid out in trenches with hordes of young men being thrown against the guns of the Somme and Ypres, had other concerns than draping pretty necks with glorious trophies.

Clouds gather

The British were increasingly worried about the security of the Trucial States against looming regional forces. The re-emergence of a strong Saudi state under Ibn Saud, the increasing unfriendliness of the government of Persia and German influence over the Ottoman Empire and its adherents in the Gulf were all of concern.

Abdulaziz Ibn Saud was the founder of modern Saudi Arabia, arguably the 'third Saudi state' and was to emerge as a huge figure with enormous influence on the region around him. Recapturing Riyadh for the House of Saud in 1902, he went on to conquer central Arabia and, by

1915 he was only held back from asserting his 'hereditary claim' to the Trucial States by British influence and subsidy and had, in December 1915, signed a treaty with them to maintain 'friendly and peaceful relations' with the Trucial Coast.³

The German and Ottoman threat was less alarming, although the British lost no time in countering any manifestations of German influence they met in the area, including successfully lobbying the Persian government to demand a German telegraph station being built on their territory be dismantled. However, events such as the huge disaster which took place at the Dardanelles – where Britain and her allies endured a massive defeat at Gallipoli in 1915 – were considered massively prejudicial to British standing in the region. British prestige, that quality which had been considered so important that it be upheld by bombarding coastal settlements, was at an unprecedented low.

Not only were pressures building outside the Trucial States: a tremendous change was now taking place within the Al Qasimi Federation, which was to shape the area irrevocably.

Sheikh Saqr bin Khalid Al Qasimi of Sharjah had seen the Federation diminished in the thirty years of his rule, with the independence of the Shihuh, of Fujairah and of Hamriyah. Although he had reasserted his rule over Ras Al Khaimah after the independently-minded Humaid bin Abdullah Al Qasimi suffered a stroke, he was later forced to appoint his Uncle Salim bin Sultan as Wali of Ras Al Khaimah in 1910 in place of his own son, Khalid. Salim bin Sultan, who Saqr had usurped as Ruler of Sharjah, was just as – if not more – independent of Sharjah than Humaid bin Abdullah had been.

Saqr bin Khalid Al Qasimi died in early 1914 and, shortly before his death nominated his cousin, Khalid bin Ahmad Al Qasimi to succeed him. In May 1914, Khalid bin Ahmad was confirmed as the new Ruler of Sharjah, albeit at the time he was struck down with the plague, which had taken thousands of lives on the coast.⁴

Recovering from his illness, Khalid bin Ahmad was left with the problem of Saqr bin Khalid's young son (still in his minority), Sultan bin Saqr Al Qasimi, who was living in Sharjah. Although Saqr bin Khalid,

Sultan's father, had named Khaled bin Ahmed as ruler, his young son Sultan would pose a potential threat to Khalid bin Ahmad as long as he lived in the town.

Khalid quickly moved against the young man and seized both property and money from him. Sultan bin Saqr was understandably embittered at this treatment and, his petitions to Khalid bin Ahmad unanswered, he eventually decamped to exile Dubai in 1921.

In the meantime, Khalid bin Ahmad tried to re-assert his primacy over the former Al Qasimi territories, putting down a revolt in Hamriyah in early 1916 with the assistance of the British ship HMS *Philomel*, which was used to induce Hamriyah to sign a peace with Khalid on 29 February 1916.[5] Having settled the status of Jazirat Al Hamra in 1914 (agreeing with Salim bin Sultan of Ras Al Khaimah that the town, home to the Zaab tribe, would be governed by Ras Al Khaimah), Khalid also moved to place his brother, Rashid bin Ahmad Al Qasimi, as Wali of Dibba, in 1919.

Ras Al Khaimah, although nominally under Sharjah's control, was in fact being ruled as an independent state by Salim bin Sultan, the former Al Qasimi Ruler of Sharjah. This arrangement was duly inherited by Khalid bin Ahmad when he acceded to rule Sharjah, and he had to accept his writ – however unwillingly – didn't run to Ras Al Khaimah.

In July 1919, Salim bin Sultan Al Qasimi of Ras Al Khaimah, formally abdicated in favour of his son, Sultan bin Salim Al Qasimi. An old man by now, Salim had long been paralysed and was considered to be close to death. Sultan, his son, had effectively been managing affairs and when Salim eventually died on 26 August, Sultan took over control of the emirate.

One of Sultan bin Salim's first moves was to petition the British for the recognition of Ras Al Khaimah as a Trucial State in its own right. Visiting Sultan in December 1919, the Political Resident, Arthur Trevor, judged that Sultan was too young to rule and his hold on power, in view of strong factions supporting the claims of his brother Muhammad, too precarious. By the following year even Trevor had to accept that Sultan was Ruler in both name and reality and on 7 June 1921, Ras Al Khaimah was officially recognised as a Trucial State, effectively establishing beyond any argument that it was independent of Sharjah.[6]

Khalid bin Ahmad of Sharjah was, it appears, powerless to intervene. That is probably because he had his hands full as a new and divisive figure emerged to dominate events across the area we know as Sharjah today. The stern figure of Abdulrahman bin Muhammad Al Shamsi was to influence Sharjah, Ajman and the east coast for some time to come. A strong and domineering character, Abdulrahman Al Shamsi was deeply unpopular with the British and took no pains to disguise his contempt for them. He was not a man to be trifled with; strong, wilful and popular with the Bedouin of the interior, a leader of men and a rebel at heart, Al Shamsi was the headman of Al Heera – today a little-known coastal suburb on the northern border of Sharjah with Ajman.

The King Maker

In 1920, Al Heera was a coastal township, nominally under the control of Sharjah but separated from the city by some three miles of barren desert and salt flats. In 1830, it was mentioned as a 'Joasmee dependency' during an account of a piracy committed by its residents, but by the turn of the next century it was a thriving port in its own right and the neighbouring port of Fasht (or Fisht) had been abandoned – Al Heera became the commonly known settlement on the northern Sharjah/Ajman border. In 1906, Al Heera enjoyed a small and active pearling fleet of twenty-five boats (each would have required a crew of some eighteen men) and ten fishing boats. Date groves stretched inland with 2,500 trees, and the populace kept herds of livestock and even sustained a few shops. The town, consisting of some 250 houses in all, was watered by relatively shallow wells and defended by a number of towers.[7] Its headman was Abdulrahman bin Muhammad Al Shamsi of the Al Bu Shamis tribe.

Al Shamsi was a formidable figure whose actions would shape the future of the Trucial States. He was driven, ambitious and forceful – and his hatred of the ruling family of Ajman was absolute. He never forgot that Ajman town had originally been settled by to his people, the Al Bu Shamis subsection of the Darawishah Na'im not, as he saw it, the crowd from Buraimi who had settled there and displaced the Al Bu Shamis. Pushed out to Al Heera and Hamriyah, Abdulrahman's people had settled for second best, but he wasn't a man to let that slight lie, even if it had taken place a lifetime and more ago. Abdulrahman could see the towers of Ajman fort from Al Heera on a clear day, shimmering on the white sands and he was drawn to them as irrevocably as a moth to a flame.

Mired in debt
The pearl seasons continued to be poor and the coastal settlements all suffered. A slight recovery took place in 1916, both the catch and the market were more lively but the Great War continued to cast a shadow over demand for pearls. The pearl fishing season was now split almost in half by Ramadan, so the fleets all sailed twice. In 1917, the Sharjah boats left for the pearl banks early, but the market in India was weak. A rare highlight was the finding of a huge pearl of unusually high quality in July of that year by a diver from Umm Al Quwain, who handed it to a Dubai man to whom he owed 10,000 rupees – the pearl was initially valued at 75,000 rupees but the Ruler of Umm Al Quwain, Rashid bin Ahmad Al Mualla, took an interest in the transaction and quarrelled with the Dubai man, asserting the pearl was worth over 100,000 rupees.[8]

It was a rare glimmer of light – following the poor first season, many boats from Dubai and Sharjah did not even sail for the second season after Ramadan – pearlers were in debt to their *nakhudas* and had no way of settling those debts. Worse, 1918 saw bad weather afflicting the pearlers and another poor season. A deadly outbreak of influenza swept across the region later in that year, the infamous Spanish flu pandemic, and 10,000 people were reported dead in Oman from the disease, which raged throughout Europe and Asia following the war.

Despite a recovery in both the catch and the market in the 1919 season, debt still loomed over the people of the coast like a cloud. Worse, the Rulers were unable to raise taxes from pearl boats on the brink of penury, already ensnared in debt and caught between the debts they owed moneymen and traders and the indebtedness to them of their divers. Food prices throughout the coast had rocketed and in December 1919 Khalid bin Ahmad Al Qasimi, the Ruler of Sharjah, was forced to raise a subscription to maintain himself and his position – the people of Layyah,[9] Sharjah and Al Heera provided him with funds, 31,000 rupees in all. Al Khan demurred and was eventually convinced, with the help of the British Residency Agent in Sharjah, to part with 2,000 rupees. At the time, a bag of rice was selling for between forty and forty-five rupees and a bag of flour thirty-five rupees.

In January 1920, the Ruler of Dubai, Sheikh Saeed, was himself forced to raise a subscription and, after much complaining – as they were themselves mired in debt – the prominent folk of the town eventually raised 21,000 rupees to help maintain their ruling family and its obligations.

The first pearling season of 1920 was again poor. Already pushed to the edge, many people were now at their wits' end. Prominent among these was Abdulrahman bin Muhammad Al Shamsi of Al Heera, whose debts had now mounted to 21,560 rupees – almost equivalent to the entire subscription raised by the town of Dubai for the maintenance of its ruling family and the tribes and others to whom Dubai paid subsidies. It was an enormous level of indebtedness for a man who commanded a small fleet of twenty-five pearling boats.

Convinced of his right to a position in Ajman, his back against the wall and debtors snapping at his heels, Abdulrahman was by now a desperate man and raised a force, which headed north and attacked the fort of Ajman on 15 June 1920. It was almost the end of Ramadan and the pearling boats would have taken to the seas once again directly after Eid Al Adha. Abdulrahman's window of opportunity was slight but his attack was a triumph and the Ruler of Ajman, Humaid bin Abdulaziz Al Nuaimi was forced to flee. Abdulrahman occupied the fort and became, briefly, the Ruler of Ajman.[10]

It was not to last. Ajman's Ruler, Humaid bin Abdulaziz, sought the assistance of Khalid bin Ahmad Al Qasimi of Sharjah and the support of Khan Bahadur Isa bin Abdullatif Al Serkal, the British Residency Agent. Abdulrahman was persuaded by these worthies of the futility of his occupation of the fort and was promised the luxury of a safe passage in return for renouncing his claim. Leaving bodies in the streets and the shops of the town's souq in flames, Abdulrahman and his men left Ajman. He had 'ruled' for less than a week.

Humaid bin Abdulaziz Al Nuaimi had his fort and town back, but he was furious at Abdulrahman's insubordination and the attack that had taken place. He swore to have his revenge if Abdulrahman should go back to Al Heera and Khalid bin Ahmad of Sharjah agreed with him that a return to Al Heera would just lead to more trouble in the future. It was looking bleak indeed for Abdulrahman, whose only recourse was to go north and take sanctuary among the Shihuh in the Rus Al Jibal, the mountainous interior of Ras Al Khaimah and Musandam.

However, Abdulrahman's debts were enormous – and a great deal of money was owed to Indian traders and merchants who were British subjects. Isa bin Abdullatif Al Serkal acted in their interests, with the backing of the Political Resident in Bushire, and offered Abdulrahman asylum in the Residency Agent's house in Sharjah. The Political Resident intervened with Humaid bin Abdulaziz Al Nuaimi, asking that Abdulrahman be allowed to set himself up in Al Khan, away from Ajman's border and that he should there attempt to repay his debts by taking to the sea for the 1921 pearling season.

Meanwhile Abdulrahman had travelled to Bahrain where he tried to gain a foothold in that country's larger and more lucrative pearling business. Failing in this, he returned to Dubai in December 1920 where his loyal subjects from Al Heera went to him and encouraged his return to his home town. Once again set up in Al Heera, Abdulrahman immediately faced the revenge of Ajman, supported by Sharjah, and was forced to defend himself, beaten back to Al Heera fort where he took shelter from the two Rulers' forces. The British, mindful of the debts owed to their subjects, now took a hand in matters, sending HMS *Triad* to enforce a peace between the three parties. A truce was signed on 8 January 1921, Abdulrahman agreeing to quit Al Heera for Sharjah for a period of one month and thereafter not to cause trouble. Khalid bin Ahmad of Sharjah agreed to act as guarantor for Abdulrahman, now pledged to be a subject of Sharjah. One signature missing on the piece of paper was that of Humaid bin

Abdulaziz Al Nuaimi of Ajman, whose opposition to having anything to do with Abdulrahman was implacable. He endured some pressure from the British over this, but held his ground. As far as Humaid was concerned, Abdulrahman was public enemy number one.

Humaid's fury at Abdulrahman's rebellion and his rejection of British attempts to force a reconciliation were to get him into considerable trouble with the British Political Resident. Arthur Trevor's initial view of Humaid as a man wronged by Abdulrahman was tempered by Humaid's refusal to come aboard HMS *Triad* and negotiate a peace with Khalid bin Ahmad Al Qasimi and Abdulrahman Al Shamsi. In December 1920, Trevor sailed *Triad* to Ajman to investigate reports that Humaid had torn up a slave's manumission certificate – a direct challenge to British authority. Humaid refused to see the Resident, who returned to Ajman in May 1921 with HMS *Crocus* and *Cyclamen*, two Arabis class navy sloops built during World War I. Trevor concluded that Humaid had, indeed, torn up the certificate and fined him 1,000 rupees. Humaid, still infuriated over the Abdulrahman incident and consequent British meddling, refused to pay the fine, despite an ultimatum and the threat to bombard his watchtowers.

The two warships opened fire, quickly destroying one of the towers. They had moved on to a second tower, damaging it severely, by the time Humaid's capitulation reached them. He was never again to defy British authority, but was left with very little reason indeed to love Abrulrahman.

The war for Sharjah

The young and dispossessed Sultan bin Saqr Al Qasimi left Sharjah in 1921, a bitter man. His father, the Ruler, had died and passed his leadership on to Khalid bin Ahmad Al Qasimi, who now ruled Sharjah – a position which Sultan bin Saqr undoubtedly saw as rightfully belonging to him. Worse, Khalid bin Ahmad had taken young Sultan's property and money, despite the disapproval of the prominent citizens of Sharjah at his actions. Khalid's rule was increasingly unpopular: he had lost control of Ras Al Khaimah and the town of Hamriyah was determinedly independent of him. Al Heera had usurped his authority, seemingly with impunity, and his taxes on the cash-strapped and struggling pearling fleet were felt to be unbearable.

Sultan bin Saqr took up residence in Dubai and it was there, in 1923 that he married. His new bride was the daughter of none other than Abdulrahman bin Muhammad Al Shamsi, headman of Al Heera and a thorn in the side of the Rulers of both Ajman and Sharjah.

The match threw Khalid bin Ahmad Al Qasimi into a fury and he immediately marched against Al Heera. Abdulrahman appealed to the British Residency Agent, who put two of his own men on guard at the gates of Al Heera Fort. Khalid bin Ahmad then appointed a Wali over Al Heera and Abdulrahman duly had the man captured, imprisoned and then forcefully ejected. It was the final straw. Khalid bin Ahmad marched, guards or no guards, on Al Heera. Abdulrahman had, in the meantime, barricaded and reinforced the town. Stopped in his tracks by the defences, Khalid bin Ahmad was now caught in a bind. The conflict with Al Heera was deeply unpopular with the people of Sharjah and, with Abdulrahman Al Shamsi so clearly settled in and prepared for a fight, was likely to be costly in terms of both cash and lives. Khalid called on the British Residency Agent, who had already worked to stop the conflict escalating. The Residency Agent wrote to tell Humaid bin Abdulaziz of Ajman to avoid being drawn into the conflict and to Sheikh Saeed of Dubai to stop young Sultan bin Saqr Al Qasimi from throwing his hat into the ring. British residency agent Isa bin Abdullatif Al Serkal and the British Resident, Arthur Trevor, now brokered a peace between Khalid bin Ahmed and Abdulrahman bin Muhammad Al Shamsi. Abdulrahman was forced to leave Al Heera and head for Dubai and the house of his son-in-law.

But not for long. By the end of the pearling season of 1924, the people of Sharjah had had enough of Khalid bin Ahmed and his conflicts and taxes. They wrote to the exiled Sultan bin Saqr in Dubai asking him to assert his right as Ruler of Sharjah and return. This he was only too happy to do, buoyed up by the Bedouin forces Abdulrahman raised. Sultan bin Saqr entered Sharjah on 1 November 1924 and, following eleven days of street to street fighting, Khalid bin Ahmad Al Qasimi conceded defeat.

Sultan bin Saqr Al Qasimi, supported by his formidable father-in-law, was now the Ruler of Sharjah.

A new broom

Sultan bin Saqr took over an unhappy town. The pearl trade continued to be depressed and *nakhudas* were having a hard time getting divers and haulers to work for the meagre advances they were able to offer (each was traditionally paid an advance on the season's haul). Up the Gulf in Kuwait, the pearlers actually went on strike, refusing to work for the 120 rupees and eighty rupees offered for divers and haulers respectively. Many, in debt up to their eyes already, absconded. By the end of May 1925, when the pearling season should have started, half the Kuwaiti fleet remained in port.[11] Things were no different in Sharjah and, to add to the problems of debt and penury, Sultan bin Saqr had to try to stabilise the town he had just taken by force and return it to some semblance of order. If he had hoped to do this in peace with a viable economy in place, he was much mistaken.

Fujairah in flames

The independently minded Fujairah had long had a fractious relationship with its neighbour, Kalba, which was an Al Qasimi dependency.

In the 1870s, Salim bin Sultan Al Qasimi, the Ruler of Sharjah at the time, had granted the Shamaliyah region, including Kalba, as a fiefdom to his brother Majid Al Qasimi. On Majid's death, Kalba was ruled jointly by his two sons Hamad and Majid. In 1902, Saeed bin Hamad Al Qasimi became Ruler of Kalba. Saeed bin Hamad's accession took place at a time when the Ruler of neighbouring Fujairah, Hamad bin Abdullah Al Sharqi, had managed to establish his independence – at least in the eyes of the other Trucial Rulers, if not the British.

Kalba, loyal to Sharjah, was a constant thorn in Hamad bin Abdullah Al Sharqi's side, but Saeed bin Hamad was an absentee ruler, living in Ajman and leaving the administration of Kalba in the hands of a slave named Barut. In the 1920s, Saeed once again took up residence at Kalba and this appears to have provoked Hamad bin Abdullah of Fujairah.

Hamad bin Abdullah now become embroiled in a fight with the British after he bought a Baluchi girl from Muscat, breaking the embargo on slave trading. The British Political Resident, Francis Bellville Prideaux, decided to enforce the rules and, in April 1925, he anchored off Fujairah in the RIMS *Lawrence* and raised the Resident's flag – the signal for a Trucial Ruler to come aboard for talks. Hamad refused and demanded a letter of safe conduct, which was issued. He then refused again and Prideaux, conscious as ever of 'British prestige' punished Hamad by bombarding Fujairah fort, destroying three of the fort's towers and killing Hamad's daughter-in-law in the process.[12]

Hamad bin Abdullah quite unjustly blamed Saeed bin Hamad of Kalba for having instigated the British bombardment and the mutual antagonism between them threatened to boil over in May 1926. Saeed bin Hamad would normally have turned to Sharjah's ruler for help against Fujairah, but Sultan bin Saqr Al Qasimi had his hands full and so it was to the Sultan of Muscat that Saeed bin Hamad eventually appealed to for help against his neighbour. A treaty was eventually signed between the two on 21 May, but Sharjah's Ruler was notably absent from negotiations – even the brother of the former ruler of Sharjah was at the negotiating table. As Ruler of Sharjah, Sultan bin Saqr Al Qasimi's standing was undoubtedly lessened by his absence from the negotiations and his inability to aid Saeed bin Hamad of Kalba. But Sultan bin Saqr had bigger and more important fish to fry – his father-in-law was accused of murder and had fled Sharjah in fear of British retribution.

Murder most foul

On 11 October 1925, Ibrahim bin Rajab, the cousin of the British Residency Agent in Sharjah, Isa Bin Abdullatif Al Serkal, was murdered by a shot fired from the closely packed houses of Sharjah town.[13] It was thought the shot was intended for the agent himself. Al Serkal initially conjectured the action was triggered by his renewal of an old insistence that a flagpole be put up at the agency house in order to fly the British flag, and blamed the Ruler of Sharjah and his retainers and family.[14]

Stuart Horner, secretary to the Political Resident, was sent to Sharjah to investigate, on board HMS *Cyclamen*. He took with him the Bahraini merchant, Yusuf bin Ahmed Al Kanoo who was, according to a note Horner wrote to the Resident, 'of very little actual assistance.'

The evidence presented to Horner came mostly from Al Serkal and was a patchwork of hearsay and conjecture, which pointed to Abdulrahman bin Muhammad Al Shamsi being the culprit, including the offer of testimony from a woman who saw a freed slave linked to Abdulrahman holding a gun nearby where the shooting had taken place.[15] Horner also spoke to a number of Indian merchants, of whom one – a Hyderabadi merchant of Dubai – was certain Abdulrahman was to blame.

In the face of the Residency Agent's fear of another attack, Horner arranged that Abdulrahman would be sent to Ras Al Khaimah where he was given into the custody of the Ruler, Sultan bin Salim Al Qasimi, who was handed the responsibility of ensuring that Abdulrahman did not abscond. At least part of Horner's reasoning was that, with the intimidating presence of Abdulrahman removed, more witnesses might come forward. None did.

After deliberations, and under increasing pressure from the Trucial Rulers as well as the heads of the Al Bu Shamis to free the accused, it was decided that Abdulrahman would be exiled to Aden for a period of four years (Karachi for five was the original suggestion of the Political Resident, Francis Prideaux). The British duly sent HMS *Triad* and the sloop HMS *Cyclamen* to Ras Al Khaimah, where the Ruler, Sultan bin Salim refused to give up Abdulrahman 'for fear of consequences to himself'. With the help of Saeed Al Maktoum of Dubai, five days later on 16 June 1926, Abdulrahman bin Muhammad Al Shamsi gave himself up to the British.[16]

Abdulrahman was transported to Muscat where he was kept in custody until 16 August 1926, when he was transferred on HMS *Lupin* to Bombay, where he arrived – and was handed over to the Bombay police

– on 22 August. On 28 August, he left Bombay on the P&O mail and passenger boat, the RMS *Kaiser I Hind*, bound for Aden (a previous passenger on this ship was T. E. Lawrence) and his four-year exile in Yemen.[17]

800 rupees was to be paid by Sharjah to the family of the agent's murdered cousin and a fine of 3,000 rupees was to be paid to the government of India 'on account of the outrage'. Among the extensive and detailed correspondence between the Residencies in Sharjah and Bushire and the Government in Bombay relating to the murder and Abdulrahman's capture, imprisonment and exile, there is no mention of any judicial process or of any finding of guilt based on the presentation of collected evidence or a confession. Abdulrahman went into exile without benefit of a trial and on no more evidence than hearsay.

Sultan bin Salim had lost his father-in-law, advisor and raiser of his military forces. He had also lost the backing of a strongman, whom he appears to have desperately needed. Abdulrahman's influence would doubtless have shaped events to follow rather differently.

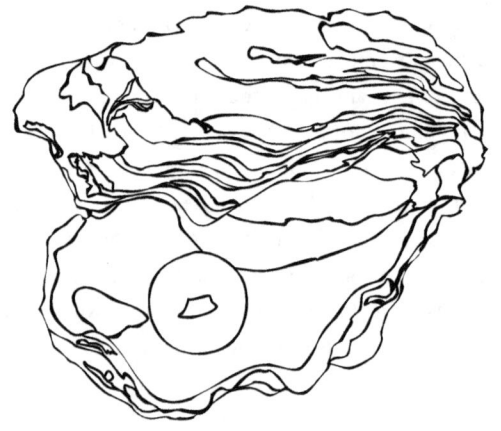

Chapter 21

THE PASSING OF THE PEARLS

"How could you reach the pearl by only looking at the sea? If you seek the pearl, be a diver."

- Jalal Al Din Rumi

As we have seen, the pearling industry did not in fact suffer a cataclysmic shock in 1929 but had been struggling with over-fishing, poor harvests, systemic debt and a febrile market since the early 1900s. We can certainly date the movement from bustling international trade to struggling penury to the year 1911, fully eighteen years before the 'doomsday date' that has been bandied about with such certitude as 'the end of the pearling industry'.

The fact is, the Trucial States were already struggling with indebtedness and penury throughout the first quarter of the twentieth century, long before the Great Depression ever took place. The people were poor, the rulers were poor and the natural resources that sustained them were at best scant. The Bedouin lived on their wits and hunting in the desert; bread, dates and camel milk were their staples. The killing of an animal, usually to celebrate an honoured guest, was a rare act of hospitality that meant weeks of hardship afterwards. Resources were husbanded and guarded jealously and conflicts erupted quickly while wounds healed slowly, both literally and figuratively. It was a harsh existence by any standard and it is hardly surprising that the Bedouin, especially as they were deprived of the brief wealth of the pearling season, would take to raiding the wealthier settled populations of the coastal settlements.

At the same time, the Trucial Rulers of the coast were truly at their wits' end – the pearling fleets were giving up and not even bothering to sail, yet there was precious little other commerce to sustain the communities other than entrepôt trade.

Dubai was the busiest trading port on the coast, but there were growing problems between the traders and money-men – often Indian and therefore British subjects – and the pearlers who were local in origin. Between them sat the Persian traders, neither protected by the British nor considered local, but whose presence was appreciated by the mercantile-minded rulers of Dubai. The Persians became subsumed into being considered Dubaians – the restored area of Bur Dubai's Creekside beside the Amiri Diwan and Fahidi Fort that is today home to galleries, teahouses and funky hotels was known as Bastakiya precisely because many of its merchants had fled to Dubai from the Persian town and area of Bastak. Here, the Persian *barjeel*, or wind tower, predominated, catching the summer breeze and channelling it down to provide relief, scant though it may be, to the sweltering people below. The adobe house and its towering *barjeel* was a symbol of considerable wealth as most people in Dubai lived in *areesh* (palm-frond) huts.

By 1926, the very existence of the pearling industry was imperilled on the Trucial Coast because the general indebtedness across the whole pearling ecosystem had risen to the point where merchants could not provide advances or supplies to divers and haulers. The Rulers, first Sultan bin Saqr Al Qasimi of Sharjah and Saeed bin Maktoum of Dubai, then the Rulers of Ajman and Umm Al Quwain, settled the advances on divers at 100 rupees and two bags of rice and haulers were to get seventy rupees and one bag of rice. This was quarter of the normal sum advanced to the pearlers. The boats started out for the banks late, on 4 July, but the season was once again disastrous and earnings for the average boat dropped 40 per cent year on year.

The situation called for desperate measures and, in November 1926, fourteen boats set out from Dubai to try for a late season around Socotra and Eritrea, with permission from the Italian government.

All along the coast there was trouble. Fujairah and Kalba once again found themselves at odds, with Kalba this time appealing to Sultan bin Saqr Al Qasimi in Sharjah. With Abdulrahman bin Shamsi still in exile in Yemen, Sultan bin Saqr was little use. Lacking his father-in-law's influence among the tribes of the interior, particularly with the Bani Qitab, Sultan bin Saqr was quite powerless to intervene and the governor of Kalba left the town. In the end, by February 1927, a truce was arranged by the Ruler of Ras Al Khaimah.

In Sharjah, the Marar and Sudan tribes found themselves at loggerheads and Sultan bin Saqr was once again unable to handle reconciling the two. The Marar had settled the Layyah area of Sharjah, removing themselves from Dubai in 1891. In January 1927, 150 members of the tribe left Sharjah for Dubai. To this day, the neighbourhood where they settled in Deira, inland of the Hyatt Regency Hotel, bears their name: Al Marar.

There were squabbles over debts and Sultan bin Saqr did little to address these. The British Residency Agent was called on by a number of Indian and Persian merchants who complained of the restless and disturbed state of the town. The Agent himself was feeling exposed and suspected an ambush had been planned against him by Sultan bin Saqr's aggressive brother as he had travelled through Al Jurf, an outlying area of Ajman (today home to an industrial estate and the Ajman China Mall). Furious at the imprisonment of his father-in-law, and clearly missing his strongman relative by marriage as he struggled to maintain his hold on authority, Sultan bin Saqr was uninterested in dealing with the Agent in response to either area of concern.

Although removed as Ruler of Sharjah, Khalid bin Ahmad Al Qasimi retained strong influence over Sharjah's eastern dependencies of Dhaid, Dibba and Kalba. Attempting to consolidate his control over Sharjah, Sultan bin Saqr removed Khalid bin Ahmad's brother, Rashid bin Ahmed, as Wali of Dibba. The move was unpopular amongst the people of Dibba, itself a divided town, with the Shihuh dominating the Omani northern part of the town, the Al Qasimi the middle part and the south belonging to Fujairah. The two northern halves were divided by a 'no man's land' dotted with ghaf trees. Rashid bin Ahmed led a revolt against his removal and subsequently remained as Wali of Dibba until his death in 1937.[1]

With his brother in control of Dibba, Khalid bin Ahmad wasn't giving up his claim to Sharjah without a fight and, if Sultan bin Saqr was looking weak and unable to act in the absence of Abdulrahman Al Shamsi, then Khalid bin Ahmad was the man to take the opportunity of using the situation to stage a comeback. Sultan bin Saqr, like the other Trucial Rulers facing constant near-penury, had sold some property belonging to Khalid Bin Ahmad (who, it may be remembered, had no problem helping himself to Sultan bin Saqr's inheritance when the young Sheikh was in his minority) and Khalid used this as the perfect *casus belli*.

As Ramadan ended, on 10 June 1927, Khalid bin Ahmed led a force of men with the support of Umm Al Quwain, Hamriyah and the Bani

Qitab, against Sharjah. Fighting broke out and carried on for another eleven days until, on 21 June, the British ship *Triad* arrived, followed by HMS *Lupin* on 25 June. Although Sultan bin Saqr had managed to beat back Khalid's forces, he was forced to parley.

An agreement was reached between Sultan bin Saqr and Khalid bin Ahmad to provide for the upkeep of the former ruler's family. Khalid was compensated for his property and awarded an annual allowance of 2,500 rupees and the fort at Dhaid and the oasis town's revenues were ceded to him. However, Khalid was afraid to take up his new desert fiefdom and repaired to the relative safety of Umm Al Quwain, whose inland town of Falaj Al Mualla abutted Dhaid.

Khalid bin Ahmad sent some of his men to Dhaid to occupy his newly acquired property, as the Bedouin who had previously manned the fort were still loyal to Sultan bin Saqr and remained active in the area. With the support of the Sheikhs of the Bedouin Bani Ka'ab and Na'im tribes, who favoured any scheme that would weaken Sharjah, it was agreed that the ruler of Ras Al Khaimah, Sultan bin Salim Al Qasimi, would possess Dhaid 'on behalf of Khalid bin Ahmad'.

This happy arrangement between the Bedouin Sheikhs was not actually supported by Sultan bin Salim of Ras Al Khaimah at all, who wanted at all costs to avoid antagonising his fellow Ruler in Sharjah, Sultan bin Saqr, and who was also convinced that Khalid bin Ahmad would bring nothing but expense and conflict. Against his better judgement, he went along with it and Khalid bin Ahmad finally took full possession of the town of Dhaid in July 1928. But Ras Al Khaimah's Ruler had been right – Khalid bin Ahmad was to leave nothing but expense and conflict in his wake.

Sultan bin Saqr dragged his heels when it came to paying Khalid's compensation and the pearling fleet was consequently stopped from leaving for the pearl banks. (Ramadan having delayed the start of the season from May to June) by the British until Sultan made the payment. Given the ambush incident against the British Residency Agent which had taken place in Ajman, the British Senior Naval Officer also took the opportunity of his visit to publicly state that

Sultan bin Saqr Al Qasimi would be held personally responsible for the future safety of the Agent.

A legacy squandered

Sharjah was not the only coastal state to have its dynastic upsets in the 1920s. The achievements and inheritance left behind by Zayed the Great of Abu Dhabi were to be squandered in a period of almost constant internecine jostling.

When Zayed bin Khalifa died in 1909, his son Tahnun took over and ruled from 1909 to 1912, when he died peacefully. He was followed by Hamdan bin Zayed, the fifth of Zayed's sons, who ruled from 1912 to 1922. Hamdan's rule saw the diminution of Zayed's great tribal federation and the tribes took to squabbling and warring between themselves. Hamdan himself paid tribute to Ibn Saud, alienating many of his intensely anti-Wahhabi subjects.

In August 1922, Hamdan was killed by his younger brother, Sultan bin Zayed, in alliance with another brother, Saqr bin Zayed. Zayed's remaining two sons disagreed with the fratricide and were estranged. Hamdan's daughter, Latifa, escaped to exile with her mother in Dubai. Latifa bint Hamdan was later to marry Sheikh Rashid bin Saeed Al Maktoum.

Sultan bin Zayed became Ruler of Abu Dhabi, but like his fellow Trucial Rulers found himself in straitened circumstances and, whether through poverty or innate meanness, he stopped the subsidies traditionally paid to members of the ruling family and other dependants. Outraged, the family resolved to act. On the night of 4 August 1926, Saqr arrived at Sultan's house, having accepted an invitation to dinner, and killed his brother. He also tried to kill Sultan's four sons, Shakhbut, Zayed, Hazza and Khalid – but failed and the boys fled with their mother to Buraimi.

The economic situation on the coast only worsened. Pearl boats had usually carried crews of eighteen men per boat, but in the 1927 season, forty men per boat were embarking for the pearl banks. Lacking capital, many were forced to take loans, the lenders charging high rates of interest. The debt trap ensnared many and there was a great wave of relief when the first dives of the 1927 season turned out to be good but that early optimism was to be short lived. By October of that year, it was agreed that the season as a whole had been yet another disaster and the earnings of divers, captains and traders alike were once again marginal.

The 1928 season proved better all round, and a number of record pearls were found. The first references to Japanese cultured pearls in the Gulf date to August 1928, when an attempt was apparently made to smuggle a 'false pearl' to the Gulf. In fact, a 1924 trial in Paris had found that 'there is no fundamental difference between natural and cultured pearls in terms of their formation and structure.'[2]

However, cultured pearls were irrelevant. The damage to the pearling ecosystem of the region was already done. Merchants, captains and divers alike were all mired in debt, traders coming from overseas for the pearling season were buying less and the whole coast was in despair. The Gulf's pearl banks, massively over-fished since the late 1800s, had hit a tipping point decades ago and were in terminal decline. Too many men and boats were scraping the shallow and denuded seabed for too few oysters. And there were all too few buyers for a luxury good whose time had passed.

The relief of 1928's happier season was to be short lived. Hard times were to follow.

Trouble in Umm Al Quwain

The Ruler of Ajman, Humaid bin Abdulaziz Al Nuaimi, died on 20 April 1928 and was succeeded by his son Rashid bin Humaid, a young man of 25. This peaceful, orderly and unremarkable accession was to contrast with events next door – Umm Al Quwain was pitched into chaos in early 1929.

Hamad bin Ibrahim Al Mualla, the Ruler of Umm Al Quwain, had himself acceded to power by questionable means back in 1923. In October of that year, a slave from Hamad's household murdered the-then Ruler, Hamad's cousin Abdullah bin Rashid Al Mualla. Immediately following Abdullah's funeral, Hamad out-smarted Abdullah's brother, Ahmad bin Rashid – who would have been expected to inherit – and occupied the government house. By the time the British Resident visited in March 1924, Hamad had consolidated his position and was clearly the accepted Ruler of the emirate.[3]

Now, six years later, Hamad found himself in precisely the same situation he had engineered for his cousin. He was shot and killed by a slave called Saeed, acting under the instigation of Hamad's blind uncle, Abdulrahman bin Ahmed Al Mualla. The whole population of the town of Umm Al Quwain rose up against Abdulrahman and Saeed, who barricaded themselves in the fort. Abandoning their initial plan of firing on the fort with a cannon, the people of the town instead elected to set a fire around the walls of the fort and in the ensuing conflagration both Abdulrahman and Saeed were burned to death.

The British considered the whole affair to be highly suspicious – Abdulrahman being blind would hardly expect to be ruler himself and was thought to have been working for the benefit of a third party. The new Ruler was to be the 18-year-old Ahmad bin Rashid Al Mualla, Hamad's cousin.[4]

There was also, unusually, instability in Dubai in 1929 – in April, the nephews of Sheikh Saeed Al Maktoum tried to appoint his cousin, Sheikh Mana bin Rashid, as Ruler of Dubai, but decisive and supportive British action confirmed Sheikh Saeed as the legitimate Ruler of Dubai.

Like others on the coast, at this time Sheikh Saeed's subjects were the target of a number of raids carried out by the Bedouin Manasir, subjects of Abu Dhabi. With the ongoing calamities of the pearling seasons and the debts brought in their wake, the traditional business of tribesmen like the Manasir, mounting caravans and carrying goods through the interior, was threatened. Now they took to raiding in an extraordinary series of lightning strikes which plundered camels, rice, dates and other goods from the coastal towns. Sheikh Saeed sent his brother Juma bin Abdulla Al Maktoum to Abu Dhabi to try to reach agreement to stop the raiding, which by now was affecting communities throughout the Northern Emirates and had effectively closed the track north from Sharjah to Ras Al Khaimah.

Trouble in the air

If the prolonged collapse of the pearling industry meant trouble at sea and the raids by desperate and predatory Bedouin were bringing trouble on the land, there was now also to be trouble in the air.

The period following World War I saw enormous advances in the technology of flight and the new reality of passenger aeroplanes brought the emergence of the first airlines. The British government was quick to appreciate the potential for this new technology in the administration of its vast and sprawling Empire, as well as the danger of competition from French and German airlines. Causing great excitement wherever they went, the Supermarine Southampton flying boats now appeared for the first time in the Gulf and in June 1929, the Political Resident toured the area in a Southampton, flying from Basra to Bahrain and then on to Abu Dhabi in a great demonstration of British Prestige, that most precious of Imperial Assets.

Apparently, the flight from Bahrain to Abu Dhabi took a mere four and a half hours. The reception of the flying boat in Abu Dhabi was ecstatic, this being the first time an aeroplane had ever been seen by the people of the town – there is little doubt that the appearance of these huge, noisy machines in the blue skies of the Gulf impressed the men far below with the might and grandeur of the British Empire as, indeed, ironclad steamships had impressed their fathers before them.

However, Ras Al Khaimah was by no means keen on the new innovation. There had already been trouble in Muscat, with resistance to motor vehicles, aeroplanes and other 'infernal machines'[5] and the imposition on Ras Al Khaimah of a 'fuelling dhow' was resented by the Ruler, Sultan bin Salim Al Qasimi, who insisted in July 1929 that once the fuel tank on board the dhow the British had positioned there was emptied, it should not be replaced.

The Southampton flying boats gave the Political Resident the flexibility to appear 'on the spot' within the day, rather than sailing out to meet trouble days after events had taken place and the dust had long settled. Furthermore, a number of pioneering experiments in aviation were taking place which would result in the creation of the 'Empire

THE EMIRATES THROUGH THE YEARS

One of three *murabaa* or defensive towers which overlook the wadi at Falaj Al Mualla. It would have been impossible for anyone to pass up the wadi without being spotted by the lookouts posted at the towers.

The eastern *murabaa* at Falaj Al Mualla, on the margins of the desert surrounding the fertile oasis.

This engraving on a Dutch tombstone from the formerly important Dutch port of Brouwershaven in the province of Zeeland dates from the 1700s and speaks to the great maritime tradition of the Dutch and their East India Company, the VOC or Vereenigde Oostindische Compagnie.

THE EMIRATES THROUGH THE YEARS

This Pre-Islamic coin mould was found in Mleiha, inland of Sharjah, and links that city to Ed-Dur on the coast of Umm Al Quwain, where coins minted using this mould were found. This was one of many finds that links the two cities closely together; the coins were Hellenistically inspired.

An incense burner found at Muwailah, dating back to 900–600 BCE. It is one of a number of Iron Age artefacts archaeologists have found which are linked to ritual and cultural practices around the distribution of water.

An Aramaic-Hasaitic inscription from Mleiha, digitised by Global Heritage. This inscription is one of a number of written records which survive from the Pre-Islamic heyday of this important city.

An extensive network dating back to an Iron Age period of snake worship in the Emirates is reflected in objects wrought in both bronze and ceramics, which depict snakes. This snake decoration is on an Iron Age pot from Rumeilah, Al Ain.

Snake depictions are common in Iron Age pottery from across in the Emirates. Similar decorations have been found in pots further afield in Europe.

THE EMIRATES THROUGH THE YEARS

This soft stone beehive-shaped vessel from Tell Abraq is typical of the Umm Al Nar era, and dates from 2200–2000 BCE.

This Iron Age pot or incense burner from Al Ain is part of the rich trove that archaeologists have found which are linked to the distribution of water and the role of water as a resource around which growing centralised communities evolved.

Dating from 100–200 CE, this tetra-drachma is from Mleiha. Coins like these show links with the ancient world throughout the Middle East and Europe.

This fragment of a fine bronze bowl from the Pre-Islamic city of Mleiha depicts horse and camel riders and dates from 150 BC–150 BCE.

An Iron Age petroglyph on display at Sharjah Archaeology Museum. These ancient illustrations are to be found dotted in locations around the Hajar Mountains and speak to the long history of commerce through the mountain.

Dating from 2000–1600 BCE, this carnelian necklace from Jebel Buhais is typical of the finer jewellery of the Umm Al Nar period and is made from stones imported from the Indus Valley, now in Pakistan.

THE EMIRATES THROUGH THE YEARS

Khan Sahib Said Aburazzak, the British Residency Agent, photographed at Al Mahattah.
[IMAGE COURTESY: NATIONAL ARCHIVES, KEW]

The RMS *Triad* was frequently used to settle disputes with, and between, the Trucial Rulers in the 1920s. [IMAGE COURTESY: NATIONAL ARCHIVES, KEW]

The Handley Page HP42 was in its time a revolutionary technology in aviation, capable of flying long distances and of speeds of up to 100 miles per hour. Carrying thirty-eight passengers, it was the backbone of the Emirate Route, from Croydon to Sydney which involved an overnight stop at Sharjah, just four days into the journey!

The Land Rover was the vehicle of choice of the Trucial Scouts as well as the Trucial Rulers. Although superseded by Japanese four-wheel drives, Land Rovers continued to be popular with the Bedouin, who prized the vehicle's endurance and indestructibility.

THE EMIRATES THROUGH THE YEARS

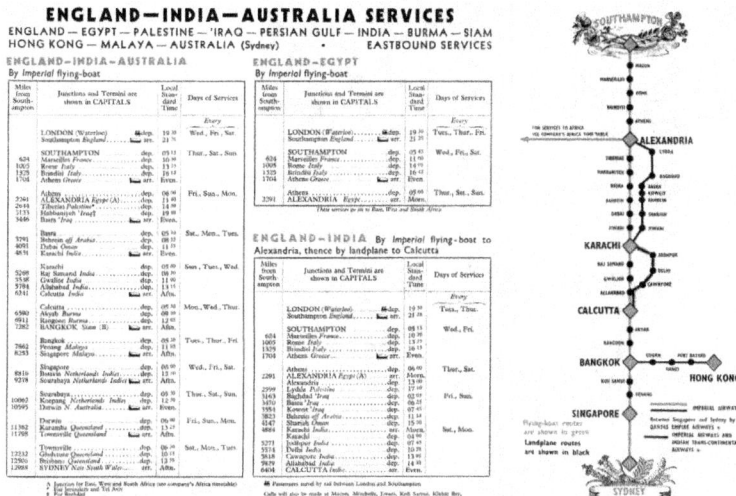

The timetable of the Empire Route. The journey to Sydney took two weeks, hopping across the world on its way. The establishment of Al Mahattah in Sharjah in 1932 was a result of the British needing to find a landing strip on the Arabian coast of the Gulf after the agreement to use the Persian Island of Hengam lapsed acrimoniously. [IMAGE COURTESY: IMPERIAL AIRWAYS ARCHIVE]

The Empire Route ran from Croydon to either Canberra or Cape Town, via Alexandria. The huge machines of Imperial Airways connected the Empire upon which the sun never set. Until, following World War II, the sun set on it.

A restored *barjeel* or wind tower at the Heart of Sharjah, a restoration of the old core of Sharjah town which aims to take it back to its 1958 condition before modern construction encroached on the heritage area.

Heritage Associations across the UAE today preserve old ways of life – including cooking the delicious little doughnuts dipped in date syrup and sesame seeds, 'loqueimat'. The shelter these ladies are using is traditional *areesh* – palm frond construction.

An *areesh* dwelling. This method of constructing housing has been common throughout the Emirates for millennia and persisted up until the 1960s.

A bedroom preserved at Ajman Fort. Typical of a wealthier home in the period leading up to the 1970s, these simple rooms contained Indian teak beds and precious objects such as mirrors and glassware.

Al Heera in Sharjah. There are few remains of what was once not only a thriving and independent community, but of a village presided over by a fearsome and warlike headman, whose dominant personality stamped itself on events throughout the region at the time.

An extensive network of tracks linking the interior of the Emirates was developed, from the pioneering efforts of the Trucial Oman Scouts through to a huge programme of public works from the 1970s onwards that built highways and byways throughout the undeveloped interior. Camels gave way to cars and petrol stations started to pop up in mountain and desert villages.

THE EMIRATES THROUGH THE YEARS

Emiratis take to the streets enthusiastically to celebrate National Day on 2 December every year. Not only is this the day that the leaders of the UAE signed the new nation into being in 1971, it was also coincidentally the day British forces arrived at sea off Ras Al Khaimah in 1819 – before they bombarded the town and reduced it to rubble.

Abras ply their trade across Dubai Creek, a form of transport which goes back to the 1800s, when Dubai was first founded as an Al Bu Falasah town under the rule of the Maktoum family.

CHILDREN OF THE SEVEN SANDS

The 'Constellation' at the Founder's Memorial in Abu Dhabi is a clever monument dedicated to the late Sheikh Zayed bin Sultan Al Nahyan or 'Baba Zayed' (Father Zayed) to the Emirati people. It is made up from 1,327 geometric shapes – Platonic solids – suspended with 1,110 cables, which combine to form a three-dimensional portrait of Zayed.

Route', the great arterial route from Croydon, in south London, through Europe to Alexandria and then down to Cape Town or across to Sydney in Australia.

The company that would fly these routes, Imperial Airways, was founded in 1924 and first flew its service to Karachi from Croydon in March 1929. Ras Al Khaimah was potentially en route, although the first flights went through Persia. Ras Al Khaimah was a desirable location for the Royal Air Force as well as a backup station for the Persian route, but Sultan bin Salim was obdurate in his opposition. The British Residency Agent waited until the Ruler was travelling and then seized his moment and convened the town's *majlis*, trying to get them to adopt 'a more reasonable attitude' and agree to the petrol store. The elders of the town agreed to the construction of the petrol store, subject to the Ruler's agreement, provided only that it would be located far away from the town, that there would be no permanent Air Force personnel stationed at Ras Al Khaimah, that there should be no land-based runway and that the flying boats would only stop to refuel and then be on their way. Lastly, they stipulated that the British government should ask nothing more of them at any future date.

In a secret minute appended to the August 1929 news summary from the Political Residency at Bushire, a laconic comment was added by J. G. Laithwaite of the Indian Government: 'It looks as though we might have a certain amount of trouble here.'

He was right, too.

The British Residency Agent, Al Serkal, had his office in Sharjah, but actually lived in Ras Al Khaimah and, on 19 November 1929, a woman took shelter in the agent's house which at the time was occupied by Al Serkal's two sons. Clearly involved in a family feud of some sort, she was followed that night by her brother and three other armed men, who attempted to remove her from Al Serkal's house. His two sons tried to resist and in the subsequent melee, the woman was stabbed.

The Political Resident despatched HMS *Crocus* to Ras Al Khaimah to investigate, the 'prestige of the British Residency Agent was involved', after all. Sultan bin Salim of Ras Al Khaimah would have had little reason to love the Residency Agent, the man who had assembled his *majlis* and tried to steamroller agreement to the refuelling station against his express will in his absence. Nevertheless, Sultan had the men who had burst into the agent's house flogged for their transgression. This action by the Ruler resulted in considerable civil unrest in Ras Al Khaimah and Al Serkal's two sons, British prestige or not, had to quit the town.

Ras Al Khaimah was by no means alone when it came to resisting the noisy new innovations the British were bringing to the Trucial Coast. For one reason and other, the flying boats – albeit impressive – were universally unpopular. In March of 1930, a flying boat touched down at Dubai but its crew was denied permission to land. Sheikh Saeed, who was ill at the time of the incident, wrote to the Political Resident and made it clear that flying boats were not welcome to land in Dubai.

Matters came to a head between the British and Sultan bin Salim Al Qasimi when the Political Resident informed Ras Al Khaimah's Ruler that the hated fuelling dhow would be replaced by an iron barge. This would hardly have been welcome news and, in fact, when the barge appeared off the coast of Ras Al Khaimah on 21 May 1930, pulled by HMS *Cyclamen*, Sultan bin Salim threatened dire consequences if it were not immediately removed. Armed men were posted on the creek and reinforcements called up from the interior. The Residency Agent arrived with the Rulers of Umm Al Quwain and Hamriyah in tow. Hamriyah's chief had already offered his own creek for refuelling if it should prove to be seaplane-friendly, in the clear hope that this would boost his claims to independence. The three of them attempted to mediate the dispute, to no avail, and were joined in this by Sheikh Saeed Al Maktoum of Dubai (who had himself objected strongly to flying boats).

Sending a clear signal to Sultan bin Salim, the British Political Resident now arrived at Ras Al Khaimah on a flying boat – touching down on 1 June, transferring to HMS *Triad* and raising his flag as a signal to Sultan that he should come aboard for talks. Sultan ignored the signal. On 14 June, the Residency Agent joined the complement aboard the *Triad* when Sultan bin Salim informed him that, as Ruler, he was no longer responsible for the Agent's safety while the barge remained in Ras Al Khaimah's waters.

The Political Agent had had enough. Eight Ras Al Khaimah boats were seized while pearling off the Sharjah island of Sir Abu Nair and the town of Ras Al Khaimah was blockaded. Every voice was raised against Sultan bin Salim (including the Sheikh of Dibba, who threatened violence) and Sultan eventually capitulated. He accepted responsibility for the barge and the seaplanes landing at Ras Al Khaimah and asked for 100 rupees per month to pay for guards to ensure it remained secure.

This was to be the last incidence of British 'gunboat diplomacy' on the Trucial Coast – from now on the British would assert their authority without resorting to force.

The island of Sir Abu Nair was itself subject to claim and counter-claim. Although generally accepted to be Sharjah territory, both Abu Dhabi and Dubai had an eye on it and both objected in 1933 when Sultan bin Saqr of Sharjah started building on the island. Home to a flagstaff (flying a Sharjah flag) and a hut, the island was a refuge for pearling boats in bad weather and otherwise entirely unremarkable – much as it is today.[6]

The flying boat was not the only unwelcome innovation to reach the coast in 1930. The reforming Shah of Iran, Reza Pahlavi, had introduced the cylindrical Pahlavi Hat as part of a Western-style dress he encouraged. Saeed Al Maktoum of Dubai, in a proclamation issued in April 1930, let his residents of Persian origin know that if they wanted to wear the Pahlavi Hat, they could go back to Persia and do so!

The pearling disaster continues

The eventual collapse of the pearling industry had become increasingly inevitable over the previous two decades. One bad season had followed another, only two brief good seasons since 1910 had offered any glimpse of hope to the indebted workers, captains and merchants. By the late 1920s, the rot had truly set in and desperation grew. Overfishing had decimated the pearl beds and something like sixty boats from Dubai's fleet didn't sail at all in July 1929. That month, with the pearling season just opening, a Dubai merchant declared bankruptcy: Muhammad bin Biyat owed 600,000 rupees. In order for his pearling fleet to sail at all, the prominent pearl merchant Mohammad bin Ahmad bin Dalmouk was forced to raise a huge amount of money, borrowing 200,000 rupees at a wicked 36 per cent rate of interest from a Hindu moneylender. Bin Dalmouk's father Ahmed had established Dubai's first school, the Ahmadiya School, in better times back in 1912 and Mohammed had finished the construction of his father's gift and legacy to Dubai. Now, far from being able to make bequests, he was struggling for his very existence.

It is likely the fact that the year 1929 is given as the 'doomsday year' for pearling – and the reasons so often cited being the Japanese cultured pearl and the collapse of Wall Street – is down to two British Residency newsletters from this time. In December 1929, the Political Residency News reported 'the slump in Wall Street has had a serous reaction upon the world's pearl trade', pointing out that the merchants that year sold very little. The second ingredient of the 'death of pearling' double whammy was supplied by the *Political Residency News Summary of March 1930*, which noted 'The most disturbing rumours are current in Bahrein regarding the Japanese cultured pearls and it is said that they have found some artificial stimulus which cannot be detected by reflection like the present mother-of-pearl centre. If this is true, the results will be very serious for the Arab Coast.'

A problem here is that these 'insights' come from the newly minted Political Resident, Hugh Vincent Biscoe, who arrived in Bushire to take up his position on 7 November 1929. TC Fowle, the Secretary to the Political Resident, arrived a day before Biscoe and took up his new post on 11 November.[7]

While both of these observations on the pearl market may well have been in their way true, they did not reflect the struggling market that had been lurching from pillar to post for twenty years while Hugh Biscoe was busy helping to run India, miles away from the Trucial Coast. This last posting was Biscoe's 'retirement post' following a long career in the administration of Indian government, with the sole exception of the post of Consul at Bandar Abbas from 1910–15. Biscoe was, in short, clueless as to the nature and state of the Gulf's pearl trade and its long history of failure and penury. Biscoe didn't even speak Arabic – he depended heavily on the Resident Agent and others for translation.

So while these new factors were no doubt felt in their way, they were by no means the core factors that had brought the market to its knees. Over-fishing, regional and world wars, poor weather, problems with debt – all of these were the factors that had been driving the market into the mire. The merchants had been struggling for decades before this – and the *nakhudas*, haulers and divers had been falling out over worsening conditions and poor yields for a very long time before 1929.

Biscoe's memos have been quoted by historians for the past century, 'the collapse of Wall Street and the Mikimoto cultured pearl both combined to destroy the pearl market in 1929'. As we have seen, this was by no means the case. The once-thriving market was now febrile beyond endurance. Throughout the 1920s, merchants went to the wall with increasing frequency. Not just pearl merchants, either. The whole economy of the coast had been in freefall long before Biscoe even set foot in the area.

Sheikh Mohammed bin Ahmad of Dubai, a leading merchant, in March 1930 sold his stock of pearls at Bahrain at a loss. Returning to Dubai, he broke up his household, dismissing staff and selling off camels. His son, furious at his actions, stole some sixty head of camels and made off with them. Saeed Al Maktoum sent his brother Juma looking for the miscreant.

In June 1930, the leading Persian merchant in Bahrain went bankrupt, absconding to avoid his debts. The son of another Dubai merchant faced the music on his father's behalf, detained in Bombay after merchants filed suit against his father. Again, he had been forced to sell his stock of pearls at a loss and was prevented from returning by the suit.

Bedouin raids, as tended to happen at any time of economic strain, now increased and Sultan bin Saqr Al Qasimi of Sharjah had a mighty falling out with his brothers over stipends when, times being grim as they were, he could not pay them the amount they were used to receiving.[8]

The 1930 season was appalling. The catch was meagre and prices in the market were down by some 50 per cent. The rot continued. A shop owned by a merchant from Hyderabad was broken into in Ras Al Khaimah, an unheard-of occurrence. Pearl sales in Bahrain in 1930 – already depressed by years of weakening demand, were a quarter of the already low volume of 1929.

In December 1930, the French pearl dealer Habib Rosenthal was bankrupted owing 8 million rupees. Hammered by years – decades – of decline, the whole commercial and social ecosystem of the Trucial States had collapsed and it threatened to take the Trucial Rulers with it.

Chapter 22

LOOK UP TO THE BLUE SKY

"The HP 42 was an aircraft that invoked the idea of a winged Cunarder and majestically emphasized Britain's own somewhat immodest perception of itself."

– Alexander Frater

If you drive down Sharjah's King Abdulaziz Street towards the Saudi Mosque and Al Ittihad Park, you may notice the road is nice and straight. Stopping at the traffic lights, with the park and the 'Blue Souq' to your left and the big 'Saudi mosque' to your right, you can see 'Smile you're in Sharjah' roundabout ahead of you. The road past the lights is perhaps a little odd if you take the time (being careful about how you drive, of course) to examine it, being made up of what seem to be patched up squares. And that is because you're actually driving on the old runway of Sharjah Airport, used up until 1977 when the current airport was opened off the Dhaid Highway.

The area around the old airport and its runway, with its many Nissen huts and other outbuildings fell into disuse and crumbled through the 1980s and 1990s, the land slowly cleared as residential blocks started to encroach on the rusting remains of aviation history. At the centre of the collection of shacks and tin huts stood an old fort, a wrecked light aeroplane parked next to its great rusty steel doors. Next to the fort were the ruins of a control tower. By the late 1990s, there was very little left of what was once the desert airport of Sharjah – a key station on the great Empire Route and home to the first airport in the Trucial States. The Al Mahatta Fort was built to accommodate guests on the overnight stop between Bahrain and the Omani-ruled territory of Gwadar in Baluchistan (now in Pakistan) in an agreement forged between the British government and Sultan bin Saqr Al Qasimi of Sharjah.

It was to be a controversial move, to say the least.

The great Empire Route established by Imperial Airways in 1927 traversed Europe to reach Alexandria, where it split to serve routes to Africa and Sydney respectively. The Sydney route was served by Imperial Airways to Singapore after which the route was operated by Queensland and Northern Territory Aerial Services Limited – known today as Qantas.

The route was flown in short hops, originally involving a mixture of flights and rail travel across Europe, together with flying boats and conventional biplanes. When it was first established, the rather negative views towards flying boats held by the people and rulers of both Oman and the Trucial States being well known, the route stopped at the Persian-owned

Hengam Island (to the south of Qeshm) on the hop between Bahrain and Karachi. However, the Persian Government withdrew the lease to Hengam in early 1932, sparking something of a crisis for Imperial Airways and its Empire Route. A furious exchange of letters between British officials followed as the Persians gleefully used the lease of Hengam as a lever to try and extract a series of concessions from the British, including recognition of Persian ownership of the Tunbs islands which the British refused. The Persian's 'most unsatisfactory attitude' constituted 'Blackmail', it was felt by horrified British administrators.[1]

However, the facts were inescapable. Even if the situation with the Persians could be recovered, they had a chokehold on the British air route to India and beyond. A solution had to be found and it clearly lay somewhere on the coast of the Trucial States. And it had to be found quickly – the lease to Hengam Island expired on 31 May 1932 and time was clearly of the essence. The flights would have to be halted unless and until an alternative route could be found.

The Trucial Rulers were approached. Would any of them agree to the establishment of facilities? The answer from Ras Al Khaimah and Dubai was a resounding 'no'. Ras Al Khaimah was already unhappy at the fuel barge installed for flying boats and Dubai had made it clear on more than one occasion that flying boats were unwelcome (Saeed Al Maktoum posted pickets onshore when the Supermarine Southampton flying boats landed).

It was at this time, March 1929, that Imperial Airways threw a spanner into the works. It had previously been seeking landing rights and facilities for its Calcutta class flying boats. Now the company reviewed the situation in light of the development of the Handley Page HP 42 class biplanes, which landed on terrestrial runways. The HP 42 planes (named Heracles, Hanno, Horatius, Helena, Hengist, Horsa, Hannibal and Hadrian) had a longer range, higher speed and more load capacity. They were simply more efficient. Imperial Airways did an about-turn and announced that it didn't want seaplane landing rights – it wanted a landing strip, for which a site at Dibba was proposed and scouted, initially being thought suitable.[2] The Residency Agent must have been appalled – it had been bad enough trying to negotiate landing rights for seaplanes, but an aerodrome meant a direct British presence on land, something he would have known would be unconscionable to the Rulers and people of the Trucial States.

Approaches were made to the Al Qasimi Governor of Dibba, harried by the Sharqiyin of Fujairah to the south and the Shihuh to the north. A desperate man, he would have accepted an aerodrome if it meant British protection against his neighbours and, in fact, requested to be able to fly the British flag.[3]

Other locations were also evaluated as the British raced for a solution to the Persia problem. Sir Bani Yas Island to the west of Abu Dhabi was proposed and rejected because it offered poor visibility and was all too easy for a pilot to miss at night or in sandstorms. Sharjah was also to be reviewed as a potential location for an airfield.[4]

A survey of both Dibba and Sharjah was carried out by a Group Captain Welsh, who reported back that Dibba was not, in fact, a satisfactory location at all. 'The ground is hard and flat over a very large area. In my opinion it would take 100 men at least two months to clear an area 500 yards by 500… 100 trees would have to be uprooted, which would make soft patches.' He noted, sourly, 'There is no labour available but Sheikh states men can be obtained from Ras Al Khaimah in two months' time when the date season starts.'[5]

This was two months the British simply didn't have – in addition to the two months Welsh had estimated the ground would take to clear. The Dibba proposal was abandoned and the hapless Governor of Dibba summarily dropped and left to his difficulties with the Shihuh and Sharqiyin.

Welsh went on to Sharjah, finding two suitable areas that were ready to be used immediately and required no land clearance. Of the two 'south and north' he preferred the northern option because of its drier appearance. Water and food were plentifully available and the town of Sharjah was about a mile and a half away. The rest house, Welsh noted, must be a fort.

Negotiations started right away.

Critically, Group Captain Welsh also pointed to the likely location of Kalba on the east coast, which he visited. A sleepy Al Qasimi town to the south of Fujairah and barely to the north of the border with Oman, Kalba offered an ideal landing strip location. Kalba and Fujairah were constantly bickering, drawing Trucial Sheikhs to their arguments like moths to a candle – something that does not appear to have been factored into thinking at the time. Despite the constant threat of instability, the idea of a landing strip at Kalba would endure

Meanwhile, the race was on to forge an agreement with the Ruler of Sharjah, Sultan bin Saqr Al Qasimi, to establish a landing strip and facilities. The British Political Resident, Sir Hugh Biscoe (the very chap who had pronounced on the collapse of pearling being a result of Wall Street and Mikimoto) had every reason to think that Sultan bin Saqr would be amenable to the idea of supporting an airport – they had not only discussed the scheme before, but Sultan bin Saqr had sent Biscoe a letter confirming he would support the establishment of an airport in Sharjah. Confident that the agreement was in the bag, Biscoe was therefore dumbfounded to arrive in Sharjah on 3 May 1932 and find Sultan bin Saqr absolutely opposed to signing any such agreement. Biscoe surmised that Sultan bin Saqr's brothers (of whom Mohammed bin Saqr was known as a strong and stormy character) had been 'got at by interested parties in Dubai'.[6]

Biscoe's theory was that Dubai, which had built itself over the past three decades into a fast-growing and thriving entrepôt port, was scared that an airport in Sharjah would mean that the British India steamers would instead call at Sharjah and this would see merchants moving up the coast to be close to the new locus for trade that an airport would undoubtedly represent. This theory persisted, despite Saeed Al Maktoum's recorded early opposition to aviation – and that of Sultan bin Salim Al Qasimi in Ras Al Khaimah. It is just as likely that the opposition on the coast was an argument against expanded British influence and presence on the ground. While the British had only ever concerned themselves with the coast they would now, with their dominance of the skies, be able to control the interior.

Sultan bin Saqr did, in fact, support the airport scheme but his rule was under remorseless pressure from the protracted collapse of the pearling industry and the poverty and debt that had ensued. He could not afford to alienate his brothers, particularly the forceful Mohammed.

But he was himself in a state of advanced penury and had even been forced to pawn family jewels to keep afloat.⁷

However, Sultan bin Saqr now played an ace card – he brought Abdulrahman bin Muhammad Al Shamsi of Al Heera into play. Abdulrahman had endured three years of his four-year exile in Aden, having been allowed back to Al Heera a year early in 1929, thanks to Sultan bin Saqr's guarantee of Abdulrahman's good behaviour. On his return, Abdulrahman had characteristically promptly got himself into trouble with the British again and had come to blows with his old enemy, the British Residency Agent, Isa bin Abdullatif Al Serkal, with whom he shared a lively antipathy. This time – on the evening of 31 January 1931 – three slaves belonging to Abdulrahman had taken refuge in the British Residency in Sharjah, seeking their manumission (release). Abdulrahman and 100 armed men had surrounded the Residency and Isa bin Abdullatif Al Serkal was forced to take refuge in Kalba until a British ship could be brought to Sharjah in his support.

Sultan bin Saqr was given two options: surrender Abdulrahman to be exiled again or pay 2,000 rupees and give up 100 good rifles. Sultan chose the latter, very expensive, option and Abdulrahman retained his freedom.⁸

Now, in May 1932, Sultan bin Saqr called on Abdulrahman to support him against Mohammed and the group objecting to the airport. Biscoe, hopeful that this would ease things (and, perversely enough, grateful for Abdulrahman's support), called for the Air Force to send a flight of Westland Wapitis to Sharjah to 'strengthen the Sheikh's hand'.⁹ The Wapiti was a versatile biplane – advanced for its time and capable of serving as a fighter, bomber and reconnaissance plane. The appearance of these fearsome machines, roaring across the blue skies of the Northern Gulf (they were based in Iraq) would have had an awesome impact on the people of the Trucial Coast.

Meanwhile, Abdulrahman swung into action. He berated Mohammed and the group opposed to the airport, calling them children. How could they stand up to the power and greatness of the British Empire? How could they stand against progress? By 11 May, it seemed as if Abdulrahman, by sheer force of character, had wrought his magic.

The Wapitis duly arrived on 20 May and their flying officers marked out the proposed runway of the new airport, but Sultan bin Saqr's brothers destroyed the marked-out landing ground soon after the Wapitis left. Sultan remade the markings but they were again destroyed. Sultan now found himself facing off against his brother, Mohammed bin Saqr Al Qasimi, backed by the Rulers of both Ras Al Khaimah and Ajman.

Biscoe called in the navy. HMS *Bideford* visited Ajman and Ras Al Khaimah and issued suitably blood-curdling warnings to the Rulers not to interfere in affairs at Sharjah. Sultan bin Saqr, said Captain Crabbe, the Senior Naval Officer for the Arabian Gulf, in his summary of the affair, 'played a master stroke by introducing Abdulrahman into the discussions'.[10]

Sultan bin Saqr held out for more concessions, more guarantees. Would the British India steamer call fortnightly to Sharjah, as it did to Dubai? This, according to Biscoe, was Dubai's great fear and it was soon enough realised following a frenzied series of telegrams between the government and the company.

And then, in the early hours of 19 July 1932, on his way to Sharjah aboard HMS *Bideford* to try and seal the deal, Sir Hugh Vincent Biscoe KBE, His Britannic Majesty's Political Resident in the Arabian Gulf, promptly suffered a heart attack and died.

Carpe diem

Biscoe had paused on his way to Sharjah to pick up the Political Agent to Kuwait, Lieutenant-Colonel Harold Dickson to help him with the negotiations in Sharjah. Dickson was an experienced Gulf hand and an Arabic speaker. Biscoe had spent a lifetime in the Indian service and wasn't an Arabic speaker, relying on the Residency Agent in Sharjah, Isa bin Abdullatif Al Serkal, for translation. Dickson was later to remark on the fact that the Residency Agent, like so many other parties, actually had a vested interest in the negotiations. An airport meant a closer relationship with the British, perhaps even European staff on the ground in Sharjah. It potentially threatened Serkal's own standing as the sole arbiter of British authority (and, remember, 'prestige') on the Trucial Coast. 'I am inclined to think that he has not given us all the support that we had a right to expect in this affair of the air station,' Dickson noted in his summation of the negotiations.[11]

It very much looks as if Biscoe had reached the same conclusion himself and decided to bring his Arabist colleague from Kuwait along for the final negotiating round rather than depend on Serkal's translating skills. Biscoe was buried at sea at noon and Dickson, on the afternoon of 19 July, sent a telegram to the Government in India – he was 'au fait' with the negotiations, could he proceed and seize the day before the Ruler of Sharjah once again got cold feet? It does seem a particularly cold-blooded move given that his former colleague Biscoe was quite literally dead in the water.

Cold-blooded or not, with the benefit of hindsight Dickson's initiative was a stroke of genius. On receiving his go-ahead, he proceeded to Sharjah and arrived at the town at 6 a.m. on 20 July 1932. When Sultan bin Saqr Al Qasimi arrived on board, he was told of Biscoe's death and was genuinely upset at the news.

Harold Dickson was a strong personality and a fluent Arabic speaker with long experience of dealing with the people of the region, both in Kuwait and Saudi Arabia. Brought up in Damascus, he had a particular affinity for the Bedouin of the region and had been Political Resident in Kuwait since 1929. In fact, Dickson's former residence in Kuwait, the 'Dickson House' is preserved as a charming little museum and cultural centre today.

Dickson immediately made a favourable impression on Sultan bin Saqr. A round of negotiations now took place at sea and on land – a nasty swell at the time forced both Dickson and the Residency Agent to flee seasickness and take up negotiations once again from the more stable ground of the Residency in Sharjah.

The argument swung back and forth, at times congenial and at times acrimonious. At one stage Dickson says, 'I told the Sheikh quite openly that it was impossible for me to continue business in an atmosphere which resembled that of chattering women rather than the deliberations of serious men.'[12]

Punctuated by the arrival of a flying boat, marked by frustration and prevarication, the two-day-long marathon finally culminated in the signing of the agreement. At 7.30 p.m. on 22 July 1932, Sultan bin Saqr

Al Qasimi signed an agreement for 'the establishment of an air station at Sharjah'. The agreement was a little odd in that it was between the Ruler and the British Government, but the beneficiary of the whole affair was to be a private company – Imperial Airways Limited.

The agreement provided for the construction of a runway and a rest house for passengers, to a design provided by the company. The rest house would remain the property of the Ruler, but would be leased to Imperial Airways. It would be used to house company staff and passengers who would not, without the Sheikh's permission, be allowed to visit the town of Sharjah.[13] The Ruler would allow the import of fuel and other resources free of taxation and would provide thirty-five guards and two head guards to provide protection 'as far as possible for marauders from outside my jurisdiction'.

In return, Sultan bin Saqr would receive monthly payments of twenty rupees per guard and forty rupees for the head guards, 800 rupees for the air station (commencing from first landing) and 300 rupees for the rest house. The funds for the construction work would be advanced to Sultan bin Saqr and these would be offset by rental income.

In a moment of uncharacteristic generosity, the British government agreed to supply such windows, doors, steel joints and corrugated iron as may be needed, free of charge.

In addition, Sultan bin Saqr was to be granted a personal subsidy of 500 rupees per month and a landing fee of five rupees for each commercial aeroplane landing. RAF aeroplanes were to be exempt from this charge. The company was only to deal with the Sheikh through the Residency Agent (Isa bin Abdullatif Al Serkal was a co-signatory to the agreement) and the renewable agreement was for a duration of eleven years.[14]

It was a momentous agreement, not only because it was to establish the first airport in the region, thereby putting Sharjah very firmly on the map, but because it was to mark the first time the British government paid a subsidy to a Trucial Ruler. It was also going to result in the establishment of a broad British presence in Sharjah, including a wireless telegraph station, a meteorological station, a post office and a fuelling depot.[15]

At 4 p.m. on 5 October 1932, the first westbound Imperial Airways flight arrived from Gwadar to Sharjah, carrying four passengers on the

Handley Page HP42 aircraft 'Hanno', which would later be celebrated in Paul Rotha's documentary film about Sharjah Airport, 'Air Outpost'. They slept in tents, the fortified rest house of Al Mahatta being still under construction. The Senior Naval Commander reported that the tents were well furnished and comfortable. The flight took off the next day, headed for Manama in Bahrain.

Sharjah airport was, finally, in business.

Barut and the fall of Kalba

In the late 1880s, Majid bin Sultan bin Saqr Al Qasimi was made Wali of Shamaliyah by Salim bin Sultan Al Qasimi. This effectively comprised Kalba and Khor Fakkan, home to the Naqbiyin tribe, which recognised Al Qasimi rule even as Fujairah asserted its independence. In fact, the Naqbiyin had moved from their traditional home in the mountainous hinterland of Ras Al Khaimah (giving their name to the Wadi Naqab there), quite possibly at Al Qasimi behest. The friction between the tribes of Fujairah and their Qawasim neighbours was to bubble away and erupt into sporadic violence for almost a century to come.[16]

By 1902, Majid's grandson, Saeed bin Hamad Al Qasimi, had become the new ruler of Kalba, even as Hamad bin Abdulla Al Sharqi established Fujairah as a broadly recognised independent state. The British, however, were to deny Fujairah formal recognition as a Trucial State, a gift granted to Saeed bin Hamad of Kalba in 1936, when the British needed to establish a back-up airstrip for the new airport in Sharjah and its Imperial Airways Empire Route flights. For the first two decades of his rule, Saeed bin Hamad was something of an absentee Wali, and lived in Ajman, leaving the effective administration of Kalba in the hands of a trusted slave called Barut. He moved back to live in Kalba in the 1920s.

In April 1937, Saeed bin Hamad's eldest daughter, Aisha, married Khalid bin Ahmad Al Qasimi, the former Ruler of Sharjah who had been deposed by the young Sultan bin Saqr Al Qasimi with the help of the able Abdulrahman of Al Heera. In his exile to Dhaid, Khalid bin Ahmad had become the recognised ruler of the desert oasis town but actually also had his house in Ajman.

Hardly had the wedding celebrations finished when Saeed bin Hamad Al Qasimi fell mortally ill while staying at Khor Fakkan. Aisha, correctly deducing that her father was close to death, gathered two companions and dashed to Kalba where she organised the defences of the fort and towers of the town, confirming the trusted Barut as the town's Wali.[17]

When news of her father's death was confirmed the next morning, 30 April, Aisha gathered Kalba's notables and they agreed to send five men to Dhaid to call her husband, Khalid bin Ahmed Al Qasimi to come to Kalba. Khalid, actually in Ajman at the time, sent his brother Abdullah and a force of ten armed men to Kalba to see if they were wanted by the people of Kalba. They found themselves blocked from entering the town.

There was now a general mobilisation of Trucial Sheikhs as news got out that Kalba was without a ruler. Sultan bin Salim Al Qasimi of Ras Al Khaimah sent a man to Kalba to evaluate the situation but his emissary was blocked, as was the Wali of Dibba, Rashid bin Ahmad Al Qasimi, who was stopped at Khor Fakkan by the Naqbiyin.

Concerned to protect Kalba, because of the backup airstrip and its Trucial status, the British Resident had the Residency Agent in Sharjah send letters to the Rulers both of Sharjah and Ras Al Khaimah warning them not to interfere with events in Kalba town. The people of Kalba had by now decided that they supported Saeed bin Hamad's 12-year-old son, Hamad, under the Regency of Barut.

The young man immediately sent a letter to Sultan bin Salim Al Qasimi of Ras Al Khaimah, confirming that he had acceded as the Ruler of Kalba. Sultan bin Salim, meanwhile, attempted to bring the Naqbiyin of Khor Fakkan onside by appointing the head of the tribe as Wali over Khor Fakkan and Kalba. Aisha's husband, Khalid bin Ahmed Al Qasimi left Ajman for Dhaid, where a force was being gathered, before proceeding to Kalba to join his brother, who was encamped outside the town.

Storm clouds were clearly gathering from all around.

At sometime around 9 June 1937, Sultan bin Salim Al Qasimi made his way from Ras Al Khaimah and arrived at Khalid bin Ahmed's camp outside Kalba, where the former Ruler of Sharjah refused to meet with him. Sultan bin Salim went on to Kalba along with some twelve men, followed by the hostile gaze of both Khalid bin Ahmed and the Sheikh of the Bani Qitab.

Sultan bin Salim strode blissfully into a lion's den. The people of Kalba had not invited him and did not want him. Finding himself effectively penned in and surrounded by unfriendly forces, Sultan bin Salim was forced to call for help from the British. A sloop was duly sent around from the West coast and stood to off Kalba to embark the interfering and embattled Ruler of Ras Al Khaimah. He was to find himself in considerable hot water with the furious Political Resident, whose careful instructions he had so insouciantly ignored. He was summarily taken to Bahrain where, allowed only one servant, he was placed in solitary confinement in Manama with two guards outside the door informing visitors that he was not to be disturbed. There he languished for two days before the Political Agent called for him and administered a thorough dressing down.[18]

He was then escorted out of the British Residency and left on the street to find his own way home from Manama to Ras Al Khaimah. It was an incredibly rude gesture to a Trucial Ruler and stands as a stark example of British paternalism and the superior sense that the Resident possessed over the leaders of 'native peoples'. That attitude, thankfully, was not to persist for very much longer.

Anyone but Barut

The British Residency Agent now gathered the notables of Kalba, under instruction from the Political Agent in Bahrain (at the time recessing at Karachi) and told them that they were required to form a Regency Council. Although nothing was said in public, in private the British were agreed that the slave Barut was not acceptable as Regent. He would not rule Kalba in deed or name, despite the fact that he had not only effectively ruled the town for some time but had done so with such a deft hand that the local notables accepted him as their choice of suzerain and thought him a safe pair of hands to look after things while young Hamad grew up.

The rent for the aerodrome at Kalba was withheld until the locals saw sense and found someone other than Barut to handle affairs in general – and treat with the British in particular.[19]

The Sultan of Muscat now crashes into the narrative with brio. It is typical of the scale of affairs and the exquisite balance in which the exercise of power could be held in the area that his action in sending six guards to Kalba and two to Khor Fakkan was to be so decisive, but it now truly electrified matters and triggered the conclusion to the whole incident.

As it happens, Muscat was trying to pursue a case involving a *nakhuda* from Umm Al Quwain fleeing his creditors. But the appearance of men from Oman at this sensitive moment resulted in the Naqbiyin appealing to Khalid bin Ahmed and resisting the unwarranted incursion from the Sultan of Muscat in Khor Fakkan. Khalid moved with alacrity, marching from Dhaid to Kalba with a force of fifty men. At the same time, his brother Abdullah moved down the Wadi Qor at the head of 200 men.[20]

A bloody conflict seemed inevitable and the situation, as Hickinbotham, the Political Agent in Bahrain, phrased it, had 'become obscure'.

The Naqbiyin invited Khalid bin Ahmed into Khor Fakkan on 12 September and the people of Kalba called for him on the 16th. An agreement was drawn up, providing for a Regency over Kalba, with Khalid bin Ahmed acting in Barut's place as Regent for the young Hamad.

The British considered the entire situation was now most satisfactory. The deposed former Ruler of Sharjah, Khalid bin Ahmad Al Qasimi, was now accepted as Ruler over Dhaid, Kalba and Khor Fakkan, which were stable and in strong hands, while Sheikh Sultan bin Saqr Al Qasimi of Sharjah appeared quite reconciled to the diminution of his territory. The Imperial Airways machines, whose flights had been suspended during the whole imbroglio, were once again free to use Kalba. All, it appears, had ended well.

Khalid bin Ahmad Al Qasimi now quietly appointed a Wali to rule over Kalba on his behalf, leaving him to go back home to Ajman.

Barut.

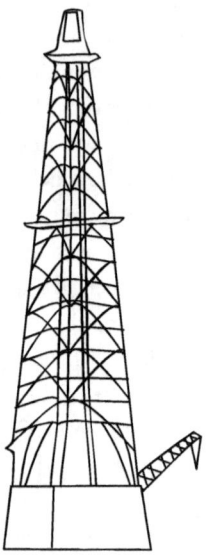

Chapter 23

OIL, REBELLION AND WAR

"My grandfather rode a camel, my father rode a camel, I drive a Mercedes, my son drives a Land Rover, his son will drive a Land Rover, but his son will ride a camel."

– *Rashid bin Saeed Al Maktoum*

There had long been tales of finds of bitumen in the warm waters of the Gulf. In fact, the material had been used as caulking for boats for millennia. But nobody could have imagined that these barren sands and the torpid sea that bordered them could contain vast quantities of oil, the new miracle ingredient of the internal combustion age. That all changed in 1932 when oil was struck in Bahrain. The concession to search for oil in Saudi Arabia was subsequently granted to the Standard Oil Company of California (SoCal) in 1933 and now there was something of an oil rush as geologists roamed the Gulf looking for the right rock formations that might harbour new finds. The science was in its infancy and the geologists, for the most part, were fumbling around in the dark.

The Trucial Sheikhs heard of Bahrain's windfall but were generally more interested in digging wells for water. They also saw the idea of 'options' (exploration rights) as a source of ready cash and were more than eager to sign these. The deal made sense, surely? You can explore for oil. If you find it, you make me rich. If you fail, you've paid me anyway. Clutching their option deals and the little wads of rupees on offer, they happily stored their windfall, (there being no banks at the time). The tiny influxes of cash made a huge difference to the impoverished Trucial Coast, where only Dubai with its port and trade and Sharjah with its airport had any form of sustainable economy in the aftermath of the long, slow decline of pearling.

The first approach to the idea of a geological survey was made by Sultan bin Salim of Ras Al Khaimah, generally the most anti-British of the Trucial Rulers, who had started talks with the French, alarming the British Political Resident, the marvellously named Trenchard Craven William Fowle. Fowle reminded the Ruler of his obligations under the Exclusive Agreement (only to do business with the British, basically) as well as the 1922 agreement only to deal with nominees of the British Government. Fowle, in what the French would surely have considered Fowle play, brought in the Anglo-Persian Oil Company (later to become British Petroleum, or BP) which promptly signed a two-year option to explore Ras Al Khaimah through its subsidiary, the

D'Arcy Exploration Company Ltd on 1 August 1935. D'Arcy went on to sign options with Sharjah, Dubai, Abu Dhabi and Ajman.

One of the key figures in the early 'wild west' years of the oil industry in the Trucial States was a colourful chap by the name of William Williamson, known throughout the area as Haji Williamson. Born in Bristol, he went to sea at the age of 13. A lifelong adventurer and sometime trader, boxer, whale hunter, brigand, gunrunner and horse trader, he converted to Islam in Yemen and went on to become a pearl fisherman.[1] In 1924, Haji Williamson was brought on board by Anglo-Persian to act as a liaison with the Gulf Rulers. An eccentric figure at the best of times, Williamson would wear a Western suit with a local headdress. He not only spoke Arabic, but was intimately involved in the various trades – and intrigues – of the region. The Trucial Rulers were initially delighted with this Englishman 'gone native' and Williamson quickly earned their trust, working for APOC in Qatar before visiting the Trucial States and signing the first round of options with the Rulers.

Williamson's great rival was a New Zealander, Major Frank Holmes. Holmes had negotiated the first concession to search for oil in the Gulf, in Bahrain, and he and Williamson worked against each other for rival companies before both ended up working for Petroleum Concessions Ltd (PCL), a subsidiary of the Iraq Petroleum Company – not, in fact, Iraqi at all, but a consortium of Western petroleum interests. Their former rivalry didn't end there and despite being employed by the same company, they continued to work against each other. Both men shared two key attributes. The first was that their contacts with Sheikhs and influential families of the region were strong, and they were very well regarded locally. The second was that British officialdom viewed them both with extreme mistrust.[2]

These initial oil exploration options provided the Rulers with an income of some 2,000 rupees per month – quite a tidy sum, but not enough to get rich on by any means – especially as Rulers were expected to pay stipends to family members and tribal leaders to keep the peace and assert their influence. However, the next round of negotiations was to involve altogether greater sums – the concession agreements granted not only the right to explore for oil, but governed the commercial extraction and payments for oil. These were the grand prize and now Holmes and Williamson vied for influence, His Majesty's Government coerced and pressured and 'the company', PCL, tried to maximise its gain and minimise its outlay. In the summer of 1936, Haji Williamson reported that Holmes was offering 60,000 rupees in cash, 20,000 rupees per annum and three rupees per ton for oil to Saeed bin Maktoum for a six-year oil concession. That sum was to rise as negotiations dragged on through 1936 and into 1937. Holmes was a dogged haggler but Saeed bin Maktoum had lived all his life in the souks and Bedouin encampments of Dubai and Holmes had certainly met his match. All of the Trucial Rulers were by now alert to the potential scale of revenue represented by this company and its 'concessions' and they were not blind to the value of competition. Standard Oil of California, in particular, was to become an influence in two ways. Firstly, the company attempted to involve itself in negotiations with the Rulers. This attempt was to run up against His Majesty's Government officials, waving copies of the Exclusive Agreement of 1892 and the 1922 agreement only to negotiate for oil with the British. Standard Oil also, having signed with the Saudis, started to encroach on the Trucial States' territory, moving eastwards from Qatar and northwards up out of Saudi territory towards Liwa and Buraimi. Any extension of Saudi territorial claims would only benefit Standard Oil and expand the scope of its concession.

The concessions the Rulers signed with PCL would consist of two parts. The first was a commercial agreement between the Ruler and PCL. The second was an agreement between His Majesty's Government and PCL, which would also be signed by the Ruler, the 'Political Agreement'.

However, negotiating the first concession with Dubai was proving difficult. Saeed bin Maktoum was dragging his heels and PCL was becoming increasingly frustrated. Saeed knew, as PCL likely knew just as well, that the person in a negotiation with time on their side will inevitably win. There was no cost to Saeed in waiting things out, besides he was also managing a number of pressures, including the constant threat of trouble from his cousins and in particular Mana bin Rashid Al Maktoum, who had himself been in contact with oil companies.[3] PCL, meanwhile, was maintaining increasingly expensive facilities, including teams of geologists. And Standard Oil was snapping at their heels, HMG or not.

Part of the ongoing negotiations now turned to the issues of borders and influence. Where did Dubai and Abu Dhabi's border lie? One question here, in 1937, was the hill of Jebel Ali, which looked likely to be oil bearing. Another was the degree of influence over the interior that the Trucial Rulers enjoyed. It was one thing signing a concession including inland areas such as Jebel Faya – it was quite another getting a team of geologists there safely, let alone setting up expensive drilling operations when the Bedouin considered the territory to be theirs. By now, every community on the coast and interior was buzzing about the fabulous sums to be gained from the oil companies.

Meanwhile, negotiations in Dubai teetered constantly at the edge of success and the brink of failure. Frank Holmes, leading the effort to clinch the deal, reported success time after time before being forced to climb down and admit he had not quite got the signature he wanted. The British Residency Agent and Political Resident both sat with Saeed bin Maktoum, appealed to his influential and forceful son, Rashid bin Saeed, cajoled and even threatened. But Saeed would not be pinned down.

While Holmes was facing frustrations with negotiating the concessions, Haji Williamson was touring the country with Anglo-Iranian's (Anglo-Persian, confusingly, had changed its name to the Anglo-Iranian Oil Company) geologists under the options he had negotiated. Not only a fluent Arabic speaker but a devout Muslim, Williamson was in constant contact with the Rulers and families of the area. Holmes, his great rival, had been selected by PCL as their concession negotiator and Holmes appears to have suspected, even blamed, the slowness of his progress on Williamson intriguing against him. He was handed a trump card to use against his rival in early 1937 when Williamson gave his opinion that Dubai had very little territory to offer in terms of concessions, as its borders with its neighbours were closer to Dubai town than Saeed bin Maktoum had claimed.

Haji Williamson was both a blessing and a curse for both sides. For the Rulers he was socially and culturally welcome, but he knew too much and understood them too well at a time when they would rather have denied their counterparts in the oil company and HMG the insights and intelligence-gathering skills that made Williamson unique. For HMG, Williamson was not to be trusted and was too close to the natives. Now Saeed bin Maktoum, furious with Williamson, banned him from Dubai.[4]

The British Residency Agent, Khan Bahadur Abdul Razzaq Al Serkal, would also have had every reason to dislike both Williamson's easy way with the Trucial Rulers and his unique insight. The negotiations over the Sharjah airport had already showed how a Residency Agent would be mistrustful of losing his position to increased British direct involvement in the affairs of the coast – what worse nightmare could be imagined than an Englishman who spoke, thought and prayed like a local? Haji Williamson, through no fault of his own, now found himself effectively banned from the Trucial States when the Political Resident withdrew his visa. He left, to retire to Basra, where he lived until his death in 1958.

To the enormous relief of all concerned, Sheikh Saeed bin Maktoum signed the concession agreement on 22 May 1937. He also signed the political agreement, although was most displeased to have a document he had never seen before flourished under his nose with a demand he sign it on the spot.

The concession agreement with Sharjah followed soon after – after a protracted and frustrating negotiation (Sultan bin Saqr Al Qasimi having observed events in Dubai closely and learned greatly from them), it was signed on 17 September 1937.

Cash and crash

There is no doubt but that times were tough in the Trucial States in the 1930s. Money was a scarce commodity on the Trucial Coast as merchants continued to struggle with the after-effects of the long threnody of the pearling industry. The boats still went out, but fewer boats employed fewer men, chasing fewer pearls (the pearl banks had been enthusiastically over-fished for much of the late 1800s and the early part of the 1900s destined for fewer merchants and, tellingly, fewer necks. Costume jewellery was big in the 1930s and the Indian market for seed pearls remained steadier than 'quality' pearls. By the mid-1930s in America and Europe, women were wearing paste and glass as costume jewellery dominated the market.

If Sultan bin Saqr Al Qasimi had a source of constant cash from the airport, he had to face down accusations from his peers that he had sold out to the British. At least some of this was driven by jealousy, but tradition in Gulf society had it that the payment of a subsidy brought fealty – and the British were, following the establishment of the airport and its fort, paying Sultan bin Saqr a subsidy. Now, with the oil concession signed, Sultan could look forward to a great deal more money flowing into the Ruler's coffers. And to having to manage the inflated expectations of tribal Sheikhs and family members.

Down the coast in Dubai, Saeed bin Maktoum was also able, at least partially, to offset the long decline of the pearl market as Dubai's trading community grew. Buoyed by the influx of traders from Persia and elsewhere, constantly scoping out new opportunities (including shipping slaves and gunrunning) and mercantile to its core, Dubai muddled through. The steamships brought bulk cargoes that were offloaded by lighters and stored for re-export to regional markets. In an echo of the trade through Hormuz, that early version of the Emirates/DP World business model, now regional cargoes came into Dubai for consolidation to other destinations, while bulk cargoes came in for breaking down and shipping to regional markets.

When the oil concessions were signed, early rumblings became more serious. The Rulers of both Sharjah and Dubai faced calls from family and other dependants to pay out larger and larger sums, often out of proportion to what was certainly a handsome – if finite – windfall.

Worse, the trouble in Dubai was that the mercantile class wasn't rooted in the Al Bu Falasah, the 'locals' of Dubai who had been ruled by the Maktoum family since 1833, or even among the members of other tribes who had settled Dubai. These had traditionally been more dependent on the pearling industry but also often could count on subsidies from the Ruler. Times were tough and subsidies not as forthcoming – and the traders of Dubai were a mixed bunch with some locals, but a great number of Indian, Persian and other nationalities. If trade was good, it wasn't necessarily benefiting Saeed bin Maktoum's core supporters as much as some thought it might.

In October 1934, it was feared an attempt was planned on the Ruler's life. Saeed bin Maktoum's cousins were fomenting rebellion. Saeed had been a staunch supporter of reconciliation among his fellow Trucial Rulers, often being seen to be aligned to British policy – to the point where even the British recognised they bore some responsibility for his safety.[5]

HMS *Lupin* was stood offshore of Dubai and the Political Resident in Bushire cabled *Lupin's* commander on 27 October, 'Please inform Sheikh of Dubai that I shall probably be able to send him some rifles and ammunition shortly should he require them. You should let the message be known in town especially to his cousins.'

The trouble was partly ameliorated by the chance arrival of three Westland Wapiti warplanes at Sharjah. Quick to spot the impact this event would have on opinion in Dubai, the Political Resident requested overflights of Dubai by the noisy biplanes over two days. They buzzed the town and HMS *Lupin*, circling low twice over Dubai as they left on 31 October. The message to Saeed bin Maktoum's cousins was crystal clear and the storm clouds over his *majlis* passed, at least for the time being.

However, more instability was bubbling under and Deira, in particular, was becoming lawless even by Dubai's laissez faire standards. It is perhaps worth noting that Deira was the side of the creek favoured by Saeed bin Maktoum's troublesome cousins, away from the Ruler's beady eye and linked to Bur Dubai at the time only by abras, the little passenger boats that plied the creek crossing. Gambling and even prostitution were rife in Deira – in 1930 Sheikh Saeed banished prostitutes from Dubai,[6] an aspect of mercantile marine cities that was clearly at odds with Muslim tradition and teaching.

On 19 January 1936, Saeed bin Maktoum appointed his cousin Sheikh Saeed bin Butti bin Suhail to act as Wali over Deira and charged him to take whatever measures he saw fit to establish the rule of law that were both in the interest of the greater good of the town and that would protect the lives of foreigners from murder and their property from loss.

Saeed bin Butti clearly had carte blanche to clean the town up and he set to with vigour. He imposed a curfew, forbidding 'loiterers' after 4 p.m. on pain of a sound beating and an overnight stay in jail. He cleaned up Deira, throwing out the gamblers and imprisoning thieves, including a gang of six miscreants who had been responsible for a string of thefts in the town.[7]

The move was highly unpopular with Saeed Al Maktoum's other cousins. Saeed bin Butti responded to their outraged protest with severity and they climbed down in the face of his righteous censure. It was not to last.

Car trouble

With tensions already high following the clean-up instituted by Saeed bin Butti and a great deal of suspicion, jealousy and greed triggered by the oil concessions of 1937, it was a row over taxis, of all things, that plunged Dubai town into crisis.

Dubai's fledgling taxi service was operated as a side-line by the Ruler Saeed Al Maktoum's son, Rashid bin Saeed. A firebrand of 26 years of age, Rashid took exception to a rival service being started up by his cousin, Maktoum bin Rashid of Deira.[8] Following the escalation of an incident when some of Rashid bin Saeed's men roughed up the driver of Maktoum bin Rashid's taxi, the Al Bu Falasah of Deira, Saeed Al Maktoum's cousins and other extended family, rose up and started to hold meetings to discuss their discontentment with affairs in general. They sent a request to Saeed Al Maktoum for subsidies to be paid, which was ignored and so they set out a list of demands for the Ruler to address, including the establishment of a 'civil list', reforms of education, sanitation, peace and order, the removal of corruption and, tellingly, the 'Grant of justice and freedom of the inhabitants in trade and other crafts'. The Al Bu Falasah of Deira wanted a slice of Dubai's mercantile pie to be handed to them on a plate and on 18 June 1938, they made it clear: if their demands were not met, they were prepared to use force.[9]

A day later, on 19 June 1938, the Al Bu Falasah in Deira acted, collecting a group of armed men who occupied the watch towers of that side of the town and took control of the whole area. Infuriated, Saeed bin Maktoum nevertheless agreed to hold back his force of 400 Bedouin as the British Residency Agent scurried to negotiate at least a ceasefire.

The Indian and Persian merchants of Dubai were secure, their interests protected by Saeed bin Maktoum in deference to the constant imprecations of the Residency Agent in Sharjah and the Political Resident in Bahrain (the British Political Resident in Bahrain was now responsible for the Trucial States, reporting to Bushire). British subjects and their property were to be protected at all costs and, despite the state of war into which Dubai was now being pitched, Saeed recognised that the safety of his mercantile community was paramount.

Saeed bin Maktoum formed a 'conciliation committee' led by his brother, Juma, to negotiate with the Al Bu Falasah and as a result, hostilities ceased and the towers were freed. Juma agreed to most of the points raised by the dissident faction, led by Sheikh Mana bin Rashid and Hasher bin Rashid Al Maktoum. Negotiations continued, but the atmosphere in the town of Dubai remained tense. Imperial Airways, which had recently started a flying boat service to Dubai, diverted its flights to Ras Al Khaimah.

On 9 October 1938, the Awlad Rashid (sons of Rashid), as the group of dissidents had become known, took over the *Burj Nahar* – Nahar Tower – in Deira. The centrepiece of a small park in the heart of Deira today, it was a significant strategic asset at that time, defending the areas of Rigga, Naif, Marar and Al Ras which together comprised the settlement of Deira.

Two days later, the group seized the Deira Customs House.

Backed into a corner, Saeed bin Maktoum agreed to the foundation of the *Majlis*, an assembly which would meet under his presidency or, if he were not present, the presidency of one of the members of the *majlis*. The assembly proposed would effectively run the affairs of the town and the Ruler would be beholden to it for any decision he took. The agreement was signed by Saeed bin Maktoum as Ruler and Mana bin Rashid 'on behalf of the Al Bu Falasah'.[10]

The *Majlis* sat and deliberated, appointing members for the management of various aspects of the town's municipal affairs. It did so largely without the participation of Dubai's Ruler. Saeed bin Maktoum quickly stopped attending when it was clear that the effort to create a consultative assembly was in fact a front for the Awlad Rashid, under Mana bin Rashid, to rule Dubai. The *Majlis*, in a final infuriation for Saeed bin Maktoum, suggested he live on a grant of 10,000 rupees a month.

And yet for a time, the *Majlis*' reforms looked positive. Dubai's customs operations were streamlined and corrupt officials who had been siphoning off significant portions of the revenue were removed. Watchmen were appointed in the town and three schools were opened.

However, the effort at reform quickly unravelled. The replacement of corrupt officials in the customs sheds was followed by the nomination of a number of individuals to roles in the management of the city. These clearly considered their new appointments to represent a series of lucrative fiefdoms and the merchants of Dubai found themselves oppressed with lightning speed. Shopkeepers were evicted and law and order, far from being enforced in a new and civilised manner, quickly broke down – with vested interests very much at play.

Saeed Al Maktoum remained aloof throughout the winter months, but by March 1939 the merchants of Deira had had enough and rose up against the *Majlis*. One, Hamad bin Majid Al Futtaim, was particularly outspoken and quickly gained the support of the guards the *Majlis* had placed on the souk as well as of other key figures. Once again, the situation in Deira was spiralling out of control and the streets were tense and fearful.

Meanwhile, the fiery young Rashid bin Saeed had fallen in love and wanted to marry the daughter of Hamdan bin Zayed, the Ruler of Abu Dhabi who had been killed in 1922. Hamdan's wife had fled to Dubai and taken refuge with her family, the Marar tribe. Her daughter Latifa caught Rashid's eye and a wedding was quickly arranged, with fifteen days of celebrations on the Dubai side of the creek and fifteen days of celebrations on the Deira side, where the Marar lived. The wedding celebrations were unusually long and festive, reflecting the status of the

Crown Prince of Dubai and, after fifteen days of feasting, displays of horse riding and enthusiastic demonstrations of Bedouin martial skill throughout Bur Dubai, on 22 March 1939, the celebrations moved to the Marar family side of the creek – Deira.

The only way to cross Dubai's creek at the time was to take an abra, the water taxis that still ply the crossing today. The members of the *Majlis* party were increasingly worried by the volume of traffic coming across the creek each day from Dubai, with large numbers of armed Bedouin flocking to join the party.[11]

They were right to be, too...

The fall of the Majlis

Concerned at the wildness of the celebrations (and the celebrants), the supporters of the *Majlis* movement occupied the towers of Deira once again. This act broke the treaty that had been negotiated with Saeed bin Maktoum the previous October. On the evening of 29 March at around 4 p.m., when hundreds of Bedouin had crossed Dubai creek to the Deira side, packing the little abras, the signal was given. A single gunshot rang out and Rashid bin Saeed's forces fell on the forces loyal to the Awlad Rashid, overwhelming the rebels and taking the whole of Deira. Something like 500 men were behind Rashid bin Saeed, including the Marar and Sudan of Deira, as well as the men of Al Ras under Hamad bin Majid Al Futtaim. The fighting into the night was fierce, with losses to the *Majlis*' forces estimated as ten dead against one on the Dubai side.

By the next morning, Mana bin Rashid's brother, Hasher, was dead and the Awlad Rashid and their supporters had either surrendered or had fled to Sharjah. Between fifteen and twenty-six people were killed or wounded, many were onlookers. Mana bin Rashid, the ringleader of the whole *Majlis* movement, escaped dressed in women's clothes.[12]

It was over. Peace once again reigned in Bur Dubai and Deira. The British Political Resident in Bahrain, Hugh Weightman, visited Dubai and gave the go-ahead for the Imperial Airways flights to resume. He met with Saeed Al Maktoum and counselled the formation of an assembly in the wake of the disastrous *Majlis* experiment and then travelled to Sharjah, where Sultan bin Saqr had given (as was customary) refuge to Mana bin Rashid and his followers.[13]

Saeed Al Maktoum did indeed establish two assemblies – one, the Advisory *Majlis* contained seven members of the Al Bu Falasah (interestingly, five of these were formerly members of the *Majlis* movement), three Sudan, two Al Bu Muhair and one Mazari. The second *majlis*, the *Majlis* Al Tujarah was appointed on 6 April 1939 and represented the merchants and traders of the town.

However, Mana bin Rashid and some forty-six armed supporters (100 originally fled with him, but his followers were starting to wander away) remained in Sharjah, hovering on Saeed Al Maktoum's northern border. This was clearly not a situation Saeed could tolerate and he pressed for Mana to be given exile far away, in Ras Al Khaimah or Abu Dhabi. Instead, Mana stayed in Sharjah and started talks with Umm Al Quwain and Ajman about granting him refuge. Neither was very keen to step forward. By 16 May 1939, Mana was running out of options, finding his overtures to Ras Al Khaimah were also rejected.[14]

Sultan bin Saqr Al Qasimi of Sharjah now claimed there was no harm in Mana bin Rashid staying in Sharjah and communicated that decision to Saeed bin Maktoum on the very next day. Saeed, furious that his neighbour was not only giving refuge to his enemy and was even permitting members of Mana bin Rashid's entourage to marry into Sharjah families, closed the traffic between Dubai and Sharjah. Sheikh Sultan reciprocated and banned Sharjah citizens from going to Dubai.

Worse, Sultan bin Saqr maintained a claim to Deira. At the height of the trouble in 1938, he had approached the British Residency Agent saying he was concerned that Dubai folk were fighting over a town to which they had no right, producing a century-old document from Maktoum bin Butti, which said that the recently sprung-up township of Deira belonged to Sultan bin Saqr – the present Ruler's great-grandfather. If the British were willing to recognise his claim, he said airily, he would be willing to grant them any oil concessions they liked.[15]

The response from Bahrain was, to say the least, pithy. 'The claim is, of course, absurd and childish,' the British Political Resident sniffed in reply.

And yet Sultan bin Saqr was convinced not only of his claim, but that having Mana in Sharjah would strengthen it and give him leverage. He was alone in thinking this was a good idea – the other Rulers and the British were all agreed it was quite the opposite. The result was an escalating conflict with Dubai in early 1940, which rumbled on across the border at Al Khan and only avoided significant loss of life because of the constant ammunition shortage which beset those on both sides of the fight. Charmingly, the conflict would pause when the charabanc carrying Imperial Airways seaplane passengers who had landed at Dubai Creek and were to be overnighted at Al Mahatta in Sharjah passed by.

At one stage, peace talks were held at Al Nahda between Sultan bin Saqr Al Qasimi and Saeed bin Maktoum Al Maktoum. Directly after, Sheikh Sultan bin Saqr's private secretary was found trying to smuggle 400 rounds of ammunition to Sharjah from Dubai concealed in a tin of nails. With trust at a low ebb between the two Rulers, the British convinced Sultan bin Saqr that he had to abandon the idea of giving refuge to Mana bin Rashid.[16]

Mana went to the Bani Qitab, but eventually was forced, his support dwindling, to travel to Bahrain and Bombay, and from his exile there, seek refuge from Abu Dhabi's Ruler, Shakhbut.

Passings and the clouds of war

The giant figure of Abdulrahman bin Muhammad Al Shamsi straddled the history of Sharjah in the 1920s and 1930s. Even as clouds were looming over Europe in 1939, Abdulrahman was threatening to go to war against his son-in-law after Sultan bin Saqr decided to build a tower between Sharjah and Al Heera, ostensibly to protect members of the Al Owais family who quit Al Heera after they had quarrelled with Abdulrahman.[17]

Abdulrahman also welcomed an old foe into his fold when Khalid bin Ahmed Al Qasimi decided to settle in Al Heera. By now Ruler of Dhaid, Kalba and Khor Fakkan, Khalid was a powerful man in his own right and his presence at Al Heera scared Sultan bin Saqr so much that he eventually prevailed on the British Residency Agent to persuade Khalid bin Ahmed to move back to Dhaid.

Strong-headed, resolute, loved by the Bedouin and particularly close to the powerful and aggressive Bani Qitab, Abdulrahman passed away on the morning of 10 August 1942. He was succeeded by his son Saif. Strangely enough, at the same moment, the exiled leader of the *Majlis* movement, Mana bin Rashid, returned from Bombay and was refused landing at Sharjah, so headed for Al Heera instead.[18]

Mana's relief at finding a landing was to be short lived. Sharjah subsumed Al Heera and Mana was once again sent away to his exile.

A change in policy

By the late 1930s, the tone of British voices was changing. Perhaps less self-assured, perhaps a little more aware that anti-British sentiment was all too easy to provoke, the British in the Trucial States also found themselves more pressured to take some sort of responsibility beyond merely chastising the children of the seven sands when they, in British eyes, erred.

The opening days of World War II saw the retirement of Trenchard Craven William Fowle. He had acted as British Political Resident in the Arabian Gulf for seven years and was to be the last of the 'Raj generation' of Residents.

Fowle recognised, as had some of his immediate predecessors, that British policy was inevitably subject to change. His retirement note of March 1939 bears close scrutiny, not because it was insightful, although it was, but because it was inspired.[19]

Although still underneath it all a typical old paternalistically inclined Imperialist, Fowle understood that goodwill towards the British was maintained mainly because British rule was indirect, that it allowed the Rulers (and their people) to manage affairs their way rather than insisting on the 'British way'. Although a breath-taking summary of a period in which the British gladly bombarded the settlements, forts and towers of anyone who did not show proper respect to that most sacred of cows, 'British prestige', Fowle was to a degree – arguably – 'carrying' his wider audience when he wrote his memo.

'The Arab States have their differences with His Majesty's Government, and on occasions I daresay they find us rather a nuisance, in connection with slavery, for example. At the same time they know perfectly well that is only His Majesty's Government who stand between them and absorption by Ibn Saud, Iraq or Persia, and would naturally much prefer to remain as they are free and independent under their own Sheikhs, and under our protection, than for their states to become mere districts of Saudi Arabia, or Iraq or Iran, with their present Rulers replaced by oppressive Saudi, Iraqi or Persian officials.'

Fowle's voice – in 1939 – would doubtless have had some resonance for the Rulers of the United Arab Emirates in December 1971, as they contemplated independence under the clouds gathering around them in the Gulf at that time.

Fowle saw the end of the era of applying 'pressure' to coerce compliance with British aims and desires and asserted the value of 'counsel' in its place. He also noted that an area which had been a 'cul de sac' in the past was now emerging 'to become an international highway of the first importance' and that even if British pressure were brought to bear to force a reluctant Trucial Ruler to the British will of the moment, the increasing voice of the people meant that they, too, needed to be considered. Fowle predicted difficult times ahead and pointed out that, above all, the British depended on the goodwill of the Rulers and people of the area.

It was all a long way from making the Ruler of Ras Al Khaimah walk home from Manama after a dressing down or bombarding the Ruler of Fujairah's fort, but it was a prescient view of the changing nature of British power and the way it was now becoming acceptable to behave towards British subjects or those under British protection.

Despite Fowle's reservations about the move, in 1939 the British Residency Agent found himself dealing with a new reality when the first British Political Officer was installed in Sharjah. It was to be a fraught time for the new appointee, as Britain, its back to the wall, prepared to defend itself against Germany and her Axis.

At this time, perhaps more than any other, Britain's handful of administrators in the Gulf would discover how important that goodwill was to be.

Sentiment über alles

Britain was at war, but it would be imposing a completely different view of the world to claim that this mattered one whit to the Rulers and people of the Trucial Coast and the interior of Southeastern Arabia. The 'phony war' followed Britain's declaration of war against Germany, months of seeming inaction leading up to the German 'blitzkrieg', the invasion of France and the near annihilation – and miraculous rescue – of the British Expeditionary Force at Dunkirk. By May 1940, the German triumph in Europe seemed complete, the British smashed and retreating to the fleeting comfort of their own shores before the Germans' killing blow would inevitably fall.

An Indian trading company's agent was heard expressing pro-German sentiment and – a British subject – he was sent summarily back to India in a move the Residency Agent clearly thought was good for that all-important quality, British prestige in the area. In the dark days of June 1940, as the tattered remnants of the British army regrouped following the evacuation of Dunkirk, expressions of anti-British sentiment would not be – could not be – tolerated by the British in the Trucial States.

It was now that the Ruler of Sharjah, Sultan bin Saqr Al Qasimi, chose to tune his radio set to the German Arabic broadcast and crank up the volume so that it blared out from the Sharjah Fort and could be heard 'for 200 yards away'. Gathering a large nightly crowd, the broadcast was clearly an attraction and the British Residency Agent assumed a disguise (likely fooling no one) and observed the proceedings. Sure enough, people were in the streets arguing passionately for and against the British as Berlin roared propaganda at them from the Ruler's palace.[20]

The Agent went to see Sultan bin Saqr, who agreed to turn the volume down. Nobody in this oriental version of an Ealing comedy (or perhaps a Western version of an Egyptian comedy) was fooled. The *majlis* was packed with visitors to hear the nightly broadcasts, the souqs were full of talk of German victory and French failure. That Britain would be next.

The Agent resolved to see who was behind this treacherous talk and soon enough found his man: the Ruler's secretary, Abdullah bin Faris. Following a series of letters and protestations, including a stage-managed circular which saw the notables of Sharjah unwittingly proclaiming bin Faris to be a fine, upstanding and pro-British fellow (which they all subsequently denied having signed) and much skulduggery, bin Faris was 'kept under observation'.

The Trucial States settled down to a wartime footing. Increased British military activity at the aerodrome and RAF station at Sharjah was an accepted symptom of the war. The British also maintained an RAF landing strip and refuelling depot on Sir Bani Yas Island in Abu Dhabi as well as smaller facilities in Kalba and Ras Al Khaimah.

The war, for the most part, passed by the Trucial States – so much so that the few incidents that took place stand out. One of the great Handley Page HP42 biplanes was lost in March 1940, en route from India to Sharjah, somewhere in the Gulf of Oman, while in February 1943 a Wellington bomber was lost at Dhadnah in Fujairah. A monument to that crash and the death of the Wellington's navigator stands at Dhadnah today. Three crashes involving Blenheims took place in 1943: one, an engine failure, in Umm Al Quwain and one plane ditched in shallow water off Sharjah. One of these three crashes, however, was fatal.

A Bristol Blenheim bomber took off from Sharjah en route to Jask on 1 February 1943 and lost an engine as it climbed over the desert. The pilot of the plane attempted a forced landing in the sand, killing the pilot and two others on board. It was only in 2017 that the crash site was located, in an area long known to locals as Nad Al Tayara – dune of the aeroplane.[21] At the time of the crash, the three dead crew were buried at the crash site – their graves have been since lost.

The war at sea in the area also contained few incidents of note – including the August 1944 sinking off the coast of Oman by the U859, a German U-Boat, of an American 'Liberty Ship' crammed with silver ingots, destined for Russia.[22]

The first sinking of a submarine was the 1940 attack on the Italian submarine Luigi Galvani. Another Italian submarine had earlier surrendered: the Galileo Galilei was taken off Aden in June 1940, and carried papers referring to the Luigi Galvani and giving an operational area for the vessel, which sparked a British search for the ship, assumed at the time to be a minelayer. The Galvani was sunk in the Gulf of Oman on 23 June with the loss of twenty-six crew (thirty-one were picked up by the British ships).

The German U-Boat U533 was sunk by a Blenheim flying out of Sharjah, on patrol off the coast of Fujairah. The Blenheim spotted the U-boat, which dived but was hit by one of four depth charges dropped by the bomber. A single crew member survived to live out his war as a Prisoner of War following a reportedly enjoyable internment at Sharjah.

Other than these excitements, the war passed by in relative peace for the Trucial States. Rationing was introduced and commodities such as tea and sugar became valuable rarities. Dubai, ever the opportunist, turned to new trade routes that opened up and smugglers and black marketeers plied the seas of the Indian Ocean, Gulf of Oman and Arabian Gulf.

Dubai's lively wartime trade continued to fund the expansion of the town and port, including a considerable trade in gunrunning. Its venerable Ruler, Saeed bin Maktoum bin Hasher Al Maktoum increasingly retreated from public affairs following the conflict with Sharjah and his son, the dynamic and assertive Rashid bin Saeed Al Maktoum took over the running of day-to-day life in Dubai. A pharmacy was opened in Deira by the town's first qualified Doctor, Dr Habib Al Redha, an event coinciding with the British appointment of a medical officer for the Gulf – a rare British nod to the development of the region rather than its usual somewhat distant form of governance.[23]

It was to be a feather in a gale when it came to addressing the health problems in Dubai and other communities in the Trucial States throughout the war years. Rationing and identity cards were introduced, but disease was rife and there were deadly outbreaks of cholera throughout the coast, sweeping through the poor, tightly packed communities and the teeming bazaars of the towns.

Dubai and the Trucial Coast also suffered from periodic and rapacious swarms of locusts, which would strip all vegetation away as they passed by in great clouds. A plague for some, the locusts were also an opportunity for others and impoverished locals would eat the insects – a rare and valuable source of protein. The British sent insecticide spraying teams in as part of a successful eradication programme.

As World War II drew to a close, an exhausted Britain started to count the cost of its greatest battle, in lives, in money and the damage to its Empire. Dubai, meanwhile, had been significantly bolstered by the profits of its wartime trade and now, buoyed up and flushed with success, decided to have a little war of its own.

The little war

Khor Ghanadah is an area of mangroves and shallows, a few minutes down the road towards Abu Dhabi from Ghantoot. It is largely unremarkable although very beautiful – and today is a (largely inaccessible) nature reserve, home to a few large houses and a resort hotel. Just to the south of the mangroves is the Emirates Global Aluminium Al Taweelah plant.

Just before midnight on 17 October 1945, Sheikh Rashid bin Saeed Al Maktoum drove through the sand flats on the coast beyond Jebel Ali to reach Khor Ghanadah. Bouncing in the car beside him were three of his cousins, who had gone with him to build two towers at Ghanadah and claim it for Dubai. Out at sea, three launches and six jollyboats made for the little inlet, packed with something like 300 men and supplies, including two huge wooden water tanks. They pitched five tents and unloaded their equipment, planting Dubai flags on the western and eastern sides of the creek. There they camped, waiting for building supplies to come up from Dubai.

The question of who owned Ghanadah had arisen before World War II, but had never been fully settled. Now Rashid set out to resolve it with typical decisiveness. His men were to build a defensive tower either side of the entrance to the creek. They would have got away with it too, had it not been for the pesky British Residency Agent, who arrived a day later from Sharjah to find out quite what was going on.[24]

Khan Bahadur Abdul Razzaq Al Razzuki, the British Agent, certainly had his ears close to the ground and the fact he was able to move so fast is testament to the effective listening network he maintained. He had already picked up information about an earlier trip by Sheikh Rashid, who had gone to Khor Ghanadah in September on a 'fishing expedition'.[25]

The British fired off a letter to Dubai and Abu Dhabi warning of dire consequences in case of any trouble causing any damage or loss of life or property to any British subjects. The Assistant Political Agent in Bahrain, Richard Bird, went to see Sheikh Saeed and Sheikh Rashid in Dubai on 22 October to know what was happening at Ghanadah. Sheikh Saeed pointed out that it was Dubai territory and outlined two substantiations to his claim.

Bird, briefed by the Residency Agent, Abdurazzak, brought up the movement of troops by boat. Sheikh Rashid, clearly seeing which way the conversation was swinging, pointed out that it was his understanding that the treaty of 1853 only applied to maritime conflict, not the movement of men by sea to another location on land. Not so, said Bird: surely Sheikh Rashid would know that sending a force of men to seize a disputed territory would constitute an act of war with Abu Dhabi?

Rashid was implacable. The claim was absolute. Bird, the British Political Officer and Abdurazzak all agreed – the action against Ghanadah would quickly escalate into all-out war involving the tribes of the interior. The British, they resolved, should interfere and step between the two potential belligerents.[26]

In the background was a quiet young man. Hamdan bin Hamdan Al Nahyan never had the opportunity to fully know his father, who was killed in 1922 by his own brother, Sultan bin Zayed bin Khalifa Al Nahyan, who had taken over as Ruler of Abu Dhabi. Hamdan's mother had fled back to her maternal family in Dubai, where her daughter, Latifa, had caught Sheikh Rashid's eye and gone on to be his wife and, indeed, the love of his life.[27]

On 26 October, the Political Agent in Bahrain was sent to visit the Trucial Coast by the Political Resident – the latest in a long line of splendidly named chaps in the British administration – Arnold Crawshaw Galloway. He was to communicate to the Ruler of Dubai that he was in breach of the 1853 Treaty and to insist that Dubai's force of men be withdrawn from Khor Ghanadah pending a review of the frontier question. The Agent was then to proceed to Abu Dhabi and tell Sheikh Shakhbut that Dubai had been instructed to withdraw from Ghanadah and that he, Shakhbut, should take no aggressive action.[28]

The exchange between Sheikh Saeed and Sheikh Rashid and Cornelius James Pelly, the Political Agent, was at best testy. 'I had no need to simulate anger,' Pelly wrote in his report of the interview, 'when I told him that the reason they were able to do so was because they had made profits out of the war which the Allied soldiers had fought.'[29]

Pelly was clearly of the opinion that the Sheikhs of Dubai were profiteers who had made good during the war and therefore would have had the lowest opinion of them – profiteering was a terrible accusation at this highly emotionally charged time, a mere month after World War II had ground to its battered close. The pragmatic view that it was not their war in the first place – let alone that trade was trade, a matter of goods satisfying a market need -- would have cut little mustard with Pelly, a staunch Irish Catholic with a lifetime in the Indian service behind him.

Nevertheless, he did his duty and conveyed the message to Dubai before sending the Residency Agent, Abdurazzak, as a messenger to Abu Dhabi. Abdurazzak stopped off at Khor Ghanadah and found that the Dubai contingent was already being broken up and removed, with perhaps a third of the men still awaiting transport. When he arrived in Abu Dhabi, he found Sheikh Shakhbut furious and demanding retribution, threatening to invade Dubai and make Zabeel his headquarters, raise the tribes and teach Sheikh Saeed a lesson. Pelly managed to placate Shakhbut with some difficulty before returning to Dubai via Khor Ghanadah, which had now been, he reported, totally abandoned.[30]

If the British thought they had brokered a peace with their speedy and direct intervention, they weren't to think so for long. Early in

November, just days after the Residency Agent had left Abu Dhabi, a group of Manasir Bedouin, allies of the Bani Yas of Abu Dhabi, looted five Dubai camels from a camp south of Dubai. Just a couple of days later, a raiding party of Awamir, again close allies of the Bani Yas, swooped and took eight camels. A few days later, on 9 November, another party took three camels from a camp near Al Marmoom (the area in the deep desert south of Dubai where you will find Al Qudra Lakes today).[31]

Attempts to resolve these incidents came to little (some of the animals were returned) and the awaited British decision on the border issue came to nothing. By January 1946, Sheikh Rashid had clearly lost patience. He mounted a raid into Abu Dhabi territory, capturing a hundred camels. Sheikh Rashid was charged by the British Agent with carrying out the attack and not only admitted it, but was 'defiant'.[32]

Sheikh Rashid now ranged a force of Bedouin across the desert from Marmoom to the Jiri Plain, estimated at some 1,500 armed men. He agreed to mediation by the Rulers of Sharjah and Ras Al Khaimah and settled in for the wait. He did not wait long.

The British tried to rein in their recalcitrant subject. Threats were followed by action and the travel documents for Dubai subjects were withheld. Resolute, Rashid's response to the British when they announced this measure was that he simply would not travel. Now the British upped the game. By April, British mediation had, by their own admission, failed. In May, the choice faced by the Political Resident was to withdraw and leave the two aggrieved parties to fight it out, or impose further sanctions on Dubai. The latter course was chosen and, on 8 June 1946, the British India Steam Navigation Company Ltd – through its agent Gray, Mackenzie – acknowledged the instruction to divert its shipping from Dubai.

Soon after, on 29 June, the British adjudication on the claims to Khor Ghanadah was made. It was ruled that the area belonged to Abu Dhabi.[33]

Faced with an economic blockade and a hard judgement by an impartial party Sheikh Rashid, as always, chose pragmatism. A payment of 200,000 rupees in restitution was made to Sheikh Shakhbut and 127 camels were returned to Abu Dhabi's men on 15 July 1946.

Dubai's traders breathed a sigh of relief as the steamships were once again sighted coming in to the town's subdued creek. Gray Mackenzie complained about 7,351 bags of wheat it had landed at Sharjah during the blockade but which the consignee, the Dubai Food Company, had declined to acknowledge or accept.

Nobody much cared. Peace was restored once again and everyone, except perhaps Gray Mackenzie's man, burdened with his thousands of lost sacks of wheat, was glad it was all over.

The peace, sadly, was not to last.

A treaty was signed in March 1947, but the peace was fragile and short-lived. The tribes had been called to arms and they had come. Now they were stood down, but Sheikh Shakhbut failed to pay them for their efforts and they decided to help themselves to some recompense. Soon a low-level conflict was once again building up, with a number of raids taking place by the Manasir, Al Bu Shamis and Awamir who once again took to seizing camels from their northern neighbours. A meeting was arranged between the two Rulers, Saeed Al Maktoum and Shakhbut Al Nahyan, but it emerged that, while Saeed had paid off his tribal allies, Shakhbut had not. Now the responsibility for the continuation of the conflict became Shakhbut's and he became evasive. 'You must realise, O Sheikh, that you cannot accept the advantages of your position of authority and evade the responsibilities,' the Political Agent in Bahrain wrote to Shakhbut.[34]

By July 1947, raiders had taken over fifty camels from Dubai since the peace was signed. The British called on Shakhbut to act, but he prevaricated and obfuscated. The trouble continued and escalated – in August and September almost 300 camels were taken by Bedouin raiders and two Dubai men were killed. Up to this point there had been no record of tribal raiding on this scale in the turbulent interior of the Trucial States.

The British resorted to their new tactic – blockade. Rationing was still in place following World War II and essential supplies were subject to a quota system. Abu Dhabi's quotas, including its grain quota, were suspended.

At this point in time, an interesting exchange took place. In early January 1948, Sheikh Zayed bin Sultan, the brother of Shakhbut and his representative in Abu Dhabi's eastern province, including Al Ain, sent a messenger to Sheikh Saeed offering to broker a peace between him and the Manasir. After careful consideration of Zayed's offer, it was decided to stick to the agreement with Sheikh Shakhbut, which bound him to be responsible for the Manasir.[35]

Further negotiations with the British (backed by sanctions) finally secured a peace by the end of April 1948. However, two key issues refused to go away. The first was the reconciliation of the boundary dispute between Dubai and Abu Dhabi and the second was the responsibility for the behaviour of the Manasir, many of whom had by now decamped to relative safety in Al Hasa in Saudi Arabia. The Manasir, reduced by the march of progress, were reported to have massed in the area of Buraimi and Al Ain in preparation for a raid against Dubai even as late as 1950, but the anticipated trouble (likely due to the intervention of Zayed in Al Ain) failed to take place. As for the boundary dispute, the British drew the line between the two emirates at Hassyan on the coast and Ashoosh inland,[36] where it remains today. Final agreement on the border would remain an unsettled issue between the two emirates until 1968.

Another incident took place in 1948 which underlined the increasing assertion of control over the interior by the Trucial Rulers when Rashid bin Humaid Al Nuaimi seized Masfout from its Na'im headman, Saqr bin Sultan Al Hamouda. Following a period of decline for the mountain community, which had long been in conflict with its neighbour Hajarain (now known as Hatta), Masfout was unable to raise a force of men to oppose Rashid and Masfout became one of two exclaves of Ajman in the interior, the other being Manama.[37] Part of Masfout, the village of Sayh Mudayrah and the nearby community of Sinadil were subject to a border dispute with Oman, settled with an agreement that had Ajman jointly governing the area under Omani suzerainty. The overall issue of the often shakily defined Oman/UAE border was finally put to rest in 1998 and the subsequent border fence, constructed in the early 2000s, split the Mudayrah/Sinadil community, with Sinadil being located on the Omani side of the border and Mudayrah on the Emirati side.

Another footnote from this settlement of the borders of the interior (often boiling down, as in the case of Musandam, to little more than tribal allegiances), is the Omani enclave of Madha, surrounded by the territories of Sharjah, Ras Al Khaimah and Fujairah and itself enclosing the second order exclave of Sharjah, the village of Nahwa.

In fact, the settlement of the borders and allegiances of the interior as the lure of oil placed a value on land previously thought to have been worthless beyond its ability to sustain the most basic of existences was to lead on more than one occasion to bloodshed. Never was this more true than in the fertile little desert town of Buraimi, adjacent to the extensive oases of Al Ain.

Chapter 24

THE BURAIMI INCIDENT

"Good morning, here is the news. We regret to announce that the Buraimi Oasis situation has deteriorated. The British garrison is under constant attack from Sheikh Rattle And Roll."

- The Goon Show: The Nasty Affair at Buraimi Oasis

As the 1940s gave way to the 1950s, the long-standing policy of British non-involvement in the affairs of the interior of the Trucial States was looking increasingly unsustainable. The conflict between Dubai and Abu Dhabi had brought this into sharp relief, involving as it had one of the more powerful tribes of the interior, the Manasir. The British mediation between Dubai and Abu Dhabi and the agreement to judge the borders between the two was an escalation in the role of the British in what otherwise would have been seen as an 'internal affair'. It was, originally, only the fact that Rashid had unwittingly broken the 1853 Perpetual Maritime Truce by sending men to Khor Ghanadah by boat that had given the British leverage to become involved at all in the dispute. And when they had become involved, they had found that imposing sanctions was the only realistic measure for them to put in place to achieve diplomatic goals – in the old days, of course, you just had to call up a sloop and bombard the Ruler's fort. That was no longer generally considered acceptable. In fact, the last such bombardment had taken place in Fujairah in 1925, when the recalcitrant Hamad bin Abdullah Al Sharqi was brought sharply into line with the reduction of three of the towers of his fort by a British warship. The last British threat of coercive action in the Trucial States had been in 1930, against Ras Al Khaimah.

Added to that was the need to make way for oil exploration. Put on hold by World War II, now the effort to search for oil was renewed but some notable pre-war failures to explore the interior still rankled – Sultan bin Saqr of Sharjah had failed to gain access to Jebel Faya for the geologists from PCL – Petroleum Concessions Ltd – and similar problems had been experienced in getting safe access to the area around Jebel Hafit, with its complex tribal associations and rivalries.

A third factor was to be provided by Britain's attempt to define its own role in the world after the war. Britain's 'sea of red', the Empire on which the sun never set, was collapsing with increasing speed and independence movements emerged – in the Middle East alone, Egypt and Iraq had become independent before the war and Jordan's independence followed hot on the heels of armistice, in 1946. Iran was newly assertive and nationalised its oil industry – a huge blow to British commercial interests in the region. In 1946, the British Residency for the Arabian Gulf was relocated from Bushire to Bahrain because of the deteriorating relationship between the British and the Iranians.

Indian independence was to have the greatest effect, however, on the Trucial States, when responsibility for their administration passed from the Indian Government in Bombay to the Foreign Office in London. The British could no longer hold the little protectorate of the Trucial States at a remove. In the eyes of the international community, if the United Kingdom was responsible for the foreign relations of the Trucial States, it was also responsible for both the moral and mercantile conduct of that protectorate. Slavery was still practised and smuggling, too. With London now in charge, there was no longer any excuse to turn a 'blind eye' and bodies like the United Nations were starting to call the UK to task.[1]

Worse, the Soviets were seeking a role and influence in the Gulf – and America was not only newly influential, it was commercial and predatory. Something had to be done.

The Foreign Office chose to pursue a new policy, born out of its colonial experience and cognisant of the need to change the way it approached its role with the Trucial Sheikhs. This was thinking born of the emerging era of the British Commonwealth. The idea was to expand the administration of the Trucial States by providing resources and expert advisors to the Rulers and promoting development. Bombardment and finger wagging was out, development was in. This was to be accomplished without sacrificing British paramountcy

The role of 'Native Agent' – the Residency Agent in Sharjah – was abandoned in 1949.

The British presence on the Trucial Coast was rearranged to reflect the increased commitment to integral involvement in the area. The role of the Political Officer in the Trucial States was expanded to become a year-round position. By 1954, this became a British Political Agency, based in Dubai – a recognition that the ever-expanding mercantile hotspot of Dubai had eclipsed its neighbour. BBME (the British Bank of the Middle East) had opened up in Dubai in 1946 and the only hospital on the coast, Maktoum Hospital, was founded in 1949. Dubai, by now, was where the action was taking place.[2]

The Trucial States Council was founded in 1952 to bring the Rulers of the Trucial States together to discuss and resolve issues and the Council met twice in that year, once in the spring and once in the autumn.

The Trucial Rulers' hold over the interior was a complex set of often tributary relationships that was as likely to break apart tomorrow as it was to hold today. This was no way to manage a modern state and when the very real prospect of oil revenues arrived, it quickly became clear to all involved that the interior had to be made safe for travellers – locals and foreigners alike.

The idea of a military force to be deployed in the Trucial States was first mooted in 1949 and took hold in the months that followed. Debates between the Ministry of Defence (MoD) and the Foreign Office – and its servants in the field – took place, arguing for and against the establishment of a British military force. The British Political Agent in Bahrain, Pelly, proposed the establishment of an Arab military force under British command. The Foreign Office consulted its foremost authority on the management of local levies – Brigadier Sir John Bagot Glubb, the founder of the famous Arab Legion in Jordan. Glubb Pasha was a legend, his soldiers known to the British regulars who served alongside them as 'Glubb's girls' because they 'wore skirts'. But Glubb's Arab Legion had proved itself a potent force and was respected throughout the region. In the battle for Jerusalem, only the Arab Legion had stood tall against the well-armed, highly trained Zionist forces during the 1948 war that led to the foundation of the state of Israel.

Glubb thought it could be done with about 200 men and a budget of some 40,000 pounds per annum. The Foreign Office listened carefully and reduced the budget to 30,000 pounds to cover 100 men. By 1950, the Treasury had agreed the plan as long as the force did not exceed seventy men.

The Arab Legion was not only to provide inspiration for this new force, it was to provide the first commanders and men as well. Major James Hankin-Turvin was appointed in March 1951, supported by two

Jordanian officers and thirty-two men. They made their initial headquarters within the RAF base in Sharjah. The Trucial Oman Levies was born.

It's just that nobody had bothered to tell the parents.

A professional army

The only Ruler consulted about the formation of the Levies was the Ruler of Sharjah, because their base would be in his emirate. The opinions or indeed reactions of the others was considered entirely irrelevant. They were informed that the action had been taken, that the Ruler of Sharjah had leased out a base for the Levies for a period of ten years, and that the new force was in situ. It was, in every way, a fait accompli.

If the Trucial Rulers had any objections to the establishment of a British military force on the Trucial Coast, it was effectively too late to voice them. Dubai was concerned that the new militia would be used to curb its 'entrepôt trade', but was assured that the Levies were purely concerned with the security of the interior.[3]

The Trucial Rulers, in all honesty, likely missed the significance of what had just occurred. The British had established a military force on their soil which was beholden to none of them, but which was bound to establish peace and the Rule of Law over the interior of 'Trucial Oman' in British interests. Reporting to the Foreign Office and its Agents, the Levies were a British force and only by British goodwill would they be deployed to the benefit of the Rulers themselves. It was a Faustian bargain and, in this case, Faust hadn't even been asked to sign the contract.

The Levies' commander reported to the Political Officer in Sharjah, and then to the Political Agents in Dubai and Abu Dhabi when the new arrangements were in place. The force was tasked with undertaking police actions against arms smugglers and the slave trade, as well as enforcing British judicial authority. At the same time, the Levies had to tread carefully – they were not permitted to do anything to usurp the authority of the Trucial Rulers and they were not permitted to act within the cities of the coast unless called to do so by a Ruler. With the passage of time, and the increasing wealth of the Trucial States into the

1960s, the Scouts (as they would become known after 1956) were also tasked with curbing illegal immigration.⁴

Initially funded by the Foreign Office, the Levies soon became the responsibility of the War Office as the force expanded and its role became more strategic. Eventually, by 1956, the two bodies shared responsibility for the force (and its budget), largely because the Foreign Office demanded it be maintained in its expanded state while the War Office refused to foot the bill.

The Levies made a concerted effort to recruit locally and train local troops, although the initial intake came from the Arab Legion. The Levies wore a similar uniform to the Arab Legion, based on a standard British uniform, but also sporting a red and white checked headdress. A steady job with a healthy income, the Levies quickly attracted local Bedouin recruits.

The force was highly effective and by the end of 1951 the slave trade had been eradicated – although the last manumission certificate to be issued by a British Resident to a runaway slave in Dubai was by Glencairn Balfour Paul in 1964. Confronted by a female slave who had run away from her master in southern Iran, Paul found an old bundle of the 'freedom certificates' that used to be issued to manumitted slaves, dusted them down and signed one for the woman.⁵

The Levies in the early 1950s experienced significant growing pains and, although popular locally (in part through the actions of its commanders, who took care to put on extravagant displays of hospitality for visitors and generally integrate well into the community), the Levies in 1953 found themselves torn internally by the recruitment of Yemeni troops, who came from the Aden Protectorate Levies. Poorly trained and lacking discipline, their commander was replaced by a British officer, Otto Thwaites. The appointment was to cost Thwaites his life.

The trouble with Buraimi
The Buraimi Oasis had long been a prize fought over by numerous claimants. Unusually lush, its date groves fed by aquifers running down from the Hajar Mountains, the oasis provides some of the oldest known

examples of the underground *falaj* or *qanat* irrigation system. Buraimi has been a centre of human settlement throughout the millennia, the mountain to the south of the town giving its name to the 5,000-year-old Hafit Culture. Saudi attempts to claim the oasis dated back to the 1800s, while Omani claims to the territory were matched by attempts to gain influence by Sharjah, Ajman, Umm Al Quwain, Dubai and Abu Dhabi alike. The tribes, particularly the Na'im and Dhawahir, had seen their influence ebb and flow until Zayed the Great had finally stamped his influence over the area and brought it decisively under his control, together with his ally, the Sultan of Muscat. By the end of World War II, Buraimi was divided into three distinct eastern settlements that were part of Oman, including the village of Buraimi itself, and nine western oases, by far the largest part of the settled area, which were part of Abu Dhabi, including Ain Dhawahir – Al Ain.

The affiliations and tributary relationships between the areas subject to Oman and Abu Dhabi had long been settled and the area was stable and free from tribal conflict for the first time in centuries. However, while everyone might have finally agreed about the division of the area's rich water resources, the question of oil brought new conflict to town.

The exploration teams from the Standard Oil Company of California had already provoked the ire of both the British and the Trucial Rulers when they had started to reimagine the limits of Abu Dhabi's western territory in order to expand the area covered by their concession from the Saudis, granted in 1933. While these attempts to expand its area of exploration had first taken place in the late 1930s, leading to the definition of the 'Riyadh line' between Saudi Arabia, Abu Dhabi and Oman by the British, a further series of movements took place in 1949 by the company's geological survey teams. Now known as the Arabian American Oil Company (ARAMCO), the company's interests were effectively identical to those of the Saudi leadership and a conference took place in Dammam in January 1952, which attempted to mediate in what had escalated into a border dispute between Saudi Arabia, Qatar and Abu Dhabi.

The conference was a failure and the Saudis decided to act unilaterally, sending the Emir of Ras Tanura, Turki bin Abdullah Al Otaishan, with a group of armed men to occupy the Omani villages, including Buraimi, whose name was still often used to describe the whole area. The force arrived in August 1952 and made its base in the Omani village of Hamasa, whose inhabitants were claimed to be long-standing adherents to Wahhabism. Whatever the merits or otherwise of Saudi claims were to be, it was certainly true that the Na'im had, following the death of Zayed the Great, asserted their independence once again from both Abu Dhabi and Muscat and had come increasingly under Saudi influence. It was arguably a convenience to have retained effective independence from their more proximate and powerful neighbours by picking more remote allies. Welcomed in Hamasa, Turki set about distributing largesse – including money and fine clothing – and held a lavish banquet to which local notables and people alike were invited. The impact was enormous on an undeveloped area that had, despite the richness of the oases, endured a long descent into poverty. Doling out gifts and fine words in equal measures, Turki set about gathering statements of support from locals, receiving some ninety-five in all.[6]

The Sultan of Muscat prepared to send a force against Hamasa but was persuaded to desist by the British, who sent in the Levies to blockade Hamasa, ensuring that no supplies, ammunition or reinforcements could reach Turki. The task was too great for the little force, at the time standing at 300 men, seven armoured cars and fourteen Land Rovers, which struggled to establish effective control over such a large area.[7] Troops were brought in from the Aden Protectorate Levies to supplement the force, taking its overall strength to 500 men.

Command of the Yemeni detachment, known to be poorly trained and to include a number of 'trouble makers', was passed to Major Otto Thwaites, who had previous experience handling Yemeni troops and bringing them up to scratch. Members of the Yemeni force now set about selling ammunition to Turki and the Saudi force in Hamasa they were meant to be blockading. Thwaites acted quickly to restore discipline and had the ringleaders sent back to Sharjah for punishment. However, there were further outbreaks of trouble, which escalated into an incident where Thwaites and two other officers were killed. The Aden

Levies were disbanded and sent home, replaced at Al Ain by a company raised from the air base in Sharjah, supplied by the Ministry of Defence.

The Levies settled down for a long siege and the Ministry of Defence became increasingly shrill about the cost it was incurring, eventually demanding the return of its company of men in March 1954. The row was escalated to the Cabinet, which ruled that the men should stay, but the issue probably prompted the British Government to act on the diplomatic front and in July 1954 a Standstill Agreement was made, which agreed to the formation of an international tribunal in Geneva and to the de-escalation of forces in Buraimi. A token officer and fifteen men would be maintained by either side while arbitration took place.

The Saudis now stepped up Turki's campaign of buying loyalty, attempting to gain as many declarations of affiliation from local notables as they could. Even Sheikh Zayed, the representative in Al Ain of his brother, Sheikh Shakhbut bin Sultan, the Ruler of Abu Dhabi, was approached four times with offers – the first time a Saudi agent met with Zayed and offered him half of the oil revenues for his support. He was subsequently offered a new car and 40,000 rupees. That offer was escalated to 400 million rupees. A final offer made on 4 August 1955 was three fine pistols – this final gift being interpreted as a stick rather than a carrot.[8]

Zayed's testimony to the tribunal on 11 September formed part of a litany of incidents in which bribes and inducements had been offered in return for professions of loyalty.

The tribunal collapsed on 4 October 1955 when the British member of the three-man arbitration committee, Sir Reader Bullard, resigned in protest at these and other attempts by Saudi Arabia to suborn the tribunal – he was joined by the other two judges, the Belgian President, Dr Charles de Visscher alongside the third member, from Cuba.[9]

The collapse of the tribunal decided the British on action. On 25 October, the Levies took control of Hamasa, capturing the fifteen Saudis and wounding their officer lightly when he resisted arrest. The Levies met spirited resistance not from the Saudis, but from local tribes and most of the fighting that took place at Buraimi did so after the

Saudi capitulation – some 200 members of the Na'im, Al Bu Shamis and Bani Kaab fought against the British force. At one point the British called in a Lincoln bomber from Sharjah but it was unable to play a part in proceedings as the close-quarters fighting was taking place in a densely settled area.[10]

A peace was eventually mediated at 11 p.m. that night between the Sheikhs of the Al Bu Shamis and Bani Kaab, obviating a planned night action by the Levies. Zayed played a key role behind the scenes during these negotiations, although he refused to be drawn overtly into a conflict between the tribes in what was Omani territory. Both Sheikhs and their families, as well as a number of Na'im, were sent by air to Bahrain to resettle in Saudi Arabia.

The Buraimi incident resulted in the formalisation of the borders of the area between Oman and Abu Dhabi and in the effective imposition of Abu Dhabi's territorial rights. It was by no means to be the last border dispute to be settled (and, in fact, wasn't settled formally until the 1974 United Nations-brokered Agreement on the Delimitation of Boundaries) in the area and the Trucial Oman Levies were to form an increasingly important force in protecting the rights of the Trucial Rulers as border issues were resolved. They would continue to maintain a full squadron at Al Ain in the years to come.

In 1956 the Levies were renamed the Trucial Oman Scouts. Between late 1957 and early 1958, the Scouts were pressed into action in the Jebal Akhdar War, defeating a rebellion against the Sultan of Muscat. They were withdrawn from Oman in 1959, but this use of the Trucial States-based Scouts to put down a rebellion in a neighbouring Arab country was deeply unpopular in the Trucial States, particularly so as the Sheikh of the Bani Riyam, one of the rebellious tribes, was close to the Rulers of Ajman and Fujairah.[11]

The Scouts expanded, establishing their main base at Mirgab in northern Sharjah (Abdulrahman bin Muhammad Al Shamsi would have been appalled – the area is part of Al Heera) and opening a school in the village of Manama as well as basing a regiment in the interior at Adhen, to the south of Ras Al Khaimah town.[12] The old TOS Mirgab base was still in use into the 2000s as the headquarters of the Sharjah Police Special Tasks Department.

By 1965, the Scouts numbered 1,600 officers and men with an annual budget of 2 million pounds and was effectively the Trucial States' army. However, they continued to report to the British Political Officer and this relationship was a constant matter of concern for the Trucial Rulers, who now faced a significant military force based in their country but beholden to a foreign power. Through intelligent management and sensitivity to local needs and sensibilities, the Scouts were not viewed as the occupying army of a foreign power but there was little disguising that – when the chips were down – this was their effective role. This led the Ruler of Abu Dhabi, Shakhbut bin Sultan, to establish the Abu Dhabi Defence Force in 1965, a move described by the Commander of the Trucial Scouts, Freddie De Butts, as a 'military absurdity'.[13] However, other Emirates followed suit, with the establishment of the Dubai Defence Force, Ras Al Khaimah Defence Force and Sharjah National Guard.[14]

It is perhaps worthy of note that Shakhbut's 'military absurdity' was somewhat prescient – his eventual removal from power would take place under the supervision of none other than the Trucial Oman Scouts.

The Scouts had not only made the interior of the Trucial States a safer place, they had used their spare time well and embarked on a basic road construction programme, blasting away rocky spurs of the Hajar Mountains to connect Masafi with Fujairah through the Wadi Ham and also with Dibba through the Wadi Abadilah.[15] Increasingly, Land Rovers packed with armed tribesmen were seen bouncing along the tracks throughout the 1960s, slowly replacing the camel.

New brooms

Sheikh Rashid bin Saeed Al Maktoum acceded as Ruler of Dubai following the death of his father on 9 September 1958. Rashid had already been effectively managing the affairs of the emirate since the late 1930s, and had refused to bow to considerable British pressure to force his father to abdicate. He had already started to implement a programme of reforms and improvements, investing the relatively limited revenues from Dubai's customs, which had itself been reformed prior to the war, in public infrastructure (in particular education and healthcare). Dubai's trading port had grown to be by far the most important on the coast and its twin souks of Bur Dubai and Deira were bustling, thriving trading centres. Although its merchants had their fingers in innumerable pies, one particularly lucrative trade was in shipping gold to India, whose government controlled the import of the precious metal. Funded by British banks, gold bullion would be shipped in, loaded onto fast dhows and taken to meeting points just outside the three-mile limit of Indian territorial waters, where it was transferred to customers' boats. Dubai was not *smuggling* the gold; it was merely *trading* it.[16] The gold trade was immensely profitable, buoyed by a lively exchange rate for the Indian rupee in Gulf markets (higher than its value in India) and 'everyone in Dubai with a rupee to his name was in on the business and plane loads of gold ingots could be left overnight, piled up unguarded on the Dubai airstrip, because no-one would steal them.'[17]

Dubai's gold trade quickly became a major international channel of funds and by 1966 Dubai was the third largest export market for gold from London, receiving some 4 million ounces of the metal. Other trading volumes were rising rapidly too: Dubai that year brought in over 15 million dollars' worth of watches and 5.5 million ounces of silver. The profits from the gold trade were phenomenal – in 1967 gold traded in the souks of Dubai at thirty-five dollars an ounce and sold in India for sixty-eight dollars an ounce.[18] The gold was sold in ten tola bars, a tola being a little over 11.66 grams. This measure gave its name to the Ten Tola Bar, the seedy Dubai watering hole owned by character Fitzroy Lodd in Robin Moore's colourful novel *Dubai*, set in the 1960s.

If Moore's novel pointed to a whiff of illegality in the whole trade, it was thoroughly international and institutionalised illegality. The gold was flown in boxes of 200 or 250 ten tola bars, consigned by Sharps Pixley, Mocatta and Goldsmid, Samuel Montagu, Bullion Exchange and the Swiss Bank Corporation. While some traders dealt with these houses directly, most managed their trades through the British Bank of the Middle East (BBME was to eventually become subsumed by HSBC, losing, in the process, the two Bedouin guards with their rifles who used to adorn the bank's Bur Dubai head office up until the 1990s), the National Bank of Dubai and the First National City Bank of New York.

Dubai's creek was busy, but it was also shallow and silting up and a plan was drawn up in 1954 to dredge the waterway. Rashid bin Saeed issued 'creek bonds' and took out a loan of 500,000 pounds from Kuwait to pay for the dredging operation, which took place in 1958 and 1959. This project allowed larger ships to put in at Dubai, up to 500 tonnes. The material brought up from the creek was used to shore up the tidal area of Ghubaiba (which could only be crossed at high tide by foot, using a series of concrete blocks as stepping stones) and also to extend the coast alongside Shindaga. Revenue from the sale of this newly created real estate went into the financing of the project.[19] A town plan was commissioned from the British company John Harris, the first example of structured urban planning ever seen in the area and a visionary move by Rashid, who was now set on a programme of construction, expansion and development that was to take on a frenetic pace of its own.

The first oil well spudded in the Trucial States was in Abu Dhabi, at Ras Sadr in 1950. It reached 13,000 feet in depth by 1951 and found no oil – hundreds of locals who had been taken on as workers in anticipation of the find were dismissed.[20] While Abu Dhabi found oil in 1958, and commenced exports in 1962, Dubai remained resolutely oil-free, much to Rashid's bitter disappointment. A well spudded at Jebel Ali, which the geologists had long fancied because of its humps, reached 12,350 feet and was abandoned. Rashid's frustration must have been bordering on infuriation.

Each penny of Dubai's scant revenue had to be raised by taxation or public subscription and Rashid's development plans meant a constant tide of debt and innovative fund-raising. Private companies were formed and Rashid started a water company, bringing fresh water into the city from the wells of Al Awir. An electricity company was founded, and a 6,400-kilowatt power station built in Deira in 1961. Grants from the British government helped. Rashid's daughter, Maryam, married the Emir of Qatar, Sheikh Ahmad bin Ali Al Thani in 1961 and his enthusiastic – yet limited – backing (as Qatar had yet to find its gas field and the transformational wealth that discovery brought) for development projects was welcomed.

An airstrip was built, with the first flights arriving in 1961. Sharjah had threatened to tax the gold imports arriving through its airport and Rashid argued with the British who saw no reason for Dubai to have its own airport. Rashid, as he was now to do in so many areas, escalated and prevailed. In May 1965, an asphalt runway was constructed, supporting modern jet airliners.

Dubai Police was founded in 1956, under a British commander, Major P. Lorimer, with its headquarters in Naif, in Deira. That force was later taken over by Jack Briggs, who moved from the Trucial Oman Scouts to take up the post at Sheikh Rashid's invitation.

A Dubai Municipality was also founded, originally as a municipal council, in 1957 and by 1961 was employing forty staff and 120 labourers. A Dubai Port Committee was established and improvements took place throughout the wharfage and coastal area, including the construction of steel piled wharves on either side of the creek. The tiny treadmill crane outside the Ruler's office, which had been installed there by Gray Mackenzie, was now supplemented by seven mobile cranes. The original little crane, at one time Dubai's only unloading facility, still stands on the Creekside by the old, whitewashed municipality buildings. It was overlooked by a mirrored window, behind which one of Sheikh Rashid's retainers would sit, taking a note of the goods unloaded to compare with the manifests later presented by the traders when paying their duties.

Maktoum Bridge was built in 1963, with a loan from Rashid's son-in-law, the Qatari Emir. The loan was repaid by charging a toll for the use of the bridge from Dubai to Deira. This first version of Salik, Dubai's road toll system today, was to cost fifty fils per crossing. Small books of blue 'chits' were issued, each costing five dirhams and holding ten chits. The theory was that drivers would stop at a toll booth and hand over a chit to pay for their crossing but they actually just opened the window and let the chit fly in the air, the accumulated compacted chits quickly turning the road surface of the bridge blue.

Rashid's prayers were finally answered in 1966, when oil was discovered offshore from Jebel Ali. The oil field, named Fateh (Fortune) was small and sixty miles offshore but it was an oil field, nonetheless. Rashid lost no time in raising credit against his anticipated revenues and building Port Rashid, a four-berth container handling port, which he had long dreamed of (the original feasibility study was conducted in 1965, before oil was found). The British company William Halcrow was once again pressed into action (Halcrow had dredged the creek and was very much Rashid's 'go to' contractor for his new projects) and awarded the 9-million-pound contract in June 1967. Neville Allen, Halcrow's manager, was soon called in to the Ruler's office – Rashid wanted the project upsized and cancelled many of the projected outbuildings and support facilities in favour of building more berths – extending the port to sixteen berths.

In order to load the oil from the Fateh field onto tankers, two onion-shaped 500,000-gallon storage tanks known locally as Khazzans were constructed on the beach to the north of Jebel Ali. When they were finally built, in June 1972, the sand around them was cut away so that they could be floated out to the field and sunk (where they are still in operation today).[21] The tanks were constructed by the Chicago Bridge and Iron Company, which gave its name both to the beach and the resort hotel which was to later be built there, the Chicago Beach Hotel. The memory of Chicago Beach was to be eclipsed in the late 1990s, when the old hotel building was demolished to make way for the Jumeirah Beach Hotel and the iconic offshore Burj Al Arab. Chicago Beach became today's Jumeirah Beach.

Rashid's aggressive expansion plans were to see a huge influx of foreign labour to Dubai and the growth of the population of the town from something like 59,000 people in 1968 to over 278,000 in 1980. A metalled road was built out to Hatta, to bring in stone aggregate and concrete from crushers in the Hajar Mountains, while roads, hospitals, schools and commercial buildings saw Dubai blossoming in all directions. The savings from using construction materials sourced from Hatta would be instrumental in Rashid's plans to accelerate the development of Port Rashid, as well as the town in general.

Abu Dhabi may have found oil first, but its revenues were not moving. The offshore Umm Shaif oilfield was soon joined by both onshore and more offshore finds but the Ruler of Abu Dhabi, Shakhbut bin Sultan Al Nahyan, was vehemently opposed to change and resisted modernisation, fearing the erosion of the values and way of life of his people.

British frustration with Shakhbut was matched with growing impatience within the Al Nahyan family. The British prevailed upon Shakhbut's younger brother, Zayed, to convince him to step aside.

As a child, Zayed had moved with his mother from Abu Dhabi to Al Ain when his father was assassinated in yet another internecine struggle. His mother, Salama bint Butti Al Hamid, made her four sons promise not to use violence against each other, fearing for them in light of the family's long track record of fratricides.

The young Zayed grew up in the oasis of Al Ain and the desert around the town, building the respect and admiration of the tribes as he flourished into adulthood. A keen marksman, he was charismatic and built a reputation for wisdom, often escorting early oil exploration parties venturing into the interior. Famed for his hospitality and easy way with the men of the desert, he hosted the British explorer, Wilfred Thesiger, at his home in Al Ain's Qasr Al Muwaiji and took Thesiger out on expeditions to hunt with falcon in the Al Khatam desert. Falconry was a lifelong passion of Zayed's, a connection to the desert roots he never left behind. By 1946, Shakhbut made him his representative in Al Ain and the eastern region of Abu Dhabi, his brother Hazza acting over the western region, including the Liwa Oasis.

Thesiger was to provide a remarkable early portrait of Zayed in his book, *Arabian Sands*:

"He was a powerfully built man of about thirty with a brown beard. He had a strong, intelligent face with steady, observant eyes and his manner was quiet but masterful. He was dressed, very simply, in a beige-coloured shirt of Omani cloth, and a waistcoat, which he wore unbuttoned. He was distinguished from his companions by his black head-rope, and the way in which he wore his head-cloth, falling about his shoulders instead of twisted round his head in the local manner. He wore a dagger and catridge-belt; his rifle lay on the ground beside him. I had been looking forward to meeting him, for he had a great reputation among the Bedu. They liked him for his easy informal ways and his friendliness, and they respected his force of character, his shrewdness and his physical strength. They said admiringly, 'Zayed is a Bedu. He knows about camels, can ride like one of us, can shoot, and knows how to fight'."

In the straitened times of the 1930s and 1940s, Shakhbut reduced the subsidies he paid to tribal leaders. Abu Dhabi itself felt the reduction in the pearling revenues keenly, although both of the inland oases of Liwa and Al Ain remained centres for agriculture and animal husbandry. When the oil concessions were signed, Shakhbut frustrated expectations that the windfall would be shared around and this became increasingly resented when the oil itself started to flow.

Upon becoming the Ruler's Representative, Zayed started work overhauling Al Ain's *aflaj*. The effort was timely: years of neglect had worn down the complex water systems that nourished the oases of the area and the distribution of water had become unfairly dominated by a few wealthier individuals.[22] He also worked ceaselessly to stop the warring tribes from raiding, a constant struggle in the aftermath of World War II, when Shakhbut's parsimony meant that tribal leaders felt they had little alternative to raiding. Zayed had played the role of peacemaker in the conflict between Dubai and Abu Dhabi and he was to do so again between the tribes. He played a key role behind the scenes negotiating with the dissident factions during the Buraimi dispute, obtaining a ceasefire and undoubtedly saving many lives.

He also worked to try to maintain unity within his own family, with his elder brothers increasingly at odds with Shakhbut, with whom even Zayed had stormy meetings as the oil flowed but progress and development stalled. By 1966, the Umm Shaif oilfield was producing a revenue of something like 8–9 million pounds sterling per annum for the Ruler and the pressure for change and reform in Abu Dhabi became overwhelming.

By June 1966, the Al Nahyan family had had enough. It was agreed that Shakhbut, now in his sixties, should step down and it was unanimously decided that Zayed would be Ruler. Following quiet discussions with Zayed, the British Acting Resident, Glencairn Balfour Paul, travelled to Abu Dhabi with two companies of the Trucial Oman Scouts (who were 'on manoeuvres') and met with Shakhbut, telling him that the family had decided he should step down and that the British government supported their position. It would be better to resign with dignity, Balfour Paul told Shakhbut. Balfour Paul's own account of the meeting relates that Shakhbut, on hearing that his family wanted him removed, went white with rage. Balfour-Paul then saw armed men carrying ammunition boxes up the stairs of the palace. He left Shakhbut, 'Glad to be able to make my escape unscathed' before the Trucial Oman Scouts closed in, shouting at Shakhbut's guards to throw down their weapons.[23] His guards disarmed, Shakhbut left quietly, with the men of the TOS forming a guard of honour, for exile in Bahrain on 6 August 1966.[24]

Zayed opened up the coffers and spent the hoard liberally, famously aiding anyone in need who came to him. He set out on a whirlwind of development, tracing the outline of projects in the sand with his camel stick. Sharp-witted and incisive, Zayed brought in a Japanese architect, Katsuhiko Takahashi, to oversee the new city plan. Takahashi was able to take Zayed's vision in the sand and turn it into blueprints and construction plans, a unique talent that helped to translate Zayed's will into built reality. Buoyed by enormous oil revenues, Abu Dhabi's march to development saw Zayed, the tribal leader, conceiving and building a modern city on the island of the gazelle with his lines etched in the sand.

Disaster at sea
The dredging of Dubai creek and modernisation of its wharves brought ever-larger volumes of maritime trade to the port and by the 1960s, those wharves were packed with increasingly heavy volumes of shipping. On 7 April 1961, an unusually fierce storm blew up from the West and gale force winds lashed Dubai, driving huge waves against the coast. A ship in port dragged its anchor in the heavy swell and smashed into the bows of the 5,000-tonne, 120-meter MV *Dara*, owned by the

British India Steam Navigation Company. Although the structural damage was minimal, the impact decided the ship's captain to leave harbour and ride out the storm in the open sea. The *Dara* made way so quickly that a number of officials and passengers' relatives were still on board as the ship left dock. In all, 819 people were on board, including 132 crew members.

The *Dara* rode out the stormy night without incident and, as dawn was breaking on 8 April, she was heading back to Dubai when a massive explosion ripped through the ship's engine room. Incapacitated and at the mercy of the battering waves, fires broke out and quickly ran out of control. The captain broadcast Mayday and ordered the ship to be evacuated. The fire prevented many of the lifeboats being deployed and the few that were launched struggled against the heavy sea. At least one capsized. Nearby shipping rushed to help, braving proximity to the blazing ship (although one nearby ship, the British naval supply ship *Guillemot*, was thought to be carrying explosives and held back), with three British frigates trying to control the blaze, putting fire parties on board and playing hoses over the blaze. An American warship, as well as several civilian boats, also helped to rescue survivors, many of whom were swimming desperately in the heavy seas.

In all, 238 of the people on board the *Dara* died in the greatest peacetime maritime disaster the world had known since the sinking of the *Titanic*. A formal investigation into the incident concluded in April 1962 that the explosion aboard the *Dara* was the result of high explosives 'practically certainly deliberately placed in the vessel by person or persons unknown'.[25]

If the sinking of the *Dara* was an act of terror, it was to be a pointless one. Despite testimony to the enquiry speculating that the 'Dhofar Liberation Front' had been behind the explosion, using a planted limpet mine with a timer, nobody ever claimed or proved responsibility.

Hard up

Dubai had its lively entrepôt trade and the very lucrative movement of gold and Abu Dhabi had oil, even if the money being earned didn't move very far in the early days. Sharjah, of course, had its airport and the revenue from the British in payment for their leased military bases, including the Trucial Oman Scouts' base in Mirgab and RAF Sharjah. Apart from this, the oil concessions brought at least some basic revenue in, but the other Trucial States were barely scraping by and any scheme that would raise money was eagerly adopted.

One source of revenue for a time in the 1950s was selling passports. Trucial States passports were single sheets of paper, richly adorned with an impressive collection of stamps and – for a short time – sold willy-nilly to any applicant. Holders of these exotic documents would carry maps with them when travelling, to show immigration officers where Umm Al Quwain and Ras Al Khaimah actually were. At one time, even Dubai passports changed hands at ninety pounds apiece, while passports from the smaller emirates were even cheaper. The trade simply wasn't sustainable – the sort of people who needed to buy passports weren't necessarily the sort of people you would *want* to be carrying your passport.[26]

Enter American philatelic 'entrepreneur' Finbar Kenny.

British management of the Trucial States' 'external relations' included the management of posts and telegraphs – the individual emirates were not members of the UPU – the Universal Postal Union. The Government of India opened its first post office in Dubai in 1941 and its operation was taken over by British Postal Agencies, a subsidiary of the GPO (General Post Office) in 1948. Stamps of the time were British stamps surcharged with rupee values, until in 1959 a set of 'Trucial States' stamps was issued from Dubai.[27]

In 1963, Britain passed the responsibility for the administration of the Trucial States' posts to each of the Trucial Rulers and opportunity came knocking. Independent postal systems opened in Sharjah in July 1963, then Ajman and Umm Al Quwain in Jun 1964 and Fujairah and Ras Al Khaimah in September and December 1964 respectively.

A white-haired, wild-eyed American eccentric, Kenny saw the chance to create a number of editions of stamps aimed at the lucrative stamp collector's market and, in 1964, signed a deal with the cash-strapped emirate of Ajman to take the franchise for the production of stamps from the government.[28] Kenny made something of a specialty out of signing these deals, also signing with the Ruler of Fujairah in 1964 and – expanding his area of influence – getting involved in a bribery case in the USA over his dealings with the government of the Cook Islands.

Kenny's issues of Trucial stamps, luridly illustrated and utterly irrelevant to the actual emirates they came from, became known as 'Dunes'. Editions included Space Research and Tokyo Olympic Games, with two odd editions issued from Umm Al Quwain including British Kings and Queens and, perversely, with summer temperatures in the emirate reaching fifty degrees Celsius, Winter Olympics.

Among these editions, following the opening of a 'post office' in Manama on 5 July, 1966, were nine editions published from 'Manama, Dependency of Ajman'. Few collectors would realise Manama was a remote agricultural village consisting of a few adobe houses on a plain overlooked by the Hajar Mountains. Similarly, Sharjah issued stamps from Khor Fakkan. Young collectors would initially have loved these exotic, unknown locations. Wiser heads quickly placed zero value on them.

The sale of these stamps briefly became the principal source of income for the Rulers of the northern emirates, with annual revenues reaching up to 70,000 pounds for the poorer states, which swiftly fell to 30,000 pounds with the inevitable saturation of the global collector's market.[29]

By this time, in 1964, the Trucial Rulers were enjoying (and spreading, through tribute and other payments) revenues from aviation, oil concessions (and, in Abu Dhabi, oil itself), stamps, customs and other commercial activities. Abu Dhabi was receiving 5 million pounds annually and Dubai just over 1 million pounds; Sharjah was making 110,000 pounds; Ajman 24,000 pounds; Umm Al Quwain 32,000 pounds; Ras Al Khaimah 44,000 pounds and Fujairah 25,000 pounds.[30] Of these, stamps made a major contribution to the five Northern Emirates' revenue. But by 1968, Abu Dhabi was bringing in 68 million pounds per annum in oil revenue and Zayed was making generous contributions to the Trucial States Development Fund and had funded electricity generation and water development schemes in the northern emirates. Dubai had also hit the accelerator in anticipation of its own oil windfall. A massive boom was now in full swing.

Kenny's philatelic philandering eventually killed itself as collectors learned to avoid the strange, gaudy issues from the Gulf and Federation was to finally end the whole racket. Federation was to realise Zayed's growing dream of a better future for the Trucial States. However, other forces in the region also had a view of the likely shape of the Trucial States' future.

The rise and rise of Arab nationalism

Sultan bin Saqr Al Qasimi died in 1951 and his eldest son, Saqr bin Sultan, acceded to rule Sharjah. Saqr was a fervent Arab nationalist. And he was by no means alone.

The Arab League was founded in 1945 and started to give voice to a growing movement in the Arab world that sought to establish a pan-Arab identity in the wake of the post-war flowering of Arab independence. As Britain focused increasingly inwards following the ruinous impact of World War II, a new generation of Arab leaders emerged, confident and energised by their new freedoms (which were not, it may be noted, to be allowed to extend in the majority of cases to their people) and this movement was given huge impetus in 1948 by the establishment of the state of Israel and the calamitous Arab effort to stop that process – known to Palestinians as the *Naqba* – the 'disaster'.

The charismatic Egyptian leader Gamal Abdel Nasser was to give voice to this vision for a new Arab world and the broadcasts of Egyptian radio's Sawt Al Arab, 'Voice of the Arabs', thundered Nasser's words out to a receptive audience across the Middle East and North Africa. In 1956, Nasser had fought off the attempt by Britain, France and Israel to collude in a military operation to take over the newly nationalised Suez Canal. The resulting fiasco was to bolster Nasser enormously in the Arab world, entirely at Britain's expense.

With the British Trucial States Development Budget under pressure and other sources of revenue producing only tiny amounts of cash, an approach from the Arab League now took place with offers of development money to the Trucial Rulers. In October 1964, an Arab League delegation visited the area, headed by Egyptian diplomat Abdel Khaleq Hassouna, on a 'mission of brotherhood'. The Arab League proposed to create a 5-million-pound development fund for the Trucial States and now Saqr bin Sultan Al Qasimi agreed to the opening of an Arab League office in Sharjah. He was joined in this by Saqr bin Mohammed Al Qasimi of Ras Al Khaimah.

Parades and demonstrations took place in the streets of the towns of the Trucial States and anti-British sentiment burgeoned. The British were dismayed, appalled at this challenge to their primacy on the Trucial Coast. Arab League money meant Nasserite money, meant Soviet influence. A concerted movement took place to convince the Trucial Rulers to reject the blandishments of the Arab League but Saqr was obdurate – even in the face of the threat of closure of his airspace and the disruption of electricity to his palace. The Rulers of the northern emirates appeared to be resolved to accept the Arab League's offer of development money. The British raised funds until the Trucial States Development Fund stood at 2.5 million pounds but, as the Ruler of Ajman, Rashid Al Nuaimi, pointed out, "5 million pounds will go further than 2.5 million pounds."[31]

From the British point of view, the standoff was becoming dangerous and something had to give. That something was Saqr bin Sultan Al Qasimi. On 24 June 1965, at the British Political Agency in Dubai, Glencairn Balfour Paul, the British Political Agent, informed Saqr that he was no longer supported by his family and was being removed from his position as Ruler of Sharjah. The Trucial Oman Scouts moved against Sharjah Fort and took the surrender of the soldiers there, as well as Saqr's brother – Abdullah bin Sultan Al Qasimi. With him was the son of the Ruler of Ras Al Khaimah, Khalid bin Saqr bin Muhammad Al Qasimi.[32]

Saqr bin Sultan Al Qasimi was sent into exile in Bahrain and, eventually, Cairo.[33]

Saqr's cousin, Khalid bin Mohammed Al Qasimi acceded as Ruler of Sharjah on 25 June 1965. The message was loud and clear – and received and understood. The British-backed Trucial States Development Fund was to be the source of development project funding moving forward – and not the Arab League.

The destruction of the Sharjah Fort

Khalid set about the destruction of Al Hisn Sharjah, Sharjah Fort, with the intent of obliterating Saqr's memory, in January 1970. His brother, the future Ruler of Sharjah, Sultan bin Mohammed bin Sultan Al Qasimi, hurried back from his studies in Cairo to try to stop the demolition of the fort. He was only able to save a single tower (that to the rear right of the current, restored fort), the 'Kubs Tower' and one length of wall, as well as some the windows and doors from the old fort. He also had a precise plan drawn from the foundations and remains of the smashed fort.[34]

The Fort was eventually faithfully rebuilt using Sultan Al Qasimi's notes, archives, photographs and reference to the 1937 documentary film, *Air Outpost*, and re-opened in April 1997. It was to become the centrepiece of the restoration of 'old Sharjah', the Heart of Sharjah.

Khalid's obsession with erasing the memory of his cousin was to prove prophetic. Because Saqr would eventually engineer Khalid's own, untimely, death.

Chapter 25

FOUNDED ON A HANDSHAKE

"The bond of mutual obligation between the tribal population and its leaders is still now a meaningful factor in the UAE's political life."

– Frauke Heard-Bey

Between 8 and 11 January 1968, the British politician Goronwy Roberts met with the incredulous Rulers of the Trucial States to let them know that Great Britain was unilaterally ending its treaty relations with them. Britain would be pulling its armed forces out of the area by the end of 1971 and taking no further responsibility for the people of the emirates or their international relations. Given Roberts' fervent assurances when he had been asked about this very matter just a few weeks earlier that this would absolutely not be the case, the news came as a hammer blow.

The unwelcome development brought incredible danger in its wake. A number of powerful forces that could decide to help themselves to some handy oil wealth surrounded the Trucial States. Sheikh Rashid and Sheikh Zayed both travelled to London to ask the government to reconsider – or at least to agree to an arrangement where the Rulers could pay for British military assistance. This latter offer prompted a sharp retort from British Defence Secretary Denis Healey, who said on the BBC TV programme Panorama that he disliked the idea of being 'a sort of white slaver for Arab sheikhs'. Healey was quickly forced to apologise for his outrageous comments.[1]

If the news left the Rulers reeling, to at least one of them it brought confirmation that pursuit of a long-cherished dream was now their only course of action. Zayed believed passionately in the wisdom of a Union between the Trucial Rulers and now he and Sheikh Rashid bin Saeed Al Maktoum arranged to meet in the desert for talks.[2]

On 18 February 1968, they met in a tent, in an area known as Arghoub Al Sedira, a short distance away from the roadside well at Semeih on the main Dubai/Abu Dhabi road,[3] each accompanied by a few retainers. As Rashid's son, Mohammed, served them little cups of cardamom-scented *ghawa*, the unroasted coffee of the Gulf, the two men talked. They had history: Dubai and Abu Dhabi had been at war twenty years before and raiding between Bedouin allied to both Ruling families had continued on and off since. Zayed had tried to mediate a peace between his brother Shakhbut and Rashid's father, Saeed, during the early years of the conflict. The border between the two emirates had long been an unresolved and contentious issue. All of this was put aside as the two settled their differences and forged an agreement for the future. They shook hands on it and in that handshake, founded a nation – in fact the only country in the world today established by agreement rather than conflict.

The result of their deliberations was the final settlement of the border between the two emirates but also the announcement that Dubai and Abu Dhabi would join in a Union, inviting other Trucial Rulers to join them. A meeting between the rulers of the Trucial Coast and of Bahrain and Qatar took place on 25 February and the other Rulers agreed to join in forming a federation, announced on 27 February as the 'Federation of the Arab Emirates'.[4]

The Rulers had a little over three years to create a modern nation state, a task that would have made lesser men quail. Negotiations between the emirates started, but the Federation of the Arab Emirates was arguably doomed from the start. While the seven Rulers of the Trucial States had become used to working together at the Trucial States Council, Bahrain and Qatar were outsiders and brought diverging views on the way ahead. Bahrain wanted representation on the basis of population figures (being the most populous of all of the potential Council members), while Qatar disagreed with the suggestion that Abu Dhabi be the capital of the new Federation. The Qataris proposed that the smaller Trucial States be rolled up into a single entity, The United Arab Coastal Emirates, cutting the number of members of the Federation to five roughly proportionate member states.[5] This was clearly unworkable and would doubtless have caused offence to the five and could well have contributed to the fact that the Supreme Council meeting planned for 30 March 1968 did not take place. A second and third meeting did take place in Abu Dhabi in May and June respectively, but by now wild ideas were being thrown up and rejected and fundamental divisions were starting to appear.

A Temporary Union Council met in Qatar in September 1968 and the Supreme Council in October 1968, again in Doha. A number of committees were set up. The Temporary Union Council met again in Sharjah that November and reached out to the World Bank for help in conducting an economic study and to the British Ministry of Defence for help in defining defence needs. It would not be until May 1969 that the nine Rulers would meet again. The Qataris tabled sheaves of proposals, their zeal alienating the less well-prepared members. The Qataris, hosting the May meeting, proposed an extensive agenda, which was rejected. However, a committee to prepare a draft constitution was named under an Egyptian constitutional expert. In October 1969, a sixth meeting of the Supreme Council took place in Abu Dhabi. While this session appeared to reflect some concrete progress in the negotiations, an extended session was found to be necessary to allow more time for wrangling about the constitution. A message was read out to the Supreme Council from the British Political Resident which immediately triggered a walk-out by some delegates who judged it patronising and offensive. This was, as it turned out, to be the last meeting of the nine-member Supreme Council.

It appeared as if time was simply running out with inconclusive talks taking place as the clock hand span. Even as late as July 1970, Sheikh Rashid was to tell *The Times of London* that he would welcome a continued British military presence.[6]

If anyone was to think that this was a period of security and peace in the Trucial States, they would be disabused by the events of that month. On 17 July 1970, a bomb was placed in the Sharjah Ruler's *majlis* and went off prematurely, detonating at 9 a.m. instead of 10 a.m. – when the *majlis* usually convened. Khalid bin Muhammad bin Sultan Al Qasimi arrived to his daily *majlis* to find it, literally, was a bombsite.[7]

With their commitment to the Union looking increasingly shaky, Qatar and Bahrain eventually withdrew from the negotiations, making their own moves to create constitutions and the machinery of state. Eventually, on 14 August 1971, Bahrain declared its independence and Qatar followed on 1 September 1971.

In the meantime, however, efforts continued to tie together the seven Trucial States. Precious time was wasted when it was thought that the Conservative government (elected in June 1970) might revoke the threat to withdraw. In February 1971, the British finally confirmed their intentions. The withdrawal was going ahead by December 1971. The

Rulers now had less than a year to play with. The frustration was palpable, even fifty years after Sheikh Mohammed bin Rashid Al Maktoum was to recall the constant amendments and discussions between consultants, which he viewed with 'the utmost disgust'.[8]

On 10 July 1971 the Trucial States Council met in Dubai. The seven rulers worked together on a twenty-two-point agenda, which aimed to transfer all former British institutions to the new state. On 18 July 1971, it was declared that the State of the United Arab Emirates would be formed, comprising Abu Dhabi, Dubai, Sharjah, Ajman, Umm Al Quwain and Fujairah.

Ras Al Khaimah was notable by its absence from the declaration.

Fear and loathing offshore

The ownership of the islands between Iran and the Trucial States was a perennial issue. The British had fallen out with the Iranian government, transferring its air route to Sharjah in the early 1930s rather than give in to Iranian blackmail to recognise its claim of title to the islands, which the British (quite rightly) disputed. The three key islands in question were Abu Musa, belonging to Sharjah, and the Greater and Lesser Tunbs, belonging to Ras Al Khaimah.

In June 1970, the American oil company Occidental Petroleum sent a drilling platform and the survey ship *Martinetta* to look for oil off the shores of Abu Musa. The company had negotiated a concession with Umm Al Quwain and was intending to drill nine miles off Abu Musa, but in September 1969, the Ruler of Sharjah, Sheikh Khalid bin Mohammed Al Qasimi extended the territorial waters of Abu Musa from three to twelve miles. Regardless of his claim, which affected the offshore rights of both Umm Al Quwain and Ajman, the British refused to allow the American company to prospect in disputed waters and Occidental's boats were boarded by men from one of four British minesweepers involved in a week-long standoff.[9]

Sharjah believed it had a stronger claim to Abu Musa and, in the face of continued Iranian determination, appealed to Arab governments in August 1971, detailing its claim. An eleventh-hour agreement was eventually reached with Iran on 29 November 1971, which handed part of the island of Abu Musa over to Iran but reserved Abu Musa's sovereignty for Sharjah. If oil were found, both states would share equally. In the meantime, Iran agreed a package of aid for Sharjah.

On 30 November, an Iranian force took over its portion of Abu Musa, greeted by Sheikh Saqr bin Muhammad Al Qasimi, the Deputy Ruler of Sharjah (not to be confused with the Ruler of Ras Al Khaimah), who visited the Iranian destroyer sent to Abu Musa for the takeover.[10] The Iranians then over-ran the two Tunbs islands, killing a number of Ras Al Khaimah nationals. The move triggered riots across the Arab world, with Iraq cutting off diplomatic relations with Iran.

Demonstrations also took place throughout the Trucial States – the arrangement between Sharjah and Iran was deeply unpopular, but Iran's unilateral action to seize the Tunbs was incendiary. On 1 December, the day after the disastrous Iranian takeover, a gunman attacked Sharjah's Sheikh Saqr bin Muhammad as he returned from Abu Musa, firing four shots at him outside his house and wounding him.[11] It was a portentous event: the backdrop to the foundation of the UAE, consensual though it had been, was massive uncertainty, fear and danger.

The next day, 2 December 1971, the Rulers of the six Trucial States met at the Guest House in Dubai and signed the agreement bringing the United Arab Emirates into being. Sheikh Saqr bin Mohammed Al Qasimi of Ras Al Khaimah attended the ceremony as an honoured guest. A Treaty of Friendship was signed with Great Britain, the former treaties between Britain and the Trucial States having been cancelled the night before.

The press of people was so great in the Dubai guest house where the ceremony took place that the Rulers had to leave through the window before attending a celebratory lunch. The rather arch tones of the last British Political Agent, Julian Walker, recorded: "The treaty was signed amid a scene of confusion remarkable even by Arab standards. Photographers and pressmen were standing on the table and it was a little short of a miracle that nobody was injured and the documents were retrieved intact."

That night at 6 p.m. Dubai time, the Soviet Mars 3 lander became the first man-made object to reach the surface of Mars. It transmitted briefly and then was silent. Fifty years later, celebrating the birth of the nation, a team from the UAE's Mohammed bin Rashid Space Centre, funded by the UAE Space Agency, designed and constructed the Emirates Mars Mission together with its academic partners in the US, launching the Mars Hope Probe from Japan to make the 600 million-kilometre journey to reach and orbit the red planet.

Uncertainty, chaos and murder most foul
The fledgling Arab state was recognised first by Jordan, on 2 December 1971. On 6 December, the UAE joined the Arab League and on 9 December, the United Nations. The Trucial Oman Scouts became the Union Defence Force when, on 22 December, the force was formally handed over to the UAE's new Minister of Defence, Sheikh Mohammed bin Rashid Al Maktoum. The timing and nature of the handover had been the subject of considerable debate between the British government and the Rulers, the British eventually agreeing to hand over all facilities, men and materiel at no charge.[12]

The Union was the culmination of three years of exhausting uncertainty for the Rulers, but now that uncertainty passed on to the people. Folk went to bed Dubaian and woke up Emirati. Some had gone to bed Bani Qitab or Manasir and woken up Emirati. What did that even mean? There was widespread concern and the Rulers of the new state met with their people, conducting their *majlis'* and answering a torrent of questions as best they could – but most of the answers lay in the future. It was all about 'jam tomorrow' – the Rulers of the Emirates asked for a huge leap of faith from their people, many of whom had little idea of nation beyond the series of loose confederations, alliances and fealties which had comprised the Trucial States. The strongest bonds of all, then as now, were those of family ('My brother against my cousin, my cousin against the stranger', as the Arab saying has it).

Patiently, the Rulers calmed people and talked to their concerns, helped both by Zayed's determination to form the Union and his largesse applied in efforts to cement the Federation together. It was a time of mixed emotions: trepidation, mistrust, hope and no small amount of sheer bravado.

At 2.30 p.m., on 24 January 1972, gunshots were heard outside the palace of Sharjah's Ruler, Khalid bin Muhammad Al Qasimi. Driving to the scene, the car of Khalid's brother, Sultan bin Muhammad, was hit by machine-gun fire. It quickly became apparent that a force of men had attacked the palace led by the exiled former Ruler of Sharjah, Saqr bin Sultan Al Qasimi.[13]

Saqr, an ardent Arab nationalist, had been ousted by the Al Qasimi family and the British in 1965, making way for the mild and progressive Khalid bin Muhammad Al Qasimi to rule. Now Saqr was back, with a vengeance.

Sultan raised the alarm with the Union Defence Force, whose units arrived and pinned the rebels in the palace. The UAE's newly appointed Minister of Defence, the youngest in the world at the time, Mohammed bin Rashid Al Maktoum, arrived and conducted negotiations with Saqr, which ended abruptly when it became clear that Khalid, the Ruler of Sharjah, had been killed in the action. Mohammed bin Rashid took Saqr's surrender and handed him over to Zayed.

Khalid was widely mourned and his brother, Sultan bin Muhammad Al Qasimi – the Education Minister of the new UAE government – acceded as Ruler of Sharjah. The attempted coup was a deep shock to the newly founded nation, and reflected the general sense of uncertainty and unease. However, it also demonstrated that, confronted with an external threat, the Rulers acted in concert and with vigour. It must have been a terrible shock for Saqr to find that his attempt against Sharjah ranged him against every Trucial Ruler acting as a single force under Zayed, and was certainly a fateful miscalculation on Saqr's part.

Disappointed in the hopes it held of an imminent oil find and scared by the casual violence of the land grab the Iranians had performed in taking the Tunbs Islands, Ras Al Khaimah chose the safety of unity and joined the Federation on 10 February 1972. However, the turbulence of the time seemed never-ending and instability continued to dog the new nation. In the summer of 1972 the Union Defence Force was called in to take control of an outbreak of fighting between two old adversaries – the Qawasim and Sharqiyin of the East Coast. The tribal dispute escalated quickly and the fighting killed twenty-two and seriously injured a dozen more before the Union Defence Force could arrive and break it up. The dispute was finally settled after mediation by Rashid of Dubai and other Rulers and a statement announcing the settlement was sent out on 17 July 1972.[14]

If the atmosphere seemed uncertain in the newly forged United Arab Emirates, the wider region was hardly at peace. The day after the UAE was founded, the Indo-Pakistan War erupted. Hijackings were taking place, principally led by the PLO and other Palestinian groups but also involving Japanese, German and other terror groups. Black September had seen many of the PLO's fighters expelled from Jordan in 1970 and now the group set up in Lebanon, leading to a period of increasing volatility that culminated in the 1976 violence that was to descend into the Lebanese Civil War.

The increasing political conflict between the Arab League, of which the UAE was now a member, and the West saw the emergence of calls to boycott Israel and its allies. The October 1973 Ramadan War between Israel and its Arab neighbours led in turn to the 1973 OAPEC oil embargo.

The hijack capital of the world

On 20 July 1973, a JAL aircraft was hijacked by Osamu Maruoka, a member of the Japanese Red Army, together with four members of the Popular Front for the Liberation of Palestine. With 123 passengers and twenty-two crew on board, the plane had been taken over just out of Schiphol Airport in Holland and one of the hijackers had killed herself by detonating a grenade. Denied landing by several governments, the plane, a 747, landed in Dubai.[15]

Over the course of three days, Mohammed bin Rashid Al Maktoum talked with Maruoka, taking personal charge of the negotiation. Maruoka demanded the release of Palestinians held by Israel, which

Mohammed bin Rashid refused. By the third day, it was agreed that the plane could be refuelled and it flew on to Damascus, then Libya, where the hostages were released and the hijackers demolished the plane.

It was to be the first of a number of high-profile hijackings to land at Dubai, leading to the airport being dubbed with the, rather unfair, sobriquet 'The hijack capital of the world'. Even as Dubai was expanding its aviation and ports, the instability of the region around it was to draw the mercantile city in. And if Dubai saw its fair share of hijackings, at the time they were commonplace around the region and, indeed, the world.

Another incident in December 1973 saw a KLM 747 hijacked and flown around the region's airports, eventually landing in Dubai where the hijack was successfully concluded.[16]

Arguably the worst incident of terror in the air took place in 1983, which the Palestinian terrorist Abu Nidal was suspected of executing. A bomb in the cargo hold of Gulf Air's Karachi to Bahrain flight GF771 brought down the plane, which crashed near Jebel Ali, with the loss of 107 passengers and five crew. A passenger had loaded a bag in Karachi and not boarded the flight. It was a bitter lesson well learned and to this day the baggage of any passenger not presenting to a flight is routinely offloaded.[17]

Boom and bust

Sheikh Rashid bin Saeed's ambitious expansion plans had led to a huge boom in Dubai, which rapidly became a magnet (as it is today) for expatriate workers. Illegal immigration was a huge problem, as indeed were poorly provisioned and over-crowded boats taking pilgrims to Haj from the subcontinent.[18] The Trucial Oman Scouts and Royal Navy had provided some degree of protection against both trades, but now the UAE had to find its own solutions. With the establishment of Port Rashid, there was an urgent need for some sort of maritime policing to be put into place and a dhow, confiscated from people traffickers by Dubai Courts, was pressed into use. Nevertheless, the area of Safa (where the park and the Canal are today) became a clapboard jungle of hopeful workers. Eventually the area was cleared, but another packing crate settlement grew on the coast near Abu Hail in Deira. It was to take a series of amnesties for illegal workers and those without a valid visa, tighter legislation of worker rights and strict border controls before the issue of illegal immigration was brought under anything remotely like control.

Port Rashid was by now fully functioning and so busy that a 15 per cent surcharge was being levied on cargoes to Dubai because of the time ships had to wait offshore to dock – Rashid's decision to expand the project halfway through construction had seemed reckless at the time and now looked visionary. His next project was to demand such a leap of faith from the town's notables that they asked his son, Sheikh Mohammed, to intercede and ask him to see sense.

One morning in 1976 at 5 a.m., Halcrow's manager Neville Allen, received a phone call asking him to travel to Ras Hasa at Jebel Ali, where Sheikh Rashid wanted to meet with him. Allen's route would have taken him past the limits of the town at Satwa and out into the open desert, bumping along a well-worn track that ran across the barren, low dunes and sabkha (salt flats) through the areas we now know as Jumeirah and Umm Suqeim.

Arriving, Allen found Sheikh Rashid and a number of retainers, including Bill Duff, Rashid's economic advisor. Rashid pointed to the sparkling waters along the deserted coast laid out in front of them and told Allen that he wanted to build a port there. He outlined his ideas and asked Allen what it would cost. Allen gave him a 'rough estimate' and got the go-ahead.[19] The sixty-six-berth Jebel Ali Port was, when it opened in 1983, the world's largest man-made harbour. It remains so today.

Rashid opened Dubai Dry Docks in 1979, with the capacity to take vessels up to one million tons. He also built the Dubai World Trade Centre, a thirty-nine-storey tower that was at the time the tallest building in the Middle East. Alongside the tower, an exhibition centre was constructed. At the time, people complained that the Trade Centre was impossibly far out of town.

Dubai's boom was to be followed by bust – the 1973 OAPEC sanctions threw the world into turmoil and drew an effective chokehold around oil exports from the region. Recovering and resuming his frenetic onward march, the outbreak of the Iran-Iraq War in September 1980 once again signalled a massive block in the path of Rashid's ambitions. Each time it seemed as if Dubai would fail, caught up in its own madcap energy and tripped up by events.

In 1979, Queen Elizabeth II visited Dubai. In a whirlwind tour, she was whisked around the city to perform a number of openings, inaugurating Jebel Ali Port and the DUBAL aluminium smelter as well as the Dubai Desalination plant and the Dubai World Trade Centre. Ever the opportunist, Rashid in fact had her opening a number of projects that had been up and running for months.

Rashid's dynamic son Mohammed was given the job of overseeing the development first of Dubai's civil defence but then of its oil portfolio and its ports and fast-growing aviation business. In 1983, Dubai Duty Free opened at the airport, an operation planned by consultants from Shannon Airport and the Irish airport management company Aer Rianta. They presented their plans to Mohammed, who agreed to them but told them to double the size of the operation. One of the consultants elected to stay and help manage the new operation – Colm McLoughlin would go on to see Dubai Duty Free become the world's largest duty free outlet, responsible for 5 per cent of all global duty-free retail revenues.

Despite the disruption of the ongoing Iran-Iraq conflict and the associated 'tanker war' which threatened Gulf shipping, the 1980s saw huge expansion in Dubai – and particularly in the emirate's aviation sector.

Dubai had an 'open skies' policy, which allowed unrestricted commercial access to its airspace. A growing number of airlines now operated flights through the busy and constantly expanding airport. The Gulf's airline, Gulf Air, was a key operator, flying from a number of regional destinations into Dubai. However, the airline was unhappy, principally because Gulf Air brought in the passengers on its regional 'feeder flights' and then waved goodbye to them as other airlines took the more lucrative long-haul business.

Gulf Air executives went to see Mohammed bin Rashid and demand that Dubai do something or they would suspend flights. In a series of 'extremely tense meetings', Mohammed refused and Gulf Air reduced their scheduled services. Mohammed called in the head of DNATA, the Dubai National Air Transport Association, Maurice Flanagan, and asked him how much it would cost to launch an airline. Flanagan was an old aviation hand who had been recruited from British Airways by Sheikh Rashid.[20]

Back when Dubai Airport first opened, in 1960, Rashid had asked BOAC, as British Airways was known at the time, to schedule regular VC10 flights to Dubai. Their man in Bombay had refused, unsure whether there was enough demand for such a flight. Rashid had offered to guarantee the revenues of the flight and BOAC's reluctant Bombay office manager finally agreed. Maurice Flanagan, for it was he, would also later accept Sheikh Rashid's offer to come to Dubai.

Flanagan's response to Mohammed's question has become famous. "10 million dollars, Sheikh Mohammed."

Mohammed wrote the cheque and asked his uncle, Sheikh Ahmed bin Saeed, to oversee how Flanagan spent it. Five months later, Emirates Airline launched its inaugural flight to Karachi.

Chapter 26

THE ACT OF UNION

"I do not impose unity on anyone. That would be tyranny. Each of us has opinions that differ from those of others. We exchange our views and melt them in one crucible and then extract their essence. That is our democracy; it is the democracy of unity."

- Zayed bin Sultan Al Nahyan

On 2 December 1972, the United Arab Emirates marked its first national day. There were displays of the new country's flag, marches and an impressive military fly-past. Returning to the silence of solitude afterwards, Zayed must have suffered moments of despair at the scale of the task ahead of him.

The driving force behind the Union of emirates, he had taken the burden upon himself of leading the way and cementing the Federation into a viable nation. Yet the truth was that the very Constitution was 'transitional', a five-year agreement that would require ratification in 1976. Many of the borders between the constituent emirates remained unresolved and each emirate had its own unique character. Zayed's noisy neighbour down the road, Dubai, was mercantile, laissez faire and thoroughly opportunistic and would undoubtedly choose what was good for business. Next door on the journey up the coast was studious Sharjah, its business community eclipsed by Dubai. Many of Dubai's workers lived in Sharjah, where rents were cheaper, commuting to Dubai along a highway that was packed every rush hour. Sharjah clamoured for the road to be expanded, Dubai saw no reason to encourage the commuters.

Further north, Ajman and Umm Al Quwain were less developed, with no oil revenues. Ras Al Khaimah and Fujairah both had agriculture, fishing and little else. Basic infrastructure in the northern emirates was almost entirely lacking – from power and water through to education, healthcare and basic community care provisions. In pursuing non-involvement in the interior, the British had indeed not interfered with these communities – but they had also done virtually nothing to develop them. A huge amount of work lay ahead – and the very machinery of state – ministries, workers, support networks and even experts who could evaluate what was needed and the best way of provisioning those needs – was utterly lacking. It was a huge task, no matter how much oil money there was to hand.

Constitution

The Provisional Constitution established five federal bodies; the Supreme Council of Rulers; the office of the President; the Cabinet;

the Federal National Council (FNC) and the Federal Judiciary. The Constitution also allowed for the Ruler of each emirate to maintain a considerable degree of sovereignty 'over their own territories and territorial waters that are not within the jurisdiction of the Union'. The exact meaning of this phrase – and other ambiguous language that had found its way into the Constitution – was to cause a great deal of debate as the lines between Union and sovereignty came under increasing scrutiny in the years to come.

One of the key proponents of Union, Rashid bin Saeed Al Maktoum was also cautious about quite how far down the road of Federation he wanted to go. A shrewd (the commander of the Trucial Oman Scouts called him 'wily') negotiator, Rashid secured political parity with Abu Dhabi in the number of seats allocated to Dubai in the Federal National Council and together with Abu Dhabi, Dubai held a veto in the Supreme Council.[1]

One of the provisions of that 1971 Constitution was the establishment of a new capital city to be built between Dubai and Abu Dhabi, to be called *Karama* or 'Dignity'. It is the reason the UAE still has no 01 telephone area code in use today (Abu Dhabi is 02, Al Ain 03, Dubai 04 etc) – the 01 code was to be reserved for the new capital.

In the end, the new capital city was a stillborn concept. With available funds stretched by the daunting task of nation-building, nobody could afford to pay for it and once the immediate danger and instability following Union seemed to be over, the UAE accepted on the international stage, everyone breathed a sigh of relief and got on with the enormous task of infrastructural and human development.

The new country did not even have a currency: the Bedouin had traditionally used silver Maria Theresa thalers, but then the merchants and traders – and Rulers – had used Indian 'Gulf' rupees. Dubai had taken to using the Qatari (and then Qatari Dubai) Riyal and, in fact, did not drop its adherence to that currency until 1973, while Abu Dhabi used the Bahraini Dinar.

The first Federal Budget was put forward in February 1972 and envisaged a spend of six million Bahraini Dinars, principally on social housing and electricity and communication infrastructure, including roads. In June of that year, the Dubai/Sharjah highway was expanded to a dual carriageway and a comprehensive road-building programme was put in place. Agriculture was always important to Zayed and he brought United Nations consultants to study the country's potential for agriculture, expanding agricultural research stations in Digdaga, Ras Al Khaimah, and Al Ain.

Zayed had a dream of transforming the desert into a green land and he built parks and gardens, greened roundabouts and central reservations as well as planting vast swathes of desert. By 1981, four million trees had been planted and municipal nurseries had been established.

For all this, the Union was still politically incoherent and struggling to find its feet as an institution built from, and representing, its parts. There was constant debate about where the writ of the emirates' rulers started and that of the Union finished and, in many cases, this translated into delay. For Zayed, a man inherently given to action, this was frustrating in the extreme.

At the end of his first term under the Provisional Constitution, in December 1976, Zayed announced he would resign as President.[2]

The public reaction was disbelief and shock. The people took to the streets in an unprecedented series of demonstrations and Zayed was confirmed as President for a second term and the Constitution strengthened. However, the issues bedevilling the process of unification continued to rumble in the background and in June 1979 a public notice was issued by the Council of Ministers and the Federal National Council (FNC) calling for the Federation to be strengthened and for its institutions to be more responsive.

It was a clear signal of frustration from Zayed and once again the people took to the streets as the debate raged, in the end requiring the intervention of a senior member of the Kuwaiti ruling family.[3] In July, in a clear signal of commitment to unity, the Vice President of the UAE, Rashid bin Saeed Al Maktoum, was appointed as Prime Minister. The move brought Rashid into a more direct managerial role alongside Zayed and served to rally the smaller northern emirates. In 1981, Zayed was re-elected President and Rashid as Vice President by the Supreme Council and the Provisional Constitution ratified. This time, there were no demonstrations. However, the Provisional Constitution remained precisely that: provisional. The fixing of a permanent constitution was a can that would continue to be kicked down the road.

Zayed's ideas of unity stretched beyond the UAE. Qatar and Bahrain's withdrawal from the Federation of Arab Emirates was a huge disappointment to him (he had even travelled to Oman to invite Sultan Qaboos to join the Federation). A great deal of Abu Dhabi's considerable oil wealth went to supporting other Arab nations and communities in need; Zayed was famously generous. He was also a believer in Arab unity and so another of his dreams was realised when, in 1981, Abu Dhabi hosted the inaugural meeting of the Gulf Cooperation Council (GCC), a political and economic union planned to include Saudi Arabia, Kuwait, Bahrain, Qatar, the UAE and Oman.

In time of war

The UAE Armed Forces first saw action overseas in 1982, with the establishment of the UN-brokered Multi-National Force in Lebanon, a peacekeeping role. UAE forces would go on to take similar peacekeeping duties in Somalia in 1992 and Kosovo in 1999.

For much of the 1980s, as the Iran/Iraq conflict and its associated 'tanker war' in the Gulf intensified, the UAE Armed Forces maintained a state of high alert. In the face of the continued threat of fallout from the Iran/Iraq conflict, in October 1983 the GCC carried out its first joint military exercises under the banner of 'Operation Peninsula Shield'. This led to the decision to create a joint military force, the Peninsula Shield Force, in 1984.

Both Iran and Iraq attacked each other's oil facilities and attempted to stifle oil exports by targeting neutral shipping. Kuwaiti tankers, in particular, shipped Iraqi oil and were attacked by Iran. America came to Kuwait's aid, reflagging Kuwaiti oil tankers with US flags and providing warships to accompany tankers through the Straits of Hormuz. Ironically, the first casualty of the operation, named 'Earnest

Will', was an American frigate, hit by Iraqi Exocet missiles. The Iranians took to laying mines in the Gulf, leading to the mining of the *Bridgeton*, a reflagged Kuwaiti tanker.

Another ship hit by an Exocet missile was the 118,000-ton tanker *Fellowship L*. The Greek-owned, Liberian-registered vessel was hit by the Iraqis some fifty miles south of Kharg Island, but the Exocet didn't explode. The ship's crew, possibly the luckiest crew in history, found themselves sitting on an unexploded missile lodged in their cargo tank and carrying 230,000 tons of oil. Doubtless moaning in fear, they sailed the *Fellowship* out of the dangerous waters of the Gulf and moored it off Khor Fakkan, where their agent asked for British assistance to remove the missile. You can only begin to imagine the relief of the crew when they finally legged it. The British were only too keen to help: the French-made Exocet was a fearsome weapon that had been used to great effect during the Falklands War between Britain and Argentina and the Iraqis had bought an advanced new type which the Argentinians were also believed to have deployed. The intelligence value of disarming and examining the missile was judged to be tremendous and a team of five experts was shipped out to help aid the stricken vessel. The British were careful to ensure that the UAE government had no objections to the defusing and removal of the missile for 'safety reasons'. They scrupulously avoided mentioning the intelligence value of the operation, which was supported by elements from the British naval patrol in the Gulf, the Armilla Patrol.[4]

The tanker war rumbled on and American forces in the region were increased. Numerous incidents took place that saw US navy and special forces involved in conflict against Iranian targets. Exocets once again made the news when the USS *Stark* was hit by two missiles fired by an Iraqi aircraft, blowing a hole in the frigate and killing thirty-seven of its crew.

The escalation continued. US forces attacked Iranian Revolutionary Guard units based on oil platforms, completely destroying three Iranian rigs. In July 1988, the USS *Vincennes* was involved in a protracted action against harrying Iranian gunboats. The *Vincennes* mistakenly targeted an Iranian Airbus A300 flying a scheduled route from Tehran to Dubai and shot it down, with the loss of all 290 passengers, and crew. Two weeks later, the Iranians accepted UN Security Council resolution 598 calling for an end to the war.[5]

Trouble in Sharjah

There was not just instability outside the UAE's borders. On 17 June 1987, while Sultan bin Muhammad Al Qasimi, the Ruler of Sharjah, was holidaying in Britain, his elder brother Abdulaziz led the Sharjah National Guard in a coup, taking over effective control of the emirate. Abdulaziz' forces posted soldiers at major intersections, occupied Sharjah Radio and TV and closed the airport. The staff of the Al Khaleej newspaper were sent home, while helicopters buzzed above the city.

Far from being the town barred to visitors flying through Sharjah with Imperial Airways, Sharjah had developed as something of a party town and became home to a large and growing constellation of hotels, bars and pubs, which served a lively traffic from Dubai. Sharjah's main street, Al Wahda Street, had more in common with Hamra or Gemmayze in Beirut than possibly any other city in the Gulf, glittering storefronts showing off the latest zany fashions, the street also home to bars, restaurants and cafés. That all changed in 1979, when the sale of alcohol was prohibited in the Emirate, a ban effected virtually overnight.

The change came as a shock to Sharjah's burgeoning tourist trade and while Sharjah today benefits from the growth of Islamic tourism, the concept had not entered people's thinking in the seventies. The move seemed to have set Sharjah back while Dubai continued to expand at breakneck pace.

Sharjah had finally discovered oil in 1980, but a drop in the oil price had seen revenues slump and the emirate was purportedly indebted to the tune of some 400 million dollars – it was this 'financial mismanagement' that was cited as the impelling reason behind Abdulaziz' coup, according to reports at the time.[6]

Sultan returned to stay in Dubai while negotiations were ongoing with Abdulaziz. Not only did Sultan enjoy Dubai's strong and vociferous support, Abdulaziz was eventually confronted with a unanimous verdict from the UAE's Rulers – Sultan bin Muhammad was the rightful Ruler of Sharjah and they all stood by him. It was a repetition of the lesson learned by Saqr bin Sultan – that despite its differences and disputes, and in spite of the growing pains and wrangling, when push came to shove, the United Arab Emirates was just that: united. As the days passed, a compromise was reached and Abdulaziz agreed to take up the post of Crown Prince, while Sultan would be restored as Ruler. A reconciliation was effected, following which the Sharjah National Guard was rolled into the UAE Armed Forces.

Breathing a sigh of relief, the UAE could once again focus on developing its Federal institutions and its member emirates their respective economies. However, if the end of the Iran/Iraq war seemed to offer peace in the Gulf, the illusion was to be short lived. In January and February 1991, the UAE's armed forces – and its economy as a whole – faced an entirely different challenge. The invasion of Kuwait.

Saddam Hussein's decision to invade Kuwait in August 1990 was to have an enormous impact on the UAE's economy. Traditionally a quiet month, with many expatriate and Emirati families travelling abroad to escape the heat, August that year came and went and business levels stayed at their summer low. A number of companies, particularly the more skittish Americans, pulled out of the UAE and other Gulf countries. Rumours abounded: Saddam was planning to carry on through Kuwait to take the whole Gulf coast; he was going to invade Saudi Arabia.

The UAE hosted thousands of displaced Kuwaitis and then, as the build-up of forces for Operation Desert Storm took place, hosted tens of thousands of soldiers. UAE brought its logistical infrastructure into play, with Jebel Ali and Dubai International Airport hosting Allied warships and planes, while Abu Dhabi's Al Dhafrah airbase played a key role in the air war.[7] In the Allied offensive to retake Kuwait, the UAE Armed Forces flew 123 sorties and led in the ground offensive to liberate the country, which launched on 24 February 1991. Under the shadow cast by the gathering clouds of war, a man's heart stopped beating and a nation mourned. Sheikh Rashid bin Saeed Al Maktoum passed away on 7 October 1990.

In a remarkable life, Rashid transitioned from being the tribal leader of a coalition of coastal and desert communities, to the head of a vibrant, modern city-state. He had worked tirelessly in pursuit of his goal, the development of a thriving and sustainable trading entrepôt, of diversification from oil. He would ride around the city on his beloved horse (and later in a Mercedes, as his famous quote noted) in the early hours of the morning, inspecting his pet projects and then harangue project managers attending his *majlis* later in the day when he thought progress was too slow.[8] As a young man he was something of a firebrand: impulsive, dynamic, ambitious and a shrewd negotiator. As a statesman, he grew to command the respect of peers around the world. His drive, his sheer verve drove Dubai into the twenty-first century with a foot slammed hard on the accelerator.

His death came at the end of a long illness, but nevertheless plunged Dubai into sincere grief. The smooth transition to the accession of his eldest son, Maktoum, reflected the fact that for years Dubai's affairs had been effectively managed by Rashid's sons: Maktoum, Hamdan and Mohammed – the fourth, Ahmed, took little role in public life.

Maktoum was also chosen as Prime Minister and elected as Vice President of the UAE. It was the second time he was to hold the former role – he had served as the UAE's first prime minister from 1971 until 1979, when his father took over the position. A natural diplomat of gentle and unassuming disposition, Maktoum maintained a steady hand on the development and management of Dubai while his forceful younger brother, Mohammed, took an increasingly public role. On 3 January 1995, Mohammed was made (after several times of asking by Maktoum) Crown Prince of Dubai. A slew of announcements was to follow, including the first Dubai Shopping Festival, a massive expansion of Dubai International Airport and, in March 1996, the first Dubai World Cup, billed as the world's richest horse race. If Rashid had a heavy foot on the accelerator, it was clearly an attribute he passed on to Mohammed, his third son.

Ways to work
The 1990s also saw changes in long-established working practices. The broadly followed working day in the UAE was traditionally built around the 'split shift', the working day broken up into two sessions, typically 8 a.m.–1 p.m. and 4 p.m.–7 p.m., allowing for an afternoon break or 'siesta'. The weekend consisted of Thursday afternoon and Friday, a 1.5-day break. With the increasing direct presence of overseas companies, particularly those in sectors such as services and technology, the private sector started to follow more 'Western' ways of work and many adopted a straight shift and a Thursday/Friday two-day weekend, then moved to a Friday/Saturday weekend, which allowed for better communication with overseas offices and clients. For a time, government ministries and, consequently, schools held out for a Thursday/Friday weekend before finally aligning with the private sector and a unified Friday/Saturday weekend was followed by all. A further move, in 2022, was to change the weekend to Saturday/Sunday, and usher in a 4.5-day week for UAE Government departments and, increasingly, private sector companies.

A series of reforms of UAE labour law provided restrictions on working hours (a maximum of eight hours a day, six days a week), allowed employees to freely transfer their visas between employers and provided protection of workers' salaries. In the face of public opprobrium, particularly in Western media, reforms of labour practises were introduced and regulations were gradually not only improved, but effectively enforced by Minister of Labour officials. Stronger regulations protecting domestic workers' rights and conditions were also introduced.

The influx of expatriate workers, from labourers to CEOs, continued at a remarkable pace, with the country's population rising from 1.39 million in 1985 to 2.98 million in 1999. Ten years later, it had shot up to 7.66 million.

Culture to the fore
If Dubai's mercantilism was driving fast growth in the city, Sharjah to the north was taking another path. Under the influence of its Ruler, Dr Sultan bin Muhammad Al Qasimi, Sharjah was investing

in education, the arts and culture. In 1997, the American University of Sharjah was founded, growing to accommodate a student body of over 5,000 and gain accreditations from global partner institutions. Recognised as one of the world's top '50 under 50' universities, AUS launched its first doctoral programmes in 2018, as well as the Sharjah Research, Technology and Innovation Park, a major innovation hub with incubators and funds to foster a programme of encouraging entrepreneurialism. Alongside AUS, the University of Sharjah was also founded in 1997, going on to become home to over 14,000 students. These two institutions would develop into Sharjah University City, a cluster of universities and educational institutions catering to a wide range of disciplines.

Sharjah's airport, long operating from its original location in the city centre, was moved to a new location outside the city in 1977. This was to become the home of the region's first low cost airline, Air Arabia, which quickly grew into a major regional operator serving over 170 destinations and operating a number of 'fifth freedom' services.

Sharjah was also to establish its Hamriyah Free Zone, suporting the further growth and development of its lively oilfield supply and support sector. A development company, Shurooq, has driven the growth of the SME sector, tourism and hospitality and other FDI developments.

The city was named UNESCO Capital of Arab Culture in 1998 (and went on to be named Capital of Islamic Culture in 2014), developing a rich mixture of museums, cultural and arts centres, as well as focusing on architecture and the restoration of the city's heritage.

Sharjah had long offered cheaper rents than Dubai and its quieter lifestyle encouraged expatriates who wanted to save money rather than keep up with the pace of the 'party town' down the road. Traffic volumes between the two emirates far eclipsed road capacities and the commute became infamous, yet the savings encouraged more and more expatriates to take up an apartment or villa in Sharjah while working in Dubai.

There was at least one exception to the prohibition against drink in Sharjah – established in 1976, Sharjah Wanderers was a members-only sports club with a strict 'expats only' membership policy. The club took its name from one of the two football teams that originated with the RAF and Trucial Oman Scouts (TOS) and played at RAF Sharjah in the 1960s, the other being the Canaries. Next to the club, originally a stiff drive out of the town, a small not-for-profit community school, Sharjah English School, was established. The school was funded, like the sports club, by locally based – mostly British – companies and built on land granted to the community by Sharjah's Ruler. It stands today as the oldest community school in the emirate.

Expansion at all costs

If Sharjah had focused on developing a more contemplative and cultured future, Dubai was determined to pursue growth and unfettered opportunism. By 1999, the projects were dropping thick and fast. The Burj Al Arab, four years in construction, was opened. On 29 October 1999, the day before the successful annual GITEX technology exhibition opened, Dubai Internet City was announced – a gateless free zone in which technology companies could operate with 100 per cent foreign ownership.

The Gulf Information Technology Exhibition, GITEX – originally called GITE, the X was added in its second year of operations – was a phenomenon which reflected the incredible growth of the technology sector in Dubai. Although old hands in the technology industry had long had distribution arrangements in place for the Gulf (IBM, Digital Equipment Corporation, Burroughs, Sperry and Rand were all early entrants), the 'new wave' PC companies like Microsoft and Intel had concerns about the rampant intellectual property theft and software piracy that characterised the Middle East market. A move to protect intellectual property by the Dubai Department of Economic Development under its dynamic Director General, Mohamed Alabbar, led to a number of confiscations of PCs loaded with pirated software. Confident of the protection offered to them, the PC companies started to establish regional offices in Dubai – the first was Oracle, followed by Ashton Tate, Lotus, Microsoft, Intel, Novell, Acer and others. Every major international technology company active in the

Middle East market opened up offices in Dubai – only one, Compaq, opened up a regional office elsewhere, establishing its office in Bahrain before moving to Dubai a year later.

As the technology sector boomed, so GITEX grew, to the point where it became the world's third largest technology exhibition, expanding from a single hall at the Dubai World Trade Centre to occupy every single hall of the expanded ten-hall complex.

When Dubai Internet City was announced, it was an immediate success. In fact, many of the companies who flocked to the new zone merely moved their operations up the road.

The first of the new breed of Free Zones, Dubai Internet City was followed by the American University of Dubai (to become the keystone of Dubai Knowledge Village later in 2002) and Dubai Media City in 2000. Together, the zones provided the keystones of an ICT development initiative that would combine technology development capability (DIC), content creation (DMC) and education (DKV).

DIC and DMC were to form the vanguard for a range of 'free zone' operations throughout Dubai, each targeting a vertical market sector. Free Zones now started to emerge in other emirates, including Sharjah's Hamriyah Free Zone; Ajman Free Zone; Ras Al Khaimah Free Zone and Fujairah's Free Zone and Creative City.

Early in 2001, Dubai Marina was announced – a new waterfront real estate development. Following on from the Free Zones, with their guarantee of 100 per cent foreign ownership and tax-free operations, Dubai would now allow 'freehold' property sales to foreigners – the first time this market opened up. The instrument used to circumvent the Federal interdiction of property ownership by foreigners was effectively an extension of the standard annual tenancy contract to a ninety-nine-year lease under the principle of usufruct. (Usufruct is a type of property transaction, similar to a lease, that actually traces its roots to the Romans, although few people have actually heard of it. Under usufruct, the holder of the lease, or the usufructuary, has the right to use the property and enjoy the fruits of that use, hence the Latin *usus* and *fructus*: use and fruit.)

The fine print, however, was not really bothering anyone: the Marina meant anyone, from anywhere, could now own an apartment in Dubai. The announcement opened up the floodgates to a huge new market as expatriates flocked to pay down payments on 'off plan' properties. The Marina announcement was followed, on 1 May 2001, with the announcement of the Palm Jumeirah and Palm Jebel Ali, two man-made islands, which would add 120 kilometres of sandy beach to Dubai's crowded seafront. Each island would see something like 80 million cubic metres of dredged sand on a base of rock brought down from quarries in the mountains.

As Dubai's fledgling property development market emerged, American Airlines Flight 11 and United Airlines Flight 175 smashed into the World Trade Centre towers in New York and the world changed.

A plea to America

In Kentucky at the time of the 9/11 atrocity, Mohammed bin Rashid Al Maktoum donated to the families of the victims, but also caught the mood in America and, on 27 September 2001, gave a lengthy statement to Reuters warning of a 'human catastrophe' if the US invaded Afghanistan.

It was to no avail, the die was cast and, on 7 October, 'Operation Enduring Freedom' was launched with a series of air strikes against targets in Afghanistan. Mohammed had often travelled to Afghanistan with his brother, Maktoum, and knew the country well. Many UAE royals had visited to hunt, both in Afghanistan and in Pakistan, including its province of Baluchistan, which lay between Afghanistan and the sea. The UAE royal families not only enjoyed falconry in these areas, but also had often donated towards local community projects. The Emirati and Omani Baloch tribe (singular Al Balushi) owe their origins to the area.

Afghanistan's complex history since the Soviet invasion had made it a hunting ground not only of falconers, but also of religious fanatics, spies and, indeed, the CIA and its proxies. Having heavily armed the Islamic militias (the fearsome mujahideen, who had for 'the price of a few Stingers' cost the Russians billions and pinned them down for years in a futile war against their shadowy foe), the CIA then found itself mounting 'buy back' programmes to try and disarm the wild men of the madrasas.[9] Born of this conflict, the Taliban harboured Bin Laden and America was determined to stamp them out. Mohammed watched the country he knew so well devastated by pounding air strikes. By 13 November 2001, Mohammed ordered daily airlifts of aid to Afghanistan. In spring 2002, he launched programmes to resettle families in the Spin Boldak refugee camps, with plans to resettle 15,000 families, providing them with food and grants to help rebuild their shattered homes and smallholdings. The aid, munificent though it was, was a drop in a troubled ocean.

If 9/11 and its immediate aftermath impacted Dubai's real estate market, it was short-lived, at least in part due to a huge signal of confidence sent out when Emirates in November 2001 placed one of the largest orders for aircraft in aviation history with both Airbus and Boeing, for fifty-eight aircraft with a value of some 15 billion dollars. If the order demonstrated remarkable brio in the face of deeply bearish market sentiment, the price negotiated demonstrated remarkable pragmatism.

The Dubai Knowledge Village educational centre launched alongside Dubai International Financial Centre. A 2.5-billion-dollar expansion of Dubai International Airport was launched, adding a third terminal to the development. Mohammed also announced two more free zone projects: Dubai Silicon Oasis and Dubai Healthcare City. The projects kept coming, thick and fast – and now real estate sales were booming and queues were forming as new projects were launched.

American rhetoric turned sharply to Iraq, where a no-fly zone imposed by the US and Britain together with sanctions against Saddam Hussein were starting to cause large-scale humanitarian suffering. Again, Mohammed reached out to the stricken and, in a little publicised gesture, brought two conjoined children out of Baghdad and paid for their operation at Great Ormond Street. Responding to a telethon held on Dubai TV in March 2003, Mohammed pledged 30 million dollars to the effort, raising the total donated to over 50 million dollars.

In an effort to avert the invasion, Sheikh Zayed bin Sultan Al Nahyan offered asylum to Saddam. Mohammed bin Rashid travelled to Iraq for an 'honest but tense' meeting to try and convince him to stand down. The mission failed and Saddam defied America to the bitter end.[10]

The US invasion of Iraq unfolded and business confidence in Dubai again took a broadside. Mohammed hardly seemed to hesitate. A huge expansion to Jebel Ali had been announced in January, adding eighty-two berths and 125 cranes to the already extensive port. Now, in May, Dubai announced 'The World', a cluster of 200 man-made islands offshore from Jumeirah and then, a month later, Dubai Maritime City – a 650-million-dirham maritime support hub. In June, Emirates once again made history, with Mohammed bin Rashid signing an order at the Paris Airshow for forty-five planes from Airbus and twenty-six from Boeing. Twenty-three of the new planes were to be Airbus' superjumbo, the A380.

The projects were beginning to blur into each other, a kaleidoscope of announcements that would coalesce into a single colour – 'Dubai Beige', the colour of Emirates' uniforms, of new villas, of entire housing developments. In July 2004, Mohammed announced a new airport was to be constructed at Jebel Ali. When Dubai's original airport was constructed, the consultants had initially focused on Jebel Ali as the preferred location, changing their minds at the last minute. Now Jebel Ali was finally to hear the roar of engines in its skies.

In September 2004, Sheikh Mohammed also laid the foundation stone of what was to be launched as the 'Burj Dubai' – the world's tallest tower.

Changes, growing pains and successions

A month later, on 2 November 2004, aged 86, Sheikh Zayed bin Sultan Al Nahyan passed away. The United Arab Emirates lost 'the father of the nation' and the outpouring of grief throughout the Emirates was as sincere as it was sustained. Children in the schools were in tears as they mourned *Baba Zayed*, Father Zayed.

The first President of the UAE and the man whose vision, dogged perseverance and limitless generosity not only created and built a nation but sustained it throughout its considerable growing pains and defended it against looming external threats, Zayed's legacy and achievement is to Emiratis what Churchill's was to the British or perhaps Lincoln's to Americans. Like Rashid, he had straddled the world of the Bedouin and the development of a modern nation state. Zayed was loved by the nomads but also took a role on the world stage as a respected peacemaker and arbiter among Arab nations as well as quietly becoming probably the world's greatest philanthropist, making huge donations to causes that were to have huge long term global consequences, from saving whale and elephant populations to funding key innovations in biosaline agriculture and solar power development.

Zayed's remarkable life and achievements are marked today by the Founder's Memorial in Abu Dhabi, an open Heritage Garden and Sanctuary at the centre of which is a cubic pavilion housing The Constellation, an artwork dedicated to Zayed's memory. Planted with some of Zayed's favourite trees (including the Ghaf, the national tree of the United Arab Emirates) and bearing a *falaj*, testament to Zayed's work in rebuilding the waterways of Al Ain, at the heart of the gardens, the Constellation artwork is a hanging of geometric 'platonic solid' shapes which form a 3D portrait of Zayed.

In a reflection of the last days of Rashid bin Saeed Al Maktoum, Zayed's son, Khalifa bin Zayed Al Nahyan had been de facto Ruler of Abu Dhabi in Zayed's last years and so the accession was smooth and seamless. Khalifa became Ruler of Abu Dhabi and, a day later, on 3 November 2004, President of the United Arab Emirates.

Khalifa's presidency was to see a coming together of the Dubai and Abu Dhabi royal families, particularly in May 2005 when Mansour bin Zayed Al Nahyan, the deputy Prime Minister of the UAE married Manal bint Mohammed Al Maktoum, Sheikh Mohammed's daughter.

Dubai, in the meantime, was hurting. The growth driven by the burgeoning real estate market was attracting investments from throughout an increasingly troubled Middle East. In times of trouble, money flies to safe havens and now Dubai emerged as the safest of them all. It ticked all the boxes – it was stable, commercial, realistic and yet still within the region. What can only be described as a gold rush was in full flow and investors from the Middle East and further afield flocked to capitalise on its inventory of dazzling projects. The road system started to creak and, in October 2004, Mohammed formed a Dubai Traffic Committee to find solutions to the problem. At the core of the issue was the simple fact that Dubai Municipality was not adapting to the fast-changing needs of the city and so, on 1 November 2005, Sheikh Maktoum appointed Sheikh Mohammed to head the new Dubai Roads and Transport Authority, which would take control of the strategic development, construction and management of Dubai's road system.

The pace of development was clearly causing cracks in the system and Sheikh Mohammed lost no time in telling government officials to pull their socks up. Dubai's construction workers, a huge influx of labour from the Indian Subcontinent brought in response to demand for real estate projects, were getting a raw deal and that was resulting in bad publicity, so Mohammed formed a Committee for Labour Affairs to manage worker rights. The move, together with the launch of a Dubai Police hotline to encourage the reporting of labour issues, was arguably too little, too late. Construction companies were chasing huge profits and fast turnarounds and the niceties of worker rights were too easy to ignore. Predatory labour companies operating in India, Pakistan, Bangladesh and anywhere else where cheap labour could be sourced were charging workers for visas and companies were withholding their passports. With events moving faster than governance or the legal system, workers were being abused and investors were relatively unimpressed about issues like worker rights. There was money to be made and it little mattered to the men in green ties and white socks quite whose sweat it was stained with.

As 2005 gave way to 2006, the slew of new projects started to become concrete reality. The Dubai International Financial Centre was inaugurated, as was the Dubai Gold and Commodities Exchange.

On 3 January 2006, Sheikh Maktoum bin Rashid Al Maktoum, the Vice President and Prime Minister of the United Arab Emirates and

Ruler of Dubai, died of a heart attack whilst staying at the Palazzo Versace Hotel on Australia's Gold Coast.

Mohammed was to remember Maktoum as 'the kindest, softest, humblest and most considerate among us all'.[11] A keen horse-owner, Maktoum's quiet nature had meant his more boisterous brother had taken a more public role, but Maktoum had been a steadying and guiding hand in the background. His passing, unlike that of his father or that of Zayed, was both unexpected and shocking – he was still a young man. Still mourning his brother, Mohammed acceded on 3 January 2006 as Ruler of Dubai and then, on 6 January, as Vice President of the UAE.

Nominated by President Khalifa bin Zayed Al Nahyan, Mohammed's appointment as Prime Minister was ratified by the UAE Supreme Council and on 11 February 2006, he became Prime Minister of the UAE.

As Ruler of Dubai, his first two actions were to change the mandate of Dubai Internet City to include research and development and innovation, and then to establish the institution which would go on to develop the UAE National Space Programme.

As Prime Minister of the UAE, he embarked on a wide-ranging process of governmental reform which, friends counselled, would break him before it saw success.

As a visionary leader driving the development of the economic miracle that was Dubai, he was to come face to face with the prospect of ruin.

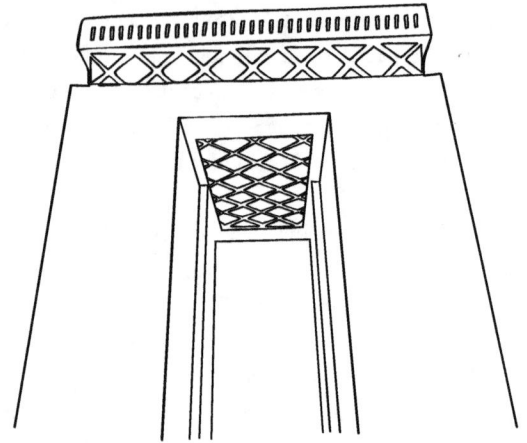

Chapter 27

WINDS OF CHANGE

"Does running water stop when it reaches a rock? Of course not. It turns either left or right, and continues its way. Likewise, a positive person is confident that no challenge will stand in the way of achieving his or her goal."

– Mohammed bin Rashid Al Maktoum

The acquisition of P&O by UAE company Dubai Ports World seemed almost routine. Dubai's ports management company had blossomed since the establishment of Jebel Ali Port in the 1970s and had grown to become not only the operator of Jebel Ali, the world's largest man-made harbour and one of its major ports, but an international ports management company with truly global operations and aspirations. If its name seemed a little too ambitious, it was at least on track to create a global footprint.

It was to be one of Dubai's trailblazers, this company that grew from bringing in expatriate expertise to manage its Dubai-based asset to signing management contracts that re-exported expertise to run ports around the world. Now Dubai was re-exporting management expertise in a way it had once re-exported saffron, cochineal, dried limes and gold. It was a trick that was to be repeated, with the luxury hotel group Jumeirah, Emirates' aviation technology arm Mercator and airports facilities management company DNATA.

In February 2006, the shareholders of British ports management company P&O (it stands for the Peninsular and Oriental Steam Navigation Company) agreed to the sale of the company to Dubai Ports World. P&O held management contracts for a number of global ports, including six major US ports including New York and Philadelphia. The deal resulted in a howl of protest from right-wing American politicians that grew into an orchestrated campaign of fearmongering. The idea of Arabs 'owning' US ports (the ports were already being managed by a foreign company) was dangerous, un-American. The fact that the UAE was a key US ally did not even get a look in – the whole campaign turned ugly, quickly and by 8 March, the Committee on Appropriations of the US House of Representatives voted against the deal. Bruised and battered, Dubai Ports World withdrew, divesting its interest in the contracts to the US-owned finance company, American International Group.

It was a harsh political lesson – and a signal that the UAE may be as moderate, open and tolerant as it likes, but that it cannot always rely on its friendly intentions being reciprocated.

Alongside announcing more new projects in Dubai such as the Dubai Metro and a slew of new road development plans, Mohammed bin Rashid quickly took up the reigns of his Federal role as Prime Minister of the UAE, chairing a renewed Cabinet and embarking on a series of visits to government institutions around the Emirates throughout March and April 2006. After a series of reviews and consultations with Khalifa bin Zayed, he launched a new Federal government strategy, a ground-up reform of the UAE's government which assigned five teams to work on developing strategies to bring government performance up to global standards. The teams were given twenty-four weeks to come back with defined plans.

Growth during this period was by no means limited to Dubai: Abu Dhabi's burgeoning real estate sector was joined by new developments in leisure and tourism, education and innovation in particular. Relentless investment in technology and higher education have sparked revolutionary growth in areas such as quantum computing, Fintech, Crypto and perhaps most notably, AI. Ras Al Khaimah's tourism sector grew around the enormous development of Al Hamra but has also now seen a major boost from new players in hospitality with the opening up of gaming in the emirate. A longstanding industrial development strategy has seen the growth of major players including pharmaceutical giant Julfar and the world's largest manufacturer of ceramics, RAK Ceramics.

While Fujairah has arguably focused its development around bunkering, oilfield support and port services, the smallest Emirate by landmass, Ajman, focused investments in its port and free zone. Long after the dust had settled on the global financial crisis, Ajman was to establish the Al Zorah Development Company, a joint venture between the Government of Ajman and Solidere International, the company that redeveloped the heart of Beirut following its long civil war. Where Zayed the Great once planned his fort, luxury hotels, golf courses, residences and a nature reserve now stand.

While every emirate was seeing burgeoning growth over this period, none were so exposed to the real estate sector as Dubai.

The trouble with real estate

Dubai's booming real estate market was not only in full swing, it was starting to create systemic problems in the city. New projects kept being piled on: in March 2007, Mohammed announced the 76 million square foot Meydan Horseracing City, a mixed-use hotel, residential and tourist destination with a 60,000-capacity stadium. Now developers were springing up, offering at times outlandish projects as they vied for attention from house buyers and investors. The city faced a cement crisis as prices shot up and a rent crisis as rents did the same. Despite the RTA's road-building and expansion programme, the city's roads were choking with clamorous lines of traffic. Efforts were made to try and manage rents but it was not enough: the whole real estate sector was spinning out of control. In August 2007, Mohammed announced the establishment of a property regulator, RERA (the Real Estates Regulatory Authority) to curb developers and bring some semblance of order to a market that reflected free market economics on steroids. With Emirates Airline expanding its operations and the airport ramping up capacity, in June 2008 Mohammed issued a decree establishing a new low-cost airline, to be named Flydubai. The announcement was an answer to Sharjah's highly successful play in low cost flight, Air Arabia, which had launched with publicity stunts including regional flights for one dirham and quickly consolidated a hold on regional travel out of the global travel hub that the Emirates was swiftly becoming.

Dubai was groaning under the strain of unfettered growth. public infrastructure could not keep up with the influx of new residents and the burgeoning sprawls of real estate. The projects had started to transition from visionary to plainly insane – an underwater hotel, a building in the shape of an Emirati man, towers with independently turning floors, new shapes that twisted and contorted concrete and smoked glass into a series of hellish conceptions. The advertising agencies were barely able to keep up. A lucrative trade in billboards put a premium on any flat space near a road as realtors scrambled to fill every opportunity in the city's print and outdoor media with imprecations to live the dream, love the life and escape to a new urban lifestyle that reflects your fantasies and desires. The rhetoric became wearing, the visions a nightmarish collection of admen's fantasies that were all too often reflected in shoddy developments with ill-considered arrangements for the carbon-based lifeforms they were supposedly designed to accommodate.[1]

School places became almost impossible to find, getting to school itself became a challenge as the roads clogged up. Dubai Municipality's sewage treatment plant could not keep up: the tankers that were used to empty the city's septic tanks were backed up along the Awir Road out to the plant, with queues over twenty-four hours long. A plan was announced to dig a huge pit in the desert for the overflow while the tanker drivers themselves took to dumping the sewage into storm drains rather than live with the constant waiting to discharge their odious loads. The result was a brown tide spreading across the sea off Jumeirah, where the drains emerged, and its luxury resorts and beaches. Hospital beds, in a city where private healthcare had meant residents could expect any treatment or procedure virtually on demand, were unavailable.

The city was breaking under the strain. When it came, the bust was almost a relief.[2]

The Global Financial Crisis was triggered by the 2007 US sub-prime mortgage crisis and emerged to dominate the world's banking markets throughout that year and 2008, resulting in the collapse of US mortgage lenders followed by banks and financial institutions around the world. While global real estate markets contracted with remarkable speed and violence, Dubai seemed deaf to the screams of pain, perhaps because it was too busy partying. For a remarkable, halcyon period, it seemed as if the power of the dream factory might actually see the city float above it all on its clouds of illusions to dare to desire new ways of luxury living. However, the truth was fast becoming all too evident.

If you could put a date on the day the party ended, it was probably 24 September 2008, the day that the Atlantis Hotel, Dubai was launched. The dream-child of the man behind South Africa's Sun

City, Sol Kerzner, the 1,500-room Atlantis was the anchor hotel on the visionary palm-frond themed land reclamation project, the Palm Jumeirah. Sitting on the apex of the palm's corona, the hotel was launched with enormous fanfare and a blitz of publicity, a light show and firework display that was Saeed to have used 100,000 shells and a party that reportedly drank the world's entire available stock of Roederer Cristal Champagne to the pumping sound of Kylie Minogue playing to a hand-picked audience of 2,000 celebrity guests.

When the party was over, the city woke up to the world's most monumental hangover.

Assuring investors of the market's stability in October 2008, Mohammed bin Rashid Al Maktoum moved 70 billion dirhams into the banking sector. A year later, having inaugurated Dubai Mall, the world's biggest shopping mall at the heart of the 20-billion-dollar Downtown Dubai development, in September 2009, Mohammed told a meeting of business people that the financial crisis was a 'passing cloud'. A few days later he inaugurated the Dubai Metro.

Three months later, Dubai World – heavily exposed to the real estate market – was restructured as part of a number of moves announced by Mohammed to mitigate the impact of the crisis which now enveloped the city. A 10-billion-dollar support package from Abu Dhabi was put into place and Dubai embarked on a fight for its life.

For years, the world's media had been covering the 'Dubai story'. Now, led by the British papers, which delighted in highlighting Dubai's woes as Britain itself struggled with the monumental impact of the global crisis, the stories of doom and gloom ran and ran. Probably the epitome of the genre was that provided by the disgraced plagiarist Johann Hari in *The Independent*. In 'The Dark Side of Dubai', a piece filed on 7 April 2009, Hari told of the 'ugly story emerging' in Dubai – of ecocide, suppression and slavery and expatriates caught up in the bust forced to live in their Range Rovers. Others soon followed suit and by July, British schadenfreude was in full force – journalists delighted in reporting that thousands of cars were abandoned at the airport as expatriates fled tides of debt in Dubai. Lurid stories of labour exploitation and the spectacular implosion of the former city of bling helped to take people's minds off their own financial woes.

The trouble was that the stories, however inaccurate and damagingly worded, were at the core of it, true. Dubai was mired in debt. Thousands had over-extended themselves, caught up in the prospect of making millions by gambling on 'flipping' property; making a down payment to gain title to an asset that was no more than a blueprint and then selling the place on before the next payment came due. With the market in full flow, healthy profits lay around every corner. When the crisis hit, the chain letter wrapped up overnight. With debt criminalised, the only alternative was flight. And fly they did, in their thousands.

On the evening of 4 January 2010, Sheikh Mohammed bin Rashid Al Maktoum inaugurated the Burj Khalifa. Right up until that point, the world's tallest tower was to be called the Burj Dubai. The spur-of-the-moment name change was a heartfelt gesture on Mohammed's part, a thank you and a sign of the unity, which a time of crisis had shown to be deeper than words. Abu Dhabi had stood by Dubai when the chips were down, when the city stood on the edge of a precipice. The Union was sovereign.

In that split second, thousands of pieces of paperwork including tenancy contracts and countless other documents as well as hundreds of road signs, all carefully prepared and ready for the launch, were trashed.

From crisis to chaos

If 2010 had started with a celebration for Dubai as it launched the world's tallest tower, it was to bring chaos to much of the Middle East as the 'Arab Spring' erupted across the region. Thousands took to the streets to protest their governments, events triggered by a young Tunisian street vendor, Mohamed Bouazizi, setting himself on fire in an act of despair and protest. It was a grim affirmation of Mohammed bin Rashid's 2004 warning to Arab leaders, 'If you do not change, you will be changed.'

Tunisia was the start of a wave of uprisings which led to the ousting of Hosni Mubarak in Egypt and the death of Moammar Gaddafi in Libya and triggered the rebellions which led to the destruction of Syria and the war in Yemen. The power of the movement across the region, spontaneous but fuelled by blindingly fast interactions across social media, was breath-taking.

Uniquely in the region, on 2 December 2010, the people of the UAE took to the streets in support of their nation. The traditional National Day parades, involving long cavalcades of gaudily painted cars and excitable kids spraying silly string, passed off without incident.

End of crisis

Dubai weathered the storm, of course, as it always had. A city of booms and busts, each rising in scale as it developed and grew, Dubai's fundamentals remained strong – trade was at the heart of the city's remarkable transformation and it was trade which continued to flow even as the realtors flew home and the developers liquidated their assets, reduced their headcount and renegotiated their payments.

Slowly, cautiously, the infrastructure projects that had been intended to address the overcrowding and traffic congestion of the boom years came on-stream. The city started to breathe easily again and projects began to resurface.

On 27 November 2013, Dubai won the bid to host Expo 2020. If Atlantis had signalled the start of the crisis, the Expo win was a signal that Dubai was once again in business.

Meanwhile, with the world's often unwelcome attention on Dubai, Abu Dhabi had quietly been laying out its plans. Sovereign investment company Mubadala rolled out the Paris-Sorbonne University in 2006, the innovative 'green' Masdar City development in 2008, built around the Masdar University, now part of Khalifa University – an institution focused on innovation and R&D in advanced sciences and sustainable technologies. Strata Manufacturing, an aerospace manufacturing company with highly sophisticated capabilities, was launched in 2010 and would become the centrepiece of the Nibras Al

Ain aerospace cluster launched in 2012. That year, satellite communications company Yahsat launched its second spacecraft following its first launch in 2011, the two spacecraft supporting connections to 140 countries.

The operations of DUBAL (Dubai Aluminium) and EMAL (Emirates Aluminium) were combined in 2014 to form Emirates Global Aluminium. The two aluminium producers had competed, with their respective plants situated either side of the Dubai/Abu Dhabi border. Together, they formed the world's largest premium aluminium producer.

Jebel Ali and its Free Zone are linked by bonded corridor to Dubai South, the site of Maktoum International Airport, a purpose-built aerotropolis that is set to overtake Dubai International as the world's busiest airport. The two airports will operate alongside each other.

In 2014, Khalifa bin Zayed Al Nahyan suffered an incapacitating stroke and his half-brother, Mohammed bin Zayed Al Nahyan, Crown Prince of Abu Dhabi and Deputy Supreme Commander of the UAE Armed Forces took over Khalifa's day-to-day duties. Close to Mohammed bin Rashid, Mohammed bin Zayed brought a new dynamism and a zest for reform and development to Abu Dhabi.

Together, MBR and MBZ, as they are known, presided over an ever-closer Union and a more assertive foreign policy role for the UAE in the Middle East. The UAE Armed Forces formed part of the Saudi Coalition against the Iranian-backed Houthi rebel forces, which had deposed the Yemeni government in 2015. They were also involved in actions in Libya following the overthrow of the Gaddafi government and the consequent chaos in the North African oil producer. Known as 'Little Sparta' to American officials, the UAE's highly trained and capable armed forces have been more active in the region than ever before. Their actions have brought criticism of the Emirates' assertive role in their wake, but there is little doubt that UAE today is willing to use both soft and hard power to promote stability and development in the region – and is also willing to balance the two in order to achieve its foreign policy goals.

With the global financial crisis behind it and with preparations for Dubai Expo 2020 underway, the country was looking forward to celebrating its fiftieth anniversary when the world faced its greatest challenge since the end of World War II: the Covid-19 pandemic. It swept the world and transformed global societies within weeks.

The pandemic had a shocking impact on some of the UAE's most iconic businesses – Emirates Airline was grounded; trade came to a virtual standstill; and food security became a critical issue as supply chains around the world fractured under the strain.

In a public message, Mohammed bin Zayed laid down an important principle to the people of the Emirates, particularly to the many expatriates who found themselves overseas in a locked down world: "I'd like to reassure every citizen and resident of the UAE that our country is infinitely able to supply everyone with all the food and medicine they could ever need."

The UAE's response was swift and decisive – a nation-wide lockdown followed by slowly easing restrictions and a vaccination programme that saw the country second only to Israel in the speed of its vaccine roll-out.

Links to Israel would also come to dominate political life with the announcement of the 'Abraham Accords', which would bring about the normalisation of relations with Israel. The move was controversial, condemned by some regional powers and yet welcomed with enthusiasm by the global community. Once again, the Emirates was showing that it had the confidence and character to play a role on the global stage.

On 13 May 2022, Sheikh Khalifa bin Zayed died following a long illness. In that period, Sheikh Mohammed bin Zayed together with Sheikh Mohammed bin Rashid had provided national leadership – now Sheikh Mohammed bin Zayed was to formally become the President of the United Arab Emirates. Acceding to the presidency on 14 May, Mohammed took the reins of a global nation, a leading soft power and one of the world's most dynamic and fastest growing economies. Diversification away from oil revenues, a pledge to deliver net zero carbon emissions by 2050 and the presidency of COP28 all became part of his first years of leadership.

New laws were passed, opening up the private sector to investment, including new classes of visas that made the Emirates a highly attractive destination for young talent. New comprehensive economic partnership agreements (CEPAs) were inked, opening global trade corridors to what had largely been considered a regional trade hub. Hard goals were set for global trade volumes, new markets were emphasised, and new investments in global strategic businesses were made.

Start-ups thrived in the open commercial environment and 'unicorns' (or start-ups with a valuation above 10 billion dollars) started springing up. As the UAE's airlines recovered from the pandemic, the movement of goods, as well as talent, increasingly saw global flows headed to the young nation and its thriving ports, airports and financial centres.

To space and beyond
When the Emirates Mars Mission was announced to the world in 2015, it appeared to be an impossible task. Few appreciated at the time that the Emirates not only operated satellites but had been involved in actively constructing and launching earth-observation satellites as part of that effort to establish a space programme. That satellite-building programme, a technology transfer initiative managed by the Mohammed bin Rashid Space Centre (MBRSC) in Dubai, was to provide the engineers and other talents for the Emirates Mars Mission. By now, learning from their South Korean partners, the fully Emirati team at MBRSC was capable of building its own satellites.

An interplanetary mission is something in the order of five times more complex than constructing, launching and operating a remote sensing satellite around the earth, and so MBRSC again sought partnerships, working together with a number of US-based academic institutions, to deliver the Emirates Mars Mission. The spacecraft, named Amal or Hope following a public consultation by Mohammed bin Rashid, reached Mars orbit in early 2021, coinciding with the fiftieth anniversary of the United Arab Emirates.

The Emirates Mars mission was followed by another, even more daring, endeavour – a mission to the asteroid belt beyond Mars, involving a number of gravity assist manoeuvres that would take the spacecraft around Venus on its journey into the yawning vastness between Mars and Jupiter to complete the largest survey of the main belt asteroids ever undertaken.

At the same time, the UAE's human spaceflight program saw astronauts visiting the International Space Station and the development of a Lunar rover by MBRSC. Ultimately, the deployment of the rover failed, a second mission followed. Alongside this, the UAE undertook to contribute elements of the NASA-led Artemis program building a space station orbiting the moon.

A new charter was released for the nation's second fifty years, the 'Principles of the 50', which outlined the core aims and goals of the nation moving forward. Of these, the third was that the Emirates' foreign policy would operate in the service of the nation's economy. It was an important assertion of the role of what had, in many ways for thousands of years, been key to the survival of the people of the Emirates – trade.

Nations can use soft power, the power of attraction, and they can use hard power, the power of coercion. The Emirates' shift to focus on asserting its soft power resulted in growing global recognition that something special was afoot in a nation that so many, over the years, had been keen to marginalise. Located in a troubled region, with ambitions and ideas way beyond its 'rightful place', the UAE was increasingly regarded as a rising soft power, home to global cities and a place where people from 195-odd nationalities could live, learn, work and play together in an atmosphere of tolerance, security, safety and opportunity.

Launching its 'nation brand', the UAE gave itself a tagline: 'the impossible is possible'.

And as the UAE moved into its second fifty years, the young nation made a decision to operate its foreign policy in service of its economy – and expand its regional leadership as a trade hub to encompass a global position. As it does so, it can look back to an incredibly colourful and varied history with the confidence to not only tell that history but delve into it, celebrate and investigate it. There are lessons for the young people of the country in those dusty pages and perhaps even inspirations for them – from the flint-knapping people of the Neolithic period through to the hardship of *bustan* plantations, nomadic tribes and the coastal trading settlements sweating under their *barjeel* (wind towers) to the foundation of the Union and the modern nation-state, the UAE is rooted in trade and cosmopolitanism. It is perhaps pleasantly ironic that it finds itself as a nation precisely where it started as a human settlement, all those millennia ago.

As a bustling and dynamic international centre for trade.

Endnotes

Preface

1. The Ealing Comedies is a series of comedy films produced by Ealing Studios, London, between 1947 and 1957. They are still regarded as treasured English classics among cinephiles.

Introduction | Crime and Punishment

1. Albion is a literary term for Britain, often used historically.
2. A Man-of-War was a British Royal Navy expression for an armed sailing ship from the period between the sixteenth and nineteenth century.
3. Pax Britannica is the term applied to the hegemonial peace and stability established by the British Empire, especially during the nineteenth century.
4. Zayed the Great ruled Abu Dhabi from 1885 to 1909. He was the grandfather of the late Sheikh Zayed bin Sultan Al Nahyan, the Founder and first President of the UAE.
5. F. Hojlund, "The First Excavations in the UAE, 1959–72", in *Fifty Years of Emirates Archaeology*, ed. D. T. Potts and P. Hellyer (Dubai: Motivate Media Group and Ministry of Culture, 2012).
6. F. Hojlund, *Glob and the Garden of Eden: The Danish Expeditions to the Arabian Gulf* (Moesgard Museum, 1999).

Chapter 1 | The Emergence of Man

1. G. Bailey, A. Al Sharekh, N. Flemming, K. Lambeck et al., "Coastal Prehistory in the Southern Red Sea Basin, Underwater Archaeology, and the Farasan Islands", *Proceedings of the Seminar for Arabian Studies*, 37 (2007), p. 3.
2. A. G. Parker, "Pleistocene Climate Change in Arabia: Developing a Framework for Hominin Dispersal over the Last 350ka", in *The Evolution of Human Populations in Arabia*, (Springer, 2010), pp. 39–49.

3. K. Bretzke, S. J. Armitage, A. G. Parker, H. Walkington, H. P. Uerpmann, "The Environmental Context of Paleolithic Settlement at Jebel Faya, Emirate of Sharjah, UAE", *Quaternary International*, 300 (2013), pp. 83–93.
4. I. Al Abed and P. Hellyer (eds.), *United Arab Emirates: A New Perspective* (London: Trident Press, 2001), p. 35.

Chapter 2 | The End of Eden

1. D. J Kennet and J. P. Kennet, "Early State Formation in Southern Mesopotamia: Sea Levels, Shorelines and Climate Change", *The Journal of Island and Coastal Archaeology*, 1/1 (2006), pp. 67–99.
2. J. I. Rose, "New Light on Human Prehistory in the Arabo-Persian Gulf Oasis", *Current Anthropology*, 51/6 (2010), pp. 849–68.
3. A. R. George, *The Babylonian Gilgamesh Epic: Introduction, Critical Edition and Cuneiform Texts* (New York: Oxford University Press, 2012), p. 70.
4. Kennet and Kennet, "Early State Formation in Southern Mesopotamia", pp. 67–99.
5. Al Abed and Hellyer, *United Arab Emirates: A New Perspective*, p. 35.
6. Kennet and Kennet, "Early State Formation in Southern Mesopotamia", pp. 67–99.
7. Rose, "New Light on Human Prehistory in the Arabo-Persian Gulf Oasis", pp. 849–68.
8. Kennet and Kennet, "Early State Formation in Southern Mesopotamia", pp. 67–99.
9. D. T. Potts, "The Archaeology and Early History of the Persian Gulf", in *The Persian Gulf in History* (London: Palgrave Macmillan, 2009), pp. 27–38.
10. H. Kallweit, "Remarks on the Late Stone Age in the UAE", in *Archaeology of the United Arab Emirates* (London: Trident Press, 2003), pp. 56–63.
11. M. Uerpmann, "The Dark Millennium – Remarks on the Final Stone Age in the Emirates and Oman", in *Archaeology of the United Arab Emirates* (London: Trident Press, 2003), pp. 74–85.
12. The stability of the sea level was relative – rises and falls of sea levels by several metres still took place after that time.
13. Kennet and Kennet, "Early State Formation in Southern Mesopotamia", pp. 67–99.
14. Rose, "New Light on Human Prehistory in the Arabo-Persian Gulf Oasis", pp. 849–68.

15. Al Abed and Hellyer, *United Arab Emirates: A New Perspective*, p. 35.
16. Potts, "The Archaeology and Early History of the Persian Gulf", in *The Persian Gulf in History*, pp. 27–38.

Chapter 3 | The Lords of Magan

17. Potts, "The Archaeology and Early History of the Persian Gulf", in *The Persian Gulf in History*, pp. 27–38.
18. D. T. Potts, *Ancient Magan: The Secrets of Tell Abraq* (London: Trident Press), 2000.
19. R. Thomas and D. T. Potts, "Atacamite Pigment at Tell Abraq in the Early Iron Age", *Arabian Archaeology and Epigraphy*, 7/1 (1999), pp. 13–16.
20. A. Hauptmann et al., "On the Making and Provenancing of Pigments from the Early Dynastic Royal Tombs of Ur, Mesopotamia", *Metalla*, 1/22 (2016), pp. 41–74.
21. Potts, *Ancient Magan*, 2000.
22. Ibid.
23. Potts, "The Archaeology and Early History of the Persian Gulf", in *The Persian Gulf in History*, pp. 27–38.
24. Ibid.
25. M. E. L. Mallowan, "The Mechanics of Ancient Trade in Western Asia", *Iran: Journal of the British Institute of Persian Studies*, 3/1 (1965), pp. 1–7.
26. Potts, "The Archaeology and Early History of the Persian Gulf", in *The Persian Gulf in History*, pp. 27–38.

Chapter 4 | Death in the Mountains

1. N. S. Al Jahwari, "The Agricultural Basis of Umm an-Nar Society in the Northern Oman Peninsula (2500–2000 BCE)", *Arabian Archaeology and Epigraphy*, 20/2 (2009), pp. 122–33.
2. Al Abed and Hellyer, *United Arab Emirates: A New Perspective*, pp. 46–8.
3. R. Carter, "The Wadi Suq Period in South-East Arabia: A Reappraisal in the Light of Excavations at Kalba, UAE", *Proceedings of the Seminar for Arabian Studies*, 27 (1997), pp. 87–97.
4. R. Carter, "Saar and its External Relations: New Evidence for Interaction between Bahrain and Gujarat during the Early Second Millennium BC", *Arabian Archaeology and Epigraphy*, 12/2 (2001), pp. 183–201.

5. R. Carter, "The Wadi Suq Period in South-East Arabia", pp. 87–97.
6. L. Gregoricka, "Human Response to Climate Change during the Umm An-Nar/Wadi Suq Transition in the United Arab Emirates", *International Journal of Osteoarchaeology*, 26 (2014), pp. 211–20.
7. P. Magee, "Beyond the Desert and the Sown: Settlement Intensification in Late Prehistoric Southeastern Arabia", *Bulletin of the American Schools of Oriental Research*, 347 (2007), pp. 83–105.
8. Ibid.
9. J. Charbonnier, L. Purdue, C. Calastrenc, E. Regagnon et al., "Ancient Agricultural Landscapes in Southeast Arabia: Approach and First Results of an Archaeological, Geo-Archaeological and Spatial Study of the Masafi Palm Grove, Emirate of Fujairah", *Proceedings of Water and Life in Arabia Conference*, 2014.
10. Magee, "Beyond the Desert and the Sown", pp. 83–105.
11. M. Mouton, A. Benoist and J. M. Cordoba, "The Snake Figuration in Iron Age Society", *Liwa*, 3/5 (2011), pp. 3–26.
12. Charbonnier et al., "Ancient Agricultural Landscapes in Southeast Arabia", 2014.
13. Magee, "Beyond the Desert and the Sown", pp. 83–105.
14. P. K. Hitti, *History of the Arabs* (London: Macmillan, 1961).
15. L. K. Handy, *The Age of Solomon: Scholarship at the Turn of the Millennium* (Leiden [The Netherlands]; New York: Brill, 1997).

Chapter 5 | The Impossible Desert Forge

1. J. T. Hermann, J. Casana and H. S. Qandil, "A Sequence of Inland Desert Settlement in the Oman Peninsula: 2008–2009 Excavations at Saruq al-Hadid, Dubai, UAE", *Arabian Archaeology and Epigraphy*, 23/1 (2012), pp. 50–69.
2. L. Weeks, C. Cable, K. Franke, C. Newton et al., "Recent Archaeological Research at Saruq al-Hadid, Dubai", *Arabian Archaeology and Epigraphy*, 28/1 (2017), pp. 31–60.
3. A. Benoist, "An Iron Age II Snake Cult in the Oman Peninsula: Evidence from Bithnah (Emirate of Fujairah)", *Arabian Archaeology and Epigraphy*, 18/1 (2007), pp. 34–54.
4. Ibid.

5. Al Abed and Hellyer, *United Arab Emirates: A New Perspective*, p. 35.
6. Charbonnier et al., "Ancient Agricultural Landscapes in Southeast Arabia", 2014.
7. Potts, "The Archaeology and Early History of the Persian Gulf", in *The Persian Gulf in History*, pp. 27–38.
8. Al Abed and Hellyer, *United Arab Emirates: A New Perspective*, p. 35.

Chapter 6 | The Rise of Mleiha

1. P. Stein, "Languages and Scripts in the Arabian Gulf in the Hellenistic Period: The Epigraphic Evidence from Mleiha (Sharjah, UAE)", in *Ancient South Arabia through History: Kingdoms, Tribes and Traders* (Newcastle upon Tyn: Cambridge Scholars Publishing, 2019).
2. Al Abed and Hellyer, *United Arab Emirates: A New Perspective*, p. 53.
3. Ibid, p. 35.
4. Pliny, the Elder, *The Natural History*, book vi: *An Account of Countries, Nations, Seas, Towns, Havens, Mountains, Rivers, Distances and Peoples Who Now Exist, or Formerly Existed*, trans. J. Bostock and H. T. Riley (London: Taylor and Francis, 1855).
5. A. Kutterer, B. Overlaet, C. E. Miller, J. Kutterer et al., "Late Pre-Islamic Burials at Mleiha", *Arabian Archaeology and Epigraphy*, 25/2 (2014), pp. 175–85.
6. D. Kennet, "The Decline of Eastern Arabia in the Sasanian Period", *Arabian Archaeology and Epigraphy*, 18/1 (2007), pp. 86–122.
7. Ibid.
8. N. S. Al Jahwari, D. Kennet, S. Priestman and E. Sauer, "Fulayj: A Late Sasanian Fort on the Arabian Coast", *Antiquity*, 92/363 (2018), pp. 724–41.
9. R. Carter, "Christianity in the Gulf during the First Centuries of Islam", *Arabian Archaeology and Epigraphy*, 19/1 (2008), pp. 71–108.

Chapter 7 | Here Lie 10,000 Men

1. D. Kennet, "On the Eve of Islam: Archaeological Evidence from Eastern Arabia", *Antiquity*, 79/303 (2004), pp. 107–18.
2. P. Hellyer interview: "Review of Arabian Archaeological and Historical Resources and Evidence" (July 2019).
3. Hitti, *History of the Arabs*.

4. S. b. S. b. Al Sirhan, *Annals of Oman*, trans. E. C. Ross (Calcutta: Baptist Mission Press, 1874).
5. Ibid.
6. A. J. M. b. J. Al Tabari, *The History of Prophets and Kings* (915).
7. Ibid.

Chapter 8 | Schism, Rift and War

1. D. Hawley, *The Trucial States* (London: George Allen & Unwin, 1971).
2. S. b. Razik, *History of the Imams and Seyyids of 'Oman*, trans. G. P. Badger (London: The Hakluyt Society, 1871).
3. Al Sirhan, *Annals of Oman*.
4. Razik, *History of the Imams and Seyyids of 'Oman*.
5. Ibid.
6. Al Sirhan, *Annals of Oman*.
7. Tabari, *The History of Prophets and Kings*.
8. Ibid.
9. Al Sirhan, *Annals of Oman*, p. 14.
10. Razik, *History of the Imams and Seyyids of 'Oman*.
11. Al Sirhan, *Annals of Oman*, p. 23.

Chapter 9 | Lords of the Seven Seas

1. T. Severin, *The Sindbad Voyage* (New York: Modern Library, 2000).
2. Potts, *Ancient Magan*, 2000.
3. P. Hellyer interview: "Review of Arabian Archaeological and Historical Resources and Evidence" (July 2019).
4. Hawley, *The Trucial States*, pp. 54–55.
5. El Masudi, *Meadows of Gold and Mines of Gems*, trans. A. Sprenger (London: Oriental Translation Fund, 1841).
6. P. Hellyer interview: "Review of Arabian Archaeological and Historical Resources and Evidence" (July 2019).
7. D. Kennet, "Kush: A Sasanian and Islamic-Period Archaeological Tell in Ras al-Khaimah (UAE)", *Arabian Archaeology and Epigraphy*, 8/2 (1997), pp. 284–302.
8. Al Abed and P. Hellyer, *United Arab Emirates: A New Perspective*, p. 35.
9. C. R. Low, *History of the Indian Navy (1613–1863)*; vol i (London: Richard Bentley and Son, 1877).

10. D. Kennet, "The Development of Northern Ras Al Khaimah and the 14th-Century Hormuzi Economic Boom in the Lower Gulf", in *Proceedings of the Seminar for Arabian Studies*, 32 (2002).
11. D. Kennet, "Kush: A Sasanian and Islamic-Period Archaeological Tell in Ras al-Khaimah (UAE)", pp. 284–302.
12. M. B. Vosoughi, "The Kings of Hormuz: From the Beginning Until the Arrival of the Portuguese", in *The Persian Gulf in History* (New York: Palgrave Macmillan, 2009), pp. 89–104.
13. P. Hellyer interview: "Review of Arabian Archaeological and Historical Resources and Evidence" (July 2019).
14. R. Kauz and R. Ptak, "Hormuz in Yuan and Ming Sources", *Bulletin de l'Ecole Française d'Extrême-Orient*, 88 (2001), pp. 27–75.
15. L. Meicun and R. Zhang, "Zheng He's Voyages to Hormuz: The Archaeological Evidence", *Antiquity*, 89/344 (2015), pp. 417–32.
16. B. Zhao, R. Carter and C. Velde, "The Chinese Ceramic Sherds Unearthed at the Julfar al-Nudud Port Site in the Emirate of Ras-al-Khaimah, United Arab Emirates", *Chinese Cultural Relics* (2015), pp. 144–62.
17. Vosoughi, "The Kings of Hormuz: From the Beginning Until the Arrival of the Portuguese", in *The Persian Gulf in History*, pp. 89–104.

Chapter 10 | The Portuguese Sword and Cross

1. S. M. Ghazanfar, "Vasco da Gama's Voyages to India: Messianism, Mercantilism and Sacred Exploits", *Journal of Global Initiatives: Policy, Pedagogy, Perspective*, 13/1 (2018), pp. 15–40.
2. D. Northrup, "Vasco da Gama and Africa: An Era of Mutual Discovery, 1497–1800", *Journal of World History*, 9/2 (1998), pp. 189–211.
3. S. Subrahmanyam, *The Career and Legend of Vasco da Gama* (Cambridge: Cambridge University Press, 1998), pp. 126–30.
4. Ghazanfar, "Vasco da Gama's Voyages to India: Messianism, Mercantilism and Sacred Exploits", pp. 15–40.
5. R. M. Loureiro, "The Portuguese in Hormuz and the Trade in Chinese Porcelain", *Bulletin of Portuguese Japanese Studies*, 5/26 (2015), pp. 5–26.
6. A. d. Albuquerque, *The Commentaries of the Great Alfonso Dalboquerque*, trans. W. d. G. Birch (London: Hakluyt Society, 1774).
7. Ibid.
8. Ibid.

9. Ibid.
10. The Xerafin was a small gold coin, a Portuguese unit of currency, developed in Goa for use in India.
11. Sublime Porte, which stood for the government of the Ottoman Empire, is French for the Turkish *Bâbıâli* (meaning 'High Gate' or 'Gate of the Eminent').
12. J. T. e. Cunha, "The Portuguese Presence in the Persian Gulf", in *The Persian Gulf in History* (New York: Palgrave Macmillan, 2009), pp. 207–34.
13. D. T. Potts, "The Portuguese on Qeshm", in *Portugal, The Persian Gulf and Safavid Persia* (Belgium: Peeters Publishers, 2011), pp. 99–118.
14. J. Hansman, *Julfar: An Arabic Port* (Oxfordshire: Routledge, 2002), p. 70.

Chapter 11 | The Company and the Prophet

1. J. Everaert, "Pourquoi les Factories?", *International Conference on Shipping, Factories and Colonization (Brussels, 24-26 November 1994)* (1997).
2. Low, *History of the Indian Navy (1613–1863)*, vol i, p. 8.
3. Ibid.
4. Ibid.
5. Ibid, p. 64.
6. Ibid, p. 78.
7. Ibid, p. 88.
8. Ibid, p. 85.
9. Razik, *History of the Imams and Seyyids of 'Oman*, p. 99.
10. Hawley, *The Trucial States*, p. 46.
11. Al Sirhan, *Annals of Oman*, p. 63.
12. It is noted by Razik that many of Rahma's followers from Ras Al Khaimah 'could not speak good Arabic', likely because they were of the Al Shihuh tribe of Rus Al Jibal, the mountainous hinterland of Ras Al Khaimah. The Shihuh had their own distinctive language, thought to have derived from an admixture of Arabic, Portuguese and Persian.
13. Razik, *History of the Imams and Seyyids of 'Oman*, p. 113.
14. Ibid, p. 111.
15. Ibid, p. 138.
16. Ibid, pp. 228–9.
17. J. G. Lorimer, *Gazetteer of the Persian Gulf, Oman and Central Arabia*, vol i: *Historical* (Calcutta: Superintendent Government Printing, 1915), p. 70.

Chapter 12 | The Arrival of Albion

1. Lorimer, *Gazetteer of the Persian Gulf, Oman and Central Arabia*, vol i, p. 135.
2. A *tranki* was a traditional Arab dhow, a 'sewn ship' – made with great skill out of hardwood and tied together with coir rope – much as Tim Severin's Sohar reconstruction, built in the 1980s; *see* Severin, *The Sindbad Voyage*.
3. Lorimer, *Gazetteer of the Persian Gulf, Oman and Central Arabia*, vol i, p. 96.
4. A Maharajah was, literally, a 'Great King' (in Sanskrit) of a Hindu state while his wife or, indeed, a 'Great Queen' ruling in her own right was a Maharani. A Rajah was also a King, although not quite as 'Great'; the title Nawab was granted to a provincial ruler of a Mughal state (Begum is the female title); Mir, or Amir, was the ruler of a Muslim Princely State. A Khansaman was the head of a household, or steward. I know this because I have an excellent recipe for a chicken curry dating from 1845 which was obtained directly from the hand of the 'Khansaman of the King of Oudh'. Pop me an email and I'll happily share it!
5. Lorimer, *Gazetteer of the Persian Gulf, Oman and Central Arabia*, vol i, p. 138.
6. Ibid, p. 95.
7. S. b. M. Al Qasimi, *The Myth of Arab Piracy in the Gulf* (London: Croom Helm, 1986), p. 31.
8. Severin, *The Sindbad Voyage*.
9. Low, *History of the Indian Navy (1613–1863)*; vol i, pp. 169–70.
10. Lorimer, *Gazetteer of the Persian Gulf, Oman and Central Arabia*, vol i, p. 158.
11. Ibid, p. 633.
12. Ibid, p. 634.
13. Low, *History of the Indian Navy (1613–1863)*; vol i, p. 209.
14. Al Qasimi, *The Myth of Arab Piracy in the Gulf*, p. 34.
15. Lorimer, *Gazetteer of the Persian Gulf, Oman and Central Arabia*, vol i, p. 634.
16. Al Qasimi, *The Myth of Arab Piracy in the Gulf*, p. 36.
17. Low, *History of the Indian Navy (1613–1863)*; vol i, p. 356.
18. F. Warden, "Historical Sketch of the Joasmee Tribe of Arabs; From the Year 1747 to the Year 1819", in Hughes-Thomas, *Arabian Gulf Intelligence* (Cambridge: Oleander Press, 1985), p. 303.

Chapter 13 | Exile and the Kingdom

1. Lorimer, *Gazetteer of the Persian Gulf, Oman and Central Arabia*, vol i, p. 180.
2. Low, *History of the Indian Navy (1613–1863)*; vol i, p. 316.

3. Razik, *History of the Imams and Seyyids of 'Oman*, p. 240.
4. Lorimer, *Gazetteer of the Persian Gulf, Oman and Central Arabia*, vol i, p. 637.
5. Low, *History of the Indian Navy (1613–1863)*; vol i, p. 317.
6. Warden, "Historical Sketch of the Joasmee Arabs", in *Arabian Gulf Intelligence*, pp. 303–4.
7. Lorimer, *Gazetteer of the Persian Gulf, Oman and Central Arabia*, vol i, p. 645.
8. Ibid, p. 182.
9. Ibid, p. 637.
10. Al Qasimi, *The Myth of Arab Piracy in the Gulf*, p. 72.
11. Warden, "Historical Sketch of the Joasmee Arabs", in *Arabian Gulf Intelligence*, p. 304.
12. Ibid, p. 305.
13. Low, *History of the Indian Navy (1613–1863)*; vol i, pp. 620–3.
14. Lorimer, *Gazetteer of the Persian Gulf, Oman and Central Arabia*, vol i, p. 643.
15. Razik, *History of the Imams and Seyyids of 'Oman*, p. 452.
16. Low, *History of the Indian Navy (1613–1863)*; vol i, p. 323.
17. Ibid, pp. 326–35.
18. Ibid, p. 326.
19. Lorimer, *Gazetteer of the Persian Gulf, Oman and Central Arabia*, vol i, p. 648.

Chapter 14 | The Trucial Coast

1. Low, *History of the Indian Navy (1613–1863)*; vol i, p. 338.
2. Lorimer, *Gazetteer of the Persian Gulf, Oman and Central Arabia*, vol i, p. 653.
3. Warden, "Historical Sketch of the Joasmee Arabs", in *Arabian Gulf Intelligence*, p. 310.
4. Low, *History of the Indian Navy (1613–1863)*; vol i, pp. 345–6.
5. Lorimer, *Gazetteer of the Persian Gulf, Oman and Central Arabia*, vol i, p. 669.
6. Ibid, pp. 673–4.

Chapter 15 | The Father of the Gazelle

1. Lorimer, *Gazetteer of the Persian Gulf, Oman and Central Arabia*, vol i, p. 763.
2. A. B. Kemball, "Historical Sketch of the Beniyas Tribe of Arabs", in *Arabian Gulf Intelligence* (Cambridge: Oleander Press, 1985), pp. 210–1.
3. Lorimer, *Gazetteer of the Persian Gulf, Oman and Central Arabia*, vol i, p. 764.

4. Ibid, pp. 685–6.
5. Ibid, p. 690.
6. Ibid, p. 690.
7. Ibid, p. 448.
8. Ibid, p. 453.
9. Ibid, pp. 681–2.
10. G. Wilson, *Father of Dubai: Sheikh Rashid bin Saeed Al Maktoum* (Dubai: Media Prima, 1999), pp. 22–3.
11. Lorimer, *Gazetteer of the Persian Gulf, Oman and Central Arabia*, vol i, p. 766.
12. Ibid, pp. 692–3.
13. Ibid, p. 688.
14. The silver Maria Theresa thaler (or dollar) was the common currency of the time, and accepted almost everywhere in the world. It was minted in 1741 and named after Empress Maria Theresa who ruled Austria, Hungary and Bohemia from 1740 to 1780. They were used for trading well into the middle of the twentieth century.
15. Lorimer, *Gazetteer of the Persian Gulf, Oman and Central Arabia*, vol i, pp. 683–4.
16. Ibid, p. 694.

Chapter 16 | War in the Sands

1. Lorimer, *Gazetteer of the Persian Gulf, Oman and Central Arabia*, vol i, p. 703.
2. Ibid, p. 718.
3. F. Heard-Bey, *From Trucial States to United Arab Emirates* (Dubai: Motivate Media Group, 2004), pp. 210–1.
4. Lorimer, *Gazetteer of the Persian Gulf, Oman and Central Arabia*, vol i, pp. 711–4.
5. Ibid, p. 706.
6. Heard-Bey, *From Trucial States to United Arab Emirates*, p. 48.
7. Lorimer, *Gazetteer of the Persian Gulf, Oman and Central Arabia*, vol i, p. 715.
8. Ibid, p. 718.
9. Ibid, p. 715.
10. Ibid, p. 718.

Chapter 17 | Of Perpetual Peace
1. Low, *History of the Indian Navy (1613–1863)*; vol i, p. 376.
2. Hennell, arguably the greatest of the Political Residents of the Arabian Gulf, was tragically to see both of his sons die in 1879 in the Second Anglo-Afghan War. Hennell himself died a year later. A memorial plaque to both young men is in the Holy Trinity Church at Ventnor on the Isle of Wight.
3. Lorimer, *Gazetteer of the Persian Gulf, Oman and Central Arabia*, vol i, p. 773.
4. Ibid, p. 773.
5. Ibid, pp. 707–9.
6. Ibid, p. 757.
7. Ibid, p. 759.
8. Ibid, p. 779.
9. Ibid, p. 622.
10. Ibid, p. 722.
11. Ibid, p. 727.
12. Ibid, p. 727.
13. Ibid, p. 759.

Chapter 18 | The Rise of the Tribes and Zayed the Great
1. Heard-Bey, *From Trucial States to United Arab Emirates*, p. 50.
2. Lorimer, *Gazetteer of the Persian Gulf, Oman and Central Arabia*, vol i, p. 768.
3. Ibid, p. 721.
4. Ibid, p. 893.
5. Low, *History of the Indian Navy (1613–1863)*; vol i, p. 557.
6. Lorimer, *Gazetteer of the Persian Gulf, Oman and Central Arabia*, vol i, p. 245.
7. Ibid, p. 723.
8. Ibid, p. 731.
9. Ibid, p. 727.
10. Ibid, p. 760.
11. Ibid, p. 726.
12. Ibid, p. 729.
13. Ibid, pp. 779–81.
14. Ibid, p. 724.
15. Ibid, p. 780.
16. Ibid, p. 821.
17. Ibid, p. 761.

18. Ibid, p. 725.
19. Ibid, p. 781.
20. Ibid, p. 771.

Chapter 19 | The Protectorate and the Darbar

1. Lorimer, *Gazetteer of the Persian Gulf, Oman and Central Arabia*, vol i, p. 736.
2. Ibid, p. 737.
3. Ibid, p. 738.
4. Ibid, p. 783.
5. Ibid, p. 740.
6. Wilson, *Father of Dubai: Sheikh Rashid bin Saeed Al Maktoum*, p. 31.
7. Lorimer, *Gazetteer of the Persian Gulf, Oman and Central Arabia*, vol i, p. 750.
8. Ibid, p. 743.
9. Ibid, p. 2626.
10. Ibid, p. 741.
11. Ibid, p. 784.
12. Ibid, p. 752.
13. Ibid, p. 752.
14. Ibid, p. 753.
15. Ibid, p. 754.
16. RIMS stands for Royal Indian Marine Service, the naval force of British India.
17. W. Shakespear, "Report of the 20th December 1910 from the Political Agent, Kuwait, to the Political Resident, Bushire", 1910.
18. J. Dick, "Report of James Dick of the HMS Hyacinth to CIC HM Ships and Vessels, East Indies", 1910.
19. P. Cox, "Telegram 33 dated 12/1/1911 to the Foreign Secretary, Calcutta", 1911.
20. P. Cox, "Telegram 35 dated 12/1/1911 to the Foreign Secretary, Calcutta", 1911.
21. P. Cox, "To the Secretary to the Government of India in the Foreign Department, 8th January 1911", 1911.

Chapter 20 | Troubled Times in Sharjah

1. P. Hellyer interview: "Review of Arabian Archaeological and Historical Resources and Evidence" (July 2019).
2. P. Cox, "Persian Gulf Residency Monthly Reports 1911–1920".

3. "The Trucial Chiefs, 1908–28", 1928, India Office Records and Private Papers, British Library: IOR/L/PS/18/B403.
4. S. G. Knox, "Persian Gulf Residency Monthly Report, May 1914", p. 51.
5. A. P. Trevor, "Persian Gulf Residency Monthly Report: April 1916".
6. R. S. Zahlan, *The Origins of the United Arab Emirates: A Political and Social History of the Trucial States* (London: Routledge, 2016), p. 51.
7. Lorimer, *Gazetteer of the Persian Gulf, Oman and Central Arabia*, vol i, p. 1,758.
8. A. P. Trevor, "Summary of News of His Majesty's Political Residency in the Persian Gulf, July 1917".
9. Layyah, today the site of Sharjah city's power and desalination plant and port, was at the time a settlement in its own right.
10. Heard-Bey, *From Trucial States to United Arab Emirates*, pp. 214, 215.
11. F. B. Prideaux, "Persian Gulf Residency – Summary of News from the Arab States of June 1926".
12. Zahlan, *The Origins of the United Arab Emirates*, p. 165.
13. I. b. A. A. Serkal, "Telegram to British Resident, Bushire: 15th October 1925".
14. Ibid.
15. S. Horner, "Report to Political Resident, 19th November 1925".
16. F. B. Prideaux, "Persian Gulf Residency – Summary of News from the Arab States of June 1926".
17. Ibid.

Chapter 21 | The Passing of the Pearls

1. Heard-Bey, *From Trucial States to United Arab Emirates*, p. 89.
2. K. Nagai, "A History of the Cultured Pearl Industry", *Zoological Science*, 30/10 (2013), p. 784.
3. Zahlan, *The Origins of the United Arab Emirates*, p. 41.
4. F. W. Johnston, "Persian Gulf Residency – Summary of News from the Arab States of February 1929".
5. C. C. J. Barrett, "Persian Gulf Residency – Summary of News from the Arab States of September 1929".
6. "Memo from Political Agent, Bahrain to Resident, Bushire: 18th June 1933".
7. "Persian Gulf Residency – Summary of News from the Arab States of November 1929".
8. "Persian Gulf Residency – Summary of News from the Arab States of September 1930".

Chapter 22 | Look Up to the Blue Sky

1. C. Baxter, "Foreign Office to Air Ministry 15th March 1932".
2. "Imperial Airways to Air Ministry, 23rd March 1932".
3. "Imperial Airways to Air Ministry, 10th March 1932".
4. Telegram: "Political Resident in the Persian Gulf to Government of India, 26th March 1932".
5. Telegram: "RAF HQ Iraq to Air Ministry, 9th April 1932".
6. Telegram: "Biscoe to Foreign Secretary, Government of India: 7th May 1932".
7. Letter: "Biscoe to Foreign Office, Government of India, Simla, 10 May 1932".
8. Telegram: "Biscoe to Secretary of State for India, 18th February 1931".
9. Telegram: "Biscoe to Government of India, 13th May 1932".
10. "Appendix No 1 to Senior Naval Officer, Persian Gulf, Communication 125/587, 10th June 1932".
11. Confidential Report: "Dickson to The India Office, 4th August 1932".
12. Report: "Political Agency, Kuwait, to India Office, London, dated 4th August 1932".
13. One did, in 1933, which triggered 'the beach pyjama incident', following which the Ruler was exhorted to enforce the 'no visits' provision by the Political Resident who feared for the safety of European passengers wandering around Sharjah's souks – particularly as the lady passenger who caused the incident was wearing 'beach pyjamas', a racy outfit for wandering around any Western town at the time, let alone the remote and conservative Sharjah! *See* T. Fowle, "Letter to Ruler of Sharjah, 30th March 1933".
14. "Agreement between Sheikh Sultan bin Saqr, Ruler of Sharjah, and the British Government for the Establishment of an Air Station in Sharjah".
15. S. b. M. Al Qasimi, *Sharjah Air Station – Between East and West* (Sharjah: Al Qasimi Publications, 2012), pp. 59–875
16. W. Lancaster and F. Lancaster, *Honour is in Contentment : Life Before Oil in Ras Al-Khaimah (UAE) and Some Neighbouring Regions* (Berlin, New York: De Gruyter, 2011), p. 550.
17. Memorandum: "British Residency Agent to Political Agent, Bahrain, 5th May 1937".
18. Telegram: "Political Resident, Bushire, to Political Agent, Bahrain, 22nd June 1937 and 26th June 1937".

19. Telegram: "Political Agent, Bahrain (in Karachi), to Residency Agent, Sharjah, 14th August 1937".
20. Telegram: "Political Agent, Bahrain, to Political Resident, Bushire, 29th August 1937".

Chapter 23 | Oil, Rebellion and War

1. S. Hope, *Arabian Adventurer: The Story of Haji Williamson* (London: Robert Hale, 1951).
2. D. Heard, *From Pearls to Oil: How the Oil Industry Came to the United Arab Emirates* (Dubai: Motivate Media Group, 2011), pp. 72–4.
3. Ibid, p. 193.
4. Ibid, pp. 232–4.
5. Telegram: "Senior Naval Officer in the Persian Gulf (SNOPG) to Political Resident, 23rd October 1934".
6. "Summary of the News from the Arab States for March 1930".
7. "Residency Agent, Sharjah, diary no. 2 from 16–31 January 1936".
8. "Note on Local Affairs, Residency Agent, Sharjah, 31st May 1938".
9. Confidential Memo: "To Political Resident, Bahrain, from Residency Agent, Sharjah, 18th June 1938".
10. Confidential Memo: "British Agency, Sharjah, to Political Agent, Bahrain, 11th October 1938".
11. Confidential Memo: "British Agency, Sharjah, to Political Agent, Bahrain, 24th March 1939".
12. Confidential Memo: "British Agency, Sharjah, to Political Agent, Bahrain, 31st March 1939".
13. Confidential Memo: "Weightman to Political Resident, Bushire, 6th April 1939".
14. "Letters from Sheikh Sultan bin Salim Al Qasimi to Mani bin Rashid, 16th May 1938".
15. "Secret and personal memo from British Agency Sharjah to Political Agent, Bahrain, 29th September 1938".
16. Confidential Memo: "British Resident Agent to British Political Agent, 31st March 1940".
17. Confidential Memo: "British Residency Agent to Political Agent, 6th January 1939".
18. Telegram: "Residency Agent Sharjah to Political Agent, 10th August 1942".

19. Confidential Memo: "Political Resident to Political Agents in Kuwait, Bahrain and Muscat – 17th March 1939".
20. Secret Memorandum: "British Agency, Sharjah, to Political Agent, Bahrain, 28th June 1940".
21. A. Iqbal, P. Hellyer and L. Garey, "The UAE in World War Two: A Forgotten Fatal Air Crash in Sharjah", *Tribulus*, 25 (2017), pp. 25–31.
22. J. Beasant, *Stalin's Silver* (London: Bloomsbury, 1995).
23. Wilson, *Father of Dubai: Sheikh Rashid bin Saeed Al Maktoum*, p. 71.
24. Letter: "From Britagent, Sharjah, to Political Agent, Bahrain, 19th October 1945".
25. Letter: "To AC Galloway from (Political Officer Sharjah?), 31st October".
26. Letter: "From RER Bird to Political Agent, Bahrain, 22nd October 1945".
27. M. b. R. Al Maktoum, *My Story* (Dubai: Explorer Publishing, 2019), p. 33.
28. Letter: "Political Resident, Persian Gulf, to Political Agent, Bahrain, 26th October 1945".
29. Confidential Memo: "Political Agent, Bahrain, to Political Resident, Bahrain, 31st October 1945".
30. Letter: "Britagent, Sharjah to Political Agent, Bahrain, 31st October 1945".
31. Confidential Memo: "Britagent, Sharjah, to Political Agent, Bahrain, 10th November 1945".
32. Telegram: "Political Officer, Trucial Coast (POTC) Sharjah, to Political Agent, Bahrain, 21st January 1946".
33. Express Letter: "Political Sharjah to Political Bahrain – 29th June 1946".
34. Letter: "C/586 from Political Agent Bahrain to Sheikh Shakhbut bin Sultan, 15th May 1947".
35. Confidential Memo: "37.0215 from Residency Agent, Sharjah, to Political Agent, Bahrain, 12th January 1948".
36. Confidential Memo: "1081/2 to Foreign office: RFG Serell to Sir Rupert Hay, 22nd May 1952".
37. Heard-Bey, *From Trucial States to United Arab Emirates*, p. 61.

Chapter 24 | The Buraimi Incident

1. Hawley, *The Trucial States*, pp. 172–3.
2. M. M. Al Hammadi, *Britain and the Administration of the Trucial States (1947–1965)* (Abu Dhabi: The Emirates Center For Strategic Studies and Research (ECSSR), 2013), p. 46.
3. Ibid, p. 56.

4. F. d. Butts, *Now the Dust has Settled: Memories of War and Peace, 1939–1994* (Padstow: Tabb House, 1995).
5. G. B. Paul, *Bagpipes in Babylon: A Lifetime in the Arab World and Beyond* (London: I. B. Tauris, 2005), p. 191.
6. Al Hammadi, *Britain and the Administration of the Trucial States (1947–1965)*, p. 69.
7. Memo: "Cabinet Office Memo C (53) 128, 17th April 1953".
8. *With United Strength: HH Sheikh Zayed bin Sultan Al Nahyan: The Leader and the Nation* (Abu Dhabi: ECSSR, 2013), p. 233.
9. Hawley, *The Trucial States*, p. 190.
10. E. Henderson, *This Strange Eventful History: Memoirs of Earlier Days in the UAE and the Sultanate of Oman* (Dubai: Motivate Media Group, 1993), p. 211.
11. Hawley, *The Trucial States*, p. 175.
12. T. Ward, *Are You the Man? Memories of Life in the Trucial Oman Scouts* (2014).
13. Butts, *Now the Dust has Settled*, p. 232.
14. Ibid, p. 194.
15. Hawley, *The Trucial States*, p. 176.
16. Paul, *Bagpipes in Babylon*, p. 193.
17. Butts, *Now the Dust has Settled*, p. 187.
18. Hawley, *The Trucial States*, p. 205.
19. Heard-Bey, *From Trucial States to United Arab Emirates*, pp. 469, 470.
20. Hawley, *The Trucial States*, p. 212.
21. Butts, *Now the Dust has Settled*, p. 235.
22. *With United Strength*, pp. 80–3.
23. Paul, *Bagpipes in Babylon*, pp. 203–5.
24. Butts, *Now the Dust has Settled*, p. 209.
25. "Judgement of JV Naisby, 19th April 1962, Court Report 8024, Investigation held at Lincoln's Inn Fields, London".
26. "Stamps are Now the Money-Spinners", *The Times* (Supplement on the Union of Arab Emirates), 1969.
27. Hawley, *The Trucial States*, p. 183.
28. G. Wilson, *Rashid: Portrait of a Ruler* (Dubai: Media Prima, 2010).
29. "Stamps are Now the Money-Spinners", *The Times* (Supplement on the Union of Arab Emirates), 1969.
30. Hawley, *The Trucial States*, p. 204.
31. Wilson, *Rashid: Portrait of a Ruler*, p. 195.

32. S. b. M. Al Qasimi, *My Early Life* (London: Bloomsbury, 2011), p. 225, 226.
33. Butts, *Now the Dust has Settled*, p. 192.
34. Al Qasimi, *My Early Life*, pp. 262–3.

Chapter 25 | Founded on a Handshake

1. N. Herbert, "Gulf Rulers' Offer Still Open", *The Times*, 1968.
2. Al Maktoum, *My Story*, p. 117.
3. M. b. R. Al Maktoum, *Spirit of the Union* (Dubai: Motivate Media Group, 2012).
4. I. Al Abed, "The Historical Background and Constitutional Basis to the Federation", in *United Arab Emirates: A New Perspective* (London: Trident Press, 2001).
5. Heard-Bey, *From Trucial States to United Arab Emirates*, p. 343.
6. D. Housego, "Dubai Asks British to Stay", *The Times*, 1970.
7. Al Qasimi, *My Early Life*, p. 270.
8. Al Maktoum, *My Story*, p. 153.
9. "Navy Men Board US Oil Drilling Ships in Gulf", *The Times*, 1970.
10. "Sheikh Shot on Eve of New Gulf Union", *The Times*, 1968.
11. Al Qasimi, *My Early Life*, p. 282.
12. G. Roberts: "Memo to Minister of Defence from FCO, 1st May 1969".
13. Al Qasimi, *My Early Life*, pp. 285–7.
14. Wilson, *Father of Dubai: Sheikh Rashid bin Saeed Al Maktoum*, p. 178.
15. Al Maktoum, *My Story*, pp. 172–7.
16. Wilson, *Father of Dubai: Sheikh Rashid bin Saeed Al Maktoum*, p. 188.
17. "112 Aboard Airliner are Killed in Crash in Persian Gulf Sheikhdom", *The New York Times*, 1983.
18. Butts, *Now the Dust has Settled*, p. 187.
19. Wilson, *Father of Dubai: Sheikh Rashid bin Saeed Al Maktoum*, p. 182.
20. Al Maktoum, *My Story*, pp. 212–20.

Chapter 26 | The Act of Union

1. M. Peck, "Formation and Evolution of the Federation and its Institutions", in *United Arab Emirates: A New Perspective* (London: Trident Press, 2001), pp. 145–59.
2. *With United Strength*, p. 208.

3. Peck, "Formation and Evolution of the Federation and its Institutions", in *United Arab Emirates: A New Perspective*, pp. 145–59.
4. Secret Telegram: "MOD UK to FCO, 22 Feb 1985" and Secret FCO Memo: "From AS Collins in Middle East Department, 22 Feb 1985".
5. Al Maktoum, *My Story*, pp. 198–9.
6. "Emirates to Act to End Coup Crisis", *United Press International*, 1987.
7. Al Maktoum, *My Story*, p. 235.
8. Ibid, p. 63.
9. S. Coll, *Ghost Wars: The Secret History of the CIA, Afghanistan, and bin Laden, from the Soviet Invasion to September 10, 2001* (New York: Penguin Press, 2004).
10. Al Maktoum, *My Story*, pp. 238–43.
11. Ibid, p. 103.

Author's notes

I have long been a huge admirer of writer Ernle Bradford, who wrote a number of histories of the Mediterranean and of some of the huge figures and empires who lived out their lives in the area around that sea. The thing that made Bradford different (and academics so very snooty about him) was that he was writing about a sea across which he had sailed since the war, when he had served in the Navy, and for years after. He knew it intimately. It gave his writing an extra dimension that crusty old men poring over manuscripts lacked – Bradford understood the sea and its seasons, the harbours and islands which crop up in history like the back of his sun-kissed hand. I can only hope that my time in the UAE brings just a touch of that feeling for the place which, to me at least, is what history is all about. It's all very well reading archives and old texts, but I do feel an appreciation of the place itself provides an invaluable lens through which those ancient words can be filtered.

Some housekeeping: I've generally gone with standardised Arabic spellings based on Google Maps and Wikipedia, unless I know a spelling to be substantively different in the real world. In general, I have already corrected many of these in Wikipedia.

The transliteration of Arabic place names into English remains a delight of life in the Emirates even to this day and we can aim to go to Mleiha, Mileiha, Malayha and any number of other places which all turn out to be one and the same. The road sign as you drive into Habhab reads Habhab and then you encounter the Hebheb Police Station. We have Muttrah and we have Mutrah – the latter is the modern Google Maps name and that's what I've gone with. Sometimes Google is wrong, but mostly it's good. One of my favourites is the

Ajmani village of Sayh Mudayrah, which is pronounced 'Muzaira' and signposted variously as Mazira, Mzairea and Muzaira.

One of a number of oddities of internet nomenclature is that dropdown menus to this day offer the options of Debbay and Al Shariqah. If anyone is interested enough in the origins of this idiocy, I'll happily share an explanation, but in general a large number of archaic UAE names survived through the medium of Wikipedia to be scraped, used and generally promulgated by all sorts of mirrors – around 150 cities, villages and other settlements that had ceased to exist decades ago, as well as a number of dodgy transliterations. I corrected that in Wikipedia, but the errors had stood long enough to create widespread online havoc and a 'virtual' Emirates that simply doesn't exist in the real world.

I've gone for a standard spelling in each case, and have chosen to avoid the old-fashioned custom of trying to render Arabic pronunciation by including mad phonetic characters in the English. It's terrible for search, for a start. So in my new world, Umm Al Nar is just that, rather than Umm an-Nar or Umm An Nar or Umm al-Nar. The danger in searching for perfect transliterations is that they kill search for the majority of the people of the world. So in English they're three words and if we want to make these things searchable and discoverable – in English and other Romance languages, we're just going to have to pick a standard and go with it. And that is precisely what I have done. Ed-Dur should by rights be Al Dur (or, as per the road signs, Al Dour or Al Door) but I ran out of energy. Occasionally my Consulting Editor, Mr Hellyer, wagged a finger and curbed my neologistic tendencies...

I have included apostrophised names (Bani Ka'ab; Na'im) where these are overwhelmingly used. Generally, (Al Zaabi), I've tried to avoid them.

As for personal names, I've again gone with a modernised standard Shakhbut is Shakhbut throughout, even though the British called each and every Shakhbout by a different spelling (Shakboot, etc). Abu Dhabi is Aboo Dhebaye and a million other iterations in the archives. I've gone with vanilla every time. The Internet has decided that Afonso Dalboquerque is Afonso De Albuquerque and I couldn't be bothered to argue. If this sort of thing interests you, and I can see every reason why it wouldn't, I would happily refer you to the letters between T. E. Lawrence and his publisher.

I have generally followed the convention of calling the Rulers of the Emirates just that, rather than use the honorific Sheikh – and have likewise used their names without the honorific. I have mainly done this in the name of simplicity, readability and – for those with a strong distaste for honorifics, relatability. I have generally tried to maintain separation between names but, try as I might, I'm sure some of the exchanges will need a careful read simply because Saqr bin Sultan calling his son Sultan bin Saqr (and having a brother called Salim bin Sultan who called his son Saqr bin Salim) is hardly helpful when trying to recount complex internecine imbroglios as they happened at the time.

I have used dates in the format 1400s rather than C15th, purely because I have found over a huge number of conversations that it confuses people unused to historical discussion – let alone using English as a second language – to observe the convention that the sixteenth century is actually the 1500s, not the 1600s. I have used BCE (Before the Common Era) rather than BC (Before Christ) and CE (Common Era) rather than AD (Anno Domini) just because there are other world views.

Wherever possible, I have gone back to the original source. Lorimer is all very well, but he wrote his *Gazetteer* and *History*, magnificent and insanely compendious works though they are, in the period between 1905 and 1915, often drawing from residency records and other histories, including, extensively, Rathbone Low's *History of the Indian Navy*. Lorimer's a bit like Mrs Beeton and Low would be analogous to Eliza Acton. The former is famous for her cookbook, the latter actually wrote 80 per cent of the recipes and Mrs B then glibly copied her work. For what it's worth, Acton herself nicked most of her recipes from a lady called Elizabeth Rundel and I have her cookbook, a much-prized possession printed in 1845 and containing that curry recipe lifted from the Khansamar of Oudh I refer to in the book. Sorry, I'm rambling.

I have tried to balance events as well as I can, giving due weight to those that shaped the modern UAE and trying to avoid pointless circumlocutions – Sirhan, the dear old Omani historian, is particularly fond of passages like 'Then Saeed went to Rustaq with his men, stayed there several days and then returned to Nizwa'. These are not helpful, IMHO. If an event results in the restoration of the status quo, I have therefore tended to ignore it in favour of events that moved and shaped the way things turned out. I have, in short, gone with the narrative.

I have also, necessarily, had to omit a tremendous amount of information that is interesting, even fascinating, in order to maintain some semblance of that narrative, so forgive me if I don't give details of how many pearling boats sailed from each emirate in 1905, which Lorimer does enumerate but which doesn't sit in a general history of the Emirates. Covering 130,000 years of human history in as many words has meant I can't tell you everything about everyone all of the time.

As with all history, you can always dig deeper and find many more forgotten and wonderful gems for yourself and if this book inspires you to do that, then I shall be beyond delighted.

Peter Hellyer

Peter Hellyer – my consulting editor in this effort – died in 2023, before this book could be published. I have left my thanks to him in the following pages, because he had read the text and knew it was coming and so I'd hate to disappoint him.

Sadly, he also knew the events of 2023 were coming. I last saw him stumping around Umm Al Quwain's Sinniyah Island in the blazing sunshine with a daft, floppy hat on his head as archaeologist Tim Power led media around the discovery of the oldest pearling village in the Gulf. Hellyer was, as usual, delightfully rancorous, his long-suffering wife, Wafa, pleading with him to moderate his language ('Please, Peter!') to absolutely no avail whatsoever. He was gone a few short weeks later.

Peter suffered fools not at all. He was often brusque and dismissive when encountering bureaucracy and stupidity, and the compelling combination of both – and fearless facing up to authority. His old comrade in arms Ibrahim Al Abed died shortly before him, and I fancy Ibrahim's passing took some of the wind from Peter's sails. They were inseparable and their contribution to the UAE's archaeology, history, media and international communications in general are almost impossible to quantify.

Peter loved the country so much, he castigated it freely and defended it fiercely. He loved its people so much, he celebrated them with gay abandon, but was equally outspoken when he found them at fault. In his dying days, he was left in tears by the generosity and love of the leaders and people of the Emirates. It turns out they were quite fond of the OB, too...

I am very proud to have known him and to have called him a friend.

Thanks and Things

This has been all rather intense, if fun, and I have to note that I am merely a scribbler of things who is happily dancing around on the shoulders of giants. They're far too numerous to lay out here, but the Globs, Bibbys, Potts, Tikritis, Magees, Kennets, Uerpmanns, De Cardis and Powers all know who they are. To all of them, digging, sifting, examining, concluding and – finally – publishing, I owe a huge debt. Still the least understood part of Emirati history is its archaeology and there is still a huge amount left to find.

I am only sad that on so very many occasions, digs have taken place in the Emirates and the objects have been left here while the knowledge gained has gone overseas to be published in journals that most people here have no access to. It's part of the reason I took this project on – much of the knowledge about this place has been taken to other places and that's simply, in my view, wrong. Alongside that, knowledge doesn't belong in crusty academic journals and flaky old bookshelves – the whole point (to me) of knowledge is that it belongs with everyone.

If you have by any chance found anything in this book that you find objectionable or discourteous, please be assured that was not my intention. History is a funny thing and particularly so in the Emirates, where it remains for many an area where exploration is discouraged. The very reason for writing this book was to bring that history to life and put it in people's hands in an accessible and readable format. If it prompts discussion and dialogue around the events of the past, it will be helping people to celebrate where they came from and the many reasons behind the shape of the modern Emirates, a place I have been delighted to call home for over three decades now.

I have to thank my wife, Sarah, for putting up with me. That's a general thing, not necessarily anything to do with writing books, but in particular she has been living with a cloud-based husband covered in archive dust for many months now and has generally been remarkably forbearing. Also the tottering piles of papers and books littering the place have caused her, a staunch minimalist, great pain. Oh, and the drone and constant weekend drives out to 'see dead people'.

Clearly, Consulting Editor Peter Hellyer spared me legion blushes and provided great insight based on his remarkable lifetime's work on the history and archaeology of the UAE. Peter was a central figure to a great deal of investigation that has taken place over the past five decades of archaeological and historical research in the UAE and his grasp of the subject was not only comprehensive, but frequently based on personal experience and insight gained in the field.

The many publications which Peter was responsible for creating and curating, from his collections of archaeological research and conference proceedings through to the periodical of the Emirates Natural History Society, Tribulus, were critical resources for me in researching this book from the Neolithic right through to World War II – and his expertise was inspirational and greatly practical. He

AUTHOR'S NOTES

was a cheroot-smoking history ninja.

Every one of his notes on the manuscript had me plunging back into my research papers in a panic and I have to say I feel privileged to have landed perhaps one punch in every ten blows we traded.

A lot of my research was made possible by the resourceful Hessa, who opened archives like an archive-opening wizardess. My colleagues Ayesha, Fatmah, Latifa, Maryam and Suha have put up with a great deal from me throughout this whole history thing, so here's a 'thank you' from me at the end of it all.

Ian Fairservice, Managing Partner and Editor-in-Chief of Motivate Media Group, listened, understood and acted. Few people do that, in my experience. His team, Robin Harvie, Vaarunya and editorial powerhouse Aswathy polished the book until it shone. Maya Smadi's chapter head line drawings have been a wee delight for me and, I hope, for you.

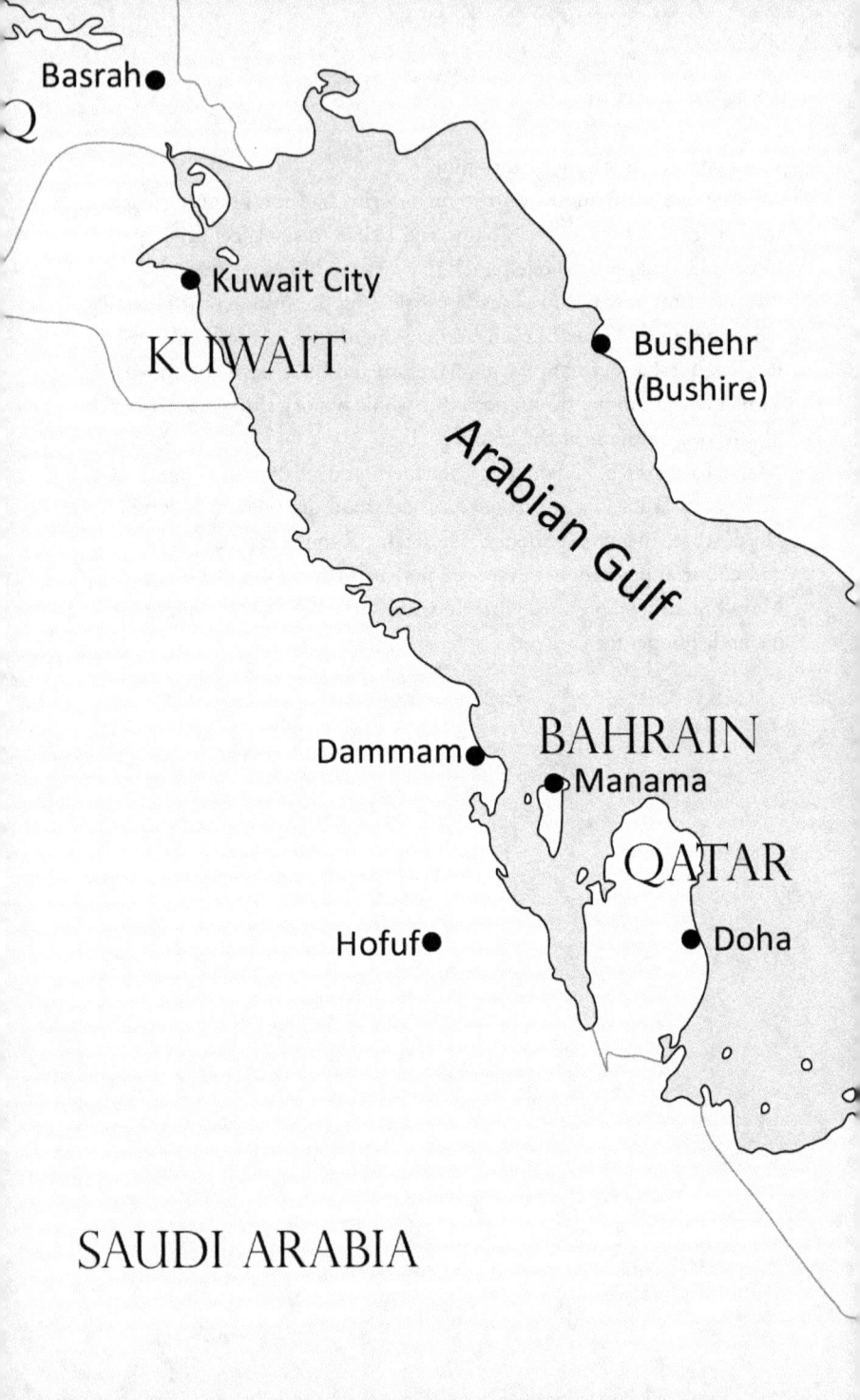

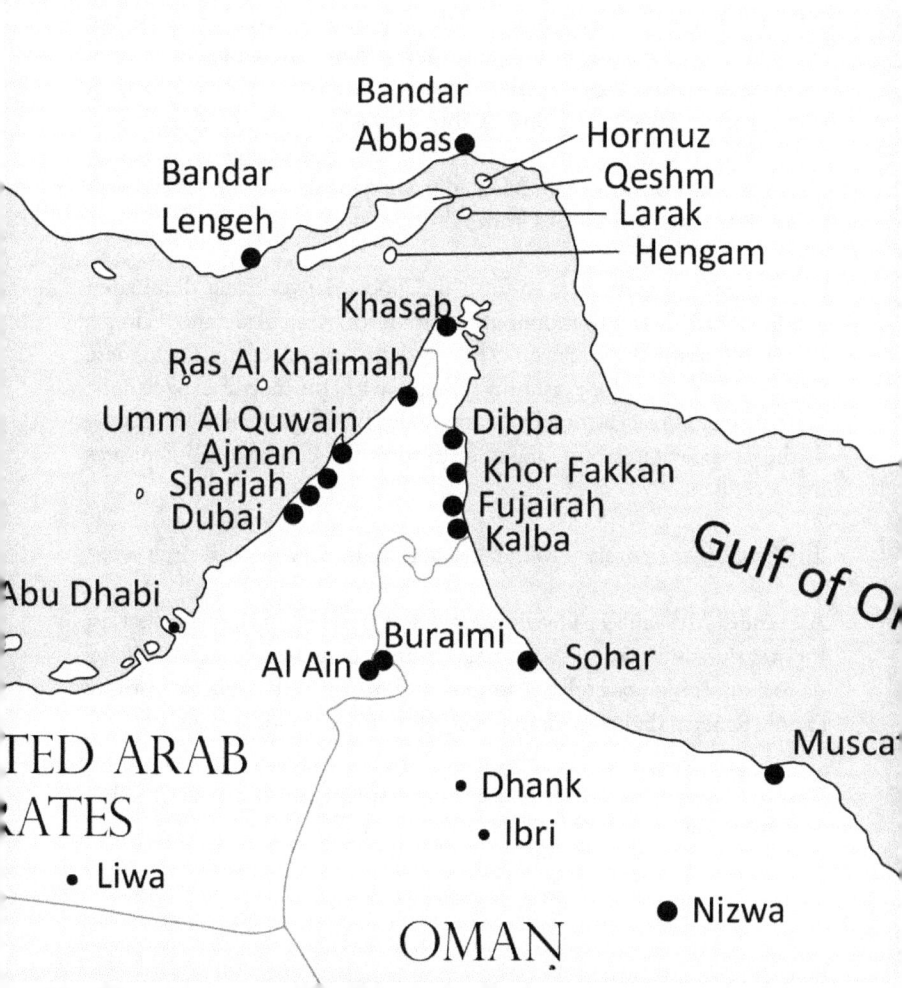

One of the world's youngest nations, the United Arab Emirates was founded based on a handshake between two men meeting in a tent in the desert between Abu Dhabi and Dubai in 1968. Yet its human history stretches back to the emergence of anatomically modern humans from Africa, a story of 130,000 years of humankind's survival in one of the world's harshest environments.

Thanks to modern archaeological and historical research, we can now trace the Emirates' story back to the Garden of Eden, the mythical floods of the Old Testament and the very foundation of the Sumerian civilisation. Known to the Sumerians as Magan, a key source of the copper that sparked the metallurgical revolution that swept Europe, the land of the Emirates was at the centre of humanity's first intercontinental trade network, linking Sumeria, Persia and the Indus Valley. This then transformed through the Iron Age into a locus for agricultural and social innovation, welcoming new religions and seeing great pre-Islamic cities blossom in the sands – from Mleiha in Sharjah's desert interior through to Ed-Dur on the coast of Umm Al Quwain.

The region's seafarers were to form the global network that dominated the fabulously wealthy monopoly of trade between Asia and Europe. Its people roamed the Seven Seas until the arrival of the Portuguese triggered a series of devastating clashes with the newly expansionist European empires. Eventually falling under British influence, the people of the Trucial States came together to form the United Arab Emirates in December 1971.

This, then, is their story – told in a single volume for the first time ever.

Alexander McNabb has lived, worked and travelled in the Middle East for over thirty-five years as a journalist, editor and publisher before moving on to a career in public relations and consulting for both public and private sector clients in digital media, publishing and international relations.

Book cover image: The gold ring – one of the numerous treasures found from the Iron Age site of Saruq Al Hadid in Dubai – that inspired the Expo 2020 Dubai logo. Image credit: Expo City Dubai.

www.ingramcontent.com/pod-product-compliance
Lightning Source LLC
Chambersburg PA
CBHW051107230426
43667CB00014B/2471